THE TSADRA FOUNDATION SERIES
published by Snow Lion, an imprint of Shambhala Publications

Tsadra Foundation is a U.S.-based nonprofit organization that contributes to the ongoing development of wisdom and compassion in Western minds by advancing the combined study and practice of Tibetan Buddhism. Taking its inspiration from the nineteenth-century nonsectarian Tibetan scholar and meditation master Jamgön Kongtrül Lodrö Tayé, Tsadra Foundation is named after his hermitage in eastern Tibet, Tsadra Rinchen Drak. The Foundation's various program areas reflect his values of excellence in both scholarship and contemplative practice, and the recognition of their mutual complementarity. Tsadra Foundation envisions a flourishing community of Western contemplatives and scholar-practitioners who are fully trained in the traditions of Tibetan Buddhism. It is our conviction that, grounded in wisdom and compassion, these individuals will actively enrich the world through their openness and excellence. This publication is a part of the Tsadra Foundation's Translation Program, which aims to make authentic and authoritative texts from the Tibetan traditions available in English. The Foundation is honored to present the work of its fellows and grantees, individuals of confirmed contemplative and intellectual integrity; however, their views do not necessarily reflect those of the Foundation. Tsadra Foundation is delighted to collaborate with Shambhala Publications in making these important texts available in the English language.

༄༅། །ཁྱོད་གསལ་རིན་ཆེན་སྐྱིད་པོ་པཙ་ལས་འབྲེལ་རུལ་གྱི་རྟོགས་བརྗོད་རོ་མཚར་སྒྱུ་མའི་རོལ་གར་ཞེས་བྱ་བ་བཞུགས་སོ།   །

Wondrous Dance of Illusion

The Autobiography of Khenpo Ngawang Palzang,
Ösel Rinchen Nyingpo Pema Ledrel Tsel

TRANSLATED FROM THE TIBETAN BY
Heidi L. Nevin and J. Jakob Leschly

Teachers consulted for transmission and clarifications:
Kyabje Chatral Sangye Dorje, Kyabje Tulku Sonam Chöpel, Gyarong Khenpo
Tubten Lodrö Taye, Lhagang Khenchen Tashi, Palyul Tulku Tubzang,
Lama Tharchin Rinpoche, Lama Tsering Gyaltsen, Tulku Thondup Rinpoche,
Lobpon Jigme Tutop Namgyal, Tulku Pema Wangyal, Khenpo Tsering Gyatso,
Khenpo Jampel Dorje, Khenpo Sonam Tenpa, Khenpo Sonam Tashi,
and Gyarong Khenpo Lhabum

EDITOR
Gyurme Dorje, PhD

SNOW LION
BOSTON & LONDON
2013

Snow Lion
An imprint of Shambhala Publications, Inc.
Horticultural Hall
300 Massachusetts Avenue
Boston, Massachusetts 02115
www.shambhala.com

9 8 7 6 5 4 3 2 1

First Edition
Printed in the United States of America

∞ This edition is printed on acid-free paper that meets the
American National Standards Institute Z39.48 Standard.
♲ Shambhala makes every effort to print on recycled paper.
For more information please visit www.shambhala.com.

Distributed in the United States by Random House, Inc.,
and in Canada by Random House of Canada Ltd

Designed by Gopa & Ted2, Inc.

ISBN 978-1-55939-427-7

This book is dedicated to the continued enlightened activity of Kyabje Chatral Sangye Dorje Rinpoche, and to all the lineage masters who uphold the living tradition of the Luminous Great Perfection.

PLEASE NOTE: This is a restricted text. It has a seal of secrecy and is guarded by the protectors of the Vajrayana. Until you have received the reading transmission and/or permission to read it from a qualified lineage master, please keep it on your shrine as an object of veneration.

CONTENTS

Foreword by Kyabje Chatral Rinpoche

OM SWASTI!

By WAY OF a brief historical introduction to this autobiography, I will
begin by saying that the great Katok Khenpo Ngawang Palzang, who
was also known as Ösel Rinchen Nyingpo Pema Ledreltsel—a name given
to him by a yidam deity[1]—was an emanation of Vimalamitra, crown ornament of the five hundred master scholars in the noble land of India, as well as
the Omniscient Longchen Rabjam, supreme among scholars in the Land of
Snows, among others. His name was as renowned as the sun and the moon.

This undisputed universal monarch of the learned and accomplished was
born in the Tibetan year 852, the year of the Female Earth Hare, which corresponds to the Gregorian calendar year 1879. He was born amid wondrous
signs into a wealthy family of grassland nomads of pure descent, in Washul
Village in the Drida Zelmo Gang District of eastern Tibet's Four Rivers
and Six Ranges region.

From early childhood, he was utterly beyond the scope of ordinary people.
He possessed miraculous powers and unobstructed clairvoyance. Everyone,
both Buddhist and non-Buddhist, honored and revered him. Right from
his youth, powerful renunciation and weariness with samsara arose in his
mind, and he entered the door to the Buddha's teachings. He attended many
authentic spiritual mentors, studied and reflected upon the teachings of the
sutras, tantras, and the five sciences, and completely eradicated all doubts.

He took novice and full ordination in the precept lineage of the Great
Abbot Shantarakshita, and his monastic discipline was so untainted by
faults or downfalls that the sweet fragrance of morality always wafted
through the air around him. Turning away from the pursuit of his own
peace and happiness, he trained to perfect mastery in bodhichitta for the
sake of others. Gathering disciples both directly and indirectly through the

four modes of gathering beings and the six transcendent perfections, his bodhisattva action was as vast as the ocean, and he worked tirelessly for beings' benefit. He was a truly great being, and everyone who made a connection with him found it meaningful.

In particular, he exerted himself with unswerving diligence in one-pointed meditation practice in remote mountain hermitages, and during his lifetime he had visions of numerous masters and exalted deities. He attained absolute confidence in his mastery of the twofold path of the Luminous Great Perfection.

Moreover, he spent nearly thirteen years as the abbot of the great Buddhist college at the victorious eastern Katok Dorje Den Monastery, the fountainhead of the Nyingma teachings. During that period, he taught, debated, and wrote about the infinite collections of scriptures and classes of tantra, thereby reviving the dying embers of the Nyingma tradition.

As a result, all the learned and accomplished saints of his day, regardless of sect or denomination, unanimously praised him as a second Buddha preaching the Buddhist teachings. He had innumerable fortunate disciples, and the vast majority of them greatly benefited the Buddhist teachings and beings. Many of them are still alive today.

This Great Master's collected works comprise ten volumes of compositions, ranging from his cycle of pure vision mind-treasures (*dag snang dgongs gter*) to his Whispered Lineage pith instructions (*snyan brgyud man ngag*) and commentaries on major Indian and Tibetan treatises. He excelled in the philosophical tenets of the higher levels and paths. He possessed untainted vision and unobstructed clairvoyant cognition, and he stated that he knew with certainty from early on that he would depart from this realm at the age of sixty-three and that his reincarnation would be born in the Dekyi Khangsarma family in Kongpo. He proclaimed these secrets with the fearless roar of a lion, and the events occurred exactly according to the truth of his infallible vajra speech.

In short, he was peerless throughout the Land of Snows from every vantage point: scholarship, virtuousness, goodness of heart, insight, love, skill, and power. This is not mere exaggeration or flattery but accords precisely with the reality presented in the Great Master's own autobiography. The majesty of its blessings is undiminished. When you read this, still warm with the breath of the dakinis and mother goddesses, you will understand, so I will cut short my wordy elaborations.

Editions of this text have been widely disseminated in every direction, so inaccuracies and errors have proliferated. This particular edition was carefully prepared and edited using three authentic editions: a genuine copy of the Great Master's own manuscript, the Markham Gyalse Monastery edition, and the Lhasa edition. Henceforth, for those who are interested, please know that there is no need to have any doubt about this.

The lowly disciple Chatral Sangye Dorje, who sat at the lotus feet of the saffron-robed emanation, the Buddhist Lord Vajra-Holder Ngawang Pel Zangpo, wrote this on the eighteenth day of the twelfth lunar month of the Earth Monkey year in the sixteenth Rabjung cycle [1969], in my room at my retreat center, Kundröl Ösel Tsey, built in the hills of Darjeeling in the state of West Bengal in north India. May it bring benefit as vast as the sky!

Foreword by Tulku Thondup Rinpoche

———

The Great Master Khenpo Ngawang Palzang, widely known as Khenpo Ngakchung, Khenpo Ngaga, or the Omniscient Ngakgi Wangpo (1879–1941), was one of the most renowned scholars and adepts of the Nyingma school of Tibetan Buddhism.[2]

Wondrous Dance of Illusion is not only a fascinating autobiographic portrait of Khenpo Ngakchung but a vivid revelation of the attainments of the Great Perfection *Ösel Nyingtik, "Heart Essence of Luminosity,"* which Khenpo received and realized, and of which he became a celebrated master.

It is believed that Khenpo was an incarnation of Vimalamitra, a fully awakened adept, who brought the Great Perfection teachings from India to Tibet in the eighth century c.e. Khenpo was born amid miracles. In childhood, he proclaimed himself an incarnation of a great adept. He attained ultimate realization of the Great Perfection even while he was training in preliminary meditations. He continually had visions of and direct communication with buddhas and enlightened masters of the past. He was especially renowned as one of the greatest masters of the Great Perfection Ösel Nyingtik. He produced many accomplished students and left a number of the most profound treatises in this field. Summarizing the Great Perfection, he wrote:

> The spontaneously present self-awareness
> Is unmodified and unchanging. It is marvelous!
> It is untouched by contrived thoughts.
> It can be realized easily through the kindness of the Lama.
> In it there is no time of wandering or not being in meditation.
> There is no mindfulness that is watching. I swear!
> So isn't it better to let adventitious concepts

> Rest today in the vast expanse of joy—
> The natural joy that is self-liberated?[3]

Nyoshul Lungtok Tenpey Nyima (1829–1901),[4] Khenpo's principal lama, was a great hermit and scholar. He taught and guided Khenpo most prudently, step-by-step, as if Khenpo were a beginner. Here readers might wonder: If Khenpo was an incarnation of an enlightened master, why was he still receiving trainings? The enlightened masters, when incarnated as students, almost always go through long, arduous, and gradual trainings as if they were ordinary beings. They thereby establish solid role models for future followers in order to train them in the sacred teachings with the correct approach. They also build a firm foundation for the tradition to last for a long time, fulfilling the needs of many. Also, we must remember that their every action—studying, meditating, teaching, or any activity—always functions as a source of spiritual guidance in one form or another.

Because of his incomparable scholarship and saintliness, Khenpo was obliged to hold the most acclaimed abbotship of the thousand-year-old Katok Monastery for thirteen years. But as soon as that obligation was over, he rushed back to his old hermitage. He dedicated the rest of his life to hermetic practice, imparting the Great Perfection Ösel Nyingtik to numerous rugged meditators and devotees, just as his spiritual mentors, the great Longchen Rabjam and Jigme Lingpa, had done centuries earlier.

The Buddha taught that every individual must earn liberation from samsara by himself or herself through the path of Dharma. Khenpo, too, shared his Nyingtik teachings, presenting himself as an example of discipline and continually urging his flock to strive for their liberation by themselves:

> If you can't liberate yourself, who else will liberate you?
> If you can't train yourself, who else will train you?
> So, pointing your finger at your own heart—
> Again and again, train your own three doors in the Dharma![5]

This fascinating autobiographic portrait is a living document that shows the extraordinary attainments of the master and generates absolute confidence in the lineage. It is a spiritual travel guide for the knowledge-seeker, a clear instruction manual for Great Perfection meditators, and a powerful testament of the highly accomplished mystic adepts—all in one volume.

Heidi Nevin and Jakob Leschly have rendered this sacred treatise beautifully and meticulously into English. It is a great cause of celebration for the students of this sublime lineage. By the kindness of the lineage masters and the Dharma protectors, may the wisdom light of this sacred life story illuminate the hearts of whomever it reaches and awaken their full human potential—Buddhahood.

Tulku Thondup Rinpoche
The Buddhayana Foundation

Translators' Introduction

KHENPO NGAWANG PALZANG, or Khenpo Ngakchung as he is popularly called, was one of the most celebrated Nyingma masters in recent history. He was a visionary saint, an eminent scholar, an exemplary monk, and a beloved teacher whose living legacy now extends far beyond Tibet. His life story, which unfolds in nineteenth-century eastern Tibet, is a wondrous narrative of liberation, rich with accounts of pure visions and astonishing deeds. Most important, it is a profound wealth of instruction, intended for those who have studied and trained in his lineage. Khenpo Ngakchung's life embodies the spirit of wisdom and compassion; it provides us with an appreciation of the nature of the Buddhist path, a practical example of its application, and a demonstration of its consummation. Recollecting such a realized master is said to invoke his presence, qualities, and blessings, so by reading and reflecting on the life and example of Khenpo Ngakchung, we plant the seed of liberation in our minds.

Khenpo Ngakchung was most famously known as an emanation of the great Indian master Vimalamitra, who helped bring the Nyingtik teachings to Tibet in the eighth century C.E. Before leaving Tibet, Vimalamitra promised to send an emanation once every hundred years to revitalize the Nyingtik teachings, and Khenpo Ngakchung first identified himself as one of these when he miraculously reversed a flooded stream at the tender age of five.

He was also renowned as a reincarnation of the brilliant and prolific Tibetan master Longchenpa (1308–64), a fact that fulfilled a prediction made long before Khenpo's birth by Patrul Rinpoche, his grandfather in the lineage.

Vimalamitra and Longchenpa are but two in the long line of accomplished beings from India and Tibet who are identified as Khenpo Ngakchung's previous lives, many of whom Khenpo encountered or experienced in pure visions and dreams. His line of incarnations, beginning with the great lay devotee Licchavi Vimalakirti, who lived at the time of the Buddha, includes a full spectrum of enlightened scholars, yogins, translators, kings, and treasure-revealers.

THE SETTING

The culture we encounter in this narrative grew out of more than a thousand years of Buddhism in Tibet. The obvious naïveté of Western romantic fantasies about Tibet left aside, few would deny that Tibet indeed upheld an extraordinary tradition of enquiry, wisdom, and compassion that served the well-being of the Tibetan people and the land. Tibetans themselves viewed their land as a sacred realm; learned scholars and realized sages were often vividly present in the lives of Tibetans, instilling in the populace an enormous appreciation of the vision and pragmatic value of enlightenment and spiritual practice—a knowledge that many Tibetans carry with them to this day. The legacy of Khenpo Ngakchung is still alive and with us to this day, as embodied by his lineage holders—among these most notably his heart-son Chatral Rinpoche.

Khenpo Ngakchung was born at the height of the Rimé or "nonsectarian" movement that began in eastern Tibet in the late nineteenth century. Despite frequent political upheavals in the region, it was a time of cultural and spiritual renaissance, inspired mainly by the illustrious Jamyang Khyentse Wangpo (1820–92) and Jamgön Kongtrül Lodrö Taye (1813–99). The famous *Treasury of Precious Revelations* (*rin chen gter mdzod*)—a vast compendium of sacred treasure-teachings that Khenpo Ngakchung received and thrice conferred during his lifetime—is one of the many important scriptural compilations that emerged during this period.

Khenpo Ngakchung's principal master, Nyoshul Lungtok Tenpey Nyima (1829–1901/2), apprenticed with the famous Rimé master Dza Patrul Rinpoche (1808–87) for twenty-eight years. From him, Lungtok Rinpoche inherited the Whispered Lineage pith instructions of the *Longchen Nyingtik, "Heart Essence of Longchenpa."* Lungtok, in turn, transmitted this tradition to Khenpo Ngakchung, who established its practice lineage at Katok Monastery, where the latter taught for thirteen years at the behest of the Third Katok Situ Rinpoche, Chökyi Gyatso (1880–1925).

It was under Nyoshul Lungtok's tutelage that Khenpo Ngakchung completed all the stages of Great Perfection practice, from the preliminaries (ngöndro) to Trekchö and Tögal. At the age of twenty-one, he was enthroned as Nyoshul Lungtok's spiritual heir and was sent to study at Dzogchen Monastery's Shri Singha College. There Khenpo met another of his Rimé teachers: the incomparable Jamgön Ju Mipam Rinpoche (1846–1912), from whom Khenpo received Mipam's famous treatise, *Gateway to Knowledge* (*mkhas 'jug*), on the very day he finished writing it.

In addition to establishing monasteries and Buddhist colleges, giving enormous numbers of teachings, and undertaking long meditation retreats, Khenpo Ngakchung was a prolific writer. His collected works comprise some ten volumes, which include Madhyamaka and Vajrayana commentaries and works on the Great Perfection.[6] Khenpo wrote his famous *kunzang lama'i shelung zindri,* published in English as *A Guide to the Words of My Perfect Teacher,* at the age of seventeen, when he first received Lungtok's oral teachings on the Longchen Nyingtik preliminaries.

THE AUTOBIOGRAPHY

Khenpo Ngakchung's 157-folio autobiography, which he composed in 1933 at the age of fifty-four (fifty-five according to Tibetan calculations), is divided into three sections, detailing the beginning, middle, and later years of his life. Through his reflections and personal experiences, Khenpo presents the entire Buddhist path, right from the birth of renunciation and bodhichitta, which spontaneously arose within him in childhood, to the pure visions and spiritual attainments of a supremely realized master. He demonstrates how to seek and attend an authentic guru; how to engage in mind training and practice the preliminary, generation, and completion stages of the path of meditation; and how to study the vast array of sutras and tantras.

Although Khenpo Ngakchung's experiences and cultural milieu may appear foreign to our own, his account depicts the most important, most universal undertaking of all: the project of relinquishing confusion and awakening innate wisdom. Founded on an empirical knowledge of consciousness, his path is a pragmatic process of uncovering a core of wisdom common to all beings. In this intimate account that outlines the actual practices of the Buddhist path, Khenpo Ngakchung guides us through his own example, inviting us to recognize our intrinsic buddha nature and discover freedom and enlightenment.

Buddhist biographies belong to an ancient genre of spiritual literature that speaks straight to the human heart, across oceans and centuries, cultures and races. Intended above all to inspire, these wondrous stories serve as guidebooks and road maps for anyone who seeks to live a conscious, compassionate, and fruitful life.

For the Vajrayana Buddhist, these biographies hold a place of special importance on the path to enlightenment. The heart of the Vajrayana tradition is the profound practice of guru yoga, or "union with the guru's nature," whereby the student invokes the presence of the master with fervent devotion and continuously merges his or her mind with the master's wisdom mind. The master, or guru, as an outer reflection of our own true nature, is the source of the blessings that enable us to progress along the path.

The term "blessing," in a Buddhist context, refers to the inspiration that permeates the ordinary confused mind and affords us a direct glimpse of an awakened mind. Receiving the guru's blessing takes place when there is genuine faith and heartfelt devotion, and this serves as the foundation of the Vajrayana path of empowerment. When the teacher's compassion and the student's devotion result in a mingling of minds, there is a transference of realization that allows the student to attain realization in this very lifetime. The guru yoga of faith and blessings lies at the core of all Vajrayana practices.

Tulku Thondup explains "blessings" in the following way:

> When our heart opens with the energy of faith (*dad pa*) and devotion (*mos gus*), the Buddha's ever-present blessings (*byin rlabs*) are there to permeate and empower us. There are two main kinds of blessing: common and supreme. Common blessings arise from the power of the Buddha to heal our sicknesses, protect us from enemies, increase our wealth, and make us joyful. The supreme blessing arises from the power of the Buddha to turn our mind to the Dharma, enable us to attain high spiritual accomplishments, and ultimately empower us to realize Buddhahood. Buddha's blessings are always there, like the sunlight is always waiting outside, and to receive them, we need faith and devotion. As soon as we open the window of our heart with the hand of devotion, the sunlight of blessings pours in, fulfilling our wishes by dispelling the darkness and filling us with light. Blessings are the special power of highly accomplished beings, such as buddhas, who can fulfill our wishes. We could perceive blessings in the form of light, nectar, peace, joy, and various levels of wisdom.[7]

Drikung Kyobpa Rinpoche says:

Unless the sun of devotion shines
On the snow peak of the guru's four kayas,
The stream of blessings will never flow.
So earnestly arouse devotion in your mind![8]

Reading the biographies of sublime spiritual masters is a powerful way to generate devotion and receive immeasurable waves of blessing. In his introduction to Dilgo Khyentse Rinpoche's autobiography, *Brilliant Moon*, Dzongsar Khyentse Rinpoche writes:

What better way to invoke the guru's blessing than by remembering him. And what better way to remember him than by reading his autobiography.[9]

Note on the Restriction and the Issue of Secrecy

Generally, Tibetan biographical and autobiographical works are accessible to anyone. In our case, however, Chatral Rinpoche set a restriction on the readership to prevent this text from falling into the hands of those who might objectify or trivialize it.

When Chatral Rinpoche granted us his blessing to translate his root guru's autobiography into English, he warned that the book consists entirely of precious instructions (*gdams ngag*) and must be translated without error to avoid corrupting all our samayas.

E. Gene Smith echoes this in his own introduction to the autobiography:

It is as a treasury of authentic instruction on the essentials of Buddhism and Rdzogs chen [Dzogchen] meditation that this work has its greatest significance.[10]

Khenpo Ngakchung himself begins by saying, "I write this autobiography for the sake of devoted individuals who would like to follow in my footsteps . . . [and] in order to demonstrate the authenticity of the lineage and the extraordinary greatness of the definitive pith instructions."

The book you now hold in your hands is an intimate account intended for those who have confidence in and sufficient familiarity with the view and practice presented in the text, as well as the intention to put the teachings into practice. Ideally, the reader's heart should be suffused with devotion and open to receiving the blessings and transmissions of Khenpo Ngakchung's wisdom mind. Each line should be read as if it were embossed in gold on the page, with a keen understanding of the importance of guarding the precious pith instructions and a genuine, selfless commitment to traversing the path to Buddhahood.

Tulku Thondup clarifies the power of the reader's intention at the outset of his book *Masters of Meditation and Miracles:*

> If . . . biographies are read as stories with intellectual and emotional perceptions, the best possible benefit that could come is inspiration. If the lives are read in order to feel and unite with the experiences of the masters, the stories will certainly arouse spiritual realization, love, peace, openness, light, and healing in the reader's heart.

We have proceeded with utmost care to ensure an accurate and inspiring translation, and we pray that our clumsy renderings have not interrupted the stream of Khenpo Ngakchung's blessings. For whatever inevitable flaws there may be, we ask the forgiveness of the dharmapalas and dakinis who guard this work, as well as the patience and understanding of our readers. It is our sincere hope that this translation finds its way into the hands of those who can comprehend it deeply and assimilate its wisdom for the sake of all beings.

ABOUT THIS TRANSLATION

We consulted four editions of the original Tibetan manuscript in preparing this translation: Chatral Rinpoche's woodblock edition, which was made using the Markham Gyalse Gön and Lhasa woodblock editions, and a handwritten copy that Chatral Rinpoche himself made from the original that belonged to Khenpo Ngakchung; Bu Kalzang's edition; and two editions published by Sichuan Minorities Publishing House in Chengdu.

As is often the case in the fledgling field of Tibetan translation, we struggled mightily with terminology choices. In the end, our words reflect a desire for accuracy, readability, familiarity, and accessibility. A key to translations is provided at the end of the book, and as far as possible we have included Wylie transliterations for key technical terms at their first occurrence. Wylie transliterations are supplied for all translated text titles at their first occurrence to avoid confusion and to assist readers who may be more familiar with the Tibetan titles. We have omitted Sanskrit diacritics for readability. Occasionally, we have retained familiar Sanskrit and Tibetan terms rather than inserting their awkward or insufficient English equivalents. Wherever lengthy lists of text titles occur, we have reformatted the paragraphs into bulleted lists for clarity and accessibility.

This work presupposes a great deal of knowledge about Buddhist philosophy and practice, as well as a general familiarity with the culture and geography of Tibet. To assist readers who may be less informed, we have included references where possible, but these are by no means exhaustive. Glossaries of place names, personal names, and enumerations are provided at the back of the book. In an effort to render the original Tibetan in natural, uncluttered English, we have avoided using square brackets to isolate words or phrases supplied for clarification. Many sections are intentionally cryptic, and we urge readers to request guidance (*khrid*) from a qualified master.

The final eight years of Khenpo's life, from 1933 when the autobiography ends, until his parinirvana in 1941, are detailed in a compendium of biographical writings entitled *Elixir That Restores and Increases Faith*, compiled by Khenpo Sonam Tenpa of Katok Monastery. This is translated in appendix 1.

A time line of major events in Khenpo Ngakchung's life is found in appendix 2. It is traditional for Tibetans to calculate age one year ahead of the Western calculation (e.g., when Khenpo writes that he is eighteen, by Western calculations he is seventeen); note that we have retained the Tibetan ages throughout this translation.

Chatral Rinpoche's edition of the autobiography traditionally includes three prayers composed by Khenpo Ngakchung: a lineage supplication, a guru sadhana, and a confession prayer. These, along with two short supplications, are provided in Tibetan and English in appendix 3.

The numerous works that Khenpo Ngakchung mentions throughout his book are listed in the extensive bibliography of texts referenced by the author at the back of the book. There is also a reference bibliography of books consulted or referenced by the translators and editors.

ACKNOWLEDGMENTS

That this precious book now rests in your hands is due entirely to the blessings of our precious Crown Jewel, Kyabje Chatral Sangye Dorje Rinpoche. There are no words to express our gratitude to him. He kindly granted us permission to prepare the English translation, and his blessings manifested in the form of a huge team of talented people who nurtured the project in all its stages.

We began the translation separately, in the spring of 2003, in distant parts of the world and unaware of each other. We did not join forces until 2008, when Ani Jinpa Palmo kindly connected us. We are deeply indebted to her for initiating our collaboration. Because we worked independently for many years, our acknowledgments at first reflect separate teams of people. However, we each received Chatral Rinpoche's permission before undertaking the project.

I (Heidi) would like to thank Kyabje Tulku Sonam Chöpel, student of Orgyen Chemchok Rinpoche (a close disciple of Khenpo Ngakchung), for granting me the reading transmission; Khenpo Sangye of Gyarong for countless hours of explanations at the outset of the translation; Lhagang Khenpo Tashi of Minyak for his patient guidance throughout the first draft; Lama Tsering Gyaltsen of Corvallis for his constant encouragement and clarifications; Tulku Tubzang of Palyul for advice and explanations of cryptic passages; Gyarong Khenpo Lhabum for help with local dialects; Lobpon Jigme Tutop Namgyal for answering many questions and for clarifying the restriction on the text; Jules Levinson and Douglas Duckworth for invaluable help on the Madhyamaka sections; Joseph Bailey and Joseph Wagner for encouragement and monetary donations to the project; Joshua Hayes and Victor Miller for helpful feedback on the introduction; and my dear vajra sister Sarah Jacoby for constant moral support and excellent, detailed feedback on the entire manuscript.

In answer to my fervent prayers, Tulku Thondup Rinpoche gave endlessly of his time and unfathomable knowledge, answering countless questions and clarifying difficult points throughout the manuscript, as well as generously composing a foreword for the book. Words cannot express my gratitude for his scholarship and support. Also in answer to my prayers, translator and Tibetologist Dr. Gyurme Dorje edited the entire manuscript line by line against two editions of the Tibetan original, vastly improving the accuracy of the translation. He systematized terminology, standardized hundreds of text titles, identified countless personal and place names, corrected and added hundreds of endnotes, and prepared a colossal bibliography of works cited by the author. I am deeply grateful for his tremendous efforts.

Cortland Dahl, president of Tergar International, was a source of constant encouragement, and he secured funding for the project from an anonymous benefactor, enabling me to dedicate myself fully to the project. For this, as well as two special grants generously awarded by the Khyentse Foundation, I am inexpressibly grateful. I would also like to thank my cotranslator, Jakob Leschly, who has been an exemplary vajra brother and a source of inestimable knowledge, insight, support, and laughter. Without him, I never would have had the courage to keep going with this project.

I would like to express my heartfelt gratitude to my parents, Kirk and Susan Nevin, and my sister, Liv Gifford, for their constant love and support. Most of all, I wish to thank my selfless husband and vajra brother, Gyarong Tsultrim Yampel, who married me shortly after I began this translation and saw it through to the end, keeping bread on the table year after year, helping me with countless passages, and cracking the whip of diligence over my lazy back. This book couldn't have happened without him. And a warm thank you to our sweet children, Clara and Tashi, whose births and early years were interwoven with this project.

I (Jakob) would like to thank Dzongsar Jamyang Khyentse Rinpoche for introducing me to this autobiography and commanding me to translate it; Tulku Pema Wangyal for the reading transmission; Khenpo Tsering Gyatso, Khenpo Jampel Dorje, Khenpo Sonam Tenpa, and Khenpo Sonam Tashi for their invaluable input and clarifications. Particularly, it is my privilege to inform the reader that the present translation is entirely due to Heidi's intelligence, pure aspirations, and steady perseverence; had it not been for her, the English-speaking readership of this work might have waited for another aeon. I would like to thank the Tsadra Foundation for their generous financial support during the first years of my work on this translation. Finally, I would like to thank my family, and especially my wife, Orgyen Chimey, for her wholehearted support and encouragement in all aspects of this work.

Jointly, we would like to express our gratitude to the accomplished translator Erik Pema Kunsang, who kindly read and edited the entire manuscript and made excellent corrections and suggestions, immensely improving the translation and giving wise counsel on the Great Perfection–related passages in particular. We would like to thank Lama Tharchin Rinpoche for his staunch support and for requesting Eric Colombel of the Tsadra Foundation to sponsor this publication, which Eric generously agreed to do. It is thanks to Eric that we were able to publish the book as a restricted text and enrich it with maps and photographs. We are profoundly grateful to him for his deep dedication to supporting the Buddhadharma. Thank you also to Tsering Wangyal Shawa for expertly preparing our maps, and to Susan Nevin for meticulously proofreading the manuscript and correcting many errors. We extend our thanks to Sonam Lhadrön (Dara Juels), Lama Changchub Dorje, Könchok Lhadrepa, and his son, Yeshe Dorje, for inputting the Tibetan font, and we owe a debt of gratitude to William Hulley (Rigdzin Norbu) for meticulously researching, formatting, and revising the many hundreds of entries in the glossaries without ever losing his sense of humor.

We are immensely grateful to Nikko Odiseos of Shambhala Publications for his kind willingness to publish this book and respect its restriction; and to our outstanding team of people: Ben Gleason, Gopa Campbell, Liz Shaw, Lora Zorian, and Florence Wetzel, whose talent and expertise made the publishing process a true joy.

Lastly, we must express our profound gratitude to all those wise and knowledgeable translators who have come before us, both in Tibet and around the world, for paving the way for this translation. Without their dedicated efforts, we could never have accomplished this work.

DEDICATION

It is with great joy that we present this mighty piece of spiritual literature, alive with blessings and heavy with the weight of an extraordinary lineage, to the English-speaking world. We especially hope that Khenpo Ngakchung's pithy advice and exemplary life will be a source of boundless inspiration for practitioners, eliminating confusion and illuminating the authentic path of study, reflection, and meditation. We dedicate any benefit that may result from our efforts to the continuity of the Great Perfection Ösel Nyingtik tradition, the longevity of the lineage holders, and the simultaneous perfect enlightenment of all beings, our mothers. SARVA MANGALAM.

Heidi Nevin and Jakob Leschly
March 13, 2013

WONDROUS DANCE OF ILLUSION

Khenpo Ngawang Palzang (1879–1941)

Benedictions for the Autobiography by Kyabje Chatral Rinpoche

Inscription in the 1987 Edition

OM SWASTI.
These sublime words, so rare to encounter in the three times,
Contain the vital essence of Sutra and Mantra, and unlock the heart
   treasury
Of ten million Indian and Tibetan pandits and siddhas.
Three Protectors of Mantra, I entrust this to your care.
Guard this, that it may not fall into the hands
Of calloused practitioners who fail to practice,
Violators of samaya, or Dharma thieves.
To those fortunate children who exert themselves
In taming their own minds in solitude,
Bestow this, dispel all adverse conditions, and assist them.
Through the merit of proofreading, printing, and distributing
The profound instructions of my perfect teacher,
May all those connected to me, and all mother beings throughout space,
Be established at the level of Buddhahood.

On the eighth day of the waxing moon in the Pushya month (Jan.–Feb.) of
the Fire Tiger year [1987], Chatral Sangye Dorje prepared this edition with
prayers of aspiration. SARVADAKALYENAMBHAVATU.

INSCRIPTION IN THE BU KALZANG EDITION

Homage to the Guru!

Here is the spiritual autobiography
Of my venerable Lord Master, endowed with threefold kindness,
Written in response to requests from many of his close heart-sons.
It contains all the profound key points of the path of the nine vehicles of
Sutra and Tantra.
It is a vase swirling with the vital elixir of Whispered Lineage blessings,[11]
A treasury of the wondrous, sublime rivers of the three lineages.
Like the sun at the center of a constellation of exemplary biographies,
This slender volume is adorned with a thousand special qualities.
All fortunate ones who wish to be liberated—please read it!
It is the "lama as your pillow," the "master who never scolds."
By reading it once, samsaric existence will be cast away in one fell swoop.
Skilled in business, the art of extracting the essence of illusory wealth,[12]
Bu Kalzang Chöwang of Dingri,
And Paljor Sonam, along with their family members,
With hearts as pure as lotus roots,
Showered us with the gift of Dharma by printing this edition.
They asked me, the old renunciate Sangye Dorje,
A lowly follower of the Master, for some verses of benediction,
Which I have written with delight.
By their virtue, may the realms of all our mother beings be dredged and
emptied,
And may everyone be liberated into the primordially pure expanse of
Samantabhadra's wisdom mind.

O PROTECTRESS OF MANTRA EKAJATI, RAHULA AND DORJE LEKPA!
SEIZE AND FEAST UPON THE LIFE FORCE OF ANYONE WHO DARES TO
SELL THIS PRECIOUS AUTOBIOGRAPHY FOR PROFIT, REVEAL IT INDIS-
CRIMINATELY TO PEOPLE LACKING FAITH, OR PROCLAIM ITS SECRETS!
KHARAM KHAHI SAMAYA RAKSHNITA.

༈ །རྣམ་ཐར་རིན་པོ་ཆེ་ནོར་ལ་འཚོང་མི་དང་དད་མེད་སྐྱེ་བོ་ལ་ཁྱབ་ བདལ་དུ་སྟོན་པ་བཅས་གསང་སྒྲུབ་མཁན་རྣམས་ཀྱི་སྒྲུབ་རྫ་སྲུགས་བདག མ་མོ་གཟའ་དང་རྡོ་རྗེ་ལེགས་པས་བཤེས་ཤིག་རོལ་ཅིག །ཁ་རོ་ཁུ་ཏི། སརྦ་ལ་རྒྱུ་ཏེ།། །།

This was written on the thirteenth day of the third lunar month of the Fire Sheep year, the fifteenth year of the Rabjung cycle. May it be cause for the eternal abiding of the Teachings of the Victorious One!
SHUBHAM MASTI SARVA DZAGATAM.

In keeping with the intention of Chatral Rinpoche stated above, a donation has been made on behalf of the Tsadra Foundation and Shambhala Publications to the Prajna Light Foundation's Animal Liberation Fund, which helps save the lives of yaks in the Himalayas. —Eds.

Homage and Author's Pledge

Homage to all buddhas and bodhisattvas!

You realized inwardly and imparted to beings
The truth of natural dependent arising,
Freeing us from the ocean of unaware existence
And setting us on the path to liberation.
Compassionate Buddha, to you I bow.

From among the infinite stages of manifold spiritual vehicles,
You compiled the teachings of the Vast and Profound:[13]
Bodhisattva heirs to the Conqueror,[14]
Manjushri, Lord of Insight,
Invincible Maitreya, Buddha's regent,
Twin Chariots Nagarjuna and Asanga,
And the masters of their lineages, to you I bow.

Within the pure wisdom of buddha-mind's true nature,
Naturally inexhaustible compassion radiates forth.
Samantabhadra—reality of self-cognizant awareness,
Buddha Vajradhara, to you I bow.

From this essential state, the lords of the five buddha families
And their retinues shine radiantly in the natural Great Perfection,
As the sambhogakaya, innumerable and inconceivable in its appearances.
Space-pervading conquerors of the Mind Lineage, to you I bow.

You who manifestly realized the ninety-six qualities of the buddhas[15]
By relying upon essential symbols,

And departed into the space of reality,
Having naturally exhausted all defilement,
Vidyadharas of the Symbol Lineage, to you I bow.

Emanating blazing clouds of wrathful dakinis,
Skilled in the yogic discipline of Secret Mantra,
You refined your disciples' minds and tamed beings in the Land of Snows.
Lake-Born Vajra, at your feet I bow.

From Samantabhadra down to my root lama,
Nirmanakaya emanations, with mastery of the levels and paths,
Have passed the words of the teachings and their meanings,
Stripped of constructs, from mouth to ear.
Assembly of Vidyadharas of the Whispered Lineage, to you I pay homage.

In the Whispered Lineage of supremely secret pith instructions
Of the precious lineage of the Omniscient Father and Son, Longchenpa
    and Jigme Lingpa,
The words are neither duplicated nor omitted, and their meanings are
    unerring.
I, Pema Ledreltsel, have understood them to be so.

Like a vase filled to the brim, without lack or excess,
This narrative of definitive, supremely secret pith instructions
Was produced without hiding, concealing, contriving, diminishing, or
    embellishing anything;
It is intended for the benefit of fortunate students.

As such, I write this autobiography for the sake of devoted individuals
who would like to follow in my footsteps. All the successive masters of the
past, from the completely perfect Buddha down to my present-day root lama,
have composed a spiritual autobiography. In accord with this tradition, I,
too, shall write something in order to demonstrate the authenticity of the
lineage and the extraordinary greatness of the definitive pith instructions.

Bearing merely the title of a Buddhist teacher in this era of spiritual
degeneration, I have done little more than wander helplessly in the city of
samsara, devoid of tangible beginning or end, with its inconceivable realms
deemed high or low, driven along by the dependent forces of past actions.[16]

I lack even the slightest positive quality or hint of realization of someone who has reached the outset of the Path of Accumulating, let alone the special manifest realizations of the spiritual levels and paths achieved by past spiritual masters and their ilk. Nagarjuna writes in his *Treatises on Human Behavior* (*lugs kyi bstan bcos*):

> To speak of one's own positive qualities
> Is dishonorable even for Indra, king of the gods.

While it is certainly not the time to proclaim my qualities, over the years many saintly people with faith in me have encouraged me to do so. The mass of faults in my mindstream is like a cloud of teeming dust particles, amid which my positive qualities are a mere speck of gold, but in order to fulfill their wishes I will tell my story honestly and concisely, without exaggeration or understatement.

I shall set forth to some extent the following three phases of my life: firstly, from my birth to adolescence; then, as the initial arising of spiritual inspiration depends upon a spiritual mentor, the period during which I relied upon a holy lama and how I studied and reflected on the scriptural traditions of the sutras and tantras without bias; and finally, though I have no experience of the fruits of spiritual practice, the responsibilities that I assumed in an effort to ostensibly benefit others.

Part One

The Period from My Birth to Adolescence

I N T H E *Khandro Nyingtik, "Heart Essence of the Dakini,"* there is a single prophecy that seemingly alludes to many of my successive reincarnations, though they are vaguely established.[17] The prophecy includes the following lines:

> To the east of Saljey Gang,
> Above what looks like a blazing iron casket,
> Upon the hip of what resembles a reclining wild yak

The region of Dokham (eastern Tibet) is known by the epithet "four rivers and six ranges." The latter include the range of Drida Zelmo Gang. Nearby is Katok Shama Porongi Rawa, one of the twenty-five most sacred power-places of eastern Tibet, and the supreme site associated with buddha activity. Here, near Lingmok Pema Drakar, which had been maintained by numerous learned and accomplished masters of the past, dwelled the lineage of Karpo Ling, that sprang from the Mukpo Dong clan, and that had in turn divided into three sublineages—large, small, and middling. Within the small lineage, there were the "seven robbers from Lharu," one of whom was known as Lingtruk Atra. From his lineage stemmed a small nomadic tribe known as Nyoshul, to which my father, Namgyal, belonged. My mother, Pema Tso, came from an area known as Juwa in Upper Dzachukha and was descended from the Khampas of the Yangtze Gorge.

I was born to them on the morning of the tenth day of the tenth lunar month of the Female Earth Hare year, known as Pramadi, in the fifteenth sixty-year cycle [1879],[18] in a place called Troda Nyakshar, which resembles the hip of a reclining wild yak. They say that when I first arrived in the world, rainbows appeared and the clashing of cymbals was heard.

Rumor has it that three days after I was born, I sat up early in the morning in the posture of absorption (*ting nge 'dzin*) and recited the Vajrakilaya mantra almost a hundred times. After that, according to my mother, I was a child possessed of extraordinary qualities: I could hold up my head, I never cried or soiled my bed, and so on. If I put my mind to it now, virtually all the things I have done from birth until today arise vividly in my memory.

As a child of only eight months, I was able to stand up and walk around without ever having to crawl. The older generation of nomads had a super-stition about children who stand early, and the elders regarded it as a very bad sign.

One night that winter, as I lay sleeping beside my mother, inside her cloak, I awoke in the middle of the night and perceived her as a black woman with a wrinkled, scowling face and bared fangs, her mass of orange hair wrapped protectively around me. The vision terrified me.

"Ama!" I cried.

"What is it?" she answered. "I'm right here." And she was just as before. From then on, I was able to talk.

One night that same winter, my mother and I were suffering from extreme cold. I took hold of my energies (*rlung*) and briefly meditated upon yogic inner heat (*gtum mo*).[19] The ensuing bliss-warmth made my mother feel as if she were sitting beside a huge fire, and it became unbearable for her. Finally, she thrust me out of her cloak, saying, "You're not like a human being, you ghostly child! Who are you?"

I sang to my mother:

I am from the direction of Labrang in the east.
I have control over both the energies and yogic inner heat.
I am an adept of the glorious *Tantra of the Secret Assembly.*
If you recognize me, I am Alak Rigdra.

"Who knows, who knows," my mother said, yanking me back inside her cloak. "From now on, don't yammer on like this in front of people, claiming to be this or that. If someone shows up one day and says, 'This is my lama' with total conviction, I will have no choice but to give you up.[20] Otherwise, don't say all these random things!" she scolded. After that, I never made any suggestions about what might be helpful or appropriate.

The next morning, the old granny who lived with us asked, "What were you and your son talking about last night?"

My mother answered, "It was not I. He was talking in his sleep."

Every night in my dreams, I found myself in an indescribably beauti-ful land that I thought must be India. I had constant visions of myself in both the charnel ground of Bhasing Forest and the great charnel ground of Tachung,[21] sometimes as a renunciate monk and sometimes as a yogin engaged in yogic discipline. The Protectress of Mantra Ekajati and the Great

Sage Rahula, both in their actual forms and in various emanational forms, guarded and protected me. Until I was thirteen years old, every evening at dusk nine huge spirit-dancers (*ging*) alighted upon the earth in the form of vultures.[22] As soon as they landed, they resumed their skeletal forms and danced around me, leaping and running. Each of them came before me, placing what appeared to be an amrita pill in my hand. Having bestowed the pills, they danced with great rejoicing and flew off into the sky. This appeared to me constantly.

When I was about a year old, the kind old woman who lived with us became my nanny, and I slept with her inside her cloak every night. During that time, just as I fell asleep, I heard what sounded like a tremendous clap of thunder, so loud that it made everything turn brilliant white, like sunlit snow. A moment later everything transformed into extremely intense red light, which enveloped me like red clouds, causing my mind to be enshrouded in darkness. Again, that appearance turned white and then into brilliant blueness. My mind went utterly blank without any recollection whatsoever. For a while, my mind remained in an unidentifiable state of emptiness and clarity, free of center and periphery. Simultaneously, the five colors flooded my entire perception, and myriad rays of light, like dense branches, shone forth, as well as inconceivable clusters of large and tiny light spheres continuously emitting rays. In particular, many spear-like light rays pierced my eyes, unnerving me so much that I could not sleep at night and told the granny. She had to hold a lamp up inside her cloak and say, "See? There's nothing there."

In the early spring of my third year, I happened upon a calf stuck in a muddy bog, scarcely alive. He had collapsed and was lowing plaintively. I thought to myself, "He got this ill-disposed body as a result of previous negative actions, and this is why he is burdened with such a load of suffering now. He has nothing but more of the same misery to look forward to in the future. Where can I find someone to rescue him from this swamp? His burden of suffering has fallen to me."

With that thought, I hauled the calf out of the mire and placed him on clean ground. Although I had not been taught the visualizations for the transference of consciousness, I imagined his consciousness as a pea-sized white light. Thinking I needed to eject it into the space above him, I called out many times, "I make offerings to the Lama and the Three Jewels! PAT! PAT!"[23] The calf exhaled, and simultaneously steam erupted from his crown aperture like a frothing geyser. They say that a clump of hair indicating the ejection of consciousness fell out, revealing a thumb-sized opening in the skull. My paternal uncle, who was an elderly lama, told me, "This is not the behavior of an ordinary person, but there is no need to tell anyone about this."

After that incident, whenever I saw or heard of a sentient being suffering, unbearable compassion spontaneously arose within me. "The apparent conditions of samsara, whether happy or sad, high or low, rich or poor, cannot be counted upon," I thought. "What means of escape is there from this endless cycle?" I felt a deep and constant sadness in my heart. Whenever I saw someone who was poor or destitute, I gave that person whatever I could find, obtaining it overtly or covertly as needed. I befriended beggars and took them around to various nomad camps to help them find alms, much to my parents' dismay. I overheard them say, "Everything about this behavior bodes ill."

I wondered constantly, "When will the time come when I can help poor beings?" This kindhearted wish was inherent in me, and I wonder if this was perhaps some hint of the Mahayana disposition. Indeed, this is the central principle of my life.

I repeated the six-syllable mantra (OM MANI PADME HUM) without cease and accumulated about ten million recitations.[24] My family owned an enormous number of livestock and was considered quite wealthy. Every year many sheep were slaughtered, and whenever I saw that happening, I fled to the mountains for the entire day. Overwhelmed with unbearable compassion, tears streaming down my cheeks, I thought with desperate sadness, "There is nothing I can do to save them!"

When I was five years old, toward the end of winter, my mother and I took our herds up to a mountain meadow and made our camp in the lower reaches of a little valley gorge called Ringmo Dilgyuk. Each day during the early summer, as the snow melted above the little valley, daily flash floods would wash away the cattle pens and the little tent my mother and I had. Every day my mother would build a dike, but it could not hold back the water, and we experienced great hardship. One day, as the water began to rise, I wielded a short kila, which I had fashioned from a piece of juniper wood, and proclaimed:[25]

In the land of India, I, Vimalamitra,
Was able to reverse the Ganges River,

So why not this little valley stream?
Mother, witness a wonderful show!
OM VAJRA KILI KILAYA HUNG PAT

As I rolled the kila between my palms, the floodwaters, as if driven by wind, flowed upstream a short distance and changed course. My mother exclaimed, "Well done! Well done!" Even today one can see the empty streambed left by the reversed flood.

When I turned seven, my uncle announced that it was time for me to learn to read. He wrote down the thirty letters of the Tibetan alphabet and read them aloud, beginning with the first letter, KA. When he pronounced the letter KA, instead of repeating after him, I proceeded to the second letter, KHA.

"Hey, don't jump ahead!" he scolded. "Look at each letter and pronounce it. Otherwise you won't learn." We did that two or three times, and I was able to recite the alphabet from memory. My uncle was displeased and scolded me further, saying that without a firm grasp of the written letters, such semblance of recitation by memory was just like the boy Litar, who was a common metaphor for illiteracy. Using him as an example, my uncle said, "You'll be no better than Litar." He aimed a wooden pointer at each letter and said, "Read!"

I did as I was told. "Goodness!" he exclaimed. "Now you may study a copy of the *Prayer of Good Conduct* (*bzang po spyod pa'i smon lam*)." For twenty days or so, he taught me letter-by-letter the *Seven-Branch Prayer* from the *Prayer of Good Conduct*.[26]

I was just a young child, so I normally fell asleep early. One night, as the others were having their evening tea, I partially awoke and spontaneously recited the entire *Prayer of Good Conduct* from beginning to end. My uncle was pleased and announced, "It is unnecessary to teach you to read." He discontinued teaching me.

Later, he gave me a copy of the *Prayer Book of Katok Monastery* (*ka thog chos spyod*) and told me to recite it. I did so, and he said, "Very well, if you can recite a *Liberation by Wearing* (*btags grol*) text, this will indicate that you are truly an excellent reader."[27]

When he handed me the text, I said, "Of course I can read this—I wrote it!" and recited it.[28] A few of the mantras in the *Liberation by Wearing* section were difficult for me to pronounce, and he corrected those, but otherwise not a single thing needed correction, which he considered extraordinary. Nevertheless, since I skipped the traditional training in spelling recitation, even now I am not very good at it.[29]

Then my uncle told me, "Now you've reached the point where you need to study the *Chronicles of Padma* (*pad ma bka' thang*)."[30] After reciting that text many times, I came to feel that for us here in Tibet, the kindness and compassion of Guru Rinpoche alone surpasses that of all the buddhas of the past, present, and future. Devotion arose in me with such certainty that no other thought could distract me. I focused exclusively on reciting the *Seven-Line Prayer* and the vajra guru mantra.[31] Even in my dreams at night, I remembered to call out, "Guru of Oddiyana, think of me!" whenever I felt afraid.

One time in a dream vision, a woman led me in a southwesterly direction, and we flew like birds through the sky. After a while, I began seeing many different lands, each of which the woman pointed out and described. Then I looked down and saw a vast kingdom encircled by a perimeter wall, and we landed at its northern gateway. Yeshe Tsogyal bestowed ablution from a silver vase, and a white man, who was in fact the Oath-Bound Protector Damchen Dorje Lekpa, led us inside through the eastern gateway of the perimeter wall. There we beheld the authentic palace of the Glorious Copper-Colored Mountain, which we entered through the southern door. In the center of this magnificent structure was a ravishingly beautiful lotus flower with eight petals, upon which I beheld the eight manifestations of Guru Padmasambhava in what looked like clay-statue form.

As I supplicated them with fervent devotion, reciting the *Seven-Line Prayer,* the clay coverings that I had seen at first vanished like mist and transformed into the actual eight manifestations of Guru Rinpoche. On each of the petals of the lotus seat, I vividly beheld the entire universe of one thousand million worlds, and in each of these were both a Shakyamuni Buddha and a Guru Rinpoche.[32] I received an empowerment from the Precious Guru, which, on subsequent reflection, seems to have been the empowerment for Ratna Lingpa's guru sadhana (*bla sgrub*). I also received this prophecy: "In your twenty-fifth year, you will be known as Lheybu Wangchuk, 'Divine Son and Mighty Lord'!" Later, when I completed my textual studies at the age of twenty-five, I thought this must have been what Guru Rinpoche had intended.

When I learned to read, I was but a child with undeveloped faculties, so it was difficult for me to grasp the depth of meaning. Still, I felt in my mind that I was able to comprehend the approximate meanings by defining the words literally and guessing what they might roughly mean.

In the summer of my eighth year, my father took me to herd a large number of pack animals. He was unable to steer them, and he grew furious and struggled with them a great deal. Seeing this, I realized that regardless of where one is born, high or low, samsara is nothing but suffering, and I knew that I had to realize the Dharma. Moreover, I saw that until I was able to firmly sever my ties to family and friends, they would be nothing but ropes binding me to samsara. From the depths of my heart, I resolved that I would wander through unknown lands disregarding loss, food, and clothing, meet an excellent spiritual teacher, and definitely realize the authentic Dharma. "I will carefully observe my mother's mood to see if she will approve," I thought, "and as soon as she does, I must go."

I explained to my mother the reasons behind this decision, but she retorted, "Have you been possessed by an evil spirit? If a little child like you were to run off to practice the Buddhist teachings, you wouldn't even be able to face a dog! You wouldn't have enough food, dogs would eat you, or you'd die of starvation. Nothing else would come of it. Stay here for a while. When you're finished growing, if you're able to practice the Buddhist teachings, you may. There are some good lamas around here." And so on. She gave a lengthy explanation of her reasoning, and it was left at that.

Realizing that whatever happiness, suffering, esteem, or lowliness one finds cannot be relied upon and is by nature nothing but suffering, my disillusionment with the world arose strongly, without needing to fabricate it. I took as my daily recitation the treasure revelation of Guru Chöwang, the *Hundred Thousand Names of the Buddha* (*sangs rgyas kyi mtshan 'bum*). When I read the benefits of reciting two names in particular, those of Sunamaparikirtanaja and Dharmakirtisagaraghosha, I thought that I, too, had no choice but to attain such a level of Buddhahood for the sake of all beings.[33] If I could become a buddha like that, I alone could liberate countless hundreds of millions of beings from samsara and establish them at the level of Buddhahood. I held that thought continuously in my mind.

From early childhood, I naturally restrained my mind from games and wild activity with great mindfulness, vigilance, and modesty. In particular, I felt that talking and playing with girls was something of which to be deeply ashamed. The elders even nicknamed me "Kid Lama."

Every day I memorized the prayer book, and each morning I was able to retain fifty short pages. Later, when I was a student at Dzogchen Monastery,

I was able to memorize the entire summer-rains-retreat recitation and the root text of the *Ascertainment of the Three Vows* (*sdom gsum rnam nges*) within a single day. Had I been a monk in the Geluk tradition, I would have been esteemed a "geshe of excellent memory."

When Shechen Rabjam Rinpoche came to our area, he recognized me with his clairvoyant mind as a reincarnation of one of the lamas from his monastery and ordered that I should be coaxed into going there. He bestowed upon me the name "Tenpa Rabpel." After that, Dzogchen Tulku Rinpoche came to our summer encampment when he was eighteen years old, and he did the hair-cutting ritual for me and bestowed the name Shönu Pema Lekdrup.[34] Later, the Shabdrung of the Eighteenth Tsiphu Rinpoche, named Khenchen Lodrö Gyatso, conferred the empowerment of Sarvavid Vairochana[35] according to the Sakya tradition and named me Ngawang Pel Zangpo. He kindly advised me that if I were to go to Penpo Nalanda Monastery, I would benefit the Buddhist teachings and beings. He had decided to return to Kham the following year and said that I should accompany him at that time. However, he passed away the next year and I never went.

One day I joined a large assembly of monks gathered at a family's house to recite prayers. I sat in a row of monks who were reciting the *Heart Sutra* (*zab mdo*) and *Praise to the Twenty-One Taras* (*sgrol ma nyer gcig la bstod pa*). When it was my turn to serve tea, an old monk named Sangye Özer got annoyed with me for not pouring his tea properly.

"Open your eyes when you pour tea!" he snarled.

"What do you mean, open my eyes?" I retorted. "Haven't we just spent the whole day reciting 'no eyes, no ears'?"[36]

"Well then," he shot back, "tell me what nonexistence means!"

"You explain existence first!" I flashed.

"My, what insolence! Heh heh!" he snorted.

I couldn't explain nonexistence either, and I sat there wondering what it meant.

Some time later, our family moved our nomad camp to a place called Kyilko. In the evening, when I went out to round up the herds on the hills at Mikchey Lakha, I happened upon a large number of thatched huts inhabited by numerous fully ordained monks. I approached one of the monks and asked, "Who are you?"

"I am Chandrakirti," he replied.

I asked him for his blessing and said, "Once, when I went to a family's house to recite the *Profound Heart Sutra*, I got into an argument with an elderly monk about the meaning of 'no eyes, no ears.' He couldn't define existence, and I couldn't define nonexistence. What do these terms mean?" I asked.

"Once you have fully comprehended the teachings on dependent arising and the definitive structure of the two truths, existence and nonexistence can be properly understood," he replied.

"What does that mean?" I asked.

He answered in verse:

> Neither eyes, nor ears or nose are truly valid,
> Nor is the tongue, bodily sensation, or mind truly valid.
> If these sensory faculties were truly valid,
> What good would the sublime path be to anyone?

"What is the meaning of that?" I asked.

"Right now you are still a young child, and the power of your intelligence is not yet fully developed, so for the time being you will not be able to understand this. Gradually reflect on these words, and you will come to understand them," he said.

"Please give me a teaching," I asked.

Placing a single volume of scripture upon my head, he said, "This is a commentary on my *Introduction to the Middle Way* (*dbu ma 'jug pa*)." Then he recited many different mantras. He gave me an old, worn yellow pandita hat and the volume of scripture, which I took. Knowing that laypeople are very superstitious, I left the items on a big rock as soon as I could see our tents.

When I got home, they asked, "What took you so long?"

I explained everything that happened in great detail, but they didn't believe me. "Don't tell lies," they scolded. "It would be ridiculous for there to be a monastery out in that barren place. And even if there were one, it would probably be for nonhumans. You can stay there, too, if you like, and if you find hats and books out there in the middle of nowhere, that's just great!"

A little while later, my uncle heard the whole story and asked me to bring him the hat and text. I retraced my steps, but there was nothing there.

This concludes the first section of my autobiography, in which I have spontaneously recounted various events that came to mind from my early childhood.

PART TWO

*How, by Relying on a Spiritual Mentor, I Studied, Reflected,
and Meditated Impartially upon the Textual Tradition
of the Sutras and Tantras*

ALL THE MANIFEST realizations of the genuine path, subsumed in the three vehicles, depend on the teacher, endowed with the defining characteristics of a spiritual mentor, whom one attends through the three methods of pleasing. Specifically, it is through the genuine insight (*shes rab*) born of studying, reflecting, and meditating upon the flawless scriptural traditions of Sutra and Mantra[37]—principally those of the two great "chariots" Nagarjuna and Asanga—that the realizations of the path are generated for one's own benefit. For others' benefit, one then teaches, debates, and composes, so that in directions where the brilliance of the Buddha's precious teachings has not yet spread, or once spread but has since faded, these vast and profound traditions come to illuminate everything like the radiance of the sun. The wondrous life stories of saintly beings are perfect illustrations of this.

In all truthfulness, such qualities are exceedingly weak in my mind. Nevertheless I have been inspired to emulate the liberated lives of the holy ones of the past, and I have protected even the subtlest points of renunciation. It says in the ordination ritual of the Mulasarvastivada for the *Vows of Individual Liberation* (*so thar gzhi chog*):[38]

> The Leader of the Shakyas—train as he did!
> Practice as he did! Do as he did!

So to begin with, here I shall explain how I first met my spiritual teacher and adviser on the path.

Peerless throughout the three levels of existence, Gyalse Jangchub Dorje, also known as Lungtok Tenpey Nyima Gyaltsen Pelzangpo, was like the orb of the crystal moon in the constellation of stellar disciples encircling the great Vajradhara Patrul Rinpoche. He was unparalleled from every perspective—the dynamism of his learning, his loving compassion, his abilities, powers, blessings, realization, and experiences. That was known and proven to be so throughout this Buddhist land of Greater Tibet.

Among the people of Dzatö, there is a saying: "Without Nyoshul Lungtok, Palgey Patrul Rinpoche would have been childless."[39] Likewise, there is a prophecy about this holy saint in a prophetic inventory discovered by Lerab Lingpa, which states that he was the embodiment of the Great Abbot Shantarakshita. The Venerable Khyentse Wangpo prophesied that he would be the embodiment of the hidden yogin Kongnyön and of the master Öntrul Kündröl Namgyal.

In any case, he followed Patrul Orgyen Jigme Chökyi Wangpo for twenty-eight years, attending him without separation. He studied, pondered, and mastered the myriad textual traditions of the sutras and tantras. In particular, as when a vase is filled to the brim by pouring into it the contents of another,[40] he received the extraordinary teachings of the vast and profound paths, as well as the ultimate key points of the path comprising the pith instructions entitled *Sangwa Nyingtik, "Secret Heart Essence."*[41] The latter have two sequential stages: Kadak Trekchö, "Cutting Through of Primordial Purity," an ultimate practice in which one is introduced directly and immediately to innate wisdom beyond the scope of conventional knowledge; and Ösel Tögal, "Direct Crossing of Luminosity," in which one is introduced to the path of the actually manifest three kayas.[42]

Moreover, he did not leave the teachings as mere hearsay but clarified their meanings by blending scriptural citations with reason, critically examining the words. Through his insight born of reflection, he established the ultimate key points. Both master and student then meditated upon these points in remote hermitages and compared their experiences. Having resolved all his points of confusion until not a single doubt remained, his mind correctly verified all the vajra points described in the tantras.

Afterward, along with Ön Tendzin Norbu, Khenpo Könchok Özer, Minyak Kunzang Sonam, and Naktar Tulku, he intended to spend the rest of his life in Nangchen and Riwoche as a mendicant renunciate. When they approached Abu Rinpoche for his permission, however, he did not give it.[43] Instead, he appointed Konchok Özer as a monastic preceptor at Dzogchen Monastery, and to the rest he said, "You three return to your homelands and stay in mountain hermitages. You, Tendzin Norbu, who are descended from the Önpo family, should teach and study as much as you can at our Gemang Monastery."

Accordingly, my gracious lama, Lungtok Rinpoche, came to this region and established his principal seat here at Jönpalung. Relying on the *Way of the Bodhisattva (byang chub sems dpa'i spyod pa la 'jug pa)* for ten years and the *Trilogy of Resting (ngal gso skor gsum)* for three years, he spent a total of thirteen years engaged in mind training.[44] He used to say jokingly, "I spent thirteen years in Shugushar doing nothing but producing and dissolving concepts, making no progress at all. If I had been meditating solely on the Great Perfection all this time, by now I bet I would have a pretty excellent view and meditation."

In addition, he lived in Dzongnak, Zangma, Karding Hermitage, Namkong, Orlima, and Gyaduk Hermitage for several years in each place,[45] and during that time he never accepted any offerings, either on behalf of the dead or the living. Later, he went to the Drubchen encampment and stayed there for nine years. During that period, he purged himself seven times of all the material belongings that had been faithfully given to him, distributing them as offerings and charities. He adopted the immaculate tradition of the great Kadampas, and his life resembled that of the bodhisattva Dromtönpa.

This Great Vajradhara of the Ultimate Meaning,[46] who lacked none of the characteristics of a spiritual mentor elucidated in the main texts of the sutras and tantras, was staying at Gyaduk Hermitage when my father took me to meet him. It was the beginning of the Water Sheep year [1883], and I was five years old. From that day forward, he cared for me with infinite kindness and compassion.

Nowadays, most of those who deem themselves learned and accomplished puff themselves up with pride over the slightest meaningless fame from their bogus activities. If they have even so much as a good worldly dream, they act as though they were highly realized, meanwhile concerning themselves primarily with the acquisition of magnificent offerings. My refuge lord Vajradhara had none of that deceitful pretention.

During the long period of time I spent with him, he would often tell me stories. Once he told me about the time he stayed at the Dzogchen Gangtrö Hermitage for three years performing long-life practices for Mingyur Namkhai Dorje. He had very few provisions.

"Dzogchen Rinpoche's estate was different back then, too," he explained. "It was nothing but a poor, ramshackle place, and retreat provisions were in scarce supply. Kind Abu, as well, gave me nothing at all, so I survived on a meager amount of food for those three years. As for clothing, I had nothing but an old monastic undershirt and my three monastic robes. Instead of a meditation cushion, I used a flat stone.

"As soon as my three-year commitment was fulfilled, I presented myself before Abu, who asked, 'Did you have enough to eat?'

"'I had hardly anything to eat,' I answered, 'but because it was your order and since I was focused on the long life of Mingyur Namkhai Dorje, I was happy.'

"Abu then quoted:

> When a yogin's samayas are uncorrupted,
> The gods and demons of phenomenal existence will provide
> sustenance.

"'That refers to people like you,' he said.

"Another time Abu said to us, 'You students ask me for teachings and then you don't bother to put them into practice. If you were to practice, superior practitioners would have results in a single day, average practitioners within a month, and even inferior practitioners would have results within a year. However, in order to practice the Buddhist teachings, one must understand the key points of practice. If nothing happens when you practice, it is an indication that you have not understood the key points. The bodhisattva Dromtönpa said, 'To blend study, reflection, and meditation is the crucial unerring key to Buddhist practice.'"

Patrul Rinpoche used to give them a session or two of teachings and then say, "Now you need to grow familiar with it." He would make them meditate for a long time.

While master and disciple, Abu and Lungtok, were staying at Ko Orma, Lungtok's mother sent him a round of butter.

"Each time she churned the summertime milk," Lungtok explained, "she set aside a scoop of fresh butter, slathering the new butter on top of the butter from the previous batch and layering it inside a bag fashioned from an animal stomach. When I received it, I offered it to Abu Rinpoche in some roasted barley flour. He sat there staring at it for a moment.

"'Why does your butter look like an official's hat made of furled rhubarb leaves?' Abu asked.[47]

"I explained.

"'Then I dare not eat it,' Abu replied, and he declined to partake."[48]

Lungtok continued, "One day Abu asked me, 'Do you miss your mother?'

"'Not really,' I replied.

"'Well, that's what happens when you don't cultivate compassion. Now go into that willow grove over there and train in recognizing all beings as your mother, remembering their kindness, and so forth, for seven days. Then come back,' he said.[49]

"I then spent seven days training in recognizing all beings as my mother, remembering their kindness, and so forth, and a genuine loving-kindness, compassion, and bodhichitta arose in my mind. I went before my lama and relayed what had happened.

"'That's it!' exclaimed Abu. 'When you train properly, these are the true signs that arise in your mind. That's what it takes. I've told you not to accept faith-offerings (*dkor*) in the past, but in this case you should accept whatever you can get and go home to see your mother for a while. Then come back.'

"I attended the funeral proceedings for Abu's mother and was given a stallion and ten silver coins. These, along with a couple bricks of tea and some cattle I obtained on an alms round from Dzachukha to Yi-Lhung, I gave to my mother.

"When you chase after those evil faith-offerings, you can't find a thing," Lungtok remarked to me, "and when you don't want them, they pile up on you!"

Another time, Abu and his students boiled "three-kaya tea" in Do Ari Forest.

"Abu was teaching Longchen Rabjam's *Trilogy of Resting*—the text *Resting in the Nature of Mind* (*sems nyid ngal gso*) and so forth—from the Great Perfection. He guided us according to our personal experience, alternating teaching with meditation training. Once, while we were meditating on *Resting in Illusion* (*sgyu ma ngal gso*), my deluded clinging to appearances as real fell away, and all phenomena arose as the manifold display of unreal illusion."

"Was that realization?" I asked.

"No, it was a good experience," Lungtok explained.

"What is three-kaya tea?" I asked.

"Our group had very meager provisions. In the morning we boiled water with a few tea leaves added, and the color, smell, and flavor were rather nice. That was called nirmanakaya tea. At midday, we added water to the leftover tea and boiled it, so it was a bit weaker than before. That was sambhogakaya tea. In the evening, we added even more water, so that there was no color, smell, or taste left at all. That was called dharmakaya tea. That's what Abu humorously called it," Lungtok explained.

"So what did you eat?" I asked.

"In the morning we mixed a little roasted barley flour into our tea, and at lunchtime we ate a little roasted barley dough. At one point even that ran out, and we had to scrounge meat off old livestock carcasses that the nomads had tossed out to the dogs.

"When we were nearing the end of the teaching period, a plague of bloody dysentery broke out. Abu announced that we had to flee, so we split up and each of us stayed at the base of a fir tree. For a long time, we had to subsist solely on azalea roots.[50]

"Some time in the fifth lunar month of that summer, Abu sent Palchen Dorje to call us, and we reconvened from our respective directions. We were all wearing our long outer robes and carrying begging bowls and monks' staffs, and Abu Rinpoche himself came out to greet us, waving incense. 'My goodness,' he exclaimed. "You look like Indian bhikshus!'[51]

"Abu had a round of cheese, butter, and barley flour that he gave to us, telling us to divide it among ourselves. That served as our meal for the day, and we didn't even light a fire.

"'You didn't have to face any hardships at all this time, but even though such favorable conditions for spiritual practice converged, you were still unable to apply the practice. What a loss!' Abu said."

Lungtok continued, "One time I went to Yel-le Gar to attend a vase-accomplishment ceremony of the New Treasure tradition.[52] During the deity invocation, the actual wisdom deities manifested to many of the monks, who in turn began to dance.[53]

"That evening, when I returned home, Abu called me before him. When I arrived, he asked me, 'What did you see at the vase ceremony today? What were they doing?'

"I told him what I had seen.

"'Oh, today was an animate dance. Sometimes inanimate dances happen as well,' he said.

"'What do you mean?' I asked.

"'In Shugushar, I performed the recitation practice for all thirteen mandalas of the Kama. While I was performing the recitation practice of Vajrakilaya according to the Rok tradition, a little copper kila that was standing as a symbolic support on the mandala in front started to dance!' he told me.

"'Why did that happen?' I asked.

"'I don't know if it was good or bad,' Abu replied.

"'Do you still have that kila?' I asked.

"'I gave it to Tertön Sögyal. Whenever he used that kila to retrieve a concealed treasure from inside any kind of rock, he said it was like thrusting it into mud.[54] Later, however, he gave that kila to the Khangsar family in Gönjo, and from then on, whenever he retrieved concealed treasures, he found the rock to be rock-hard. It seems that after he became famous, he did not care for anything but bronze-alloy treasure kilas and was no longer satisfied with mere copper ones.'"[55]

Lungtok continued, "Kind Abu said to me, 'Do not teach the Great Perfection to others until you are fifty years old. Then, if you are able, you may teach it.' Unfortunately, before I turned fifty, Gemang Ön Tenga insisted that I teach him, so a little slipped out of my mouth. Other than that, I have never transgressed Kind Abu's word for even an instant, and our lineage is a golden chain untarnished by the rust of corrupted samaya."[56]

Gracious Lungtok Rinpoche was quite reserved and endeavored to keep his inner qualities completely concealed throughout his life.[57] Nevertheless, every tiny drop of nectar that fell incidentally from his lips reflected his manifest realization of the three vehicles: he relied on moral discipline as the foundation, he became accomplished in absorption as his objective, he connected with loving-kindness and compassion as the essence, and he completed the practice of all the ordinary and extraordinary key points of the generation and completion stages of meditation. These qualities can be patently verified through the authentic tantric texts.

Dromtönpa once said, "This lineage of mine is like a mountain stream descending from the snows: from the perfect Buddha down to my own lama Atisha, one can point to each lineage holder in succession, naming every one. The practice of precious bodhichitta has been uninterrupted, which is why the lineage retains its blessings. The pith instructions of Profound View and Vast Practice are utterly complete, and thus the key points of the path of the Mahayana are complete and lacking nothing." Likewise, our own lineage reaches back to this authentic source.

I was two when my father took me to meet the holy master Lungtok at Gyaduk Hermitage.[58] He was delighted to see us, and gave me a painted wooden bowl filled with green and purple grapes and brown sugar, as well as long-life pills, a protection cord, and a blessing scarf, which he put around my neck. He placed both his hands, graced with the glory of ten million merits, upon my head, bestowing his blessing and making aspiration prayers for manifold auspiciousness. He instructed my father to bring me back to receive teachings as soon as I had grown up a little, clearly revealing our future auspicious connection.

Over and over again, Lama Lungtok remarked to my uncle Jangchub, who lived there at the encampment, "That little boy today certainly was amazing . . ." I later heard that Uncle Jangchub sent a message to my family that said, "You probably ought to keep him in very sanitary conditions. Our precious lama never comments on the positive or negative qualities of anyone who comes to see him, no matter what their status, so this is very significant."[59]

When I turned nine years old in the Female Fire Pig year [1887], my father and I went with a large group of men and women from our region to a hot spring called Chukol Tsatok, where one of the heart-sons of the great accomplished master Nyakla Pema Düdül, who attained the Rainbow Body, had come to bathe. His name was Chomden Dorje, otherwise known as Lama Taye. For a period of seven days, he gave teachings on the preliminary practices from the *Profound Teaching: All-Pervasive Natural Liberation* (*zab chos mkha' khyab rang grol*). At the time, my mental faculties were not yet developed enough to penetrate the depths of what he was saying, but merely seeing his face inspired such devotion that my whole mind seemed to transform. I was certain that he was a teacher connected to me from previous lives, but shortly thereafter he passed away to the pure realms.

When I was eleven, I studied a commentary on the Manjushri supplication *You Whose Intelligence* (*gang gi blo gros ma*) with my uncle Lama Dorje Samdrub.[60] I memorized the root text and its commentary by the venerable Jamyang Khyentse Wangpo. That winter, since the upper and lower monasteries we have now did not exist back then, a makeshift assembly of monks from Ta and Trom gathered in a place called Dzongkar to perform a patron-sponsored ceremony. I gave a discourse to the assembly on the *You Whose Intelligence* prayer, and the elders present were astonished.

When I was twelve, my uncle Trachung, who was a very good lama, needed a copy made of a volume containing the *Sadhana of Lord Vinayaka* (*mgon po tshogs bdag*) according to the Katok tradition. I prepared the paper, and Lama Dorli scribed.[61] When we did the proofreading, I recited the original text. When I came to the line, "Chant the statement before purifying the poison," I had some difficulty pronouncing the words. I asked Lama Trachung about it, and he berated me.

"I told you there is no need for you to be a monk; just be a layperson. Now you're acting like a monk, but you can't even read!" He scolded me like this many times.

That evening I prayed fervently to Lord Manjushri, and at dawn the roaring sound of AH RA PA TSA NA resounded from the depths of my being. I perceived myriad orange AH RA PA TSA NA syllables rising up from within me like boiling milk, and just when I thought they would gush out of me, I fainted.[62] From that day forward, my ability to read aloud was far superior to what it had been, and I was able to accurately recite the whole of the sublime *Prajnaparamita in Eight Thousand Lines (shes rab kyi pha rol du phyin pa brgyad stong)* in half a day.

When I was twelve, a female naga gave me what she said was a wish-fulfilling jewel, and at thirteen I discovered a single-volume medical text in Dzongkar.[63] I returned them to their respective treasure-protectors and never considered such things of any particular importance.

When I was fourteen years old, I received elaborate guidance on the *Mid-Length Commentary on the Preliminary Practices (sngon 'gro'i 'bring po)* according to Longsel Dorje Nyingpo from the great treasure-revealer Ngawang Tendzin, also known as Jigdral Tutop Lingpa. He had been a direct disciple of the Fourth Drime Shingkyong, Rigdzin Mingyur Tenpey Gyaltsen of Katok,[64] and he was an undisputed, prophesied emanation of Shübu Palseng. I gained a true understanding of the need to link whatever great or small roots of virtue one accomplishes to the three supreme methods. I effectively completed each stage of that particular guidance tradition, including the generation of bodhichitta, the mandala offering, the inner and outer recitations of Vajrasattva, the devotional guru yoga, the *Supplication to the Hundred Thousand Names of the Buddha (mtshan 'bum gsol 'debs)*, and the loud, extended recitation of the syllable HUM for dispelling obstacles.

Then, in my fifteenth year, from the same great treasure-revealer, I received the complete empowerments and oral transmissions for the eleven volumes of Longsel Dorje Nyingpo's *Profound Treasures (zab gter)* and *Supplemental Collected Works (zhal skong gsung 'bum)*. On the first day, the day of preparatory rituals, he said to me, "Observe your dreams tonight. You will need to tell me about them in the morning."

The next morning, in the early dawn hours, I dreamed I was at the base of a large willow tree beating a big gong, which summoned large crowds from far off in the distance.

That morning I related my dream.

"The willow tree was Katok Monastery," the great treasure-revealer explained. "The ringing of the gong is a sign that you will study and teach the Buddhist teachings at Katok." From this I understood that he could see the future.

During the main section of the empowerments, when the wisdom deities actually descend, he instructed the students in the sequential visualization, whereby we generated ourselves as the deity.[65] Without any mental fabrication, my karmic body instantly transformed into the body of the wrathful deity, complete with all its glorious accoutrements.[66] In what seemed to be the state of consummation of the three aspects of objective perception, I experienced such firm divine pride that I could actually hear the sound of my vajra wings flapping.[67]

That year I went to the Khangtsik encampment. Gracious Lungtok Rinpoche's spiritual son, Khenchen Gyaltsen Özer, who possessed unimaginably excellent qualities of scholarship, virtuousness, goodness of heart, insight, love, and power, served as my ordination preceptor. The master of the ordination ceremony (*las slob*) was Kulung Khenpo Tsultrim Norbu; the master who explains the significance of the time of ordination (*dus go ba*) was Karma Damchö Özer; his assistant (*grogs dan pa*) was Tsewang Rigdzin; and the auxiliary master of ceremonies (*las kyi kha skong*) was Dordzin Namdrol Gyatso of Mindroling. These five comprised the requisite quorum of devout monks, and in their presence, I received the vows of the novitiate, which are conferred in three stages.[68]

Gracious Lungtok Rinpoche then summoned me, and when I arrived, he was utterly delighted. "You are very fortunate to have received the vows of a renunciate," he remarked. "The ritual ordination text of the *Novitiate of the Mulasarvastivada* (*gzhi chog*) says:

> Immediately after one has taken the vows of the novitiate,
> One becomes an object of homage and prayer for all householders.

"As this explains, you have been released from the ties of the householder life and have laid the foundation for unsurpassable qualities. Arya Nagarjuna once said:

> Just as the Earth supports both the animate and inanimate,
> Moral discipline is said by the Buddha
> To be the foundation of all qualities.

"Therefore, since the monastic precepts bring such inconceivable benefits, it is imperative that you uphold them with certitude. It also says in the *Ascertainment of the Three Vows:*

Killing, taking what is not given, sexual misconduct,
Lying, drinking alcohol, eating after noon,
Dancing and so on, jewelry and the like, high luxurious beds,
And accepting gold and silver—
These comprise the ten coarse acts to renounce, the Buddha said.

"The acts of renunciation and commitment should be correctly implemented in accordance with the four basic precepts and the six branch precepts. The detailed listing of the thirty-six precepts is subsumed within these," he said. With these words, he imparted detailed instructions and kind advice, and gave me five squares of red silk.

From then on, I heeded the precepts mindfully and conscientiously. There is no mention of a "downfall of separation" for novices, but I wore my formal monastic cloak and patchworked lower robe without separation.[69] I gave up eating after noon and so on, and renounced the mere touch of gold and silver, let alone accepting it as mine. In these ways, I precisely observed the ten coarse precepts. Moreover, without any hypocritical pretense and inspired by feelings of renunciation, I trained with immense respect for the monastic precepts.

In fact, my pure moral discipline is the only reason people respect and honor me as a lama these days. So it is very important that my followers properly control their minds with vows and mindfully uphold the points of the precepts. Karma Chakme Rinpoche once said:

An old monk with pure vows—
This is the greatest of all signs of accomplishment.

This is absolutely true.

Thereafter, I lost about two years, preoccupied with distractions.

At seventeen, I read the expanded version of the *Prajnaparamita in One Hundred Thousand Lines* once through and was overjoyed at the meaning of "the emptiness of emptiness."[70] When I came to the part that reads, "The illusory mind hankers after illusory objects...," I felt strong conviction that appearances are unreal and dreamlike.

One day early that winter, I became certain that nothing truly exists, either as a single entity or as many parts, and after thoroughly searching for the so-called "identity" of individual beings and phenomena, I concluded with stronger certainty than ever that they do not truly exist at all, in any place, direction, or time. I arrived at a clear and definitive understanding that whatever emerges through dependent arising lacks any inherent existence, just as Chandrakirti intended when he said to me earlier, "Neither eyes, nor ears or nose are truly valid."

In that state of recognition, I rested in one-pointed equipoise. First, the grasping mind ceased and mere appearances remained before me. After a while, even those appearances faded away, and my mind perceived only a clear and empty field, the union of emptiness and clarity. Then this, too, vanished, and notions of ordinary consciousness and emptiness both fell away. Like pouring water into water, ordinary consciousness and emptiness became of one taste, at which point I was left without any thoughts.

As I began to emerge from that state back to coarse-level mind, all appearances arose as unreal, dreamlike illusions. Were I to evaluate this process, in which clinging to substantial reality occurs only occasionally, I would surmise that even for those who have attained the sublime bodhisattva levels, such clinging to substantial reality, while it might occur only for very brief moments, probably does not entirely cease to occur. But that refers merely to direct nonconceptual cognition of objective emptiness.

Later, when I turned twenty-seven and all the indications of the culmination of awareness were complete, I established through genuine personal experience that there is a vast distinction between awareness-wisdom—the abiding reality of the subject-object dichotomy—and the above-mentioned direct cognition that arises through its expressive power, insight.[71]

In the post-meditative state, when emotional obscurations are eliminated, there are varying degrees of the insight that thoroughly apprehends phenomena, which are awareness' expressive power (*rtsal*).[72] This is something that I feel could be elaborated upon. I say this lovingly to those nowadays who maintain that the two paths of seeing in Sutra and Tantra are the same, as are the insights that apprehend them.

After spending nine years at Drubchen Gar, the Gracious Lungtok Rinpoche decided to return to his native land. He went to speak with Lama Özer about it. "At this point, I have finished putting eyes and mouths on your egg-like tokdens.[73] I have dreamed many times of a great golden stupa lying on its side in the lower reaches of Sershung Valley. Each time I'm right on the verge of standing it up, so I must go," Lungtok explained.

The following year, at the end of the fifth lunar month, he came down from that high encampment and stayed near a hot spring. All the lamas and monks of Ta and Trom came on horseback to welcome him. At Chukhol Tsatok, everyone received his audience, and he stayed for a few nights. On the day of his departure, he called down from his horse, "Now everyone needs to line up in a horseback procession. Ngakli and Sangye Kyab, come stand to my right and left as my attendants."[74]

In Mokong Maklam Gang, we met a welcoming party from Gyashö. When we passed by the place where Lama Ngawang Tenpa had died, he made prayers of dedication and aspiration, and had tea. Ngawang, an emanation of the great Vidyadhara Adzom, came as well, and in offering he presented Lungtok Rinpoche with a silver crown adorned with the eight auspicious symbols, and a fine bell and vajra that belonged to the late Lama Ngawang Tenpa.

After relaying the immense joy and gratitude they all felt that Lama Lungtok had returned to his homeland, Ngawang implored Lungtok to consider the devotees of this region, particularly those of Ta and Trom, and to accept them as his followers. "Our sole wish is for you to show us the unerring key points of the path of the sacred Great Perfection, only this. Please turn vastly the Wheel of Dharma and remain firmly among us for a hundred aeons! Please, please do not accept the invitations from the people at Dzogchen Monastery. If you try to go elsewhere, this old monk will grab hold of your shawl and not let go!"

Lungtok Rinpoche listened to both his mundane and his spiritual requests, which were not mere flattery but humble appeals straight from the heart, and he promised to stay. He settled into a tent complete with kitchen, seats, and so forth, beautifully prepared for him by the monastic community, on the upper side of the field at Yel-le Gar. Those who had come to welcome him dispersed.

After a few days I went to see him. "We are going to perform an amendment feast offering on the tenth day of the sixth lunar month," he announced.[75] "Go see if there are any faithful people around here, and bring back whatever feast offerings you can gather."[76]

I went door-to-door carrying the message. "We need to make this a grand and elegant occasion," I explained. The people of Ta and Trom, communities that were much more populous than they are now, offered numerous sacks of butter and cheese, and many others offered butter, Tibetan cheesecake, milk, and yogurt. Lungtok Rinpoche recited an elaborate amendment feast-offering ceremony according to Ngari Panchen's profound treasure, entitled *Guru as a Treasure Trove of Qualities* (*gu ru yon tan gter mdzod*). To me he said, "This autumn I plan to teach a set of preliminary practices, so please come." He stayed there for several months.

On the thirteenth day of the eighth lunar month, he set up camp at Pema Rito, "Exalted Lotus Mountain." One day I went to visit him, and he said, "This place is pretty small. Since many people have come to attend the teachings, we need to divide up the area." He allotted places to the fifty or so people who had gathered to receive teachings. "This is your tent site," he would say, and he had me pound a stake into the ground to mark each person's site. No one was allowed to stay in the area beyond Lungtok's own tent because many lamas and tulkus would be arriving, he explained, and he went on his way.

At the beginning of the ninth lunar month, he began teaching *Words of My Perfect Teacher* (*kun bzang bla ma'i zhal lung*). However, my tribal group was camped in the lower Trom valley, so I didn't hear about it. One day I received a message from Lungtok Rinpoche and went immediately. He had already begun teaching the cultivation of bodhichitta according to its application stage.

"May I join you now?" I asked.

"I sent you many messages," he replied, "but it seems you did not receive them. Yes, you may join us."

The next morning, I offered him three silver coins, a full tub of butter and cheese, and a whole sheep carcass as a symbolic mandala offering, and I joined the assembly.[77] As soon as the teaching session was over, Lungtok Rinpoche repeated many times, "The most important thing is not the fact that supreme bodhichitta *should* be cultivated, but the fact that it has actually *been* cultivated. Oh my, what a wonderfully auspicious note on which to take our session break!" he exclaimed with great excitement.[78]

He completed the remaining sections of the text within a month. Concurrently, each day he summarized the key points starting from the beginning of the text. I composed a guide to the *Words of My Perfect Teacher*, commencing from the cultivation of bodhichitta. When the entire teaching was over, I asked his advice.

"You have not received teachings on the preliminary practices before, so you need to accumulate a full cycle, reciting each of the five sections one hundred thousand times.[79] However, in your case these will not follow the traditional order. This winter, you will recite the hundred-syllable mantra of Vajrasattva. I will train you step-by-step in how to do the recitation," he replied.

He then had me recite the hundred-syllable mantra.[80] During my session breaks, he explained in detail the visualizations pertaining to the four powers. In particular, he told me, "It is through the power of support that the mind is trained in the generation stage. You should familiarize yourself with it. You should visualize the deity as a unity of appearance and emptiness, like the moon's reflection in water. In terms of the apparitional aspect, visualize even the white and black of the eye and the hair pores on the skin; and in terms of the empty aspect, understand that this visualization lacks even a speck of true existence."

I meditated accordingly, but when it came to the dissolution at end of the session, where one chants, "Vajrasattva melts into light and dissolves into me . . ." I had some difficulty dissolving the visualization. I asked Lungtok Rinpoche about it, and he said, "Oh, that's what happens when you fixate too hard on solid material reality. 'Vajrasattva' is nothing more than a name mentally ascribed to a configuration of face and hands that has no substantial existence whatsoever. If you examine the face and hands individually, is there anything there?"

I investigated accordingly and discovered with conviction that the deity appears, yet lacks any true existence. I completed over one hundred thousand recitations of the hundred-syllable mantra within fifty days. As a sign that my negative actions had been purified, my body felt light both in dreams and in actuality, my mind acquired the clarity of absorption, and so forth. Every indication of successful practice described in the scriptures manifested.

"What shall I recite now?" I asked.

"There are four supports explained in the *Way of the Bodhisattva,* and of these, the support of relaxation is what you need right now, so rest for a while," he told me.[81] I then rested for ten days.

"Now, the practice of Vajrasattva and the mandala offering may be substituted for the merits accrued over one incalculable aeon on the Paths of Accumulating and Joining, according to the Mahayana," he explained.[82] "For the guidance on the main practices, an introduction equivalent to the wisdom of the Path of Seeing is required, so you should first accumulate a mandala offering. It is this practice that marks the outset of the bodhisattva's Path of Accumulating, so take these sacred representations as supports for your mandala offerings." He lent me a bronze-alloy statue of Shakyamuni to represent buddha body, the *Verse Summation of the Prajnaparamita* (*mdo sdud pa*) and root text of the *Guhyagarbha Tantra* (*gsang ba snying po*) to represent buddha speech, and a Kadam-style stupa to represent buddha mind.[83]

"This Kadam-style stupa is traditionally explained in terms of the stages of the path for the three capacities of practitioner," he said,[84] and he went on to explain the way in which the three main parts of the stupa correspond to the three trainings, starting from the lotus cluster of its base.

Then he fell silent and sat for a moment. He held up a statue of the Great Omniscient Longchenpa and said, "This was given to me by Jamyang Khyentse Wangpo. It contains a brain relic of Omniscient Longchenpa and the hair of Jigme Lingpa. Take this, too! Longchenpa is the most precious spiritual teacher of the Nyingma school, so pray to him and you may even meet him in a vision. Since this will be your initial accumulation of merit, you should amass as much as you can of all five kinds of offerings. You are the son of a wealthy family, so you will need to offer as many butter lamps as possible. I will provide the wick cotton." He gave me cotton, a bundle of one hundred sticks of white and red Mindroling incense, and saffron mixed with the five bovine products.[85]

I arranged the sacred objects on a flat stone, and from that day forward I never went a day without sweeping my room and offering food, butter lamps, and each of the five kinds of offering substances, which I set out on a small board. I rinsed and cleaned about four dry measures (*khel*) of grain, removing all the stones, chaff, bird droppings, and dirt until it was pristine. Each day, I doused the grain I needed that day with saffron water. I never used the same offering grain two days in a row.[86]

When I had completed just over thirty thousand repetitions of the *Billionfold Mandala Offering* according to the *Longchen Nyingtik*," I was summoned before Lungtok Rinpoche.[87] When I arrived, he asked, "How many have you done?"

I told him, and he said, "Now you should accumulate the remaining seventy thousand plus the amendment, using either Jamyang Khyentse Wangpo's prayer that begins 'I and others,' or the one that begins with the words, 'The ground is sprinkled with scented water.' You may choose."[88]

"Although there is no reason *not* to use the Khyentse prayer, I think

I would prefer to recite the one first spoken by the great Buddhist king Trisong Detsen," I replied.

"That's fine. The peerless Jowo Atisha said, 'Whatever your current means of accumulating merit and aspirations, it is crucial to recite the authentic words of the buddhas, such as the *Prayer of Good Conduct*. Alternatively, you may recite something like the *Prayer of Maitreya* (*byams pa'i smon lam*), the Buddha's regent, who abides on the tenth bodhisattva level, or the words of one who abides on the first bodhisattva level, such as the *Prayer in Twenty Verses* (*smon lam nyi shu pa*) by Arya Nagarjuna. It makes a significant difference to rely upon the teachings of those who have mastered words of truth.[89] The words and rhymes of ordinary people, however eloquent, have no real essence.'

"What Trisong Detsen said is indeed true. However, Khyentse Rinpoche is the undisputed reincarnation of that great Buddhist king, so it doesn't make much difference. You do as you wish. The prayer that begins with the words 'The ground is sprinkled with scented water' is famous because the great Buddhist king Trisong Detsen composed it when he offered his entire kingdom and subjects to Guru Rinpoche. Moreover, with regard to whatever practice you are engaged in, if you analyze and examine it beforehand, that will make a big difference when it comes to not mistaking the key points of the paths of Sutra and Mantra." He gave me detailed advice, explaining things such as why getting involved with the teachings indiscriminately and impulsively, like a dog who finds a lung, is a recipe for ruin.[90]

Then I came back down to my retreat room. So I wouldn't feel discouraged about how many days it would take, I recited a *Calling the Lama from Afar* (*bla ma rgyang 'bod*) prayer and accumulated one full set of the refuge, bodhichitta, and Vajrasattva recitations, each with its required visualization. Then, during the mandala offering, I began each session with ten repetitions of the *Seven-Branch Prayer* from the *Prayer of Good Conduct,* conjoined with prostrations. During the final repetition of the *Seven-Branch Prayer,* I filled and offered the mandala plate, and after a long time I finished this accumulation. During my breaks, too, I accumulated as many mandala offerings as I could.

During that period, I had a dream in which a woman who seemed to be Yudrönma said, "Come, let us go meet the Great Omniscient One." She led the way, and we arrived at a cave on the eastern face of what looked like a golden hill in Golden Valley. Inside the mountain, there was a tunnel shaped like the throat of a white conch. We went in, spiraling to the right. When we reached the peak of the mountain, there was a meadow of golden-green grass about the area of a house foundation, where the Great Omniscient One sat facing east. Staring at the sky with a fixed gaze, he chanted AH AH. He placed a crystal the shape of a sheep's heart on my head and spoke these words:

> AH The nature of mind is self-existing awakened mind. AH
> AH Supreme emptiness is Samantabhadra's expanse. AH
> AH Awareness, wide and penetrating, is the dharmakaya. AH
> AH Everything unfolds from its five great radiances. AH
> AH The nature of awareness transcends view and meditation. AH
> AH Today, may this remain within your heart! AH

Overcome with devotion, my mind fainted for a time into a thought-free state. When I arose from that state, I awoke in my bed. After that, some tiny pearl-like relics emerged from the statue of Longchenpa.

When I completed the mandala offering, I went before Lungtok Rinpoche to return the sacred objects.

"Did you meet the Omniscient One?" he asked.

"No, actually I didn't," I said. I had forgotten about the dream and neglected to tell him about it. He took the pearl-like relics, and I departed.

Some time later he asked me again, "When you were doing your mandala offering practice, did you meet the Omniscient One?"

"No, I did not meet him," I replied.

"Did you have any dreams?" he asked.

Suddenly remembering, I described my dream, and he asked, "Did the Great Omniscient One not bestow the word empowerment of the three classes of the Great Perfection?"

"I don't know," I replied.

He did not say anything, but later I came to know that he had praised me in front of some of his students, saying, "Ngakli met the Great Omniscient One in a vision!"

Another time during that same period, he quoted:

> Ultimate innate wisdom
> Comes about solely as a result of accumulating merit and purifying
>   obscurations,

And the blessings of a realized master.
Know that relying on any other method is foolishness![91]

"Regarding the accrual of the requisite accumulations of merit and wisdom, the texts of our tradition talk about common and uncommon mandala offerings,[92] whereas Abu spoke of the mandala of the nirmanakaya, which is the apparitional mode of reality, the mandala of the sambhogakaya, which is the abiding mode of reality, and the mandala of the dharmakaya, which is all-pervasive. There is much to be understood in that," he said, and he gave me an elaborate explanation.

"Now," he continued, "there is a practice for accumulating merit based upon the practitioner's own body, which is called the *Kusali's Accumulation.*[93] This is easy to do and extremely effective. Although the Great Omniscient One, in his *Resting in the Nature of Mind,* taught this in conjunction with guru yoga, the Omniscient Jigme Lingpa taught it in combination with the outer and inner methods of accumulating merit in the mandala offering practice. Regardless, it is an important practice in its own right," he said. He gave me an elaborate description of the stages of visualization for the four great feasts.

"You should undertake the white feast offering in the morning, the variegated feast offering at noon, and the red feast offering in the evening. The black feast offering is unnecessary at this point. One is actually supposed to go to a haunted place and remain there until spiritual eruptions have ceased to arise over a prolonged period of time, or, if not, until they have been overcome, or otherwise, at least until they have settled.[94] However, there isn't anyone who knows how to distinguish this sequence."

With that, he gave an oral explanation, combining the *Coming of Age of the Six Transcendent Perfections* (*phyin drug lang tsho*), which is an explanation of the *Object of Severance: Wild Laughter of the Dakinis* (*gcod yul mkha' 'gro'i gad rgyangs*), with Abu's explanation, entitled *Profound Pith Instructions of the Object of Severance: Wild Laughter of the Dakinis.*

Accordingly, I did the mandala offering practice in conjunction with the body offering of the *Kusali's Accumulation.* Every night I dreamed of a large charnel ground filled with fresh and rotting corpses and myriad birds and wild beasts. There, I ejected my consciousness out of my body, transformed it into the Wrathful Black Mother Khrodakali (Tröma Nakmo), and made a feast offering of my body to the many birds, beasts, and charnel-ground guardians.

When I told Lungtok Rinpoche about it, he asked, "Were you afraid?"
"I wasn't afraid at all," I answered.

"That was Utsala Charnel Ground. Even the glorious Lord of Secrets Vajrapani was so frightened that the vajra almost slipped out of his hand, so how can it be that you were unafraid?" he teased.

"When I ejected my consciousness into space, I transformed it into the Wrathful Black Mother Krodhakali, and since the teachings say that she is the mother of all buddhas, I figured there couldn't possibly be a god or demon more powerful than a buddha. My mind was suddenly empty and fresh, but beyond that I can't remember feeling any kind of fear."

"Boy, are you ever full of yourself! So you think you're better than Vajrapani?" he asked. But later he said, "Such experiences derive from the power of the body offering. Whether they are good or bad, I can't say."

Early that summer, Lungtok Rinpoche transmitted the liturgy for the preliminary practices of the *Longchen Nyingtik,* conjoined with Jamyang Khyentse's *Two Stages of Visualization* (*dmigs rim rnam gnyis*) to everyone at the encampment. Once then and twice later in my life, I took the bodhisattva vow to cultivate bodhichitta according to Abu Rinpoche's method of combining it with the fourth chapter of *Way of the Bodhisattva.*[95]

Lungtok Rinpoche said to me, "Leave guru yoga aside for the time being. You need to gradually train your mind in the four thoughts that turn the mind. In order to become a true Buddhist practitioner, these preliminaries are crucial. If you are intent on the so-called 'main practice' as a superior path, remember the words of Shantideva:

> Deflate the eight ordinary concerns for your own sake, and great loving compassion for others' sake will automatically arise.

"That's how it is. When one genuinely realizes emptiness, one will discover with profound certainty that emptiness arises as dependent arising, and dependent arising returns to emptiness. Confidence in this infallible relationship between cause and effect will inevitably ensue. Arya Nagarjuna has said:

> Understanding that phenomena are empty,
> The results that arise dependent on past actions
> Are more wondrous than any other wonder!
> More marvelous than any other marvel!

"And the bodhisattva Dromtönpa once said:

The realization of emptiness and the birth of compassion occur
simultaneously;
The birth of compassion and the renunciation of nonvirtuous acts
occur simultaneously."

"So why is it that nowadays people who claim they have realized emptiness haven't reduced their disturbing emotions?" I asked.

"They've strayed into mere rhetoric," he explained. "In evil times such as
these, those who claim they have realized emptiness or the nature of mind
and who hold a high view have become more and more arrogant about their
nonvirtuous actions, their behavior has become more and more crude, their
disturbing emotions have become stronger and stronger, and they entrust
themselves to a chaff-like view. However, when they reach the threshold of
the intermediate state between death and rebirth, any kind old lady will
be much better off than those lowly scoundrels. What they say and what
they do contradict each other, such that nowadays when you say you are a
Nyingmapa, people consider you a Bönpo.[96] We act as if our view were so
high, yet we fail to mix our minds with the Buddhist teachings. This is how
we have destroyed ourselves.

"So, first train your mind with teachings such as those given in the
Great Perfection's *Resting in the Nature of Mind,* which clarify the stages
of the Nyingma path. Once the genuine experience of the Great Perfection's abiding nature has dawned in your mind, you should maintain this
experience continuously, broaden the horizon of your view, and ensure that
your actions are meticulous and precise. In fact, Rigdzin Jigme Lingpa was
esteemed as a perfect master by Ganden Tri Rinpoche, the abbots of East
Peak and North Peak at Ganden Monastery, and the head of the Sakya
school, Ngawang Palden Chökyong, because he united the Nyingma scriptures with the *Stages of the Path.*[97]

"Now, you and I need to make time to train our minds again and again
in the preliminary four thoughts that turn the mind. According to Abu's
technique, one may either train the mind for the number of days prescribed
in his *Essential Guide to Resting in the Nature of Mind* (*sems nyid ngal gso'i
don khrid*), or one may train for 146 days, starting with the preliminary
contemplation on the difficulty of finding a human body endowed with
freedoms and advantages, and continuing all the way through the precepts

associated with the application stage of the cultivation of bodhichitta and the six transcendent perfections. By practicing in this way, superior individuals will attain the fourth concentration, average ones will attain the first concentration, and at the very least, one will inevitably achieve the ability to focus the mind one-pointedly on whatever one wishes.[98] Having accomplished that, if one is then introduced to awareness, in accordance with the original Great Perfection, the integration of Calm Abiding and Higher Insight will definitively emerge.[99] As Shantideva said in his *Way of the Bodhisattva* [ch. 8, v. 4]:

> Insight, when fully integrated with Calm Abiding,
> Completely annihilates disturbing emotions.
> Knowing this, one must first seek Calm Abiding.
> This will be realized by delighting in detachment from mundane
> concerns.

"The path of Higher Insight that fully liberates the mind, whether with reference to the sutras or tantras, must achieve as its support a level of Calm Abiding endowed with definitive characteristics, free from distraction, like the clear brilliance of a butter-lamp flame untouched by the wind. Also, motivated by genuine disillusionment, which is the basis for detachment from ordinary concerns, one should maintain a pure ethical discipline. Having gained a genuine understanding of the rules of the three trainings, those who do not act accordingly and instead go about making exaggerated claims regarding Calm Abiding with and without characteristics in a feigned attempt to teach Mahamudra and the Great Perfection, all the while boasting about the years and months they have spent meditating, will not only fail to accomplish the true foundation of concentration, they will not even be able to focus one-pointedly on a chosen object. What a great loss to waste one's life on such a course!" he said.[100]

"Yes," I said, "but the methods for practicing Calm Abiding with and without characteristics aren't mentioned in the Mahamudra or Great Perfection scriptures, are they?"

"The Great Omniscient One never mentioned Calm Abiding with characteristics in his pith instructions of the Great Perfection. Mahamudra does seem to contain such instructions, but back then there were many authentic teachers who knew the key pith instructions and taught a genuine Calm Abiding, which entailed abandoning the five faults, relying on the eight applications, using the nine techniques for sustaining mental calm, and focusing on a piece of wood, a token, or some other item. Nowadays, however, despite the dearth of such key pith instructions, people just arbitrarily stare at a stick or token, and this does not produce even the faintest whiff of Calm Abiding. The precious Lord Tsongkhapa said, 'Those who fail to understand that the sustained aspect of absorption needs to be accomplished with mental consciousness and instead practice with visual consciousness are the laughing stock of the learned.' I believe this is true.

"There are two approaches to giving this guidance: one in which the view is sought through meditation, for those inclined toward using a referential object (*dmigs pa yul gyi blo can*), and the other in which meditation is sought through the view, for those inclined toward personal experience of awareness (*rig pa rang snang gyi blo can*). The latter seems to be the Great Omniscient One's general mode of guidance, although he himself explained that due to its meditation methods, employing the former can be more effective. Therefore, while it may be difficult to achieve a genuine Calm Abiding endowed with definitive characteristics through this preliminary mind training, one inevitably attains the ability to focus the mind one-pointedly on whatever one chooses. Beginning with motivation, one trains the mind in stages.

"As for recognizing all beings as one's mothers and remembering their kindness, one should begin by reflecting on one's mother in this present life. This reflection is not divided into practice sessions or session breaks. Lord Atisha taught a meditation on the sevenfold pith instructions of cause and effect, whereas in Abu's tradition these are subsumed into the fivefold practice of recognizing one's mothers, remembering their kindness, and so forth. 'Affectionate loving-kindness' is subsumed in the wish that all beings who have been one's mother might be endowed with happiness, and 'pure higher altruistic aspiration' is also subsumed in connection with the bodhisattva vows," he explained.

In every teaching session, he taught the methods of mind training. He had me contemplate each point for many days, and it took nearly two years. During those years, Lungtok Rinpoche gave elaborate teachings on the preliminary practices to Lama Sögyal and his son, and to Lama Ngawang Tendzin and his son, which I too received. At that time, I also composed a guidebook on his teachings.

While I was practicing the preliminary mind-training, the mind's uncontrolled pursuit of objects calmed, and I achieved with ease whatever analysis or mental placement I did.[101] On one occasion, when my mind was settled in one-pointed absorption, I naturally relaxed into a state of mental clarity and emptiness, where there was nothing to analyze and no mental placement to be done. All appearances transformed into vital nuclei, and finally these, too, subsided in the face of that absorption, giving rise to a state free of any appearances whatsoever.

I shared this with my lama, who said, "Who knows? Perhaps it was the universal ground (*kun gzhi*)."[102]

When he said that, I thought I had better be careful. I applied sharp concentration to every detail of the mind-training visualizations, but even that intense focus left my mind free of thoughts and appearances, and I remained in a state of vast openness.

Again, I asked my lama.

"I have no idea what that could be," he replied.

Later, when I received guidance on the main practice and he was explaining the distinction between mind and awareness, he said, "This distinction is identical to the one between equipoise with and without appearances that you described earlier when you were engaged in mind training, though I didn't introduce you to it as such at the time. They say that if you get tipped off too early, you'll lose the focus of your meditation and become a 'worthless dog'—I was concerned that would happen!"

During that early period, he forbade me to read even one text about the nature of mind. Then Khenpo Gyaltsen Özer came, and I was told to study with him. He gave extensive teachings on Gyalse Shenpen Taye's *Analysis of the Five Psychophysical Aggregates* (*phung lnga'i rab dbye*) and its *Summary* (*sdom byang*), as well as a commentary on both, written by Khenpo Jigme Samten of Dzogchen Monastery.[103] These I studied until I understood at least the meaning of the words. Then Khenpo Gyaltsen Özer taught Geshe Drapa Ngönshey's *Advice on the Ten Cardinal Treasures of the Kadampas* (*bka' gdams phug nor bcu'i zhal gdams*), as well as *Staircase to Liberation: Seven Mind Trainings according to the Longchen Nyingtik* (*sems sbyong rnam bdun gyi don khrid thar pa'i them skas*), and its instructions—the *Practical Application of the Common Preliminaries* (*lag len*) and the *Foundations of Mindfulness on the Uncommon Preliminaries* (*dran pa nyer bzhag*), along with *Wondrous Ocean of Advice on Mountain Retreat* (*ri chos zhal gdams ngo mtshar rgya tsho*). I also studied *Ascertainment of the Three Vows* and the *Way of the Bodhisattva* intensively and gained a rough understanding.

Around that time, my lama said to me, "Now, you should request *Spike of*

Unity of the Stages of Meditation (*zung 'jug snye ma*) from Atob. Although it does not offer any especially valuable profound points for comprehending the theory of the generation and completion stages, it will be necessary for any retreat you undertake in the future."

"Which major text is best for illuminating the profound points of the generation and completion stages?" I asked.

"*Resting in the Nature of Mind* is not a textbook, but it is a precious instruction that contains the complete and unerring stages of the path for those of great capacity, including the profound and vast paths of Sutra and Mantra, along with the generation and completion stages. However, after the time of Terdak Lingpa, the great treasure-revealer of Mindroling, and his spiritual heir, Minling Lochen Dharmashri, its explanatory transmission became scarce. Kind Abu taught it to us once. Indeed, I have explained its key points to you in the context of the preliminary practices. See if you can receive more detailed instruction on this work in the future," he said. Following his advice, I requested teachings on *Spike of Unity*.

My lama then asked, "With your mind training, how many recitations of the refuge and bodhichitta prayers have you completed?"

"I spend two-thirds of each practice session doing mind training, and one-third accumulating refuge prayers. So far I have recited the refuge verse three hundred thousand times and the bodhichitta verse one hundred thousand times," I replied.

"You only need to recite the bodhichitta verse thirty thousand times. Training the mind is the important part. As for your accumulations of the provisional commitment refuge prayer, that will suffice. But you should continue to practice the fourfold refuge prayer at all times. Apart from the Lama and the Three Jewels, what other friend, companion, or shepherd can free us from the terrors of samsara and nirvana?[104] In order to protect others from the sufferings of samsara and nirvana, one must be free of such sufferings oneself. Otherwise, one will have no such ability. The Buddha actualized the level of nonabiding in these extremes, so therefore he is able to protect us if we embrace him as our teacher."

"The Dharma, subsumed in the two noble truths of cessation and the path to Buddhahood, is present within the Buddha's enlightened mind.[105] In Dharmakirti's *Exposition of Valid Cognition* (*tshad ma rnam 'grel*), Buddha is established as reliable because he knew what to adopt and reject based on the Four Noble Truths. If you embrace these teachings as your path and practice accordingly, they are capable of granting protection."

"The Sangha comprises all those who have attained a sublime bodhisattva level. They have practiced the path revealed by the compassionate Buddha, so their minds are endowed with all the various qualities of renunciation and realization of the Buddhist path. For this reason, we should follow their example and take refuge in them as friends and mentors on the Buddha's spiritual path. Without Sangha, we are like the wealthy merchant who travels a terrifying road without a strong escort. We will not reach our destination. It says in the *Verse Summation of the Prajnaparamita:*

> For anyone who holds the perfection of insight in hand,
> Demons delight in creating obstacles.

"There are all kinds of obstacles that can befall bodhisattvas. The absence of both insight and diligence is the work of demons, and indicates that one has already been inundated with obstacles. A diligent person who lacks insight will also encounter obstacles, but demons have no ability to create obstacles for those endowed with both insight and diligence. Nevertheless, as it says in the *Verse Summation:*

> When a mother of many children falls ill,
> All of them will worry and say healing prayers for her.
> Likewise, the Conquerors dwelling throughout the ten directions
>   of the universe,
> Care for their mother, sacred insight.

"Since you possess faultless insight and diligence, it is crucial to take refuge with conviction in the Three Jewels in order to dispel obstacles from the path. Taking refuge by practicing in accordance with the path means that whatever practices you undertake should not transgress the boundaries of the refuge vows. From the outset, without hankering after the so-called main practice, thinking it is a higher teaching, you need to establish a firm foundation for the path with these preliminaries. As Geshe Potowa said:

> A fine hook is certainly nice, but a hook with a strong neck is
> what matters.

"So you definitely need to transform your attitude with this mind training. How much progress have you made with your mind training?" he asked.

"Well, it has been difficult for the four mind-turnings to arise in exactly the right way in my mind, but ever since I was a young child I have had little interest in the delights of this world. During this period of time, through my lama's compassion, a well-reasoned disillusionment with ordinary existence has emerged without my having to fabricate it at all. A sincere and heartfelt faith in the Three Jewels has arisen. As for bodhichitta, the basis of the Mahayana path, by recognizing all beings as my mother and understanding that all enemies and friends of this present life have been my mothers in the course of my successive past lives, I am motivated by the sublime wish to secure their happiness and free them from suffering, and if an opportunity arises, I will gladly give up my life to be of benefit. I am not embarrassed to say that the desire to attain Buddhahood for others' sake has been inherent in me since childhood," I replied.

"Well done. However, even if a virtuous attitude comes about through the power of mind training, it can very easily revert back again if we fail to train the mind over and over. For this reason, it is imperative to keep in mind each aspect, starting with the difficulty of finding the freedoms and advantages, their nature, numerical comparisons, sequences, and so forth. Learn *Words of My Perfect Teacher* by heart," he said, and he gave me a copy.

I did as my lama said and memorized it, which pleased him.

"Well done," he said. "Fools insist on the importance of focusing the mind, but such 'great meditators' will not succeed. It is true what they say: superior meditators become superior teachers, mediocre meditators become mediocre teachers, and poor meditators become poor teachers. As far as possible, you should memorize my explanations, too, so they are not lost, and think them over. As the *Seven-Point Mind Training* states:

> There is greater merit in retaining a single word spoken by one's teacher than in studying and expounding the teachings of all the buddhas of the three times.

"The Whispered Lineage of the Nyingma school has been largely lost due to those who simply say whatever they want, without analyzing and investigating the words of their lamas. To ensure that the precious Buddhist teachings endure, it is crucial that the pith instructions of the lineage not be lost," he said.

Keeping in mind what he had said, I memorized each and every word, and wrote everything down in a guidebook. Even now, the Gracious One's close disciples tell me that regardless of what they are practicing, the preliminaries or the main practice, my commentary remains the most useful.[106]

Later, Lama Atob said, "In the earlier part of his life, our Gracious Lama did not impart Abu's oral transmissions much, so the teachings he has now given you are exceedingly profound. My own ears have run out of merit. Many have come to see me, claiming that they are reporting their realizations. They each describe something that resembles the nature of mind, but not one has been able to discriminate between mind and awareness, and purely recognize the face of awareness. I cannot show them what I know. Even if I try to explain, since I lack the exact instructions of the Whispered Lineage, communication is difficult." After he said this, I transmitted to him the Gracious One's guidance.

The thought occurred to me that the guidance of Abu's oral transmission, including both the generation and completion stages, had been given to me alone. It was apparently not widely disseminated. Early in the Gracious One's life, his students were Sögyal and Atob Tubten Gyaltsen Özer. In his middle years, they were Khenpo Dorli, Lingda Norkho, Sa-ngen Wangchen, Lakha Tulku, Tulku Alo, Sertok Tulku, and Peltsa Lama Yönten. Later in his life, they were Peltsa Pema Dorje, Sonam Norbu, Pema Losal, Takko Pema Dorje, and Sa-ngen Konchok. These were his foremost disciples. However, after he gave me the vital quintessence of all the pith instructions, he emphasized the importance of not allowing this oral transmission to deteriorate even slightly. He reiterated many times that his genuine lineage had been entrusted to me, so that I was clear about this.

In conversations with his senior disciples, Lama Gyaltsen and Lama Yönten, Gracious Lungtok mentioned that "Abu Rinpoche told me that Vimalamitra promised to come back once every century to restore the teachings of the *Nyingtik,* and that he sensed the time was drawing near. Abu said that while he himself would not meet him, I would. I wondered if perhaps it was the Dzogchen Tulku, but that doesn't seem likely, since Abu not only met him but imparted the *Guhyagarbha Tantra* to him. So if it's not our Ngakli, then I have not met him, either. Judging from Ngakli's keen insight and the way the signs of his progress on the path have emerged, it seems quite probable."

Hard as it is to determine the actual emanations of Vimalamitra, I do have clearly visible markings on my body, such as an OM syllable on my crown, a HUM between my eyebrows, an AH on the tip of my nose, and the hand emblems of the five buddha families on my body. Also, when I first began to impart the teachings of the Great Perfection, a dome of rainbows arched overhead and a rain of flowers fell, and other such excellent signs have appeared time and time again. In fact, most of my devout followers have seen me manifestly take them into my care at the time of their deaths. So, if all these wondrous supporting indications are taken into account, it seems that I might be somewhat worthy of my followers' devotion and respect.

I received the complete empowerments and transmissions of the new treasures from Lama Terchen,[107] and at the outset of my guru yoga practice, I received the complete empowerments and transmissions for the two volumes of revelations according to the *Longchen Nyingtik* from Lama Atob.[108]

Then my gracious lama said, "Now you need to undertake guru yoga, by means of the recitation practice (*bsnyen pa*) and the preliminary practices.[109] In our *Nyingtik* tradition, the stages of the guru sadhana, through which blessings are conferred, are as follows:

"First, there is the outer sadhana (*phyi sgrub*), through which one trains the mind according to the guidance of the outer and inner preliminaries.

"Next, there is the inner sadhana (*nang sgrub*), the *Guru Embodiment of Vidyadharas* (*bla ma rig 'dzin 'dus pa*). Through this, one achieves the seven impure bodhisattva levels according to the common generation stage, which is the intent of the sixty-fourth chapter of the *General Sutra That Gathers All Wisdom Intentions* (*spyi mdo dgongs 'dus*), the main scripture of the Anuyoga transmission.[110] The remaining three higher levels are achieved through the *Path of the Wish-Fulfilling Jewel: A Scroll of the Whispered Lineage* (*snyan brgyud shog dril yid bzhin nor bu'i lam*).[111] First, one generates the impure illusory body and the illustrative luminosity, and then gradually one traverses the stages of unity, from the paths of learning to the Path of No-More-Learning.[112] Then there is the practice of Mahayoga, which emphasizes the five phases of the generation stage. This is achieved through the *Oral Transmission of Great Glorious Heruka* (*dpal chen zhal lung*), a commentary on the *Mind Attainment of the Vidyadharas: Embodiment of Great Glorious Wrathful Heruka* (*rig 'dzin thugs sgrub drag pod pal chen 'dus pa*)—along with its explanatory commentary entitled *Staircase to Akanishta* (*'og min bsgrod pa'i them skas*), and its *Commentary on Difficult Points Entitled Guidance on the Deities of the Generation Stage* (*dka' grel*), composed by Abu Rinpoche, which is the wisdom intention of the *Tantra of Glorious Heruka Galpo* (*dpal chen he ru ka gal po*).

"Then there is the secret sadhana (*gsang sgrub*), entitled *Great Compassionate One: Natural Liberation of Suffering* (*thugs rje chen po sdug bngal rang 'grol*), and the supremely secret *Guru Sadhana Sealed with a Vital Nucleus* (*bla sgrub thig le rgya can*), along with the *Transmitted Teachings of the Mother: Queen of Great Bliss* (*yum ka bde chen rgyal mo*).

"The instruction manuals on these principal sadhanas include the main scripture of the widely renowned *Longchen Nyingtik,* entitled *Tantra of the Wisdom Expanse* (*ye shes klong gi rgyud*), its subsequent tantra entitled *The Experience of Samantabhadra* (*kun bzang dgongs nyams*), and their explanatory commentaries, entitled *Yeshe Lama* (*ye shes bla ma*) and the *Words of the Omniscient One* (*kun mkhyen zhal lung*).

"We have had this practice tradition of ripening instructions since the time of the Omniscient Jigme Lingpa. Normally we say that the approach-mantra supplication should be recited ten million times in guru yoga, but in your case you must recite it thirty million times."

Accordingly, I exerted myself in the practice of guru yoga on the basis of the five knowings, and I accumulated one hundred thousand full-length prostrations in conjunction with the *Seven-Branch Prayer.* Indeed, ever since the first moment I met the Gracious Lungtok and received a Dharma connection to him, I have perceived him as a buddha and prayed to him with respect and devotion, never once negatively thinking of him as an ordinary human being.

During the first half of each practice session I recited the supplication for attaining accomplishments (*dngos sgrub bsgrub pa*), and during the second half I recited the supplication for invoking accomplishments (*dngos sgrub bskul ba*). During the first ten million siddhi mantras, I recited the supplications after each mala cycle, and for the final twenty million I inserted them after every thousand mantras.[113]

Once during the recitation period, I had gone to attend my lama during his daily rounds, which he made twenty-five times around his house after his noon meal. When he visited the bathroom, the bootlace strap fastened to his wolf-skin waist-wrap would dangle down behind him like a tail.

"Pull up my tail," he would say. This kept his robes from sliding down, which made his visit to the toilet easier. On this particular day, he said nothing and went about his business as usual. He seemed to be quite uncomfortable.

"Would you like me to pull up your tail?" I asked.

"Oh yes," he said. "I forgot. Go ahead, pull it up."

Then he looked at me out of the corner of his eye and said, "Son, you cannot be blamed for repeating my vulgar language and saying 'tail.' However, the teachings say that the lama should be viewed as the dharmakaya, not as a form body with particular characteristics. That being so, how could it be acceptable to say 'tail'?"[114]

He then quoted the verse that begins, "Whoever perceives me as form . . ." and explained, "If you don't know how to perceive the lama as the dharmakaya, and instead regard him or her as an ordinary person, endowed with form, sound, smell, taste, and feeling, this negative conception will obscure you to the point where it will greatly hinder your ability to attain the supreme accomplishments. It is said one should 'perceive all guides as reality.'[115] Therefore, from the rational perspective of reality, you should perceive your lama as the dharmakaya buddha."

When he said that, I thought, "He really is the true Buddha Vajradhara," and an uncontrived certainty was born in me.

"Regardless of how near or far away he is, or what time of the day or night it may be," I thought, "there is nothing that goes unseen by his eyes of pure wisdom. I am always in his sight." Terrified and anxious about having even the slightest negative thought, I remained perfectly mindful and attentive. I think this must be what is meant by the teaching, "Remember the Lama and the Buddha."

By establishing the five knowings—knowing the lama as a buddha and so on—through scripture and logical reasoning, I achieved both contrived and uncontrived devotion, the latter having been imprinted in me from previous lifetimes. From then on, I viewed all the lamas to whom I was connected through empowerments or teachings as having infinite kindness and compassion. In doing so, I only ever pleased them and never upset them for even an instant, and they held me in their hearts. Later, Khenpo Söchö of Dzogchen had only praise for me, saying that I was so skilled at following spiritual masters that I emulated the life of the sublime bodhisattva Sudhana. Not only have I respected my lamas, I cannot recall ever uttering the slightest disparaging, offensive, or slanderous remark about my vajra brothers and sisters. Therefore, I am confident that my samayas are most immaculate.

Nowadays, as a natural effect of this degenerate era, practitioners criticize and scorn their teachers and the spiritual siblings with whom they are connected through Buddhist teachings and samaya. Bootlicking and backbiting, they are short-tempered and envious, cruelly insulting each other in an atmosphere of mutual hostility. Whatever learning and teaching they undertake is done to procure the splendor of worldly enjoyments. Taking refuge in mere material acquisitions and credentials, they haughtily maintain that their samayas are intact. Masquerading as accomplished masters and bestowers of ripening empowerments and liberating instructions, these fated "practitioners" entertain high hopes of gaining signs of accomplishment and special powers, yet they focus on none other than the causes of corrupt commitments and rebirth in the lower realms. Therefore, in this Secret Mantra vehicle, pure commitments are vitally important. It says in the *Tantra of Peaceful Deities* (*zhi ba lha rgyud*):

> The teacher, the deity, and one's spiritual siblings
> Are to be attended without separation.
> This is the principal sacred commitment.

Indeed, this is very true.

Then, when I finished guru yoga, my lama said, "Now, it would be good for you to train in a generation-stage practice." He gave me an extensive explanation of the pith instructions on the "four stakes that bind the life force," entitled *Display of the Three Realms: The Melodious Voice of Brahma* (*khams gsum rol pa tshangs pa'i sgra dbyangs*).

He then explained, "*Staircase to Akanishta,* its *Commentary on Difficult Points,* and especially the five phases commonly understood in both Mahayoga and Anuyoga are most essential. The latter are enumerated in the *Tantra of Glorious Heruka Galpo* as follows:

> The recitation of vajra syllables,
> The focusing of the mind in visualization
> Self-consecration, luminosity, and unity—
> These five are called the five phases.

"The only one who has explained these thoroughly is Kind Abu," he said, and he proceeded to give me an elaborate explanation. I composed a short guidebook on this.

During that period, I clarified many doubts on this topic and asked numerous questions, whereby I gained a genuine understanding of the two stages of meditation (generation and completion) according to the Vajrayana.

Immediately after that, Lungtok Rinpoche imparted essential guidance (*don khrid*) on the *Trilogy of Resting* at the request of an artist named Lama Rigdzin, and I received this guidance along with him. My lama explained that we needed to train our minds for several months in the essential guidance of the *Trilogy of Resting*, so we gradually practiced the contemplations.

At one point during the generation-stage training, my lama explained, "The remedy for attachment to common appearances is threefold: clarity of visualized features, recollection of purity, and steadfast divine pride. On this basis, one needs to meditate until one reaches consummation of the three aspects of objective perception (mental, sensory, and physical). Although other traditions may adopt a contrived path, relying on the generation stage in isolation, and make no mention of the view at the outset, in our tradition of the Early Translations, from the very start one needs an unswerving conviction in the view of great purity and evenness (*dag mnyam chen po*).[116] In this regard, it is said in the eleventh chapter [v. 2] of the *Guhyagarbha Tantra:*[117]

> The single basis and the manner of seed-syllables,
> Blessedness and direct perception:
> Through this fourfold thorough realization,
> Comes the great Truly Perfected King.

"And [ch. 11, v. 15]:

> The world, its contents, and the mindstream
> Are realized to be pure.

"And [ch. 11, v. 15]:

> Through the twofold evenness
> And the twofold superior evenness . . .

"Although this text mentions the three purities, the four modes of evenness, and the logical argument of Great Identity (*bdag nyid chen po*),[118] the key points of all these nuances of view are subsumed within the logical argument of the four kinds of realization,[119] through which all things are established as the 'great king, manifestly perfect.' This is the established viewpoint or philosophical tenet. Now, the object to be negated through the logical argument of the single basis is unawareness, the ordinary mind that apprehends things as truly existent, which is the root of samsara. Elsewhere, the same text says [ch. 3, v. 22]:

O! The flaws that are the basis of conditioned existence
Extend from the notion of self.

"And [ch. 2, v. 15]:

EMAHO! From the essential buddha-nature,
Individual thoughts are projected by past actions.

"What is meant by this? When you recite the liturgy of the *Peaceful and Wrathful Deities,* you say, 'May all conceptual obscurations be purified.' It is this rigid pattern of thought that is referred to as clinging to the notion of self. To negate this, one must establish through reasoning that its basis is emptiness. This is easier to establish if one initially ascertains the lack of true existence of person and phenomena using the reasoning of the Vehicle of Definitive Characteristics (*mtshan nyid theg pa*)—either according to the Prasangikas or Svatantrikas, as appropriate.[120] Otherwise, except for those with superior acumen, it would be ineffective to simply cite the logical argument, 'It is because they have a single basis, emptiness,'" he explained.

"So which is superior—the reasoning of the Prasangikas or the Svatantrikas?" I asked.

"What are you saying? When it comes to ascertaining the nature of phenomena as emptiness, it makes no difference. The debate is merely about how the two posit conventional reality. However, in terms of the ultimate goal of Mantra, which is the unity of genuine luminosity and illusory body, when the energies and mind are purified within the central channel, by means of the completion-stage refinement of energies and vital nuclei, the result is the convergence of the illustrative and genuine luminosities. Appearances then dawn as unreal and illusion-like in the postmeditative state. At that point, regardless of how they delineate conventional reality, in truth both approaches are equal in their lack of clinging (*bden zhen*) to true existence.

"Lord Maitripa was an exponent of the Mind Only philosophical system.[121] The master Vajraghantapada was a Svatantrika, and Shantideva was a Prasangika. Yet, there was no difference between the kind of realization they experienced during the attainment of supreme accomplishment on the Path of Seeing."

"How can that be?" I asked.

"At that point, when even the eighty inherent thought processes must cease, an apprehension of conventional reality is not a big deal!" he said.

"Well, if that is the case, are there no qualitative differences between the two traditions of Prasangika and Svatantrika based on their positing of conventional reality?" I asked.

"What? Of course there are differences between them on the level of conventional appearances, in terms of whether or not doubts are resolved. But that does not pose a big hindrance on the path," he answered.

"Well then, why is everyone arguing with each other nowadays?" I asked.

"They don't understand how to traverse the path, so they end up arguing about who has the best view," he explained.

"So, does that mean that Buddhapalita and Bhavaviveka did not understand how to traverse the path?" I persisted.[122]

"Not at all. They were simply debating the methods of resolving misconceptions about conventional reality, according to the wisdom intent of Arya Nagarjuna. Regarding ultimate truth, they did have differences in terms of the emphasis they placed on the expressible ultimate and the inexpressible ultimate.[123] However, you should know that once beginners have acquired certainty in the expressible ultimate truth (*rnam grangs pa'i don dam*), they embark on the Path of Accumulating, where they achieve an authentic experience of Calm Abiding in addition to that previous understanding of the expressible ultimate truth. On that basis, they expand their experience of the path (*lam la goms pa bsring ba*). It is this that enables them to traverse the Greater Path of Accumulating and subsequently gain some experience of Higher Insight, thereby progressing to the Path of Joining. Inexpressible ultimate truth (*rnam grangs ma yin pa'i don dam*) is established from the first bodhisattva level onward. The first bodhisattva level has emptiness as the object of its realization, but that does not mean that each of the ten bodhisattva levels has its own distinct object of realization. Indeed, this hierarchy is established through the capacity of the bodhisattvas' mental fortitude.

"These days, people claim that even Prasangika beginners need to establish the inexpressible ultimate, free of all philosophical positions and in conformity with the equipoise of the three classes of sublime being. However, there are said to be substantial differences between the realizations of the three kinds of sublime being, so how can one possibly practice three kinds of equipoise without differentiating them at all? Since mere thought-free equipoise (*mnyam bzhag rtog med*) is no different from the concentration and absorption of the formless realms, it does nothing to undermine adherence to the notion of self, or adherence to the notion of true existence. It is said:

Loving-kindness and so forth do not contradict delusion.
Hence they do not eradicate the most serious fault.

"That's right. Making all sorts of bogus spiritual claims like, 'From the start I have had no philosophical position—I'm free of constructs (*spros pa*)!' does nothing to undermine the two notions of self or the ways in which we adhere to them. For instance, if we announce, 'I have no belief in either of the two kinds of self-clinging—I'm free of constructs!' what good will that do? Avoid making lofty claims. We should regard ourselves as followers of the Great Abbot Shantarakshita, for by emphasizing the view of the Madhyamaka Svatantrikas, we establish an excellent auspicious connection.[124]

"Of course, the highest of all the views propounded in the Vehicle of Causal Characteristics is that of the exponents of the Madhyamaka Prasangikas, but it is difficult to ascertain that without error. On this basis, you may say, 'I am a Prasangika,' and then go about citing various Prasangika scriptures to justify your personal opinions in debate, but why reference scriptures? Scriptures are like deerskins that can be stretched in any direction to suit your particular standpoint.

"Henceforth, you need to engage in logical analysis to arrive at a definite understanding. The objective of this realization is endowed with great merit, for the reasoning and logical arguments of the Madhyamaka cannot be understood merely by looking outside oneself and engaging in arguments and debate. One must proceed inwardly, focusing on the main objects to which one clings as truly existent. This way, one sees that objects lack true self-identity, and this inevitably undermines the ordinary intellect that adheres to the notion of true existence.

"For example, if we see a mottled rope in the shadowy darkness, we might mistake it for a snake. But by shining a lamp and revealing that it is in fact a rope, we can reverse the misperception of a snake. Since this misperception of a snake was not with us for very long, a single reversal prevents it from recurring. The habit of clinging to things as truly existent has been deeply ingrained over a long span of time. So if we fail to apply our minds for a prolonged period to the certainty gained through the power of analysis, we will be unable to reverse this habit. This is why one should rely upon a qualified teacher, a spiritual mentor who is authentic and genuine.

"If you apply a scrupulous analysis, like eyes with perfect vision, for a prolonged period, you will gain understanding. Indeed, there are two kinds of beginners' views. The 'view of certainty' emerges when an unswerving certainty is produced through logical analysis using our tradition's Sutra and Mantra view. For those who first ascertain the Mantra view of great purity and evenness, and who subsequently meditate on a generation-stage practice, this view may also be termed 'unity of generation and completion.'

"On the other hand, there is what is called the 'view of devotion,' noticeable when people say, 'Lama So-and-So said this, it's in such and such a text,' without having any of their own definitive reasoning. This view is unreliable and can easily change. Therefore, it is imperative to acquire the view of certainty. Nevertheless, the teachings say that 'The path of the Secret Mantra is forged through devotion,' so to assume that this simple devotion is ineffective would not be right, either.

"Now, if you lack the intelligence to discern the true path from bogus paths, you must at least avoid blindly following and imitating others, and doing whatever they say.

"Abu once said, 'If you are wondering whether a genuine understanding of the true path has arisen in your mind, fervently supplicate the lama and your yidam deity. Accumulate the provisions of merit and wisdom in numerous ways. Examine the Buddha's transmitted teachings in conjunction with their treatises. Investigate with a straightforward mind, and you will gain understanding! I began by grasping the wisdom intention of the Buddha's teachings. Then I grasped the wisdom intention of the treatises composed by his learned followers. Like an eagle soaring in the sky, I acquired a vast view of the land and then alighted on the earth. You people are like stone carvers, taking pains over every single syllable.[125] When you come across scriptures of another tradition, rather than remaining impartial, you think, "How can I refute this?" You never think, "I am not familiar with this, so how might it enhance my understanding?" That attitude will do you no good at all.'

"His words are very true. He was a sublime being who achieved realization simply through grasping the wisdom intention of the Buddha's teachings and their treatises. His *Benefits of Reading the Mahayana Sutras* (*theg chen mdo mthong phan yon*) alone provides ample evidence of this. While it is difficult to be like that, you must not resort to repeating what others say. You must be able to investigate things for yourself through reasoning. Abu would point out to us just the very tip of awareness (*rig pa*) and then tell us to keep investigating it through reasoning (*rigs pa*). Likewise, using the logical argument (*gtan tshigs*) of the single basis of emptiness, you need to establish that all phenomena are essentially uncreated."

"Does this imply that if one has certainty with respect to emptiness, one does not need the wisdom of the Mantrayana?" I asked.

"What are you saying? When you apply logical reasoning regarding the absence of singularity and multiplicity, what can you find that is not empty?[126] Here is what I mean in terms of the logical argument of the four kinds of realization:

"Firstly, when you ascertain that all phenomena, ranging from the aggregate of form to omniscience, are empty, this refers to the abiding nature of all phenomena in general, or principally to the abiding nature of objects.[127] After that, when you establish the abiding nature of the subjective mind, it is the unity of the space of reality (*dbyings*) and wisdom (*ye shes*) that will be established, and this is known as the spontaneous presence of the seven aspects of spiritual wealth in the essential nature (*ngo bo nyid*). These aforementioned logical arguments, cited in the *Guhyagarbha Tantra,* can be comprehended on a mere intellectual level, but they are difficult to realize directly and nonconceptually. Therefore, at this juncture it is important to understand emptiness while acquiring the understandings of those logical arguments on the Path of Accumulating and so forth.

"Secondly, when you apply the logical argument of the manner of seed-syllables, we see, for example, that the seed-syllable OM is formed by combining AH, OO, and MA. Just as in the sutras, where emptiness is established as the arising of unceasing dependent arising, here too in the tantras, this is paralleled by the arising of the display of wisdom as the unobstructed perception of deity (*lha rtog*).[128] The certainty will arise that our present impure perception *is* the display of wisdom, and that this display is inseparable conception and deity. But to proclaim that appearances are deities, without ascertaining the reasons at all, is just like Lama Dönpa saying that the mouth and the nose are the same thing.

"Thirdly, when you apply the logical argument of blessing, wisdom and its display (*rol pa*) validate each other. Just as the sutras affirm that emptiness and dependent arising are indivisible or mutually nonexclusive, here this display of wisdom does not arise from anything other than wisdom, like waves arising from water, or ice that is water even when it appears as ice. Likewise, at the very moment when impure appearances arise, it is certain that in essence they are the display of wisdom, so one need not superimpose appearances onto emptiness, or emptiness onto appearances. From the very start, you need to develop a positive conviction that the display of wisdom is the indivisibility of deity and conception. By realizing and experiencing this, you will be able to actualize it. Generally speaking, you will not need to actualize all the constructs or imputations of the intellect, but rather, in this case, you should first realize the inseparability of the two superior truths by way of the view, and then you will have to actualize this through meditation. This is the key point of the inseparability of reality and the two truths.

"Fourthly, when you apply the logical argument of direct perception (*mngon sum*), just as in the sutras, where the intelligence required for attaining realization is the direct perception of sublime beings, here too in the tantras, you must establish the direct perception of the wisdom of individual self-awareness (*so sor rang rig*). Although for beginners there is not actual direct perception of individual self-awareness, one must certainly understand the need for such realization. Although this wisdom of individual self-awareness can be discussed in different contexts, I shall explain it later in the context of the main-practice guidance," he explained. "But right now you need to undertake the recitation practice based on certainty of the view that the two truths are indivisible.

"The four logical arguments explained above are the remedies for attachment to ordinary impure appearances. Of these, the first will enable you to ascertain the inseparability of the space of reality and wisdom, which is known as the superior ultimate truth (*lhag pa'i don dam*). For this reason, it has to be realized through the insight that analyzes ultimate truth (*don dam dpyod byed kyi shes rab*).

"The second will enable you to definitively establish through conventional valid cognition that sights, sounds, and awareness are the magical display of wisdom, in which unobstructed dependent arising, deities, and thought processes are indivisible. This is called the superior relative truth (*lhag pa'i kun rdzob*).

"The first of these two logical arguments will not only negate attachment to true existence, insofar as this mundane view of independent substantial existence is concerned, but it should also impede, through the realization that the space of reality and wisdom are nondual, the two modes of attachment to impurity—attachment to substantial existence (*rdzas grub*) and attachment to the notion of self (*ngar 'dzin*).

"The second is the valid cognition that principally obstructs this ordinary impure perception and conventional delusory consciousness. These two logical arguments emphasize the view that ascertains ultimate truth.

"The third logical argument is a method for cutting through doubts if

negative thoughts should arise, such as, 'Once I have thoroughly familiarized myself with the view, will I be able to actualize it? And if so, will I then
regress?'

"As for the fourth logical argument, in order to realize the inseparability
of the two superior truths as the great dharmakaya, you will require the
conventional knowledge that ascertains through the direct realization of
wisdom—the individual self-awareness—that in pure relative appearance,
deity and conception are indivisible, just as they are in the minds of sublime
beings. Even though you may not apprehend appearances as truly existent,
if you still apprehend them as impure perceptions, you will misconstrue the
superior relative truth. Therefore, in this context of the Vajrayana, it will be
vitally important to ascertain the inseparability of deity and conception. It
is said that one who understands these methods and puts them into practice
may rightly be called a tantric yogin.

"Although this inner sadhana, *Guru Embodiment of Vidyadharas,* resembles Anuyoga in terms of its tantric classification, from the standpoint of
the descent of the Treasure Revelations it is classified as a guru-blessing
sadhana (*byin rlabs bla ma'i sgrub pa*), one of the Three Roots of Mahayoga.
Although the verse that reads, 'The state of uncontrived awareness, empty
and clear . . .' does refer to the Anuyoga meditation on the vibrant display
of nondual space and wisdom, at this point it will be best for you to focus on
absorption according to Mahayoga, by means of the three modes of absorption. Visualize that the essential nature—emptiness and its radiant expression (*gdangs*), great compassion—arises as the seed-syllable HUM, from
which the mandala is generated, complete with its celestial mansion and
deities. At this juncture, you should meditate, keeping in mind the logical
arguments of the single basis, the manner of the syllables, and the blessing.
Furthermore, do not rest your hopes merely on the number of days spent
reciting the approach mantra.

"'Approach' means to intimately acquaint yourself with the visualization
again and again. So, from the moment you begin meditating on the form of
the syllable HUM until the entire mandala is perfectly present, make your
meditation solid and concrete. That is what Guru Rinpoche said. Moreover,
you must meditate that objective appearances arise as divine, endowed with
the seven vajra qualities—invulnerability, indestructibility, reality, solidity,
and so forth—and that subjective consciousness is absorbed into emptiness.
Why should increasing the solidity of the visualization be equated with the
misconception of true existence? As for the divine pride that is associated

with pure appearances, it is said that 'One should meditate without distraction, the mind clearly visualizing its divine object.'[129] Therefore, you should meditate on this clear vision until all mental, sensory, and physical objects are mastered.

"As for the divine pride of emptiness, it says, 'Visualize things as apparent yet devoid of self-existence.' Even as phenomena appear, you must understand that they lack even a hair's tip worth of true self-existence. Nowadays, without a proper understanding of the distinctions between these two (appearance and emptiness), people explain that the words 'Apparent yet devoid of self-existence, like an illusion, a reflection of the moon in water, a rainbow' suggest that visualizations should be hazy and indistinct. But these explanations are mistaken and reflect a lack of understanding. Not only would an illusory, blurry deity be useless for authentic generation-stage practice, it would also hinder progress to maturation through the completion stage, the advanced path of meditation. Those who lack an understanding of the key points of the generation and completion stages may claim that the generation stage is a fabricated path and a deviation from the Great Perfection. Even if they have meditated through these two stages, they overemphasize the rainbow and illusion similes. This is a sign that the Nyingma teachings are deteriorating. The number of days you undertake mantra recitation and the number of mantras you recite are not the main point; successful cultivation of the generation stage is what counts.

"Since this is your first recitation practice, stay in strict retreat, but not for long. If you quit before the end, you acquire the defect of starting things and then quitting, which then prevents you from completing anything throughout many lifetimes. So stay in retreat for only forty-nine days," he said.

Accordingly, I entered retreat to undertake the recitation practice of the *Guru Embodiment of Vidyadharas*. For almost half of each of my four daily practice sessions, I trained primarily in the three stabilities, apprehending the focal point of my visualization with sharp clarity. The latter half of each session was devoted to reciting the approach mantra, while visualizing the entire mandala—the principal deity and the retinue, the supportive celestial mansion and the deities within it, either in rotation or all at once as I saw fit. During those periods, when I was visualizing the deities as a remedy for impure perception, it seemed that I simply transformed into them, and a stable clear vision arose without my having to concentrate and fabricate it.

At one point, Lungtok Rinpoche called me before him. "How is your generation-stage practice going?" he asked.

I explained how I had been meditating.

"That sounds about right," he said. "The statement that 'Sights, sounds, and awareness are the display of deities, mantras, and wisdom' does not mean that you must visualize all appearances as deities. Just as there are enlightened forms, enjoyments, and activities in a buddha realm, likewise visualize your home as a celestial mansion in a pure realm. To transform your body, speech, mind, and activities into buddha body, speech, mind, and activities, you must know how to apply the pith instructions on the four stakes that bind the life force in all such circumstances.

"The meditations you did earlier on the clarity of the deities' features will suffice. That is a direct remedy for impure perception.[130] Now, as the remedy for clinging, you must meditate on both the recollection of purity and steadfast divine pride.

"There are two kinds of clinging—clinging to things as real and clinging to the notion of self. These have two corresponding remedies. The remedy for the first is clear visualization of the deities. If clinging to the deities arises in your mind, then you should develop certainty by recollecting the purity of the symbolism—their three faces represent the three kayas, their six hands represent the six transcendent perfections, and so forth, confident that the qualities of fruition (*'bras chos*) are visualized as the celestial palace and the deities within it.

"On this basis, steadfast divine pride becomes the remedy for attachment to the notion of the self as truly existent. Sometimes during your mantra recitation, after precisely visualizing all the features of a deity, you should generate divine pride, thinking, 'I am such and such a deity.' At other times, without visualizing any deity, you should generate the divine pride of Guru Rinpoche, identifying with the ultimate deity of reality and the wisdom in which ground and result are indivisible. These are the most essential points of the generation stage," he said.

I trained accordingly, and gained stability in the clear vision of the generation stage.

When I had completed ten million vajra guru approach mantras and four hundred thousand Vidyadhara accomplishment mantras (*rig 'dzin spyi dril*), my lama announced, "Now, since no obstacles have arisen, this is an excellent time to stop."[131] So I ended my retreat and went to see him.

"That's right," he said. "Generally speaking, the generation stage accomplishes Calm Abiding and is indispensible for performing myriads of ordinary ritual activities.[132] It also matures one to progress toward the higher paths of the completion stage. Also, when accomplished meditators assume the pure or impure illusory body, they are able to assume the form of the deity, because the power of the generation stage has been perfected and projected in their minds. In general, it will not help you to think that all deity visualization is solely to be understood in terms of the generation stage. For example, when one engages in the practice known as the isolation of speech, the preliminary stage entails meditation on the isolation of body, and this is quite different from the generation stage.[133]

"Now, the Yumka dakini practice (*Khandro Yumka*) is a method of deity visualization that accords with the instantaneously perfected recollection (*skad cig dran rdzogs*) of the Atiyoga tradition, as the text itself explicitly indicates.[134] All the vidyadharas of the Nyingtik lineage have relied on this method to attain supreme accomplishment, and all Tibetans owe Yeshe Tsogyal a huge debt of gratitude. Since she is the sovereign of all the tantras of the secret Vajrayana, and since the *Transmitted Teachings of the Mother* (*yum ka*) are very closely linked to the *Transmitted Teachings of the Father* (*yab ka*), you need to undertake this recitation practice.

"In general, the generation stage purifies the habitual tendencies of birth, death, and the intermediate state. All the various kinds of habitual tendencies can be subsumed in the habitual tendencies of the four modes of birth. These are purified on the paths of the generation and completion stages, and the ensuing results include the provisional attainment of the four kinds of vidyadhara and the ultimate level of unity.[135]

"First, according to Mahayoga, one purifies the habitual tendency for egg-birth by means of the extensive visualization known as 'taking others as one's own child and taking oneself as another's child' (*bdag sras gzhan sras*).[136] These are revealed in the sadhana of the *Embodiment of the Sugatas of the Eight Heruka Sadhanas* (*bka' brgyad bde gshegs 'dus pa*) and the *Peaceful and Wrathful Deities of the Magical Net* (*sgyu 'phrul zhi khro*). In the *Embodiment of Great Glorious Heruka*, on the other hand, there are only a few passages that may substitute for that, but nothing elaborate.

"For the practice called 'taking another as one's own child,' one meditates in order to bring forth the superior qualities of awareness, which is the seed of buddha nature, and absorbs the pure-essences (*dwangs ma*) of samsara and nirvana, taking them as one's own child.

"Then, in the case of the practice called 'taking oneself as another's child,' in order to ensure the continuity of the ancestral line of fully enlightened buddhas, one first visualizes the manifestly pure buddha as the fruitional heruka—the father and mother aspects in union. Then, in order to be born as a child of the mother consort, one supplicates the father consort, whereby one's psychophysical aggregates, sensory bases, and activity fields dissolve into light, transforming into a vital nucleus, which is inhaled through the father consort's nostrils. One then visualizes that it mingles in a single taste with the vital nucleus of supreme bliss and emerges from the secret space (*mkha' gsang*) of the mother consort, complete with ornaments, accoutrements, and symbolic handheld emblems. From then on, one will be established in the abode of the mandala.

"The mid-length visualizations, which generate the five or four awakenings and the three ritual activities of vajra reality, are used to purify womb birth. As such, they are designed to purify the habitual tendencies of the five elements, the five psychophysical aggregates, the eight modes of consciousness, the energies and mind present within the intermediate state prior to birth, and the moment of conception when sperm and ovum intermingle, along with all the worldly resources enjoyed from the time when the sense faculties first become aware of their sense objects. These techniques are explained in the *Staircase to Akanishta,* and you must certainly apply them.[137] The vast majority of the oral traditions and Treasure Revelations of Guru Rinpoche contain only the threefold vajra visualization. Consequently, you must definitely understand the progression of ritual practices: from the outer sadhana (which is Mahayoga), through the inner sadhana (which is Anuyoga), to the secret sadhana (which is Atiyoga). The current practice of designating these yogas based merely on the length of their liturgies is the talk of fools.

"The visualizations designed to purify the habitual tendencies for birth through warmth and moisture are effected merely by repeating the name mantras found in the Anuyoga texts, and by visualizing them as the dynamic display (*rtsal snang*) of nondual space and wisdom as the deity. This twofold progression is as previously described.[138]

"The visualizations designed to purify the habitual tendencies for miraculous birth entail an introduction to the view of Atiyoga, whereby one sees awareness as the dharmakaya and the expressive power of awareness as the display of the dharmakaya. One thereby discerns that all phenomenal existence is primordially present in the ground, in great purity and evenness. By cultivating this certainty as the path, the visualization is perfected in a single instant of recollection.

"In fact, if one purifies any of these four modes of birth, the others will be automatically purified as well. This is firstly because their basis of purification (the wisdom of luminosity) is identical; secondly, because their objects of purification (the habitual tendencies of samsara) are of the same type; and thirdly, because their means of purification are all effected through the extraordinary key points of the generation and completion stages. This is how you should understand the elaborate and concise teachings on the generation stage.

"In *Resting in the Nature of Mind,* the Great Omniscient One explains these four aspects of visualization as a modality of meditation, whereby an individual becomes initially familiarized, moderately familiarized, well familiarized, and supremely familiarized. In terms of the path of definitive perfection (*nges rdzogs*), these stages are extremely important.

"Devotional meditators have nothing that correlates with the progression of the three inner tantras. They are like Adön at Katok, who, saying that he recalled the meaning of the words after reading them, always recited the ritual text that explains how to teach the *Guhyagarbha Tantra.* Even so, such people must surely be establishing some positive propensities for the future.

"Now, in the *Transmitted Teachings of the Mother* from the Atiyoga tradition, the visualization should be perfected in a single instant of recollection. However, since you have not yet received guidance on the main practice, it will not happen exactly like that for you. Rather, it will be important for you to perfect the visualization of the celestial mansion and its deities as the dynamic display of the nonconceptual nature of your intrinsic mind (*sems nyid*). When visualizing a deity in accordance with any of the three approaches—generation, completion, or Great Perfection—other than the initial varying degree of detail, there is no difference between them when it comes to the need to produce a clear vision (*gsal snang*) of the deity and then to acquire stability in that. Given your latent propensities from previous lifetimes, I think you will have no difficulty training in deity visualization.

"So, this time when you undertake your recitation practice, there are four modes of mantra recitation to consider. Among them, the two known as 'moon encircled by stars' and 'emissaries of the king' are Mahayoga styles of recitation. Alternatively, the method known as 'emissaries of the king' may be used for recitation in all three classes of inner tantra.

"The 'palanquin recitation' or 'swing recitation' is the Anuyoga method.[139] Also, when employed as a remedy for mental drowsiness, you should imagine that the string of mantra syllables at the heart center ascends through the upper body and out the male deity's nostrils, before reentering through the female deity's nostrils, exiting through her secret space, and dissolving once again into the root mantra string.

"When these recitation techniques are employed as a remedy for mental agitation, as you recite the mantra, you should visualize the cycle in reverse: the mantra string descends through the lower body, exits from the secret space, reenters through the nostrils, and circles continuously like a whirling firebrand. The primary purpose is to induce the wisdom of bliss and emptiness, and it is especially important for inducing the descent of the vital nuclei. If you become extremely proficient in the generation stage, you will be able to induce the wisdom of great bliss merely through the 'swing recitation,' while meditating on the principal father and mother deities in union. Furthermore, one will have an opportunity to discuss the Buddhist teachings with the principal deities and their entourages, and to receive sensory enjoyments directly from the offering goddesses who are positioned on the outer ledges of the celestial mansion. Furthermore, the touch of the offering goddess Dharmavajra will induce the wisdom of great bliss.[140] This and other such experiences will occur.

"By attaining supreme mastery of generation-stage absorption, energies and the thinking mind are conjoined in a single essence, so one is able to focus the mind on whatever one chooses. At that point, it will be easy to train in the completion-stage practices of the energies and vital nuclei. Even without such supreme mastery, by meditating on the energies and yogic inner heat, you will chiefly gain control over the energies and vital nuclei, and simultaneously your mind will become extraordinarily pliable. Through the force of this practice, you may gain clairvoyance and other supernormal cognitive powers or miraculous abilities.

"However, nowadays there are those who merely put on an act, claiming that they have refined the energies and vital nuclei in the dead of winter. Huddling in the freezing cold with no understanding of the key points of this practice, they are no different from non-Buddhists who believe that they will achieve purification, liberation, and deliverance by adopting the austere lifestyles of dogs and cattle. Do you have any wrong views?" he asked.

"No, sir," I ventured.

"Your pure perception is quite strong. Now train in having pure perception of everything. To properly investigate what is and is not valid, you need the intelligence to distinguish between bogus fabrications and the key points of the genuine path. At this juncture, you should undertake your recitation practice using the Atiyoga recitation technique known as beehive bursting (*bzlas pa bung ba tshang zhig lta bu*), while clearly visualizing the buddha realm, complete with celestial mansion and deities. Most importantly, you should perceive all sounds as the natural resonance (*rang gdangs*) of mantra," he said.

Accordingly, I spent a month performing the recitation practice, day and night, until whatever sounds I perceived vividly arose as the resounding tones of mantra, without the need for deliberate mental focus. Simultaneously, there emerged in me an extraordinary certainty that deities and appearances are nothing more than a mere magical display (*cho 'phrul*) of the mind, lacking any inherent existence apart from their mere names. I understood this to be the most supreme kind of accomplishment that can be attained.

Then, when I turned twenty, during the waxing moon of the first month of the lunar New Year [February 1899], my lama told me to request the vows of full monastic ordination from Lama Atob.

I protested, saying, "Since I can properly guard the points of the precepts based on my current novitiate ordination, and since it will be difficult to correctly implement the numerous facets of the precepts of full ordination, will the novitiate ordination not suffice?"

"No, it will not," he said. "At present you have obtained a human body endowed with the freedoms and advantages, and in order to make it meaningful, you have no choice but to follow the teaching of the Buddha and take the vows of full ordination in their entirety. Full ordination is also the supreme support of the Vajrayana. The *Tantra of Hevajra* (*'gyes rdor*) states:

> Of the three, fully ordained monks are supreme;
> Middling are those known as novices;
> Compared to these, householders are inferior.

"There are vast numbers of precepts for fully ordained monks to observe, so full ordination is more powerful for perfecting the accumulations of merit and wisdom. Moreover, full ordination is more powerful for purifying obscurations. Indeed, there is a unique direct correlation between the increase of power to perfect the accumulations and purify obscurations, and the arising of the extraordinary manifest realizations of the bodhisattva levels and paths. As it is said:

> The precious lamp of the Buddha's teachings
> Blazes within the vessel of the ascetics,
> The saffron-clad heirs of Shakyamuni,
> For they are holders of full ordination.

"Full ordination is the sublime support for the three trainings, and like a jeweled lamp, it is the most exalted support for the extraordinary manifest realization of the training in insight. It says in the *Kalachakra Tantra* (*dus 'khor*):

> Except for those who have attained the bodhisattva levels,
> Householders shall not be teachers of the king.

"As such, the Tathagata told the Buddhist king Suchandra that apart from a sublime being dwelling on the bodhisattva levels, he should take as his lama a fully ordained monk rather than a lay householder. The very existence of the Buddha's precious teachings depends on the presence of fully ordained monks. Shantideva said:

> As the root of the Buddhist teaching are fully ordained monks . . .

"So it is of utmost importance to become fully ordained. I will make the necessary preparations. Although we live in an outlying border region, the quorum must be as large as those in the central region.[141] We need to assemble ten officiating monks, headed by Thubten Gyaltsen Özer," he explained. He then convened a quorum comprising ten members of the monastic community.

"We need monastic robes, a begging bowl, and a renunciate's carpet, and they must be proper and authentic. Here, take this extra robe of mine, and this begging bowl and carpet," he said, lending them to me. In these empowering circumstances, I received the complete vows of a fully ordained monk.

From that day forward, I have done my very best to guard against the five classes of downfalls that may confront a fully ordained monk. I have had all my monastic articles consecrated, either as actual items or as token symbols.[142] I have relied upon Panchen Lobzang Chögyan's *Remembrance of*

Circumstances (*dus dran*) concerning the proscriptions against eating food cooked in an unconsecrated kitchen (*mtshams btsos*); handling and keeping food that has not been properly given or received (*lag nyal*); consuming raw and uncooked food (*rjen btsos*); making fires (*me la reg pa*); or touching precious gems and metals (*rin po che la reg pa*).

Later on, I received a great magnitude of material goods and worldly wealth, nearly all of which I turned over to my lama and the Three Jewels. I also entrusted such objects to my preceptors, my excellent spiritual brethren, and my patrons. Other than my consecrated objects, I have no possessions. In fact, I have very little desire for material belongings, and I am content with what I have. I have no greedy feelings about others' wealth. Vigilantly maintaining an attitude of contentment with few needs, I have sought to emulate the liberated lives of sublime beings. Thoughts of hoarding money and possessions for the future—such as "I'll need this if I fall ill, I'll need that when I'm dying"—have never even crossed my mind. No matter what I have seen of others' prosperity and grandeur, none of it has inspired admiration or wonder in me. I realize that this is the result of having meditated on revulsion.[143]

Once during that period, Gracious Lungtok showed signs of illness. According to Tertön Sögyal's prophetic divination, one hundred thousand recitations of the *Tantra of Immaculate Confession* (*dri med bshags rgyud*) were needed to restore his health, so all of the nearly 150 disciples residing in the community set about reciting the *Tantra of Immaculate Confession*. Twenty or so were skilled readers who could recite the text eighteen or nineteen times in a day, but most were unable to do very many per day, so it took us several months to finish. I personally offered eleven hundred recitations of the *Tantra of Immaculate Confession* for his long life. Individual disciples pledged to rescue some three thousand animals as a means to stabilize Gracious Lungtok's health. Due to all this, his health began to improve. All the disciples decided to complete one hundred days of longevity practice to restore our lama's health, and they went into retreat.

I went before my lama and asked him, "How many more recitations of the *Tantra of Immaculate Confession* shall I offer for your health and long life?"

"I am old now," he replied. "The aggregates of this illusory form are like an old tree at the end of its season, and there is no telling when I will have to cast them away. But if you would like to offer long-life prayers for your lama and Dharma siblings, the *Seven-Branch Prayer* contains the branch of supplication to remain in the world without passing into nirvana. This will dispel any immediate threats to life. For the longer term, you can stay in retreat to undertake Rigdzin Jigme Lingpa's *Longevity Sadhana: A Drink from the Vase of Immortality* (*tshe sgrub bdud rtsi'i bum bcud*), since it contains a particularly essential practice for achieving a full life span. Don't worry about finding a long-life vase, skull-cup, and ceremonial arrow."

He handed me an envelope, saying, "Here are some long-life pills made by Jamyang Khyentse. Perform the sadhana using just these and a torma offering cake. In general, it is very important to amass the substances described in the Secret Mantra texts. Indeed, substances, mantras, and absorption all have their own specific purposes. However, at this point you need to focus on the amendment for the *Guru Embodiment of Vidyadharas* recitation practice that you completed earlier, so it would be good if you could integrate that longevity practice here. In the first half of each practice session, you should accumulate the recitations, and so forth. In the second half, you need to undertake a *Longevity Sadhana,* based on the refinement of the channels, energies, and vital nuclei, so the common channels, energies, and vital nuclei practices you already covered in the preliminary practices will suffice.[144] At this point, you should train in the yogas of the energies and inner heat, just so as not to omit this aspect of Anuyoga practice.

"In Buddhist phenomenology, 'life' is defined as a state that lasts as long as warmth accompanies consciousness. However, in the present context of the Vajrayana, we refer to 'life' as that which is conceived when the body, mind, and energies first converge in the mother's womb. The white element, which resembles a thread of spider silk, forms inside the central channel at the heart center. If the thread is long, one's life span will be long; if it is short, one's life span will be short; if it is crooked, one will have many illnesses, and so forth. This is what we refer to as 'life.' If this diminishes, one's life span diminishes. If it is exhausted, one's life span is exhausted. In order to prevent it from diminishing and to lengthen the life span, one must engage in longevity practices by refining the energies and vital nuclei.

"There are three reasons why beings die: they die when their life spans are exhausted, they die when the driving force of their past actions is exhausted, and they die when their present store of merit is exhausted. When only one of these is exhausted, death can be reversed, but when two or all three are exhausted, there is no turning back. If yogins have control over the energies and vital nuclei, they can prevent the life-sustaining energy—the support for the consciousness at the heart center—from transmigrating, thus gaining power over the life span.

"In general, according to the Mahayoga, the rank of 'Vidyadhara with Power over the Life Span' is attainable from the Path of Seeing onward. However, according to the Vajrayana, once one has reached the Path of Joining and is empowered to traverse the subsequent paths, if one can prevent transmigration *before* reaching the Path of Seeing, this is also considered power over the life span. Such people, upon reaching the Path of Seeing, may do as they like, because the intrinsic characteristics of birth and death are absent.

"On the Path of Joining, one gains control of the two life-sustaining energies at the heart center and the crown center. One then has the power to prevent the threefold assemblage—the white and red vital nuclei and the energies, which are the subtle aspects of the coarse channels and energies—from transmigrating.[145] When control over the life span is attained on the Path of Seeing, those coarse channels and energies will have already been abandoned. However, because the wisdom of sublime beings is the mastery of the subtle channels, energies, and vital nuclei constituents, there is a significant difference between these two (i.e., the contexts of the Path of Joining and the Path of Seeing). On the other hand, the immortality attained by non-Buddhist sages, which depends on god-granted boons and the potency of long-life elixirs, does not qualify as a valid means for attaining the vidyadhara level of longevity according to the Vajrayana.

"Through the path of the Supreme Vajrayana Vehicle, Guru Rinpoche purified the residual impurities of the elements, which are the ripening of past actions, with the fire of wisdom, and he actualized a divine body (*lha sku*), formed of the natural elements of ultimate truth (*don dam pa rang bzhin gyi 'byung ba*), which is the unique state of Buddhahood. Hence the verses, which begin:

O Lotus-Born Guru, Vidyadhara with power over the life span!
Glorious subjugator of phenomenal existence, at your heart center . . .

"It is a grave error to presume that all those with mastery over life are identical."

He then imparted pith instructions on the fourfold application of vase breathing and the stages of yogic inner heat and subtle vital nuclei, and said, "Now, go meditate and don't come see me for a hundred days."

So I undertook the recitation practice according to his instructions, and after a time, rays of light began radiating from the long-life pills, and the torma offering cakes and pills melted into light. I had dreams of enjoying many kinds of fruit from a celestial tree, and so on. Even so, I let all constructs of hope and fear rest in the space of reality.[146]

Through prolonged familiarization with the energies, I gradually perfected the signs of entry, abiding, and absorption, and I was able to hold the energies in whatever way I wished.[147] When I then meditated on yogic inner heat, the force of the blissful warmth in my body and the melting of the white vital nuclei caused an experience of bliss and emptiness to arise in my mind. All external sensations, hot or cold, stimulated the warmth and bliss.

Then, after only a brief period of familiarizing myself with the subtle vital nuclei, all thoughts and mental states ceased. But this was not like being enveloped in the darkness of deep sleep, for the initial perceptible object of that nonconceptual mind was lucid emptiness, and then even that vanished. The state that followed was unidentifiable, such that I could no longer even say, "This is the empty mind." I was able to sustain this for a whole practice session.

When a hundred days had passed, I concluded my retreat and went to offer my sadhana substances to my lama. He partook of a little and said, "If this old man sticks around, it will mean nothing but hardship for my attendants. You are young, so it would be good if you stayed for a while. I will give you a long-life empowerment." He recited the life-summoning liturgy once through and gave me the remaining substances.

"Eat all of it," he said. "Don't give any of it away."

Then after a pause, he said, "Eating rotten tormas will only make your stomach hurt. Heh, heh! Now tell me, did any sort of signs appear when you trained in the channels and energies?"

I recounted everything in detail.

"It seems that you have awakened some propensity for channels-and-energies practice from a past life," he said. "Don't let it make you proud, and speak of this to no one. Never abandon your practice. Now do you understand the distinctive swiftness of the Secret Mantra?" he asked.

Then he added, "Now, continue with your mind training and resume your meditation on guru yoga. As it says in *Answers to Tsogyal's Questions* (*mtsho rgyal zhu lan*):

If you fail to meditate on the four thoughts that turn the mind in each and every practice session, you may be a Buddhist practitioner at the beginning of a session, but by the end of the session you will be bound only for this life.

"So this mind training is crucial if you aspire to be a practitioner who is consistent inwardly and outwardly. Abu Rinpoche used to do the mind training in each of his practice sessions, to the point where he would beat his chest with his fists and wail, 'I'd rather die than . . .'[148]

"Once he said to me, 'My dear Lungtok, I simply cannot bear contemplating the sufferings of the three lower realms anymore. When I meditate on the defects of samsara, I can think only of the sufferings of the three higher realms.'

"While we were staying in Do Ari Forest, in the morning when the nightingale sang, he would sit and lament with it, saying, 'You boo-hoo, me boo-hoo.'[149] We need to emulate that. If you listen to lofty talk about the so-called guidance on the main practice, and then reach for 'high' teachings, you will end up as the saying goes: 'If you tie your head to a high place, your neck will get cut from below.' There's a story about the monk Tangpa, who despite having gained control of his mind and energies, failed to bring a single evil thought onto the path and ended up a warlord in a foreign land. That's what can happen."

"Abu Rinpoche gave guidance on the main practice to all his other students once they had properly completed the five hundred thousand preliminary accumulations, but he withheld them from me for a very long time. Sometimes I wondered what my lama had in mind, but I never chased after the main-practice guidance or tried to forcefully gain access to the essential precious instructions.

"However, after many months and years had passed, I presented a symbolic mandala offering and made this request: 'In your compassion, kindly bestow upon me a preliminary or main practice, whichever would be most auspicious and suitable for my own mind and needs. I would be most grateful.'

"Guidance on the main practice is not a casual matter," he replied. "The Great Omniscient Longchen Rabjampa said:

At present, the teaching of the Great Perfection is coming to the end of its time. To access it, one must have superior accumulations and an extensive background in study and reflection. This domain is not the lot of others.

"This is true. The key points of the view, meditation, and action of the Great Perfection are the domain of sublime beings alone, and they cannot be casually understood by ordinary men and women," he said.

In the summer of my twenty-first year, I made plans to return home. At noon on the day my welcoming party was to come and receive me, I went to offer a little butter and cheese to my lama and request his blessing. He was sleeping, so I stepped outside to offer prostrations while I waited. As soon as I had finished and sat down, he arose. I went before him and presented my offerings.

"What's with all the butter and cheese?" he asked.

"I plan to go home today," I said. "My mother says she needs water tormas offered on her behalf, so I probably won't be back before autumn."[150]

Gracious Lungtok replied, "I just had an amazing dream . . ."

He repeated this several times, but I did not have the nerve to ask him what he had dreamed.

"If I were to analyze my dream, who knows . . . maybe if I were to teach you the guidance on the main practice, someone might come along for you to teach as well. Don't go home. Stay here. I need to give you extensive guidance for one hundred days or so," he said.

"Yes, sir, but my mother needs someone to do the water tormas for about ten days. May I take leave for that time and come back immediately afterward?" I asked.

"No, you may not. It is unacceptable to be lazy or procrastinate when it comes to receiving the extraordinary teachings. It is said:

The precious teachings are rare, and hostility toward them abounds;
Until one has found this rare and precious jewel,
Demons will delight in creating obstacles.

"This being the case, we'll start the guidance tomorrow. Observe your dreams tonight," he said.

Merely hearing him say that made all the hair on my body stand on end, and my eyes filled with tears of boundless devotion and joy. I was so excited I could scarcely sit still. From this, I knew for certain that he possessed the blessings of the lineage.

That night in my dream, someone who said she was Yeshe Tsogyal gave me a long, slim volume, the title of which read *Heart Treasury of the Guru Vidyadharas of the Three Lineages* (*brgyud gsum rig 'dzin bla ma'i thugs mdzod*). I dreamed that when I opened it, the pages were entirely filled, margins and all, with tiny letters that appeared to be in symbolic script.

The next day, I went before my lama carrying a symbolic mandala offering.

"So, what did you dream last night?" he asked.

I explained everything in detail.

"Could you understand the symbolic script?" he asked.

"No," I replied.

"The text filled with writing might indicate that you will be a supremely capable meditator, while the lack of margins might indicate a weakness in the virtuous practices of body and speech. Beyond that I don't know," he said.

That day he began the guidance on the main practice.

"These steps of guidance (*khrid rkang*) have been exclusively passed down to us from Rigdzin Jigme Lingpa, through a whispered mouth-to-ear lineage like a long chain of excellent golden mountains. Foremost among all the disciples of that great vidyadhara who came to Kham[151] was Dodrubchen Jigme Trinley Özer. The latter's disciples included the four of the Vajra lineage, the six Buddha brethren, the thirteen named Namkha, and the hundred or so holders of the mandala. Among them, the foremost of the thirteen named Namkha was Mingyur Namkhai Dorje, from whom I received the *Precious Treasury of Reality* (*chos dbyings rin po che'i mdzod*). Jigme Gyalwey Nyugu's two main disciples were Jamyang Khyentse and Kind Abu. From them I received guidance on the *Khandro Yangtik*, "Dakini Quintessence," entitled *Cloudbanks of the Ocean of Profound Meaning* (*zab don rgya mtsho'i sprin phung*), as well as firsthand guidance on the *Essence of Ultimate Meaning* (*nges don snying po*), and the *Demonstration of the Vajra Path of Secret Conduct* (*gsang spyod rdo rje'i lam bstan*).

"In fact, Rigdzin Jigme Lingpa prophesied, 'In this lineage of the Ösel Nyingtik, the son will be more excellent than the father, the grandson more excellent than the son, and the great-grandson more excellent than the grandson.' Thus far, there have been no embarrassments except for me. Now it seems that you have arrived as the great-grandson.

"Kind Abu taught me this guidance over a long period, one or two steps at a time, and I integrated it thoroughly and definitively within my being. Whenever I didn't understand or was confused about something, I went to

Abu himself, and he resolved my doubts verbally through scripture and rea-soning. These teachings, which delight the learned, are perfectly articulated, accurately reflect authentic experience, and are endowed with the blessings of the lineage. Therefore, to ensure that even the words remain uncorrupted, you must commit everything to memory," he explained.

First, he taught me by summarizing the key points of each step and had me reflect on each one for several days. Then he gave me an elaborate expla-nation, resolved my doubts, and again had me reflect for several days.

"Are you memorizing the words?" he asked.

"Right now I have them memorized, but I'm afraid I might forget them later on. Would it be all right if I took notes?" I asked.

"Nonsense! Have you not understood what is meant by 'Do not set forth the Whispered Lineage in writing'?" he asked.

After a while he said, "If you are still concerned that you will forget, they say that there is nothing wrong with writing a guidebook on the root stanzas only. Hence, the Great Omniscient Longchen Rabjampa wrote down the secret unwritten cycles of the Great Perfection, under the titles *Trilogy of Whispered Lineage Instructions from the Lama Yangtik* (*bla ma yang tig gi snyan brgyud skor gsum*) and *Guidance on the Secret Unwritten Whispered Lineage of the Zabmo Yangtik* (*zab mo yang tig gi gsang ba yi ge med pa'i snyan brgyud kyi khrid*). However, it would be inappropriate for the two of us to try to emulate him. Setting forth this Whispered Lineage guidance in writing would be disastrous, yet its disappearance would be disastrous, too."[152]

Because he said that, I later composed two guidebooks, one extensive and the other concise.[153]

When he explained the view of the wisdom of equipoise in the context of the main practice, I could find nothing whatsoever to ask. I was so dis-traught that I fervently supplicated the lineage lamas, took the four empow-erments associated with guru yoga, merged my mind with my lama's buddha mind, and rested in that state. Previously, during the preliminary practices, Lungtok Rinpoche had said that my experience of thought-free mind, in which all apparent objects vanished, was just the alaya, the universal ground. But examining it now, I found it to be completely unsullied by any thoughts whatsoever—past, present, or future, virtuous, nonvirtuous, or neutral. Nor was this one of the five thought-free states. I thought to myself, "There is nowhere to go beyond this stripped-naked empty awareness." Totally con-vinced of this, I went to tell my lama.

He chuckled. "Of course that's what it was, but I didn't want to give you any hints. The Great Omniscient Longchenpa stated:

To ascertain the heart of the wisdom realization of the Nyingtik, awareness must be stripped naked. If one does not understand this, no amount of Trekchö or Tögal practice will be of any use.

"That is certainly true. And now it has happened!" he exclaimed.

He was thrilled. "A son was born to the father, and the son will carry on the lineage! Today we must have a celebration!" He gave me large amounts of jaggery and fruit. "Here, drink some of my tea!" he said, and he spontaneously spoke a great deal.

"While you were doing the preliminary mind training, you described what sounded like unperceiving equipoise (*snang med mnyam bzhags*). That was it! During the equipoise of sublime beings (*'phags pa'i mnyams bzhags*), the first of the two aspects of the subject-object dichotomy—the concept of subject—disappears. As the concept of object has not yet disappeared, this perception is directly present as an object of equipoise. Next, the concept of an object disappears, and even that mere perception then becomes imperceptible in the face of equipoise. The former is known as perceiving equipoise (*snang bcas mnyam bzhag*), and the latter as unperceiving equipoise.

"Some contemporary scholars recognize the perceiving and unperceiving equipoise found in the literature of the *Prajnaparamita* to be the absorption of emptiness and the illusion-like absorption. However, such talk reveals a lack of experience and should be dismissed as false.

"You mentioned that when you arose from that equipoise you initially heard something that sounded like a chime (*ting shag*),[154] which caused appearances to arise with vivid clarity. It is said in the *Tantra of the Sole Heir to the Buddhas:*

With the ringing of cymbals, the natural resonance of appearances,
You will return to your former state and perceive things mistakenly.

"These indications are normally said to occur when the body of transformation (*'pho sku*) arises, but in this instance they seem to have occurred when you reached the inner consummation of awareness (*nang rig pa tshad phebs*). Do not be proud or conceited. Are you feeling proud?" he asked.[155]

"No," I replied. "In the postmeditative state, appearances all seem untrue and worthless, and I feel nothing but incredible sadness."

"That's how it should be," he said. "As the Great Omniscient One says:

> By familiarizing oneself with this reality,
> Qualities and experiences will emerge:
> A heartfelt appreciation of impermanence, short-term aims,
> Unceasing loving-kindness, and compassion,
> Pure perception, faithful devotion, and impartiality will all arise.[156]

"One must have all of these. Saraha said:

> In front, in back, and in the ten directions,
> All that one sees is this reality!
> Today, O Lord, my ostensible confusion has ceased.
> Now I shall question no one.

"You have arrived at the place he describes. Kind Abu gave me an introduction to the nature of mind at Nakchungma Hermitage near Dzogchen Monastery," he began.

"What was that like?" I asked.

"I had always been very fond of meditation, so Trom Drubtop gave me an introduction to the path of sudden or 'one-step' realization (*gcig char ba*).[157] Then I went up to the grasslands. I described my meditative experience (*rtogs 'bul*) to Lama Garab of Yi-Lhung and was told that I was on the path of 'two-step' realization (*gnyis char ba*).[158] Then I went to see Gemang Kyabgön Rinpoche, who offered me some yogurt.

"'I have no bowl,' I said.

"'Use your spontaneously appearing skull-cup,' he said.

"I held out my cupped hands.

"'You're smart!' he said.

"I described to him my meditative experience and was told I was on the path of 'three-step' realization (*gsum char ba*).

"Finally, I met with Abu, described my meditative experience, and was told that I was on the path of gradual realization (*rim gyis pa*).

"'What do "two-step" and "three-step realization" mean?' I asked.

"'That's precisely what I was poking fun at,' Abu replied. 'Without a single essential technique for conveying the pith instructions of the Whispered

Lineage, the teachings of these supposedly highly realized masters will get you nowhere. It is difficult for a student with a gradualist bent to receive an introduction. The current trend of bookishness is also ineffective.'

"Abu and I went up and sat at the base of a pine tree on the slope of Nakchungma that faces the valley. Every day, Abu went to a new isolated spot to do his practice sessions. When I brewed tea at the base of the pine tree, he returned and sat down.

"I had been having a recurring dream about a ball of black yarn that I had to hold very carefully to avoid unraveling it. One night I dreamed that Abu took the end and unraveled the ball of yarn completely. Inside it was a gold statue of Vajrasattva, which he gave to me. Had I known earlier what was inside the ball of yarn, I thought to myself, I wouldn't have struggled so hard to keep it from unraveling.

"Every evening at dusk, Abu went to a tiny clearing just big enough for his body, spread out his new wool mat, and stretched out on his back to do a session of threefold sky practice (*nam mkha' sum phrug*). One night, when he had finished doing his practice, he asked me, 'My dear Lungtok, did you say that you don't know the nature of mind?'

"'Yes, sir, I did,' I replied.

"'There is nothing not to know,' he said. 'Come here.'

"I went over to him, and he said, 'Lie down like I am and look up at the sky.'

"I did as he instructed.

"'Do you see the stars shining in the sky? Do you hear the dogs barking down at Dzogchen Monastery? Do you hear the two of us talking?' he asked.

"I answered each of his questions.

"'Well, that is meditation,' he said.

"From the depths of my being, an unshakable certainty arose, releasing me from the chains of doubt, and right then and there I was introduced to the wisdom of naked empty awareness. This recognition came entirely from his blessing. As Saraha says:

> When the words of the guru enter your heart,
> It is like seeing a treasure in the palm of your hand.

"That's true. In retrospect, it would seem that he merely told me that visual consciousness and auditory consciousness are both awareness. However, you must understand that the pinnacle of realization, according to the wisdom intention of the Nyingtik, the actual ultimate meaning, comes about solely through the transference of the blessings of the lineage. Abu once spent a day and night at a haunted charnel ground near Minyak Lautang, and he experienced many paranormal disturbances. He supplicated his lama and gained perfect confidence in the wisdom realization of the Great Perfection. He described his spiritual experience to Do Khyentse Yeshe Dorje, who said, 'You have cut down all four demons in a single blow!' It really seems that this was true. He said that after this, his disturbing emotions never amounted to much. Therefore, in this lineage, realization must be gained solely through faith and devotion to the lama. As they say:

> The way to attend the guru
> Is through faith and devotion, not polite language;
> The way to practice the guru sadhana
> Is through faith and devotion, not supplications.

"Jigme Gyalwey Nyugu meditated for many years at the sacred place of Chikchar in Tsari, undergoing many hardships. One day he went outside in the sun and gazed in the direction of Lhasa. Recalling his root lama and the lamas of the Nyingtik lineage, he prayed with such faith and devotion that he fell unconscious for a brief spell. When he came to, his previous need to control his meditative state disintegrated into the space of reality. Left with nothing to view and nothing to cultivate, he arrived directly at the abiding nature of awareness, free of distraction and delusion.

"However, he was not satisfied with that and thought to himself, 'Oh no! If only I hadn't come out here in the sun, I would still have a meditation practice. Now I have nothing at all! I need to resolve my doubts again, and my lama is elderly, so I should really go see him. On the way, I'll stop to see my old mother again . . .' and he started out.

"His body was emaciated from the hardships he had endured, and that first day he was unable to go farther than the riverbank below his hermitage. That evening, the local guardian deities, male and female Ksetrapala, appeared in the form of a Mönpa couple and offered him roasted wild-maize flour and venison.[159] The next day, they sent the leftovers along with him as provisions. After he had walked a few more days, a wealthy nomad, wishing to serve him, slaughtered a sheep and offered him the meat. He felt like a child whose own mother's flesh had been set before him, and an overwhelming compassion surged up in him. He could not even bear to look at the meat, much less eat it, and after that he never ate meat again.

"When he arrived before Rigdzin Jigme Lingpa, he described his spiritual experience. His lama was pleased. 'Son, that is exactly right. You have reached the level known as 'exhaustion of phenomena in reality' (chos nyid zad pa'i sa)."[160] Jigme Gyalwey Nyugu then stayed there for one year, and in the presence of his lama, he resolved nearly all his uncertainties concerning the topics of precious instruction he had previously been taught.

"His lama then said, 'I never knew you had such keen insight. Now stay with me for a long time, and you will become a great scholar.'

"Jigme Gyalwey Nyugu declined, saying, 'If my mother is still alive, I wish very much to see her. If I am able to practice the guidance of the preliminary and main practices, then I am contented with the kindness you have shown me, Lama.' With his lama's consent, he went off to Kham and visited his mother. He then meditated in Dza Trama for more than twenty years, where he became known as the Trama Lama.

"So it is not enough to have some realization; you have to cultivate it. Your experience must be thoroughly perfected. Until you have reached perfect mastery, you need to exert yourself in formal practice sessions. At some point, for your own sake, you will gain realization of the Great Perfection, which is the exhaustion of phenomena in reality, and the insight that thoroughly discerns all things—the expressive power of awareness—will burst forth from the expanse of reality. You will automatically be able to differentiate between the spiritual vehicles and the structure of philosophical systems, as distinctly as the gills of a mushroom.

"When an unconditional great compassion spontaneously emerges, the time will have come for you to teach, debate, and compose for the sake of others. Therefore, base your life on the exemplary lives of past saints, gain full confidence in your own experiences and realizations, and with discerning insight, identify the path and the hidden flaws of that which is not the path. Through these means, if you continue to practice, this alone will encompass everything.

"When you teach others, you must know how to summarize the key points of the pith instructions based on what you feel is sufficient for each individual. From now on you should align your mind with the wisdom intention of the Great Omniscient One's Seven Treasures (mdzod bdun) and the Four Nyingtik Mother-and-Child Cycles (snying thig ma bu).

"When an old lama says, 'Nonsense! Listen here. The *Seven Treasuries* and the *Four Branches of the Nyingtik* (*snying thig ya bzhi*) are just textual explanations, so put them aside. I hold an unexcelled Whispered Lineage given to me by Lama So-and-So,' and he goes about giving a newfangled interpretation of Calm Abiding with and without characteristics, and the three stages of stillness, movement, and awareness, he is tricking all of his students, high and low. These types are heretics blessed by demons. The Great Omniscient One admonished such people who practice idiotic meditation, devoid of the key points, saying:

Those whose view of emptiness is blankness,
And whose meditation on emptiness is like throwing stones in the
    dark,
Are left behind, thinking that these are the true view and
    meditation.

"You possess a flawless insight, so always make sure you thoroughly grasp these consummate key points of the path, the secrets of the Great Omniscient One's speech, and check your own experiences and realizations against them. These Abu aphorisms of mine could not be found even if you went around carrying a month's supply of provisions in search of them. Someday you will understand whether they can be found or not.

"When I offered guidance on *Yeshe Lama* to Lama Mipam, Tartse Pönlob, Solpön Pema, and Lama Tenpel, I gave them a rough outline of this oral tradition, but with the exception of the Pönlob, they were not particularly interested. If you look at their writings ever since, though, you will recognize what a difference there is in the way they express the precious instructions." He then proceeded to systematically impart the remaining guidance.

Then he said to me, "Now the time has come for me to introduce the main practice, so observe your dreams tonight." That night I dreamed of an enormous perimeter wall, of inestimable size, square with a large door in each of the four cardinal directions. The interior was filled with many different kinds of beings, and many lamas stood outside each door as gatekeepers. Above the western door was Orange Manjushri, holding a sword and a volume of scripture. To his left was Arya Nagarjuna, white and dressed in the robes of a fully ordained monk with a protuberance on the crown of his head.[161] I stood next to him, and beside me were many lamas, all carefully protecting the beings, making sure they did not get out.

The next morning I described this to my lama. Without offering any interpretation at all, he simply said, "That is a good dream."

Later he joked, "If those beings had escaped and Manjushri had whacked them with his sword, he would have killed them. Hitting them gently would probably not have stopped them. What was in Nagarjuna's hand?"

"Nothing," I answered.

"Oh well, what could of a bunch of unarmed people do anyway? What else did you dream?" he asked.

"In the latter part of the night I dreamed of a stupa in the form of a chaitya, apparently built by the religious king Ashoka, which had collapsed on the west side and was being swept into the western ocean by a flood, turning the waters deep red.[162] From the sky came a voice that said, 'Ten million creatures in the ocean have seen the truth!'" Lungtok Rinpoche said nothing about it being good or bad.[163]

"Now, traditionally, this introduction commences with just a lineage prayer, but in this case I will confer the two *Yeshe Lama* empowerments for the expressive power of awareness (*rig pa'i rtsal dbang*)," he said.[164]

"What implements do we need?" I asked.

"You are supposed to offer a gold mandala, but since you don't have one, take my mandala plate with the gold flowers on it and offer that, along with a few of your silver coins. I shouldn't use the skull-drum and bell, or everyone will say, 'The lama is giving an empowerment!' and come running."

He conferred the expressive-power empowerments for both the Trekchö and Tögal sections of *Yeshe Lama*. "In this lineage there is nothing more excellent than these two empowerments," he said. "I have hereby fulfilled whatever hopes you have had for receiving empowerments from me.

"In fact, I have not given many empowerments to anyone in this life. I once gave an empowerment to Khenpo Ngawang and Damchö of Dodrubchen Monastery, and they both vowed to take the *Guru Embodiment of Vidyadharas* as their daily practice, promising to accumulate one hundred million siddhi mantras each. Later I received a letter from Sershul Ngawang saying he had finished three hundred million siddhi mantras. When you receive an empowerment, you need to make use of it like that.

"In Khangtsik Gar, I conferred all the empowerments and reading transmissions for the liturgies of the *Nyingma Transmitted Teachings* (*rnying ma bka' ma*). I had hoped that the proverb 'The Transmitted Teachings should form the mainstream, and the Treasure Revelations their accessories' would come to pass, but instead they took the Treasure Revelations as the mainstream, and they did not even adopt the Transmitted Teachings as an accessory. Lama Atob later conferred and disseminated the empowerments and reading transmissions for the *Nyingma Transmitted Teachings* several times, but beyond that I don't think it brought much benefit to the encampment as a whole. Last year, while teaching *Yeshe Lama,* I gave an empowerment to Lama Ngawang Tendzin and Lama Dorli based on Khyentse's ritual arrangement, but other than these I have not conferred many empowerments.

"The two *Yeshe Lama* empowerments of the expressive power of awareness are for the extraordinary purpose of the practice entitled *Guru Sadhana Sealed with a Vital Nucleus.* You are henceforth permitted to undertake the recitation practice of *Sealed with a Vital Nucleus,*" he explained. Then he gave me an introduction, based on the guidance manual to the main practice.

"Since this is the actual word empowerment, it is not customary to give it more than once. However, in the coming days, I will explain it in detail," he said.

He then taught me the preliminary, main, and concluding practices, giving me one topic of guidance each day and making me contemplate it for a long time. Applying all the intellectual strength I possessed, I assimilated both the meanings and the words, and in places where I had hesitation or difficulty, I asked as many questions as I could. I felt contented thinking that this could not compare to receiving the guidance superficially.

The first portion of the teaching sequence went like this:

Day 1: How to apply the guidance of the main practice, having properly trained the mind through the common and uncommon preliminaries.

Day 2: How to develop the mind as wisdom through the common and uncommon teachings of the sutras and tantras.

Day 3: The importance of explaining and studying the teachings of the Secret Mantra by way of the five perfections.

Day 4: The differences between the transmissions and lengths of the three lineages particular to the Great Perfection.[165]

Day 5: The distinctions between the view, meditation, and action of the greater and lesser vehicles.

Day 6: The qualities that distinguish the Secret Mantra, the Vajrayana, from those greater and lesser vehicles.

Day 7: The distinctions between the view, meditation, action, and result of each of the vehicles from Kriyatantra through Anuyoga.

Day 8: Distinct from those, whatever tantras of the Great Perfection have come into being are compiled into three classes: mind, space, and pith instruction;[166] and how their respective wisdom realizations (*dgongs pa*) are assimilated.

Day 9: The superiority of the class of pith instructions to the preceding mind and space classes.

Day 10: Of the four cycles of pith instructions—outer, inner, secret, and innermost secret—the extent of the fourth, the unexcelled innermost secret tantras, which comprise the *Seventeen Tantras* (*rgyud bcu bdun*), plus the *Tantra of the Wrathful Protectress of Mantra* (*sngags srung khros ma'i rgyud*), making eighteen, and the *Tantra of the Brilliant Sun of the Clear Expanse* (*klong gsal 'bar ma nyi ma'i rgyud*), making nineteen, in addition to the contents of the *Mother and Child Cycles*. With regard to the latter, the wisdom intention and practice of the *Mother Cycles* were disclosed by the two preeminent masters, Vimalamitra and Padmasambhava. Specifically, Vimalamitra's *Sangwa Nyingtik*, "*Secret Heart Essence,*" and Padmasambhava's *Khandro Nyingtik*, "*Heart Essence of the Dakini,*" contain the complete, unerring requisites of the spiritual path that a single individual may follow.

Day 11: The *Child Cycles* comprise the Great Omniscient Longchen Rabjampa's *Lama Yangtik*, "*Guru Quintessence,*" and *Khandro Yangtik*, "*Dakini Quintessence,*" which perfectly elucidate the wisdom intentions of the two *Nyingtik Mother Branches*. They also include his *Zabmo Yangtik*, "*Profound Quintessence,*" which essentializes those two compilations, but is not counted separately from them because in the inventory it is referred to as "belonging to the secret *Khandro Yangtik* and its *Mother Branch.*" This explains why the *Four Nyingtik Mother-and-Child Cycles* are renowned as such.

Day 12: The *Longchen Nyingtik,* which integrates the wisdom intention and practice of the *Four Nyingtik Mother-and-Child Cycles*. The reason for this name is as follows: While Rigdzin Jigme Lingpa was staying in the remote forest solitudes of Chimpu, he encountered the writings of the Great Omniscient One, which for him was like meeting the Buddha in person. Having entered the holy citadel of unshakable devotion, he supplicated Longchenpa and engaged in essential practice (*snying po'i sgrub pa*) for three years. On three occasions, the Great Omniscient One blessed him with his buddha body, speech, and mind, and thrice accepted him as his disciple. On the final occasion, the Great Omniscient One spoke these words: "May the wisdom realization of expressed meanings be transferred to your mind! May the lineage of expressive words be complete!" He repeated this three times, whereby the wisdom realization of the authentic lineage was transferred to Jigme Lingpa. Resting in equipoise, he directly perceived the abiding nature of the Great Perfection, free from any mental speculation. In his postmeditative state, the wisdom that knows all things burst forth, and without him having to study them at all, all the key points of the vast and profound paths of the sutras and tantras appeared as clearly as a fresh myrobalan fruit placed in the palm of his hand.[167] This occurred through the transference of the Great Omniscient One's wisdom blessings (*byin rlabs kyi dgongs pa*), so it is for this reason that these teachings are renowned as the *Longchen Nyingtik, "Heart Essence of Longchenpa,"* as well as the fact that they resemble the pure-essence of the vital nucleus of Longchenpa's buddha mind.[168]

Day 13: The methods of guidance these teachings employ, corresponding to the stages of the path appropriate for individuals of the three distinct capacities (superior, middling, and inferior), combined with the Great Omniscient One's *Resting in the Nature of Mind*.

So for the first thirteen days, he made me contemplate and analyze the framework for the guidance.

Secondly, three days were then spent on the divisions of the three continua—ground, path, and result—which constitute the topics of guidance in the main practice.

The third portion of the teaching sequence went as follows:

Day 1: In order to specifically present the continuum of the path,[169] one day was spent identifying the two stages—the empowerments of the ripening path and the instructions of the liberating path—and their superiority to the common empowerments and teachings of the generation and completion stages presented in the lower vehicles.[170]

Day 2: How, in the context of the stage of liberating instructions, the interconnected methods of two kinds of guidance are skillfully applied, namely Trekchö, through which lazy practitioners are effortlessly liberated, and Tögal, through which diligent practitioners are liberated with effort; and how these two techniques facilitate the acquisition of the Dharmakaya and the Rupakaya, respectively.

Day 3: In order to guide the two kinds of practitioner—those whose minds are inclined toward referential objects (*dmigs pa yul gyi blo can*) and those whose minds are inclined toward the personal experience of awareness (*rig pa rang snang gi blo can*)—according to the stages of their individual capacity, there are two systems of Trekchö guidance: one that pursues meditation through the view, and another that pursues the view through meditation. Those whose minds are inclined toward referential objects should first meditate using the mental focusing appropriate for gods and humans, which is found in *Resting in the Nature of Mind*.[171] They should then apply the mental focusing on the symbolic white syllable AH, along with the mental focusing on the energies and vital nuclei, which are mentioned in the *Treasury of the Supreme Vehicle* (*theg mchog mdzod*), in the section on meditation and training that guide practitioners whose minds are inclined toward referential objects. There follows an explanation of the inaccuracy of the contemporary conflation of this technique with the so-called practice of Calm Abiding with characteristics, and an elaborate argument employing refutation and established reasoning, as to why those comments do not accord with the wisdom intention of the Great Perfection.

Day 4: First, the Trekchö guidance entails the memorization of: the preliminary practice that destroys the dwelling place of the mind; the main practice that introduces the awareness of one's own nature (*rig pa rang ngo sprad pa*); and the conclusion that reveals how to sustain this experience; along with their subcategories.

Day 5: Then comes cutting the root of the mind (*rtsad bcad pa*).

Day 6: Searching for the dwelling place of the mind (*mthsang btsal ba*).

Day 7: Its seven subcategories.[172]

Day 8: Knowledge about mind's origin, dwelling place, and destination[173] serves to identify the object of negation, grasping onto true existence (*bden 'dzin*), and to develop certainty about lack of self.

Day 9: Then one begins by investigating the place from whence the mind arises.

Day 10: What arises.

Day 11: Where the mind abides.

Day 12: What abides.

Day 13: To where the mind goes.

Day 14: What departs.

Day 15: One gains certainty about the fact that mind is free of the three phases of arising, abiding, and departing, is apparent yet empty, and lacks inherent existence because it is dependently arisen. These constitute the analytical view, or in the terminology of the Great Perfection, the subjective view (*chos can lta ba*) rather than the view of reality (*chos nyid lta ba*). The former, the view of direct self-awareness (*mngon sum rang rig lta ba*), is directly perceived through the key points of the channels in Tögal practice, although the luminosity produced through the skillful means of Mahayoga and Anuyoga may also be designated as a form of direct perception. These divisions of the view are explained in great detail in Vimalamitra's *Illuminating Lamp* (*snang byed sgron ma*).

The fourth portion of the teaching sequence includes two uncommon teachings, namely the investigation of the actual nature of the subjective mind and an introduction to the wisdom that is thereby established.[174] The first of these has four sections: view, meditation, action, and result.

Among these four sections, the view examines three distinctions: the distinction between the universal ground and the dharmakaya; the distinction between mind and awareness; and the distinction between relative and ultimate truth. Then, in order to come to a resolution (*la bzla ba*) of the view, one must recognize one's subtle conceptual attachment to that which is resolved. In itself, resolution encompasses the resolution of the effortful view, meditation, action, and result of each of the vehicles up to Anuyoga, as well as the view, meditation, action, and result of our own path, the Great Perfection.

Having made these distinctions and resolutions of the view, one then focuses on meditation. Here, one must distinguish between effortful, tenacious, grasping mindfulness and effortless, genuine, innate mindfulness. So meditation in this case refers to the wisdom intention of the four ways of freely resting, which naturally occur, and to the wisdom intention of the threefold motionlessness.

Action includes both the action of yogic discipline, which refers to the yogic practices associated with the path of skillful means, and the careful action of the path of liberation, which is also known as the action of harmonious skillful means.[175] Of these, the latter is emphasized here.

As for result, initially there is the explanation of the reason why provisional result requires the completion of all the thirty-seven factors of supreme enlightenment; and how these can then be subsumed in insight and great compassion. If the latter two factors are present, this is known as the result of the provisional path. Then, there is the ultimate result, which is definite liberation, attained either in this lifetime, at the time of death, or in the intermediate state after death. These explanations were given in conjunction with Garab Dorje's *Foundation Manual Recording Signs of Realization and Degrees of Progress* (*rtags yig tshad yig gzhi*). All this lasted three days.

The second part is the main practice [see above: Day 4, p. 91], otherwise known as the presentation of natural liberation in actuality (*rang grol mngon sum du ston pa*). Here, one is introduced to the awareness of one's own nature (*dngos gzhi rig pa rang ngo sprad pa*). Since this has several subdivisions, it lasted five days.

Then the third part is the concluding practice [see above: Day 4, p. 91], which reveals the method for sustaining the experience of awareness and has seven sections.

Together, these preliminary, main, and concluding practices constitute the complete instructions and guidance through which those of highest acumen may attain liberation in this very lifetime.

Next there follow the instructions through which those of middling acumen may attain liberation in the intermediate state after death:

Day 1: The instructions for entering the sphere of luminosity.[176]

Day 2: The ejection and transference of consciousness into another body.[177]

Day 3: The transference for entering the sphere of luminosity.

Day 4: Enhancing (*'bog 'don*) with the threefold sky practice.

Then, for those of inferior capacity, there is the instruction for attaining liberation in the intermediate state of becoming (*rnam smin srid pa bar do*),[178] along with the accompanying instructions on how to mount the consciousness on the energies (*rnam shes rlung zhon*).[179]

During his teaching sessions, Lungtok Rinpoche taught a single topic of guidance on any given day, and in the intervals between those sessions, he had me contemplate for many days. The Great Omniscient One said:

> In this teaching lineage of mine, one must attend the lama for a long time and listen to the precious instructions for a long time.

Accordingly, I earnestly attended my lama with the three methods of pleasing for a total of six years, thoroughly scrutinizing the precious instructions and putting them into practice. For this reason, I can say that in the future, if there are individuals who are genuinely focused on their next life and practice the Dharma from the heart, it will be necessary for them, too, to attend their lamas for a long time and listen to the precious instructions for a long time.

Then Lungtok Rinpoche said, "Now the guidance of the main practice, Trekchö, is complete. You should undertake the recitation practice of the *Guru Sadhana Sealed with a Vital Nucleus* for one hundred days, because this is the secret guru sadhana and the sadhana associated with *Yeshe Lama*. Each day you should recite about ten thousand mantras, primarily meditating in accordance with the threefold motionlessness. Your retreat does not need to be strict; come see me every few days and carefully resolve your uncertainties about the key points of the main practice," he instructed.

I entered retreat, and after three weeks I had a visionary experience in which the Great Omniscient One appeared in the sky, as vividly as if he were there in person. Loving-kindness, compassion, and bodhichitta arose within my cognitive experience (*shes nyams*), seemingly innate in my mental consciousness, and inseparable from me even at night when I was sleeping.[180]

When I related these experiences to my lama, he said, "Those are good visionary and cognitive experiences. It is as Shantideva said in the *Way of the Bodhisattva* [ch. 6, v. 14]:

> With practice, there is nothing whatsoever
> That does not become easy.

"However, these are in no way signs of attainment associated with the higher levels and paths. If you do not clearly distinguish between experiences and realization, it will be as they say:

> Perfecting the natural expressive power of insight,
> And losing one's mindfulness—
> These two are so similar, so similar—so easy to err![181]

"That's what will happen," he said, and he gave me the pith instructions of the *Three Statements That Strike the Vital Point (tshig gsum gnas du brdeg pa)* and also the *Lion's Roar That Cuts Through Errors and Deviations (gol shor tshar gcod seng ge'i nga ro)*.

At another point, he conferred guidance on the *Golden Rosary of Nectar (bdud rtsi'i gser phreng)*, a question-and-answer text from the *Khandro Nyingtik*.

Then he said, "Now you should end your retreat, for Lama Ah-ngak is going to give the reading transmission of the *Seven Treasuries*, which you should receive."

Accordingly, I came out of retreat and received the oral transmissions for the *Seven Treasuries*, along with the *Trilogy of Resting*. As soon as this was finished, I went before Gracious Lungtok, who asked me, "Do Longchenpa's *Seven Treasuries* and your own realization have some points in common?"

"How could they have points in common? I have nothing but mere intellectual understanding," I replied.

He was pleased. "Well done! It is very important to know the progression of the five paths and the ten stages by way of intellectual understanding, experience, and realization. Nowadays, mere intellectual understanding is introduced as realization. Avoid straying into lofty babble, claiming things like, 'This unwavering nonmeditation suffices for both view and meditation.' It is crucial to have absolute certainty regarding the presentation of the stages and paths.

"The *Precious Treasury of the Space of Reality* (*chos dbyings rin po che'i mdzod*) is considered a portrayal of the Great Omniscient One's realization: the first nine chapters present the view, the tenth presents meditation, the eleventh action, the twelfth the provisional result of the path, and the thirteenth the ultimate result. Now read the book while keeping this authentic understanding in mind," he instructed.

I fervently supplicated the Great Omniscient One and read the book, but I didn't understand much.

At one point my lama asked me, "What have you understood?"

"Sir, there are too many scriptures of the three classes—mind, space, and pith instruction—and especially within the mind class. Just trying to understand the differences between the mind class and the key points of the pith instructions of the secret cycle has greatly increased my confusion," I replied.

"Texts can be interpreted in any way. However, it is improper to quote higher scriptures when explaining lower ones, whereas lower scriptures may be quoted when explaining higher ones.[182] Now, let us see if I am able to explain the *Precious Treasury of Reality*," he said, and he gave me guidance.

"You are very fortunate," he said. "You are allowed to receive these teachings sitting down. When I received this guidance, Abu Rinpoche stopped sleeping. He taught me at Gangtrö Hermitage above Dzogchen Monastery. If he sat down he would fall asleep, so I opened my copy of the *Precious Treasury of Reality* and held it out in front of me so Abu could see it. I walked backward, and Abu followed me, reading from the book. He taught for many days and nights in a row. He said that this *Precious Treasury of Reality* is the quintessence of the Buddhist teachings. Indeed, this was the core of

Abu Rinpoche's spiritual practice (*thugs dam*), and I pretend that it is mine, too. You need to hold this in your heart as well. When you gain a genuine understanding based on these explanations, it will be impossible for you to confuse it with the mind class. *Absence of Letters* (*yi ge med pa*), which is a tantra belonging to the most secret unsurpassable cycle, as well as the final testaments of the buddhas and vidyadharas adorned with pith instructions, and the two traditions for introducing the nature of mind—one based and the other not based on the key points of Shri Singha's *Great Garuda Soaring in Space* (*khyung chen mkha' lding*)—are all included in the *Precious Treasury of Reality*. For this reason, it belongs to the Whispered Lineage of pith instructions. You should read and scrutinize the book accordingly," he explained.

I studied the book again and again, but my understanding improved only slightly. I explained this to my lama, who said, "That's right, you need to gradually improve your understanding. I once made Lingda Norkho read the book, and when I asked him what he had understood, he said he had understood the passage that reads:

> Whether or not there is wandering in samsara, with its three realms,
> Whether or not the fruit of Buddhahood is attained,
> The expanse of Samantabhadra
> Has neither samsara nor nirvana, neither cause nor result.

"He is a realized being, so for him such a thing is possible, but that kind of talk is a bit boastful and should be avoided. In general, it harms the integrity of the Buddha's teachings. In particular, it harms individuals, because they end up squandering their lives. It especially harms those students with meager merit. This is why they say:

> One needs courage for the view; one needs cowardice for the action.

"That's really very true," he said.

At one point, I requested guidance on *Yeshe Lama*, but Lungtok replied, "I am old and my eyesight is poor, so instead I will explain the classifications of ground, path, and result according to the unsurpassedly secret cycle." Over an extended period, he bestowed the extremely secret *Absence of Letters Tantra*, which belongs to the Whispered Lineage of Tögal and has a vast number of topics. Later, I also wrote a guidebook on this.[183]

In the meantime, I trained periodically with Lama Atob in mandala construction, according to the *Transmitted Teachings* (*Kama*) and *Treasure Revelations* (*Terma*) in general. I learned how to mark out the lines, apply the colored sand, and build three-dimensional scaled models, as well as build the three-dimensional model of the mandala palace of the *Magical Net* (*sgyu 'phrul drwa ba*), and so forth. In particular, he asked me to build a three-dimensional *Magical Net* mandala out of wood, which I did, and although it took me a long time, I am grateful. Now, whenever I explain or meditate on mandala formations, I have the confidence that comes from practical experience.

During that period, we saw a hunter shoot and kill a deer. Our assembly recited the *Heart Sutra* and slapped our religious robes to shame the hunter. Then we went to see our lama, who asked, "What's going on?"

We told him what happened.

"Oh, your compassion is misdirected! The victim is experiencing the result of a past action, and so the retribution exacted for past actions is being cleared bit by bit. The killer, on the other hand, is experiencing the cause of suffering, and from now on, for five hundred intermediate aeons, he will endure the miseries of hell and lose his life five hundred times as retribution. That begins today. So if you have compassion, it should be for him. You people think you have some understanding, but the fact that you have not even understood compassion is really stupid. It looks as though understanding the higher levels and paths will be far too difficult for you," he said.

One day Lungtok said to me, "Although you hold a potent view (*lta shed*), at this point you need to do a wrathful recitation practice. Otherwise, when you need it, you will be like a defenseless person facing a ferocious dog. I, too, have held a high view, but that doesn't help," he said.

"Which wrathful deity should I practice?" I asked.

"Generally speaking, Vishuddha Heruka, as presented in the *Nyingma Transmitted Teachings,* has been the main yidam deity of past Nyingma vidyadharas. Guru Rinpoche attained accomplishment by combining Vishuddha Heruka, who resembles a merchant, and Vajrakilaya, who is like a guardian escort. This, therefore, is foremost among the meditational deities.[184]

"In particular, if you want to show off some clear proof of the efficacy and power of the Early Translation school, a recitation practice based on Matarah, Yamantaka, and Vajrakilaya will be critical," he explained.[185]

"Which Vajrakilaya practice is the most profound?" I asked.

"The *Three Razor Scriptures* (*spu gri rnam gsum*), but what good will that do us? In these parts it is hard enough to find the texts, let alone the empowerments and reading transmissions," he said.[186]

"Which Yamantaka practice is the most profound?" I asked.

"There are no Yamantaka practices more effective than *Imitation Meteorite* (*lcags 'dra*) and *Meteorite Scorpion* (*lcags sdig*).[187] Lama Atob has the texts for *Matarah according to the Gangshar Tradition* (*ma mo sgang shar*) and for both of these Yamantaka practices, but leave them aside for the moment. Keep in mind that you will need to receive them later.

"Right now, pay close attention to your lama's pith instructions. Later, you will need to go to pursue your studies at a college. But if you go to a Geluk institution, you will fritter your life away in the science of dialectics.[188] Katok is our monastery, but at present there is nothing much happening there. They say that even in the Dzogchen area there is nothing but a dying residue of explanation left, and it is not like it was at Gemang when Abu was there," he said.

Then one day he announced, "Now you need to go and study at Dzogchen. I just received a letter from Lama Mipam Rinpoche's attendant Ösel, saying that Lama Mipam Rinpoche is coming to Dzogchen at New Year and intends to give teachings, primarily on his own writings, for the next few years. You must go."

"Sir, it would be wonderful for me to receive Lama Mipam Rinpoche's promulgations of the Wheel of Dharma, but I am just a young student, and I'm not sure how much I would understand of such a great scholar's discourses. And even if I were to understand something, I would just end up spending my life in distraction. Now, by all means, Lama, you are elderly—I beg you, please allow me to stay with you for as long as you live! I would be grateful if you could teach me some more key points of practice, but if not, I am completely satisfied with the teachings you have given me, and I can practice them just as they are. Later, I can wander through unknown lands and spend the rest of my life in solitude. Which of these would please you most?"

"Nonsense!" he exclaimed.

Those who renounce their homeland lack shame.
The best meditators are expert at collecting and hoarding.

"That's right. If you wander around in unknown lands, one day you'll get bound up with a woman. If you stay here and meditate, it will serve only your own purposes. While that is not wrong, the sun of the unified theory and practice of the Buddha's teachings is about to set in the lap of Varuna.[189] So failing to pursue your studies for the benefit of others would not be right. You have great hopes of benefiting others, so don't just wait around for me to die. Don't come back here until you have completed your studies, even if I fall ill! Even if I die, don't come back! You must go!"

His command was issued with such intensity that I dared not say a word. I thought to myself, "It is so rare to meet a qualified spiritual mentor like this! Now that I have met him, if only I could stay with him for as long as he lives, or at least for a little while longer, then it wouldn't matter if I didn't benefit others!" I burst into tears.

"There is no reason to cry," my lama said. "If you had not met a genuine spiritual mentor, you would have reason to cry. If you had met one but had not received the precious instructions, you would have reason to cry. If you had received the teachings but had not resolved your uncertainties, you would have reason to cry. You, however, have met a lama who holds the extraordinary lineage of the Ösel Nyingtik. You have received the pith instructions of the lineage, the profound teachings that have been passed down from mouth to ear, as if the contents of a full vase had been poured into you. You have resolved your uncertainties in relation to your own experience until not a single doubt remains. You have reached the level of self-reliance in your practice. I have entrusted to you the teaching of the *Nyingtik*. You have arrived at the threshold of being able to benefit others, so you must definitely go."

"What if Lama Mipam doesn't come?" I asked. "What should I do then?"

"It doesn't matter if he doesn't come. I assure you that there will be someone with whom you can study at Dzogchen Monastery. Now gather your things."

After that, I dared not contradict his words and made the decision to go. I went home briefly and gathered clothing and food supplies. When it was time to leave, I received a message from my lama requesting me to come. I arrived around noon, but he told me not to come until dusk that evening.

When darkness fell, I went to see him. There is a tradition of analyzing the line break in the lama's chanting that coincides with one's arrival. My arrival coincided with the line at the end of Padampa Sangye's *Thirty-Verse Prayer* (*smon lam sum cu pa*) that reads: "Through the enlightened activity of the nirmanakaya, may the benefit of others be perfectly accomplished!" After repeating this several times, he said, "The perfect accomplishment of others' benefit through nirmanakaya activity is the level of Buddhahood . . . that might be a bit too high for you." He said that several times.

"What should I do if I reach Buddhahood and it's too high?" I asked.

"I was just joking," he laughed. "When I analyze the auspicious coincidence of the line where I stopped chanting, it seems that in this life you will have no obstacles at all to your work to benefit beings and your enlightened activities."

He then prophesised, "As a bodhisattva, you will perfectly accomplish the welfare of beings."

"I am old now and have many illnesses," he went on, "so I don't know if we will meet again. Abu told me not to teach the Great Perfection until I was fifty. In your case, from today forward you should go ahead and teach whatever is requested, be it the preliminaries or main practices, as elaborately or concisely as you deem appropriate for your students' mental capacities.

"When you go to Dzogchen, you will get an education. But don't linger there, for it is Katok that is the fountainhead of the Nyingma teachings. Gyalse Shenpen Taye had planned to go there, but unfortunately he passed away. Right after that, Abu Rinpoche went there, but he did not bring much benefit to anyone aside from the previous Situ.[190] Abu told me to go, too, and I did stay some years in retreat at Jangsem Hermitage, but beyond that no one even realized I was a lama. Now, if someone comes in the future to invite you there, it would be of benefit if you went. The truth and power of our predecessors' aspirations are unfailing.

"Both Mindroling and Dzogchen monasteries think they are quite excellent and act very impressive, but there is really not much there. With only a few generations of lamas, they are recent establishments. Katok is entirely different. Ever since the Dharma Lord Dampa Deshek and his spiritual heir Tsangtönpa came and established the transmitted teachings of the Sutra, Magical Net, and Mind, which constitute the teachings of the Early Translation school,[191] the lineages of their students, extending from the regions of the white and black tribal groups of Khyungpo down to the Chinese border,[192] have produced learned and accomplished individuals, many hundreds and thousands of whom have attained the Rainbow Body.[193] They say that at its high point, the monastic assembly at Katok convened 1.8 million monks. Indeed, when they gathered every fortnight for the ceremony to restore their monastic vows, the light reflected from their saffron robes could change the color of the sky. This is true.[194]

"In those days, in the eastern ranges beyond Khyungpo, only the lineages of Dampa Rinpoche's students were extant. The teachings of the Sakya, Geluk, Kagyü, and so forth did not exist, having not long since taken root in the provinces of Ü and Tsang. This was the period when here in Dokham, the teachings of Katok flourished and thrived. When people nowadays claim that a certain lama has vastly benefited beings, it is really not much compared to how things were back then! Katok also offered moderately good prospects as a monastic seat for both Gyalse Shenpen Taye and Jamyang Khyentse, but the auspicious connections did not materialize. It has been a calamity for the teachings.

"When you meet the lamas at Dzogchen, do not go empty-handed. Regardless of their status, you must offer a mandala to each one of them. When you study, don't get stuck on a single text, but rather request as many different textual explanations as you possibly can. Once you have received the explanatory transmissions and textual commentaries, the word-for-word commentaries will be easy. You need to know how meaningful topics are investigated through the insight that arises from reflection (*bsam byung shes rab*),[195] and how the key points of the Sutra and Mantra vehicles are then condensed. For your own personal practice, that will suffice. However, if you are to teach others, you must arrive at a certainty in which you think, 'The key points are subsumed in this presentation.' You must do as Abu said: 'Study the philosophical systems impartially. Biased study causes distorted understanding. If you study the teachings impartially, you will know what is true and what is not, what is profound and what is not, what accords with the buddhas' wisdom mind, and so forth. From then on, you will understand through your own insight.'

"It is clear from each of their biographies that the earlier masters of the Nyingtik studied the textual explanations and precious instructions of all philosophical systems without sectarian bias, such that it seems there was nothing they did not receive. The Great Omniscient One, too, seems to have written a treatise on most of the systems of guidance extant here in Tibet.

"Now, the master who nurtures our minds and the parents who nurture our bodies are the ones to whom we owe the greatest debts of gratitude. Therefore, without ever forgetting your lama, pray constantly with devotion, and we will never be apart. That is why the link between the lama, who lovingly looks after the disciple, and the disciple, who has devotion to the lama, is vital. It is this that distinguishes our master-disciple relationship from others. Later, as long as your parents are alive, remain in your homeland in whatever remote hermitage appeals to you. After that, you will know what to do. I hereby wrap your nose-rope around your own head. Now go."[196]

He returned the money that I had given him, adding about twenty silver coins and fifty silk scarves.

As I made my way outside, offering prostrations, he called me back in. When I went inside, he said, "Give me your hands, and I will make a prayer of aspiration." He recited the supplication from the *Lama Yangtik,* along with aspirational prayers. "Now go," he said.

I went outside and offered prostrations, and again he summoned me. When I went in, he said, "Son, we shall not meet again. Do not let the instructions of my Whispered Lineage go to waste. Spread them as much as you can! Nowadays, it is indeed difficult to find a worthy recipient for the teachings of the Great Perfection. But anyone who hears even the name of the Great Perfection, not to mention receiving its empowerments and guidance, will go on to become a student of Khandroma Palgyi Lodrö (Dakini Glorious Intelligence) in the future, when the human life span is ten years, and they will definitely attain a degree of liberation, whether in life, at the time of death, or in the intermediate state after death, whatever the case may be.[197] This is clearly elucidated in the scripture entitled *Great Array of the Highest* (*a ti bkod pa chen po*),[198] and is therefore infallible.

"When you give Great Perfection guidance, at best your students should have received the empowerments for the *Four Nyingtik Mother-and-Child Cycles.* If not, they should at least have received an empowerment for the *Guru Sadhana Sealed with a Vital Nucleus.* Otherwise, it is not appropriate to teach them. You may confer the empowerments yourself or have another lama confer them," he explained. He gave me thirteen rounds of jaggery and a silk scarf inscribed with the auspicious "good-day" motif,[199] and said, "I am now empowering, inspiring, and acclaiming you at the thirteenth level, Holder of the Vajra!"[200] He then recited an elaborate benediction of auspicious excellence, and I in turn chanted the aspirational prayer that begins "In all my lives . . ."[201]

When I went outside, I was so overcome with grief that I fell unconscious. When I came to, tears streamed down my face. I went to spend the night at the home of a Dharma friend and wept all night.

The next day, I wondered to myself many times, "What would happen if I didn't go . . . ?" But thinking that there is no worse crime than defying the lama's command, I left.

On the twenty-ninth day of the ninth lunar month of the Mouse year [1900], I arrived at Dzogchen Monastery and settled into Tokden House at Shri Singha College. That night, the Great Yaksha Tsimara,[202] dressed in a brocade hat, gown, and boots, offered prostrations and respects, and presented me with a silk scarf.

"Why are you giving me these things?" I asked.

"Indeed, it is due to a past sacred commitment," he replied. "In a previous life, when you were Ngari Panchen, I appointed you as senior spiritual adviser (*dbu bla*) to the Sakya Dakchen. Then, when you were Lobzang Gyatso, I appointed you as the officiating lama (*bla'i mchod gnas*) in the court of the Mongol king Gushi Qan. Do you remember?"

"No, I don't remember," I said.

"Heh, heh, the stains of the womb have obscured you! Henceforth, I shall offer you my assistance," he said. I took that as a sign that the protector of the Buddhist college was pleased.

Lama Mipam had not come. I heard talk of his coming the following year. A few days later, from Lama Ngawang Tendzin, I received a concise explanation of the topical outline and word-for-word commentary of the *Ornament of the Middle Way* (*dbu ma rgyan*), which he had composed based on Mipam's *Great Commentary* (*'grel chen*).

Every day he praised the text, saying, "This *Ornament of the Middle Way* is like a pair of lions seated with their necks entwined (*seng ge mjing bsnol*)."[203]

Near the end of his explanation, I asked him, "Will you kindly explain to me what is meant by the expression 'lions seated with their necks entwined'?"

"Whatever assertions are made through conventional valid cognition are negated through the analytical reasoning of the ultimate truth. Whatever standpoints are held through analysis of the ultimate truth are negated through conventional valid cognition," he explained. (162.2)

That did not sit well with me. I quoted:

While riding the chariot of the two approaches,
Hold on to the reins of reasoning.[204]

"Your explanation does not accord with this. Does what you say not render the presentation of the two truths baseless?" I asked.

He was so gentlehearted that he sat there without the slightest annoyance and said, "Well then, tell me how you understand it."

"As I see it, the innate apprehension of things as truly existent (*lhan skyes kyi bden 'dzin*) is negated through the analytical reasoning of the ultimate truth, whereas concepts such as 'primal matter' (*gtso bo*) and 'almighty' (*dbang phyug*),[205] which are philosophically imputed, are negated through conventional authentic valid cognition. All of the Madhyamaka's own presentations of the conventional are thereby established through the authentic valid cognition of an unerring rational mind. With respect, Sir, that is what I think."

He thought for a moment and said, "Yes, that's right, that's right!"

After that, he questioned *me* about difficult points. I later heard that he announced to his colleagues, "That new student is extremely intelligent. You had better teach him carefully, because if you idly rattle off a word-for-word commentary, he won't be satisfied."

Soon after that, Minyak Lama Rigdzin Dorje arrived. He had spent thirteen years at the feet of Lama Mipam and was widely renowned for his extraordinary erudition. From him I received the root text and Jamgön Mipam's commentary on the *Ornament of the Middle Way*, Sakya Pandita's *Treasury of Valid Logical Reasoning* (*tshad ma rigs gter*) along with Mipam's annotations, and the *Sword of Insight That Thoroughly Ascertains Reality* (*don rnam par nges pa shes rab ral gri*), with a commentary by Tokden Lhaksam. These I more or less understood. I also received Jamgön Mipam's *Sword That Cuts Through Doubts about Symbolism* (*brda shan 'byed the tshom gcod pa'i ral gri*) and his own guidebook on that text, but as I had not yet studied Dharmakirti's *Exposition of Valid Cognition*, I could not reach a full understanding.

From Lama Pema Wangchen of Ku-sey, I received:

▶ Jamgön Mipam's *Explanation of the Deities of the Eight Heruka Sadhanas* (*bka' brgyad rnam bshad*);
▶ his *Overview of the Guhyagarbha Entitled Luminous Essence* (*gsang snying spyi don 'od gsal snying po*); and
▶ his *Secret Commentary on the Sadhana of Vishuddha Heruka* (*yang dag sgrub pa'i gsang 'grel*), along with the *Synopsis of the Secret Commentary* (*gsang 'grel don bsdus*).

Then, from Khenpo Losal I received:

▶ Lochen Dharmashri's *Great Commentary on the Ascertainment of the Three Vows, Entitled the Wish-Fulfilling Spike* (*sdom gsum rnam nges kyi 'grel pa dpag bsam snye ma*); and

▶ Jamgön Mipam's *Short Commentary Entitled Definitive Excellence* (*nges legs 'grel chung*).

After that, Khenpo Losal moved to Guhyagarbha House above the assembly hall at Shri Singha College. There he conferred a delightful empowerment for the *Peaceful and Wrathful Deities of the Magical Net* and taught me:

▶ Maitreya's *Ornament of the Sutras of the Greater Vehicle* (*theg pa chen po mdo sde'i rgyan*);
▶ the commentaries of Rongtön Sheja Kunrig on the *Two Distinctions* (*'byed rnam gnyis*);
▶ Dölpopa Sherab Gyaltsen's *Commentary on the Unsurpassed Continuum of the Mahayana Entitled Rays of the Sun* (*theg pa chen po rgyud bla ma'i bstan bcos legs bshad nyi ma'i 'od zer*);
▶ Longchen Rabjampa's *Commentary on the Guhyagarbha Entitled Dispelling the Darkness of the Ten Directions* (*gsang 'grel phyogs bcu mun sel*);
▶ Rongzompa Chökyi Zangpo's *Rare and Precious Jewel Commentary on the Guhyagarbha Tantra* (*dkon mchog 'grel*);
▶ Yungtön Dorjepel's *Ornate Flower Commentary on the Guhyagarbha Tantra* (*g.yung tik rgyan gyi me tog*);
▶ Rongzompa Chökyi Zangpo's *Introduction to the Mahayana Way* (*theg chen tshul la 'jug pa*); and
▶ his *Establishing Appearances as Divine* (*snang ba lhar sgrub*);
▶ the root text of Rigdzin Jigme Lingpa's *Precious Treasury of Qualities* and its *Commentary* by Alaksha Tendar (although there is no extant transmission of guidance for this text, he told me it was very important to understand);
▶ *Drop of Water in the Ocean* (*rgya mtsho'i chu thigs*) by Dodrub Jigme Trinley Özer, along with Abu's *Commentary on Difficult Points;*
▶ the root text of the Great Perfection's *Resting in the Nature of Mind,* along with its commentary and essential guidance; and
▶ the root text of *Resting in Illusion,* along with its commentary and essential guidance.

He is a lama to whom I feel tremendous gratitude.

From the resident abbot, Khenpo Sonam Chöpel, also known as Shedrub Chökyi Nangwa, I received:

- Abu's *Word-for-Word Commentary on the Ornament of Emergent Realization of the Transcendent Perfections* (*sher phyin mngon rtogs rgyan a bu'i tshig 'grel*), along with its *Overview* (*spyi don*);
- Je Rinpoche's *Commentary on the Ornament of Emergent Realization Entitled Golden Rosary of Eloquence* (*legs bzhad gser phreng*);
- Abu's *Stages of Meditation on the Transcendent Perfections* (*sher phyin sgom rim*);
- Tokmey Zangpo's *Commentary on the Way of the Bodhisattva;*
- Kamalashila's *Three Stages of Meditation* (*sgom rim gsum ka*);
- Lama Mipam's *Commentary on the Insight Chapter Entitled Water-Purifying Gem* (*sher 'grel ke ta ka*); and
- Kunzang Sonam's *General Explanation of the Insight Chapter* (*sher le'i spyi don*).

During that period I gained tremendous faith in the view of the Prasangikas, but a deep understanding had not yet dawned in me, so I supplicated my lama and my yidam deity. One day during a break between teaching sessions, I went out for a walk, and up on the mountainside I found a woodblock text of the *Insight Chapter* wrapped in black brocade. From that moment on, my understanding was quite different than before.

Then Khenpo Sonam Chöpel taught Lochen Dharmashri's *Ornament of the Lord of Secrets' Wisdom Mind* (*gsang bdag dgongs rgyan*) in Shri Singha's main temple, saying that this accorded with the tradition of explanation for an assembly for the *Guhyagarbha Tantra*. Next, he taught the same commentary to just a few of us, saying that this tradition of scholarly explanation stemmed from Ön Rinpoche Tendzin Norbu. I received both of these.

After that, he did a six-month retreat on the *Eight Heruka Sadhanas* (*sgrub pa bka' brgyad*), during which time I offered my services as his retreat attendant. During his breaks, he taught Nagarjuna's *Fundamental Stanzas of the Middle Way, Entitled Insight* (*dbu ma rtsa ba'i tshig le'u byas pa shes rab ces bya ba*), along with its auto-commentary entitled *Total Fearlessness* (*ga las 'jigs med*), the *Clearly Worded Commentary* (*tshig gsal ba*) of Chandrakirti, and the *Commentary* of Majawa Jangchup Tsöndrü.

In the early dawn before the teachings began, I had a clear vision of Arya Nagarjuna, wearing the robes of a fully ordained monk and resembling a tathagata who was enchanting to behold. In his hand he held a volume of the *Fundamental Stanzas of the Middle Way,* which he placed on the crown of my head, reciting its verses of obeisance, which begin, "To him who taught that things arise dependently . . ."[206] To that he added, "May you realize the meaning of dependent arising!" and repeated this three times. Consequently, dependent arising and the lack of inherent existence—the ordering of the two truths—however they were expressed, became easy for me to understand.[207]

Then I received:

- Nagarjuna's *Five Collections of Reasoning of the Middle Way* (*dbu ma rigs thogs*) one after the other;
- followed by Chandrakirti's *Auto-Commentary on the Introduction to the Middle Way;*
- Orgyen Tendzin Norbu's *Annotated Commentary* (*mchan 'grel*) on Chandrakirti's auto-commentary;
- Avalokitavrata's *Commentary on the Lamp of Insight* (*shes rab sgron ma rgya cher 'grel pa*);
- Master Dharmapala's *Commentary on the Four Hundred Stanzas on the Middle Way* (*dbu ma bzhi brgya pa'i 'grel ba*), which emphasizes the Mind Only tradition; and
- Chandrakirti's s *Commentary on the Four Hundred Stanzas on the Middle Way.*

These final texts Khenpo Sonam Chöpel conferred after explaining that while their explanatory transmissions are no longer extant, the reading transmissions do exist within the *Tengyur.*

He then taught:

- the root text, commentary, and essential guidance of Longchenpa's *Treasury of Wish-Fulfilling Gems* (*yid bzhin mdzod*);
- Lama Mipam's *Summation of Philosophical Systems from the Treasury of Wish-Fulfilling Gems* (*grub mtha' bsdus pa*);
- his *Commentary on Difficult Points in the Eighteenth Chapter of the Treasury of Wish-Fulfilling Gems* (*le'u bco brgyad pa'i dka' 'grel*);
- Abu's *Discourse on Virtuous Action in the Beginning, Middle, and End* (*thog mtha' bar dge'i gtam*);
- his *Benefits of Reading the Mahayana Sutras*
- his *Drumbeat of the Gods: Advice for Retreat* (*dben gtam lha yi rnga sgra*);
- his *Guide to the Seventeen Foundations of Monastic Discipline* (*gzhi bcu bdun zin bris*);

▸ his *Guidance on the View of the Middle Way according to the Maha-yana* (*theg chen dbu ma'i lta khrid*); and

▸ his *Selected Works of Kadam* (*dka' gdams gsung gi gces bsdus*).

I received his guidance on all these texts, and mostly reading transmissions for other miscellaneous writings, in addition to his firsthand guidance on the channels and energies according to the Nyingtik. For these reasons, he was the second lama at Dzogchen to whom I felt deep gratitude.

After that, from the reincarnation of Alak Kalden Gyatso, I received the middle chapters from *Mirror of Poetics* (*snyan ngag me long*), concerning poetic ornaments, along with the commentaries of Bokhepa Gelek Namgyal and Khamtrul Ngawang Kunga Tendzin.

Then, from Lama Menlha I received Abu's teachings on astrology, including the five planetary aspects and the fivefold calculation, as well as his teachings on the *Grammar of Sarasvati* (*brda sprod pa dbyangs can gyi mdo*), and on prosody.[208] He also taught me synonymics according to the system of Shedrung Pema Namdak.

From Tongza Bakwa Lama Do-ngak, I received:

▸ Mipam's *Commentary on the Verse Summation of the Prajnaparamita Integrating the Sutras and Treatises* (*sdud 'grel mdo sbyar*);

▸ his commentaries on the *Two Distinctions;*

▸ his *Manjushri Offering Ritual* (*'jam dpal mchod chog*); and

▸ his *Praise and Sadhana of Manjushri* (*'jam dpal bstod sgrub*).

He also offered the teachings of Situ Chökyi Jungney on Tibetan orthography and Tibetan grammar.

Then Mura Tulku Pema Dechen Zangpo arrived. From him I received:

▸ the extensive empowerment for Karma Lingpa's *Peaceful and Wrathful Deities: Natural Liberation of Wisdom Mind* (*kar gling zhi khro dgongs pa rang grol*), which is entitled *Natural Liberation through Encountering All Four Empowerments* (*zhi khro dbang bzhi phrad tshad rang grol*);

▸ the *Mid-Length Empowerment Entitled Natural Liberation of the Six Classes of Beings* (*dbang 'bring pa 'gro drug rang grol*); and

▸ the *Concise Torma Empowerment Entitled Meaningful to Touch* (*gtor dbang reg pa don ldan*).

All of these were given in accordance with the primary lineage of Dzogchen Monastery's own liturgical arrangement. Along with these, I received the *Guidance Manual to the Six Intermediate States* (*bar do drug gi khrid yig*) from the same cycle. In addition, he conferred:

- ▸ Rigdzin Jigme Lingpa's *Naked Perception of the Abiding Nature* (*gnas lugs cer mthong*);
- ▸ the reading transmissions of the two volumes of the *Longchen Nyingtik;*[209]
- ▸ guidance on *Yeshe Lama;*
- ▸ and Ngedön Tendzin Zangpo's teaching entitled *White Path to Liberation: Guidance according to the Khandro Yangtik* (*mkha' 'gro yang tig gi khrid thar lam dkar po*).

Then, in the Shri Singha temple, he conferred the bodhisattva vows according to the tradition of Profound View, conjoined with an explanation of the fourth chapter of the *Way of the Bodhisattva* according to Abu's practical technique. Later, at the residence of Khenpo Sonam Chöpel, I received them according to the tradition of Vast Action.[210]

He then conferred an elaborate empowerment for the sadhana from Sangye Lingpa's *Embodiment of the Master's Realization* (*bla ma dgongs 'dus*) upon all those who were staying in the retreat center. This took many days.

Khenpo Sonam Chöpel was the resident monastic preceptor, so he often had to give full and novitiate ordination, and whenever he did I was required to go as the ritual officiant. I felt that my homework was more important and asked him if he could look for some other monk to fill the rank, but he said, "That won't do. After all, it is important for you to see how this is done in our lineage, and you need to master the procedures. For you, too, the time will come one day when you will find this useful. If you have to learn the procedures at that point, it will be hard for you," he said.

At one point, I served as overseer at the monastic school of Dzogchen.[211] I had to clarify everyone's confusion and help everyone with their studies, which I found very tiresome.

From Khenpo Yeshe Gyaltsen, I received both Gyurme Tsewang Chokdrup's *Explanatory Guide to the General Meaning of the Guhyagarbha Tantra, Entitled Ocean of Eloquence* (*gsang spyi bshad legs bshad rol mtsho*) and

Orgyen Chödrak's *Guide to the Ornament of the Lord of Secrets' Wisdom Mind* (*gsang bdag dgongs rgyan spyi don zin bris*).

I requested Khenpo Könchok Norbu to give me an explanation of the *Way of the Bodhisattva,* adorned with Abu's oral transmission. He had received this text from Abu thirteen times and had spent his entire life focused solely on the cultivation of bodhichitta.

"I don't know how to give impressive Buddhist teachings," he said. "Nowadays, students do nothing but roam around checking out what people have to say, so there is not much point in teaching them. But you are not at all like that, so don't tell anyone and tomorrow I will teach you."

He recited the root text and topic outline of the *Way of the Bodhisattva,* directly from memory, interjecting comments such as "Here, Abu's oral transmission states such and such . . ." and "You need to analyze like this and reflect like that . . ." For an entire month he gave me a delightful explanation, combined with pith instructions on how to traverse the paths of both Calm Abiding and Higher Insight.

"What do you think of this style of teaching?" he asked me.

"It's wonderful," I said.

"It really is. At Dzogchen Monastery they say I don't know the curriculum. I actually do, but what's the use? There is no one here who is concerned with future lives or with practice, so from early on I have refused to teach," he explained.

Then he asked me, "Have you received Gunaprabha's *Root Sutra of Monastic Discipline* (*'dul ba mdo rtsa*)?"

I replied that I had not and requested the holy master to grace me with his kindness.

"That wouldn't be good," he replied. "From the start, I have trained my mind solely in bodhichitta, and I have done little contemplation or analysis of any other subject. My eyes are bad, too, so I am unable to rely upon texts. It is important that you receive it, but from someone else. Monastic discipline is like the foundation of all good qualities. In the past, this monastery had fairly strict monastic discipline, but nowadays things are becoming more and more lax. Their debate on the Prasangika and Svatantrika approaches of the Madhyamaka is completely externalized; indeed there is not a single person who turns inward to look within the mind. According to this monastic discipline of ours, one needs to have a good character and a stable mind, as well as superior intelligence. Without straying into pretense or exhibitionism, one needs an attitude of uncontrived disillusionment with ordinary concerns. Although it is difficult to have that right now, you must rectify your discipline and enter the path. I heard from Sonam Chöpel that you have a flawless character. See if you can get the *Root Sutra of Monastic Discipline* from Sonam Chöpel." I kept his words in mind.

From Khenpo Sonam Chöpel, I then received:

- the *Root Sutra of Monastic Discipline;*
- Ön Rinpoche's *Annotated Commentary* on the latter;
- Gendün Drubpa's *Commentary on the Root Sutra of Monastic Discipline Entitled Jewel Garland* (*'dul tik rin chen 'phreng ba*);
- Tsonawa Sherab Zangpo's *Ocean Commentary on Monastic Discipline* (*'dul ba mtsho tik*);
- Gendün Drubpa's *Hundred Thousand Anecdotes of Monastic Discipline* (*'dul ba'i gleng 'bum chen mo*);
- Je Tsongkhapa's *Precepts for Fully Ordained Monks and Novices Entitled Soaring the Vaults of the Heavens* (*dge tshul slong gi bslab bya gnam rtsad lding ma*);
- the *Annotated Sutra on the Vows of Individual Liberation* (*sor mdo mchan 'grel*);
- Shakyaprabha's *Commentary on Monastic Discipline* (*'dul tik*); and[212]
- Vimalamitra's *Commentary on Monastic Discipline* (*'dul tik*).

He gave me his copies of both the *Jewel Garland* and the *Hundred Thousand Anecdotes,* saying, "Study both of these. Nowadays, in these parts, people are all caught up in annotated commentaries. No one engages in the study and comprehension of the great canonical scriptures. Regarding the classifications of past actions and their results, other than explanations given in the works of monastic discipline, there is no way to analyze them through logical reasoning," he said.

Then Geshe Kunzang Sonam's attendant Ah-pel was invited to Dzogchen to establish the explanatory tradition of Vasubandhu's *Treasury of Abhidharma* (*chos mngon pa'i mdzod*). Dzogchen Rinpoche chose ten of the brightest monks among the resident and visiting students, and told them to study hard.[213] I was placed on the list, so I began my studies of Buddhist phenomenology.

Ah-pel was a high-level geshe, so he recited virtually all of the root text and commentaries from memory.[214] He incorporated the first section of

Vasubandhu's *Auto-Commentary on the Treasury of Abhidharma* (*chos mngon pa'i mdzod kyi bshad pa*) into his teachings, as well as other Indian commentaries by Jinaputra and Purnavardhana, and the indigenous Tibetan works known as the *Greater and Lesser Commentaries on the Treasury of Abhidharma* by Chim Jampelyang and Chim Lobzang Drak. For the first few days, we could not even grasp the word-for-word commentary, and everyone was shocked and dismayed, convinced that we would never understand.

I went up the mountainside behind Shri Singha to a rock that resembles a teaching-throne, where Kind Abu had sat when he taught Buddhist phenomenology. I thought to myself, "Even though I don't understand the Abhidharma, I'll recite the root text a few times and pray that I can establish some positive propensity." I sat at the base of the teaching-throne and made many prayers of aspiration that I might be able to comprehend the holy teachings of Buddhist phenomenology, exactly in accord with the wisdom mind of Acharya Vasubandhu himself.

After that, I fell asleep for a short while, and in my dream I met Acharya Vasubandhu attired in a sleeveless blue vest, the three religious robes, and a hat with short flaps resembling a hermitage hat. Instantly, in what I knew was a region of India, I had a hazy recollection of my previous life as Acharya Sthiramati. At that moment, Acharya Vasubandhu recited the words of homage that begin, "He who has, in an ultimate manner, destroyed all blindness . . ." and so on.[215] Then he explained, "This *Greater Commentary on the Treasury of Abhidharma* by Chim Jampelyang precisely explains the wisdom intent of phenomenology, so take that as the basis of your studies and you will understand Buddhist phenomenology." Then I awoke.

Right away, I borrowed the *Greater Commentary on the Treasury of Abhidharma* by Chim Jampelyang from Kusho Labrang and read it, whereupon I gained a little understanding.[216] When we reached the middle of the text, trouble erupted between the monks from Golok and Dzogchen, and most of my classmates fled. Only four of us actually completed the study of phenomenology: Yongshar Khenpo, Gey-gye Lama, Dorli, and myself. Later, when Khenpo Lhagyal was beginning his term of service as abbot, I offered him the teachings and was able to at least prevent the explanatory transmission from being interrupted in that region.

From Khenpo Ah-pel, I also received:

▸ the Fifth Dalai Lama's *Compendium of Eloquence on Mind Training* (*blo sbyong legs bshad kun 'dus*);

▸ Padmasambhava's *Narrative History Entitled Heap of Precious Gems* (*gtam rgyud rin chen spung pa*);
▸ Kunzang Sonam's *Prayer for Mind Training* (*blo sbyong smon lam*); and
▸ Patrul Rinpoche's *Selected Works of Kadam*.

Early that summer, Lama Mipam came from Denkhok to Dzogchen. Dzogchen Monastery welcomed him with an elaborate procession of monks, and he took up residence. On that occasion, I just caught a glimpse of him. He stayed upstairs, above the Shri Singha Temple, and through his attendant Ösel I was able to obtain a close audience. I requested the kindness of a teaching connection, but he said it was not yet time.

It was there that he began composing his treatise *Gateway to Knowledge*. After about one month, he moved uphill to Nakchungma Hermitage. Sometime during the fifth lunar month, that summer, I went to see him. He had finished writing *Gateway to Knowledge* that very day.

"Today, when the constellations Cancer and Jupiter have just gone into alignment, your arrival coincides with the completion of my philosophical treatise. What an excellent auspicious sign for you!"[217] he exclaimed. "It is called *Gateway to Knowledge,* for it is like the threshold to the three ways of the wise. The difference between this and Sakya Pandita's *Gateway to Knowledge* is that this one is more extensive. This summary (*sdom byang*) should be committed to memory. It is a summary, not the root text."

He gave me the reading transmission for the main text along with the summary, starting at the beginning, adding brief comments, and leaving out certain sections. Continuing in that mode, he finished by early evening. As soon as he had finished, he placed the text on top of my head and said, "I entrust this to you. Even though I was unable to recite the whole text from beginning to end, you have obtained authorization from the author of the treatise, so from today forward you may teach it. If you give explanations based on this text, many erudite scholars will emerge.

"I received many letters from dear Lungtok explaining how the two of you needed teachings, but I've been constantly afflicted with this nervous disorder, and I am old and weary of teaching.[218] I had hoped that by leaving behind a few treatises, it would bring benefit to the Nyingma school, (176/1) but because of the times, that may be difficult. Had the lotus feet of Gyalse Shenpen Taye remained firmly upon this earth, the great philosophical tradition of the Early Translation school would have spread, but because our shared merit has been weak, he passed away. After that, of all those who comprehend the Nyingma teachings, Lama Lungtok is most excellent. After him come Sögyal and Dodrub Tenpey Nyima, both of whom have a pretty faultless understanding. Other than that, there is no one who is learned.

"Earlier, I went to Katok and gave a few teachings to Situ Tulku Chökyi Gyatso, primarily the *Five Treatises of Maitreya* (*byams chos sde lnga*). At the time, I had aspirations for their college, but nothing came of it. Now Situ Tulku has his own aspirations for the college and has sent me messengers and letters inviting me to come, but I doubt I'll be able to go. In the future, if his aspirations mature, please don't be deterred from helping him," he said.

He gave me a volume of the *Tantra of the Litany of Manjushri's Names* (*'jam dpal mtshan brjod*) wrapped in cloth, as well as seven blessed Manjushri pills. His attendant Ösel, as well, knowing that I was Gracious Lungtok's student, always looked after me lovingly.

Again one day he told me to come, saying it was time to complete an offering of ten thousand butter lamps. I went and helped them for a few days. During our breaks, I received the reading transmission for many sections from his cycle entitled *Instructions on the Mind: Holding Buddha in Your Hand* (*sems don sangs rgyas lag bcang*), about forty pages in all.

Through Ösel, I requested the permissory initiation (*rjes gnang*)[219] for the *Praise to Manjushri Entitled You Whose Intelligence,* so one day Lama Mipam conferred the permissory initiation for his *Manifold Light Rays of the Praise Entitled You Whose Intelligence* (*gang blo ma'i 'od zer dgu phrug*), along with the sadhana of praise. "My *Manjushri according to the Mahayoga Tantra Tradition* (*'jam dpal rgyud lugs*) has had a seal of secrecy until now," he explained. "Its flow of blessings is more powerful than any other. If you would like to copy it, you may borrow this text, but do not show it to anyone."

I took the text and copied it under a rocky overhang on the hillside above Shri Singha. When I was done, I returned the text and asked, "If there is an empowerment for this, will you kindly confer it?"

"There is no empowerment except the one of Sarben Chokmey. Nor am I able to bestow it. I will give you the reading transmission."

He read a little, starting from the beginning, including the sadhana, its amendment, the longevity practice, the technique for making white and red torma offerings, and the ritual activities. The rest I received from Ösel.

Mipam Rinpoche then said, "Until you have completed the requisite recitations for each part of the practice, do not transmit this to anyone."

Later, I accumulated three times the requisite number of recitations. When I had nearly completed the recitations of the ritual activities, I began to propagate this practice.

Then, from Khenpo Sonam Chöpel, I received:

▶ teachings on Jamgön Mipam's *Light of the Sun: Response to Critiques* (*brgal lan nyin byed snang ba*);
▶ the *Compendium of Abhidharma* (*mngon pa kun btus*), with the commentary of Sabzang Mati Panchen;
▶ reading transmissions for Asanga's *Five Sections of the Yogacharya Levels* (*sa sde lnga*);
▶ his *Summary of the Mahayana* (*theg pa chen po bsdus pa*);
▶ Vasubandhu's *Dissertation on the Thirty Verses* (*sum cu pa'i tshig le'u byas pa*); and
▶ Kamalashila's *Three Stages of Meditation*.

From the Fifth Dzogchen Tulku, I received all the empowerments and reading transmissions for the supremely profound *Union of All Precious Jewels* (*dkon mchog spyi 'dus*).

From Drukpa Kuchen Chöying Rolpey Dorje, I received the extensive root empowerment, as well as the ultimate empowerment, for Sangye Lingpa's *Embodiment of the Master's Realization*.

In short, for a period of twenty-four months spanning three lunar years, I exerted myself night and day exclusively in academic studies.

One day in the autumn of the Tiger year [1902], as I was preparing to return home, I received a note from Drukpa Kuchen, who was staying at Pematang. It read: "I need someone to shave my head today. Bring your bell-metal razor and come." So with my bell-metal knife in hand, I went to see him.

Laughing, he said, "I wanted to bestow an empowerment for the *Khandro Yangtik* today, but I thought if people found out, then everyone would crowd in. So I came up with this trick. Now you and Buluk Kyitar should sweep the room well. We need plenty of decorations and ritual articles, as well as elaborate tormas for feast offering. While you finish all that, I'll be out in the meadow."

He went out and sat on a carpet inside the wood-fenced enclosure. The two of us did as instructed and around midafternoon, just as we had finished getting everything ready, he came inside.

"The *Khandro Yangtik* is the reason why an individual such as Dzogchen Rinpoche can hold the title 'Accomplished Master of the Great Perfection' (*grub dbang rdzogs chen pa*).[220] This is a one-to-one transmission wherein the lineage of empowerment is entrusted to a single heir. Mingyur Namkhai Dorje entrusted it to me. Now I would like to entrust it to you," he said.

"Drada Karma prophesied that if I went to Rudam Gangtrö this year and stayed for three years, my life would be long and my practice would reach fruition. If I didn't, there would be many obstacles this year—my forty-fourth year. According to my own divinations, if I don't die this year, I will remain for a long time and then go to the Palace of Lotus Light. If I do die this year, I will depart for the Palace of Lotus Light after one rebirth in the region of Yarlung."

"Please, if you are able to stay for a while, do not withhold your kindness!" I begged him. "You must fulfill your life's aspirations! I will most certainly undertake whatever longevity prayers you deem appropriate, for however many months and years are necessary, and I will accomplish whatever you ask of me," I promised.

"Nonsense," he scoffed. "No one wants to die, but this year I have had many indications of approaching death and many visions of dakinis coming to receive me. I need to give you this empowerment," he said.[221]

"In that case, may Lama Dorli receive it?" I asked.

"If no one else hears about it, he may," he replied.

He began the preparations for the empowerment, with me serving as his shrine assistant while Kyitar went to call Lama Dorli. When I carried a feast-offering torma outside to offer it, the area behind the wooden fence was filled with a large number of unusual-looking women. I told the lama, saying, "I didn't tell a soul there would be an empowerment. I wonder if Kyitar said something. Where did all those women come from?"

"Do you recognize any of them?" he asked.

"No," I answered.

"Ah, those are not human beings. It is probably an assembly of dakinis. In the evening when we invite and serve them, we need to offer plentiful feast offerings on the rooftop. When we make the remainder offerings, many spirit-dancers will come to dance. They are guardians of the *Nyingtik,* so keep your mind undistracted. At that point, you should behold them with your wisdom mind. I will check to see if your wisdom realization is high or not," he said.

A moment later the two others arrived from Shri Singha. "Tonight I will perform the preparatory phase (*sta gon*) and tomorrow the main section," he explained. At the beginning, when the empowerment's seal of entrustment (*gtad rgya*) is imparted to the students, he said to us, "Until each of you makes a mandala offering indicative of your commitment, I dare not recite this empowerment."

Kyitar pledged to undertake the recitation practice of the *Guru Sadhana Sealed with a Vital Nucleus* for one hundred days, and Lama Dorli pledged to undertake the practice of Tögal for one hundred days. As for myself, all the movements of past and future thoughts dissolved into the space of reality, and I was left stunned in the state of wisdom of naked empty awareness (*rig stong rjen pa'i ye shes*). The flux of ordinary sensations ceased, and I could say nothing at all.

"So what is your pledge?" he asked me. (182/1)

"Nothing is coming to mind, so whatever you deem best," I answered.

"Well then, you should teach the guidance on the *Khandro Yangtik* thirteen times. It won't do to teach it casually, either. Only after you have practiced it and received permission from the lamas and dakinis should you teach and propagate it," he said.

I pledged to do so, and he bestowed the empowerment for the seal of entrustment, along with prayers of aspiration. When the time came to offer the feast remainders, many skeletons appeared and danced on the periphery of the mandala. Just when I thought to offer them the remainder tormas, the lama said, "Now take out the remainders!" I went outside to offer them, and there, outside the door, I saw Dorje Yudrönma in the form of a graceful and seductive young woman.

When the empowerment was finished, the lama said, "Now Kyitar and Dorli, you two may go. Ngakli needs to stay and pack my bags." He sent them home, and I stayed the night with him. In the morning, as I was gathering and organizing the empowerment articles, he asked me, "What did you see yesterday during the empowerment?"

I described everything to him.

"Were you afraid of the skeletons or attracted to the woman?" he asked.

"No, sir, nothing like that occurred. My consciousness became free of reference points and I felt like a child watching a spectacle, unable to identify anything in particular," I offered.

"Oh, that's it, that's it! When all phenomena are spontaneously subsumed within one's wisdom mind, the expanse of reality, this is called bringing the dakinis under one's control. Henceforth, you shall have no obstacles," he said, and I realized he was foreseeing the future.

After that, I returned to my homeland and learned that Gracious Lungtok Rinpoche had passed away on the twenty-fifth day of the fifth lunar month of the previous year [1901].

The whole world became like a desert of sorrow and despair. I went to his residence and made prostrations and offerings before his reliquary. At the very top of the reliquary, I beheld the figure of Vajrasattva within a sphere of rainbow light, like a pool into which a pebble had been tossed. I exerted myself solely in the practice of devotional guru yoga there at his monastic seat. I saw my lama's form and heard his voice many times, and gained absolute confidence that he was protecting me constantly and inseparably with his compassion.

Then, two people came to request teachings, one from Tahor Rong and the other from Markham. With these two as the principal recipients, I gave some teachings on works such as the *Five Treatises of Maitreya* to a few individuals. In the morning of the first day, as I taught Rigdzin Jigme Lingpa's *Precious Treasury of Qualities*, rainbow light filled the entire valley. As I taught the *Precious Treasury of Qualities*, we performed one hundred thousand feast offerings. To fulfill the wisdom intentions of Gracious Lungtok Rinpoche, I also gave a brief explanation of Chandrakirti's *Introduction to the Middle Way*.

In front of my lama's reliquary, I made one hundred thousand prostrations and mandala offerings. I dedicated them to the spread of the precious Buddhist teachings and recited Mipam's *Prayer for the Spread of the Teachings* (*bstan rgyas smon lam*) many times. I heard the voice of Gracious Lungtok say:

> Great glorious Vajrakumara
> Has accompanied you for thirteen lifetimes.
> All those who make a connection with you, positive or negative,
> Will be led to the realm of Lotus Light.

I entered retreat for three months to undertake the recitation practice of *Vajrakila: Subjugator of the Hordes of Demons* (*phur ba bdud dpung zil gnon*), from the *Longchen Nyingtik*. I perfected the wisdom realization (*dgongs pa*) of the four transfixions (*thal 'byin bzhi*), the essence of the generation stage. During that period, many external curses (*phyi gling gi byad ngo*) were directed against me, but the Protectress of Mantra Ekajati guarded me with her compassion.

After finishing that, I undertook the recitation practice of Yama Dharmaraja, a subdivision of the *New Treasures: Three Aspects of Wrath* (*drag po rnam gsum*), applying the wisdom realization of the four wheels (*'khor lo bzhi*).[222] I concluded with a torma ritual to avert negativity. I sent a monk named Lhagyal outside to offer the exorcism torma, and he said the torma spontaneously burst into flames.

That evening, excellent omens appeared in the sky, on the earth, and in the atmosphere. Stars streaked and swirled through the sky like a meteor shower, which all the students witnessed. When we put the ash and coals from the amendment fire offering into the water, it made a thunderous sound. In the frigid cold of deep winter, the ash and coals melted all the ice the distance of an arrow-shot in every direction. Many such extraordinary signs of blessing occurred.

In those days the fighting in Nyarong was severe.[223] It was no longer comfortable to stay at my lama's residence, so I visited nearly all the places he had stayed during his life. I undertook the recitation practice of the *Mind Attainment of the Vidyadharas: Embodiment of Great Glorious Wrathful Heruka* and *Consorts Mahakala and Shri Devi* (*ma mgon lcam dral*), from the *Longchen Nyingtik*. The Protectress of Mantra Ekajati showed me in a clear turquoise mirror the image of Samantabhadri with an AH syllable at her heart center and spoke these words: "The time has come to propagate the teachings of the Great Perfection. I will assist you." Her locks of matted hair then became flat, like bird feathers, and I felt them wrap around me. Instantly, I experienced a thought-free lucid wakefulness without center or periphery.

Soon after that, I had a vision of Vajrasadhu, the great tsen-spirit of Tsang, giving me a wooden basin filled with various smiths' tools.[224] When I looked at them, they all turned into gold and iron hammers. I hesitated, uncertain of which one to choose, and he said, "The gold hammers bring vast riches and abundance. The iron hammers tame enemies. You may choose only one." I chose a gold one.

At one point during that period, I had the recurring thought, "If only this *Longchen Nyingtik* practice of the channels and energies had a detailed oral tradition, then the fundamental pith instructions of the three inner tantra classes would be complete. What can be done?" One night, I dreamed of the valley of Chimpu, which resembled a lotus in full bloom. At its center, Rigdzin Jigme Lingpa, dressed in the white garb of a yogin, bestowed the *Path of the Wish-Fulfilling Jewel: A Scroll of the Whispered Lineage,* along with the practice of yogic inner heat and the esoteric yogic exercises (*'khrul 'khor*). This vision occurred continuously for several days, but because I did not receive the practical instructions in a useful form, I chose not to propagate them.

Then I went to Karding Hermitage and undertook the recitation practice of both the *Peaceful and Wrathful Deities of the Magical Net* and *Manjushri according to the Mahayoga Tantra Tradition.* I accumulated one hundred thousand activity mantras, along with the heart mantra of dependent arising,[225] and although it was the middle of the coldest part of winter, the grains that were scattered about from my mandala offering sprouted six-inch shoots in the ground. From this, I grew certain of the meaning of dependent arising and the lack of inherent existence.

Following that, I gave the empowerment for both the *Peaceful and Wrathful Deities of the Magical Net* and the explanation of the *Ornament of the Lord of Secrets' Wisdom Mind* to a gathering of twenty or so.

Right after that, I entered strict retreat and engaged in the practice of Tögal both morning and evening. After a while, five spherical empty lamps appeared, the size of bell-metal bowls, stacked one on top of the other; and when I recalled with devotion the *Nyingtik* lineage lamas, visions of peaceful and wrathful sambhogakaya deities and buddhafields became all-pervasive. Then vajra-chains of light, which are the expressive power of awareness (*rig rtsal rdo rje lu gu rgyud*), dissolved into the inner space of subtle insight (*phra ba'i shes rab nang dbyings*). All the veils of mental grasping onto experience fell away, and I arrived at the natural condition (*gshis*) of the wisdom of naked empty awareness. Objective and subjective grasping dissolved, and I remained deeply immersed in great nonconceptual luminosity for nearly half a day.

In the late afternoon, Lama Özer came in and wondered whether I was ill. Concluding that I must be asleep, he blew on the fire, and the crackling sound reawakened my sense faculties to their sense objects. In that postmeditative state, I arose into open and unimpeded wakefulness (*ye shes zang thal*), which shattered my grasping on to appearances as truly existent. Within that perception of insubstantiality, there were no reference points for identifying anything. I was able to directly perceive the instantaneous production and cessation of extremely subtle atomic particles. All thoughts of coarse and subtle disturbing emotions vanished without a trace. The expressive power of awareness—the insight that thoroughly discerns all things—burst forth. Through these and other authentic experiences of the full measure of uncommon inner and outer signs, which indicated that I had reached the higher levels and paths, I reached a definitive understanding.

As proof that appearances arise without any true existence, one time my bell fell on a rock, and both the rock and the bell left reciprocal impressions—the bell on the rock, and the rock on the bell. When I offered naga tormas at a dried-up spring, my butter sculptures shaped like fish and frogs actually came to life before my eyes, and water instantly began to flow from the spring.

After that, Gyakor Tulku Kunzang Tekchok Tenpey Gyaltsan came to receive essential guidance on the *Treasury of Wish-Fulfilling Gems* and *Resting in the Nature of Mind*. When the guidance was completed, I received from him all the empowerments and reading transmissions of the extant Kham lineage of the *Four Nyingtik Mother-and-Child Cycles*. Proportionate to my personal finances, I made as grand and elaborate a symbolic mandala offering as I could. After that, he departed.

I went into retreat to practice the *Khandro Sangwa Nyingtik, "Secret Heart Essence of the Dakini."*[226] I undertook the recitation practice of the inner, outer, and secret dakini sadhanas, as well as that of the protector Shenpa Sokdrub.[227] I also composed an offering liturgy for the treasure-guardian Danglha, and then I did extensive recitation practice of the Three Roots according to the *Lama Yangtik,* along with the elaborate and unelaborate empowerments.

The following year, while I was in retreat at a remote place in Kyilko doing the recitation practice of the *Khandro Yangtik,* a terrifying red woman appeared one night as I was falling asleep. She had fingernails curved like hooks, and I felt her scratching me with her claws. My consciousness, like an arrow shot into the air, was propelled to the eastern gate of Bhagavati Vajravarahi's palace in Akanishta. There a white woman held up a lapis lazuli vase and gave me ablution, whereupon she chanted three times the request for admission from the *Khandro Nyingtik* itself, which begins, "O fearsome form of unbearable wrath . . ."

Then the gate of the mandala swung open, and I suddenly beheld countless spirit-dancers—eater-spirits, drummer-spirits, runner-spirits, power-spirits, liberation-spirits, and union-spirits—swirling like dust particles in a sun ray. My perception seemed distracted, and for a moment I fell unconscious. Once the spirits' leaping and dancing had quieted down, I did not arise in my present form but in that of Princess Pemasel, my body swathed in maroon silk and adorned with precious gems, a tiara of flowers upon my crown. The first woman gave me a red flower the size of a helmet and said, "Take my hand."

She led me inside, where I beheld the peaceful Vajrakrodhi surrounded by tens of millions of dakinis of the five families. Before the principal dakini was an empowerment stool, a red lotus with a "joy whorl" (*dga' 'khyil*) of red light on top, spinning clockwise with a humming sound. I sat down on it and was about to take off my flower crown when the first woman said, "You shouldn't take that off. That crown was given to you by Guru Rinpoche."

Then the principal dakini successively conferred empowerments, beginning with the *Precious Torch of Power* (*rin po che dbang gi sgron ma*) from the *Khandro Sangwa Nyingtik*. I offered her the flower I had been given earlier, and she gave me the secret name Ösel Rinchen Nyingpo Pema Ledreltsel, "Precious Luminous Essence, Power of Karmic Links to the Lotus."[228]

After the vase empowerment, she conferred the three higher empowerments, conjoined with the main commentary on these empowerments. The verses of the two higher-awareness empowerments were chanted by the principal dakini's main face, while the mantras were recited by the sow head upon her crown. She also gave the guidance for the great *Khandro Nyingtik*.

Afterward, all the dakinis recited the concluding benediction for these empowerments and exclaimed, "This is your inheritance!" They then bestowed upon me a silver-white divination mirror, a maroon brocade robe embroidered with gold and turquoise adornments, and a dark-red skull-cup with fifty-four bone segments, upon each of which a section of the *Khandro Nyingtik* appeared, as in a mirage. Then, after rotating the empowerment vase, she said, "Now go."

"The human realm is such a difficult place to live," I protested. "May I stay here?"

"Not for now. That would cause an obstacle to your life. In the future you may come, but for now, go to the realm of humans. You are the lord of the *Khandro Nyingtik* teachings, so you must work for the welfare of beings." To the principal dakini of the north, she said, "Lead him back down."

We suddenly emerged from the northern gate and went down to a terrifying charnel ground. We entered a palace of skulls, where the five families of the Wrathful Black Mother Krodhi were seated. The principal dakini picked up my mirror and a skull-cup and said, "OM OM OM." She gave the

Tögal empowerment for the expressive power of awareness, but after a while, instead of reciting the entire empowerment liturgy, she made an auspicious declaration of truth, whereupon a great rain of flowers fell, covering our feet. The sounds of SHRI SWASTI resounded throughout all directions.[229] To the green Krodhi of the north, she issued a command: "Accompany him back to his home without obstacle."

She and I landed like vultures descending upon victuals. The dakini of the karma family alighted on top of my body, and from my crown aperture the beautiful protectress Durtrö Lhamo, the color of a red hollyhock flower, emerged and stood in front of me.[230] I reentered my body through the crown aperture, and when my sense faculties reawoke to their sense objects, the dakini of the karma family proclaimed a contract to Durtrö Lhamo, appointing her as protectress of the dissemination of the *Khandro Sangwa Nyingtik*. Then she departed. For some time afterward, I constantly perceived Durtrö Lhamo's presence.

At that same hermitage, I performed a *Great Display Torma Exorcism* (*rol pa chen po'i gtor bzlog*), and in a clear vision that night, I arrived at the feet of my Gracious Lama Lungtok Rinpoche in a pure realm. I prostrated myself before him and requested his blessing.

"Here, sit on this carpet at the head of the row," he said.

"Ever since you passed away, Lama, I have been exerting myself in practice. May I offer you my realization?" I asked.

At first he didn't listen and sang out Abu's *Calling the Lama from Afar* in melodious meditative tones. I made my request a second time.

"Your realization is good," he said.

"I find the Great Omniscient Longchenpa's teachings—their sacredness, the style of his precious instructions, and his way of illustrating the pith instructions—truly amazing," I said.

"What is so amazing about the Omniscient Lord of Dharma Longchenpa?" he replied. "The carefree renunciate deeds of my lama Patrul Rinpoche, now *they* were amazing." He spoke words of praise and exaltation.

"Is there anything still more amazing than that?" I asked.

"Your lama Kumaraja was more wondrous than that," he replied.

Instantly, a young girl and boy appeared and said, "Let's go and see Lama Kumaraja!"

I followed them. We arrived in the holy place of Yartö Shampo Snow Range, on a plain as smooth as the face of a mirror, just outside a white tent in which the great Vidyadhara Kumaraja dwelt. Its entrance was tightly closed. I prostrated myself and made supplications, and a voice called three times from within: "Who are you?"

I was unable to say a word, so my boy companion answered, "This is a fortunate heart-son named Ngakgi Wangpo!" For a moment, I perceived myself as the Great Omniscient Longchen Rabjampa.[231]

The door of the tent opened, and we went inside. The tent was a celestial mansion of incomprehensible design in which Lama Kumaraja sat, dressed in renunciate's garb. When I approached to receive his blessing, he transformed into the great Vidyadhara Garab Dorje, above whom the Twelve Teachers of the Great Perfection were preaching the Dharma. All the courtyards of the palace were pure realms, mainly the sixty-four pure realms, and inconceivable manifestations of buddhas and countless students, as well, appeared like shimmering illusions.

I rested in equipoise, beholding the face of the ultimate lama, the true nature of reality, and my boy companion made this exhortation: "When the tathagatas teach the 6.4 million tantras of the Great Perfection, listen without distraction!"

I listened, and the resonances of the tathagatas' voices blended into one, reciting A AH E EE, and so on.[232] But then I could hear nothing except Garab Dorje proclaiming the title, "Herein is contained the *Tantra of the Wheel of Lightning (nam mkha'i glog gi 'khor lo'i rgyud)*."

I thought to myself, "If there were a tantra with a name like that, anyone could grasp it and put it into practice. I wonder how many stanzas it has."

My boy companion transformed into the protector deity Lekden Nakpo,[233] holding a staff and a skull-cup, and the girl transformed into Ekajati, the Mistress of Mantra, holding a corpse staff *(zhing dbyug)* and a magical pledge staff *(dam shing)*. They spoke these words:

According to the divisions of conceptual minds,
Such are the titles of the tantras that have come, are coming, and
   will come.
You should now learn a few stanzas!
In the space of reality, where nothing has been taught
And there is nothing to teach,
They appear variously according to the faculties of students,
Transcending the extremes of "one" and "many,"
Yet they are entirely complete in the wisdom intention
Of the three classes of the Great Perfection.

When one considers the appearances of the pure realms, buddhas, and trainees, they would seem to be endless. However, these are not separate autonomous entities; they are inseparable from the display of the lama's wisdom and compassion. Hoping for accomplishments from an external source, like a child carried away by a spectacle, is pointless. One must merge with the wisdom mind of the ultimate lama, which is inner self-awareness.

I prayed, "Great Vidyadhara Kumaraja, heed me with your wisdom mind!" Then the appearances, like streams flowing into a river, dissolved into the great master Garab Dorje, who in turn vanished into the universal vital nucleus of all-pervasive blueness. Then, Kumaraja appeared as before, dressed in monastic robes, seated upon the hide of a spotted antelope.[234] I supplicated him fervently and asked him to accept me as his disciple.

"I have already given you all the empowerments and precious instructions for the *Seventeen Tantras of the Great Perfection,* along with the *Four Nyingtik Mother-and-Child Cycles,* which are the pith instructions of the Whispered Lineage. However, I will now once again confer the consecration," he said. On my head, he placed a bamboo pen with a peacock feather affixed at its tip and a ribbon of yellow silk wrapped around it, upon which was written in vermilion ink, "Great Omniscient Longchen Rabjam, expressive power that naturally liberates all that arises." With his eyes fixed in a meditative gaze, he focused his wisdom mind and said, "AH AH AH."

I suddenly remembered the teachings the Great Vidyadhara Kumaraja had given me in the past.[235] All the difficult points spontaneously became clear, and I gained a certain understanding, such that I no longer needed to rely on anyone to explain either the words or their meanings. This was clearly due to the kindness of the Great Vidyadhara Kumaraja. I write this here for the sake of my future followers, to inspire their confidence that the fountainhead of our lineage does indeed reach the pure mountain snows.[236]

When I was nearly twenty-nine years old, in the twelfth lunar month of the Horse year [1907], my dear kind mother, who gave me my body, suddenly fell ill with a liver tumor. None of the medicinal treatments or longevity rituals we arranged for her helped. The great treasure-revealer Rinchen Lingpa's divination indicated that one thousand recitations of my *Offering Liturgy of the Five Great Kings (rgyal chen sku lnga'i gsol mchod)* could help, so a few of my students and I undertook the recitations.

On the night when we completed the thousand recitations, I was drifting between the waking state and sleep when I heard the sounds of horses' hooves and the tinkling of small bells, and I saw many horsemen appear. I noticed that the Five Great Kings, protectors of the Buddhist teachings, were with them as well, riding mounts adorned with silks and brocades, their saddles studded with precious gems. They all wore robes of gold and maroon brocade, and sported noblemen's hats with iron arrows. After humbly paying me their respects, they said, "You have made a very insistent request, so we have now come from Pekar Kordzö Ling. We come here this once, due to our past solemn oath. The impact of past actions cannot be reversed; this disease is not a sudden ailment."

A moment later, they vanished. Then, a woman, whom I thought was Dzeche Pemakye, said to me, "Your mother has reached the end of her life, and there is nothing we brothers and sisters can do. Look over there!"

Beside my mother's sickbed, I saw a black woman with shiny orange hair and beard, naked except for a tiger-skin skirt, seated upon a stool in noble posture. Next to her, many women were preparing to lift my mother onto a litter. The clear vision then disappeared.

My mother said she had dreamed of a monk with a fine gold lancet who announced that I had sent him to be her doctor. He made an incision between her ribs and extracted many long strands of what looked like hairs from a horse's tail.

For thirteen days, she appeared to be completely cured. Then the illness reemerged, and I nursed her for four months, meditating day and night on compassion, the giving of happiness and the taking of suffering. I feel that this was a time of purification of my own negative actions and obscurations.

On the evening of the tenth day of the third lunar month of the Sheep year [1907], I had a vision just as I was drifting off to sleep. On the north face of Lhari Yerpa Cliff, in a cave just big enough to hold a person, I perceived myself as Nyangben Tingdzin Zangpo, engaged in practice. A beautiful woman came before me, wearing fine, layered garments of the five colors, with a slightly stained blue garment outermost. As I was wondering who she might be, the woman said:

I am a girl who has come from the twenty-four sacred lands.
I have one essence yet various appearances:
Vajravarahi, Yeshe Tsogyal,
The Mistress of Secret Mantra Ekajati:
If I am not they, then who is?

She conferred the empowerment of the *Tantra of the Great Magical Net of Manjushri,* as well as an explanation of the tantra. "From now on, you have authority over all the ripening empowerments and liberating instructions associated with the profound treasures hidden below the earth in the land of Tibet. There is little need for new material treasures. Teach and study the old ones," she said. In this mirage-like vision, she shed her inner garment, warm with the heat of her body, and wrapped it around me, whereupon I became deeply immersed in the nonconceptual state of bliss and emptiness.

After that, external heat, cold, and tactile sensations of smoothness and roughness, such as rocks, sticks, and thorns, all felt pleasurable. This experience lasted for an entire month. Through her blessings, there was never the slightest obstacle during the three occasions when I transmitted the *Treasury of Precious Revelations,* or on any other occasion when I conferred the ripening empowerments and liberating instructions for any aspect of Vajrayana. Indeed, this is due to the compassionate power of this Sublime Mother of the Conquerors.

On the tenth day of the fourth lunar month, the earth quaked and rays of light appeared as my dear mother succumbed to the nature of time. Numerous extraordinary signs appeared throughout the cremation, but so as not to offend the people of this degenerate age, I will write no more than that.[237]

I returned to Jönpalung, where I offered ten thousand butter lamps and recited the *Prayer of Good Conduct* three thousand times. I think my intention must have been pure, but at any rate, the melted butter increased, the dharani of offering clouds (*mchod pa'i sprin gzungs*) spontaneously appeared on the altar, and on top of the frozen butter there appeared vivid motifs of the eight auspicious symbols and the eight auspicious substances. These were visible to everyone.

From the great treasure-revealer Ngawang Tendzin Rinpoche, I received the reading transmissions for the *Nyingma Collected Tantras* (*rnying ma rgyud 'bum*). One day the great treasure-revealer said, "You and I, master and disciple, have been connected to each other for many lifetimes, alternately as teacher and student. Therefore, tomorrow I need to receive from you Lochen Dharmashri's *Oral Transmission of the Lord of Secrets* (*gsang bdag zhal lung*), and a brief explanation of the *Ornament of the Lord of Secrets' Wisdom Mind.*" These I offered to him.

After the completion of the reading transmissions of the *Nyingma Collected Tantras,* I made a visit to Dzogchen Monastery. From Khenpo Lhagyal, I received Dharmakirti's *Exposition of Valid Cognition.* In the chapter on inference for the sake of others (*gzhan don rjes dpag*), I had some difficulty mentally engaging the topic, but by supplicating my yidam deity, a precise understanding arose. I also composed a praise to Manjushri at that time.

From Khenpo Shenga, I received:

▶ Gorampa's *Commentary on the Introduction to the Middle Way, Entitled Dispelling the Darkness of Inferior Views* (*'jug tik lta ngan mun sel*);
▶ his *Overview of the Middle Way according to the Mahayana* (*theg mchog dbu ma'i spyi don*); and
▶ his *Commentary on Difficult Points in the Ornament of Emergent Realization Entitled Explanatory Clarification* (*mngon rtogs rgyan gi dka' 'grel rnam bshad rab gsal*);
▶ a Nyingma commentary on the *Introduction to the Middle Way*, which Khenpo Shenga himself had authored; and
▶ instruction on the channels and energies according to the *Longchen Nyingtik*.

I offered him and Khenpo Lhagyal the *Three Words That Strike the Key Points* and the *Lion's Roar That Cuts through Errors and Deviations*.

From Khenpo Sonam Chöpel, I received Jamgön Mipam's *Gateway to Knowledge* and his *Reply to Lobzang Rabsel's Letter* (*rab lan*). I offered him Trekchö guidance according to the Whispered Lineage and a synopsis of the essential guidance of *Yeshe Lama*. In addition, over a period of eight months, I offered individual teachings to a few bright students according to their wishes. I had to teach the *Insight Chapter* from the *Way of the Bodhisattva*, the *Root Sutra of Monastic Discipline*, and the *Ascertainment of the Three Vows* at night by the light of a butter lamp.

I had planned to stay at Dzogchen for some time, but everything was so busy and distracting that I found it difficult to relax and so I resolved to leave. Dzogchen Tulku Rinpoche then said, "Generally speaking, we don't have a tradition of appointing outsider monks as abbots, but seeing as the Önpo family and Lungtok are no different from the lamas of our own mother monastery, I shall appoint you as abbot after Khenpo Lhagyal has finished his term of office. You need to stay. I will give you whichever of four houses you prefer—Tori House, Pedrak House, Lugyal House, or Lutruk House."

The bursar said the same thing, specifically mentioning that he would give me a room in Lugyal or Lutruk, complete with all amenities.

However, my gracious teacher Lungtok had told me earlier not to stay at Dzogchen for long, so in accordance with his words, I stuck to my plan to stay for a short time. With the chant-master Penor and the shrine-master Kunzang Tenpel, I trained in the practice of the great-accomplishment ceremony (*sgrub chen*) for Karma Lingpa's *Peaceful and Wrathful Deities*, following the ritual arrangement of Chöying Rolpey Dorje. I also studied the practical techniques for making consecrated medicine (*sman sgrub*), according to the *Gathering of the Great Assembly* (*tshogs chen 'dus pa*).

In Takhokma, the Katok-sponsored ceremony for the *Peaceful and Wrathful Deities* used to last only a few days, but I rearranged it into a proper great-accomplishment ceremony, which I eventually performed about nineteen times. On that particular occasion, a column of rainbow light streaked through the temple, the feast-offering liquor overflowed endlessly, the original blessed pills multiplied, and even though it was autumn, numerous long-stemmed white flowers bloomed on the hill at the base of the mandala. Many buddha images spontaneously formed on the consecrated medicine within the medicinal palace of the mandala, and numerous small black myrobalan fruits suddenly emerged from within the medicinal powders. I felt that these were clear indications that the medicine would be beneficial for all who encountered it.

Later, at the command of the Lord Refuge Katok Situ Chökyi Gyatso, I changed the medicine ritual of the *Peaceful and Wrathful Deities* to that of the *Eight Heruka Sadhanas*. Following the practical methods of Mindroling, I conducted the medicine ritual of the *Eight Heruka Sadhanas* nearly fifteen times.

I had planned to go stay at my hermitage in Jönpalung for a while, but a large number of monks had gathered from near and far, so that winter I gave the reading transmission for Longchenpa's *Seven Treasuries*. I began by conferring an empowerment for Rigdzin Jigme Lingpa's *Transmitted Teachings of the Mother: Queen of Great Bliss*, during which the water in the skull-cup transformed into liquor with an excellent color, smell, and flavor. The five seed-syllables of the five mother dakinis (BAM HA RI NI SA) spontaneously appeared, embossed upon the mirror.

On the day I began the reading transmission of the *Seven Treasuries*, a woman adorned with precious gems and pearls appeared and attended one session before vanishing without a trace. Apparently, the resident monks thought she was bringing provisions for one of the visiting monks, and the visiting monks thought she was a local woman. In fact, I knew it was a sign of Dorje Yudrönma's delight.

I gave a teaching on *Resting in the Nature of Mind*, and that day all the mountains and valleys filled with rainbow light. A rain of white flowers like wild roses descended from within countless swirling spheres of rainbow light in the sky. By evening, most of the rainbows had dissolved into the ground, while some rose up into the sky. All were wonder struck. As for me, the elaborations of conceptual mind were severed in the true nature of reality, and grasping onto "good" and "bad" appearances with hope and fear dissolved. Everything transformed into an expanse of evenness—the supreme state of equalness and perfection.

One evening in my visionary experience, a woman whose entire back was adorned with a blanket of gem-grade amber ornaments came riding up on a mule and said, "It's time to go."

"Who are you? Where are we going?" I asked.

"I am the Mistress of the Early Translations' Sutra, Magical Net, and Mind.[238] I am called Remati.[239] The time has come for you to go to Katok and work for the benefit of beings, so let's go," she said.

"I am not at all worthy of such a great monastic seat," I protested. "It would be better for me to look after the occasional humble student who comes to me for teachings."

"I know whether or not you are worthy," she replied. "Ride this." She dismounted, pulled an exquisite silk mat made of what looked like Chinese gold brocade out of her cloak pocket, and spread it over the saddle. I dreamed that I took hold of the reins and mounted, and I awoke wondering, "What was that about?"

The next day I received a letter from Katok Situ Rinpoche saying that he wished to establish a school and requesting me to come. However, I delayed going for a while, and a few years passed. Every so often another letter would come, and each time the same woman would appear and tell me I had to go. One day, I asked her, "If I go, will it be of any benefit? What are Situ Rinpoche's aspirations?"

"He is a great bodhisattva of the tenth level.[240] He has established the Buddhist teachings in general and the lineage of ordination in particular at this monastic seat. He is upholding, maintaining, and propagating the nonsectarian teachings, and has founded colleges and retreat centers. Such are his magnificent aspirations. Indeed, you yourself looked after that monastic seat continuously when you were Wu Öd Yeshe Bum and Zangri Bumpa, so wouldn't you like to return to your own people and your own home?" she urged.

From that moment, I made the decision to go. One night in a dream vision, I saw Dampa Deshek and his spiritual heir Tsangtönpa, surrounded by many monks, seated inside a large mansion. Many texts were stacked at the door. I went inside and recited the supplication that begins, "Lord like the sky, free of center or periphery . . ." I requested his blessing and asked, "What are all these texts?"

"These are the scriptures of Sutra, Magical Net, and Mind. For a long time I have had no one to whom to entrust them, and some have been lost entirely. Situ Tulku has taken care of some of them, and these are the ones that are left," he explained.

"There still seem to be quite a few," I said.

"Without a son, what use is a father's great wealth? If there were an heir, I would give these to him," he replied.

"Well, will you grant me a volume from the Sutra, Magical Net, and Mind?" I asked.

"In my time, I emphasized the *General Sutra That Gathers All Wisdom Intentions,* and during that period my teachings brought great benefit. I doubt that sutra would be of much benefit now. As for the mind class, what you have is sufficient. Permit me to give you an explanation of the *Tantra of the Magical Net.*" He began by reading the title *Guhyagarbha, King of Tantras, Definitive with Respect to the Real* (*gsang ba'i snying po de kho na nyid nges pa'i rgyud kyi rgyal po*), and ended with the verses from the *Prayer of Maitreya,* which begin: "With the resounding of the great drum of the teachings . . ."

Then the clear vision faded.

Before I left for Katok, I received Rigdzin Godemchen's *Unimpeded Realization of the Great Perfection* (*rdzogs pa chen po dgongs pa zang thal*), along with Longchen Rabjampa's *Khandro Yangtik* and *Lama Yangtik* from the Great Vidyadhara Natsok Rangdrol. I offered him my realization, and he expressed great delight: "The two of us can even compare our realizations! We can even offer each other our realizations!"

He told me how he had gone to Katok at the age of thirteen, and from Situ Chökyi Lodrö he had received the preliminary practices of Longsel Nyingpo's *Vajra Essence* (*rdo rje snying po*). During that time, a certainty about death and impermanence had arisen in his mind, so he engaged in the purification of obscurations for several years. Then, from the previous Situ he had also received guidance on the channels and energies, and on the

Great Perfection. At the age of twenty-one, he had directly perceived the essential nature of awareness (*rig pa'i ngo bo*), and until the age of thirty-four, his practice had solely focused on that awareness.

"This old man achieved his present realization at that time," he said. "Since then, I've made no progress at all." His explanation of how he had gained realization made me think that this was the way to be a yogin of the Great Perfection.

He asked the students living in his encampment to come offer me their realizations. Nearly all of them came to present their experience, and I resolved their doubts to the best of my ability. He then taught the guidance for the preliminary and main practices of the *Vajra Essence,* and for an extended period he taught me and most of his senior students directly from Longsel Nyingpo's original guidance text (*khrid rgan*). He imparted many topics of guidance from the Katok tradition, an extraordinary lineage which he had received directly from the previous Situ.

"If you go to Katok, you should undertake this cycle of preliminary practices once every year, without interruption," he said. Then he added, "You must offer me an explanation of the guidance of the *Khandro Yangtik* according to the revelations of Minling Trichen Terdak Lingpa, mustering whatever expressive power of insight you possess."

"You have undoubtedly already received this in the past. The only thing I can offer you is the reading transmission. I dare not offer you an explanation," I protested.

"Don't worry," he replied. "This is a matter of vitally important auspicious connection." His request was so insistent that I could not refuse him, so I offered him an explanation of that teaching.

To the treasure-revealer Rinchen Lingpa, I offered the reading transmission of Longchenpa's *Seven Treasuries* and an explanation of the *Trilogy of Resting.*

In turn, he conferred the empowerments for *Yama Dharmaraja* (*gshin rje chos rgyal*); *Black Manjushri: Lord of Life* (*'jam dpal tshe bdag*); and *Variegated Vajra Garuda* (*rdo rje khyung khra*), all from his own *New Treasures,* and he prophetically recognized me as the principal master of his teachings. He gave me a longevity prayer, the verses of which relate to my purported lives in the incarnation line of the great Dharma king Trisong Detsen, along with a mountain of gifts.

After that, the treasure-revealer of Godzik, Yeshe Jungne, arrived. I offered him the reading transmission of the *Seven Treasuries,* and then I returned to Jönpalung.

That summer, the caretaker of Katok, Rigdzin Dorje, and his attendant came to escort me to Katok, but they were stopped by the flooding Tromchu River and made it only as far as Adzom Gar. So they tied Situ Rinpoche's letter to the horn of a yak and sent it across to the other shore. In reply, I sent a letter promising that I would come to Katok the following year, the year of the Monkey [1908].

For a year, I undertook the recitation practice of *Peaceful and Wrathful Manjushri* from Rinchen Lingpa's new treasures. After one week, I had a vision of Black Manjushri, a rain of blue flowers fell and covered the floor of my hermitage, and the pills on the shrine melted into nectar. When I had recited seven hundred thousand EY mantras during the recitation practice of the wrathful Manjushri (Yamantaka), I dreamed that I ate the hearts of all the eight classes of haughty spirits at once, which was a sign of accomplishment.

Later, when Situ Rinpoche proclaimed Rinchen Lingpa to be a false treasure-revealer, I did not lose faith. It seemed to me that he was authentic. I took his unusual behavior and minor falsehoods to be part of the natural disposition of a treasure-revealer, and all the words and meanings of his treasures were perfect.[241] One cannot establish falsity merely based on the modality of a treasure-teaching. Most of the undisputed treasure-teachings of the past do contain vocabulary approximating that of the revelatory language of Nyang-rel Nyima Özer and Guru Chöwang, but how can one possibly prove others to be false merely on that basis?

In the beginning of the sixth lunar month of the Monkey year [1908], a welcoming party arrived. I left immediately for Katok, and we arrived for the Tenth-Day celebration.[242] The entire congregation gave me a festive welcome, and the Lord Refuge Situ Rinpoche came to the door of his residence at the Tantric College to greet me. We exchanged silk greeting scarves, and he led me inside to the front of the assembly row, where we had tea and dined together for our noonday meal.

"I had hoped you would come when the Tantric College was first established, but you never came. Now, two years after it opened, you have finally come. It is so wonderful that you are here! Tomorrow, during the Tenth-Day celebration, you must offer us a mandala of eloquent teachings," he said.

The following day, to an assembly in which Situ Rinpoche himself sat, along with Venerable Öntrul, Lama Atob, and Khenpo Kunpel, I gave an explanation of the wisdom intention of my *Sadhana of Guru Vidyadhara* alongside the Eight Heruka Sadhanas (*bka' brgyad bla ma rig 'dzin sgrub pa*), demonstrating how most topics of the nine vehicles are subsumed within the profound key points of the path of devotion.[243] It was an eloquent lecture to gladden the hearts of the learned. Situ Rinpoche and Venerable Öntrul both placed silk scarves around my neck.

On the evening of the Tenth Day, in front of the image of the First Drime Shingkyong, Situ Rinpoche gave both the empowerment and reading transmission of Düdül Dorje's *Vajrakila* to me alone. He informed me that as of the next day, I would serve as the overseer of the college curriculum.

The next morning, Situ Rinpoche enthroned me in the temple of the Tantric College and gave me a gilded copper Buddha statue, a bell and vajra, a ritual vase, a pair of offering cups for symbolic nectar and rakta (*sman rag*),[244] a wooden torma, a set of white conchs, a wooden cane, a stick for removing ceremonial blindfolds (*mig thur*),[245] a silken whisk with an iron vajra handle, a saffron-colored religious robe, a monastic shawl, a vest, a lower robe, a carpet, and a brocade coat, as well as a single volume of scripture containing Katok Dampa Deshek's *Commentary That Binds All the Vehicles* (*theg pa spyi chings*); three volumes containing Jamgön Kongtrul's *Treasury of Knowledge* (*shes bya kun khyab mdzod*); and a small stupa.

"Teachings should resemble the one you gave yesterday," he said. "If one fails to elucidate meaningful content, word-for-word commentaries alone get one nowhere. Please be kind enough to extract the key points for the sake of the newer students as you teach." He presented me with a silk offering-scarf and empowered me as a genuine regent of the Buddhist teachings upon the teaching throne. Such was my great good fortune.

Khenpo Kunpel presided over the summer rains' retreat. He taught the *Analysis of the Three Vows* (*sdom gsum*) with Ngawang Chödrak's *Commentary*, Gorampa's *Commentary on Difficult Points in the Analysis of the Three Vows* (*sdom gsum gyi dka' 'grel*); Shakya Chokden's *Golden Lancet of Questions and Answers* (*dris lan gser thur*); and Ngari Panchen's writings on this subject.[246]

In the autumn, Khenpo Kunpel taught Dharmakirti's *Exposition of Valid Cognition* and Sakya Pandita's *Treasury of Valid Logical Reasoning* (*tshad ma rigs gter*). In the *Treasury of Valid Logical Reasoning*, once the philosophical assertions of Sakya Pandita's opponents Chapa Chöseng, Tsangnakpa Tsöndrü Senge, and Denkokpa Dharma Lodrö have been presented, there is a section refuting their assertions. These Tibetan opponents of the past differ from those Indian logicians whose views are found in the *Exposition of Valid Cognition,* in that they argued such extremely subtle points that I had difficulty following their reasoning.

At one point, while I was studying Sakya Pandita's *Auto-Commentary on the Treasury of Valid Logical Reasoning,* I dreamed that I arrived at the residence of Gorum Temple in Sakya, where I supplicated the Dharma Lord Sakya Panchen and requested a blessing from the Dharma Lord Drakpa Gyaltsen, who sat on a throne in monastic garb, his slightly protruding crown covered with snow-white hair. I requested an explanation of the *Treasury of Valid Logical Reasoning* based on Sakya Pandita's own manuscript, and Drakpa Gyaltsen said, "Oh, in a past life when you were Nesar Jamyang Khyentse Wangchuk, you and Tsarchen Losal Gyatso were great boons for the tradition of the Path and Fruit,[247] and you composed numerous manuals on the *Masters' Explanation of the Pith Instructions (man ngag slob bshad).*[248] However, in this particular incarnation you will not benefit this Sakya teaching, and nor will you give exegeses on the *Treasury of Valid Logical Reasoning.*"

"Well then, will you kindly grant me a single Sanskrit folio from among the manuscripts of the Dharma Lord Sakya Pandita?" I requested. .

He lifted a single page out of one of the volumes and looked at it. "This is my text entitled *Parting from the Four Clingings (zhen pa bzhi bral).* Since I happened to choose this, I will explain it," he said, and he gave me a teaching. I understood the dream to be a sign that the Dharma Lord Drakpa Gyaltsen had symbolically blessed me.

Khenpo Kunpel then gave us explanations of Longchenpa's *Treasury of Wish-Fulfilling Gems, Treasury of Pith Instructions (man ngag mdzod),* and *Precious Treasury of Reality.* At the very beginning of the Bird year [1909], fighting broke out with the Chinese in the region of Dzachukha, on account of which Khen Rinpoche Kunpel had to travel up there.[249]

Part Three

The Responsibilities That I Assumed While in an Effort to Ostensibly Benefit Others

A Brief Description of How I Worked for Others' Benefit

In the wake of Khenpo Kunpel Rinpoche's departure, I took on the role of khenpo and looked after the monastic college at Katok. I finished the remaining three years of his earlier course in the tantric school, and subsequently completed two other five-year courses, offering my services for a total of thirteen years. During that period, the number of monastic ordinations alone that I conferred totaled around 3,400, or so I am told by Venerable Öntrul Rinpoche, who kept a running tally. I had thirty-seven students who definitely became able to work for the benefit of others, and there were countless individuals who made a connection to me through empowerments and teachings.

During this time, the curriculum of the tantric college included over two hundred large and small works. These I taught to enormous gatherings of students, large numbers of whom came from Gyarong Tsakho, Golok, and Serta, as well as the region of Jang, the upper and lower regions of Ü-Tsang, and Bhutan. I taught an average of seven sessions every day, and never fewer than three or four. I gave the empowerments and reading transmissions of Longsel Nyingpo's *Vajra Essence* three times, Longchen Rabjampa's *Four Nyingtik Mother-and-Child Cycles* twenty-seven times, and his *Seven Treasuries* thirteen times. All in all, I ostensibly worked for the sake of others on a colossal scale.

On several occasions I asked permission to step down, but it was not granted. Situ Rinpoche had vast aspirations, so despite enormous personal hardship, I focused on the continuity of the teachings and the purification of my own obscurations. I willingly accepted the difficulties and never once turned anyone away, high or low, who came to receive teachings.

Empowerments, Reading Transmissions, and Guidance Received

Incidentally, during that period I, too, received some teachings. From the Lord Refuge Situ Rinpoche, I received:

- the *Three Cycles of the Eight Heruka Sadhanas* (*bka' brgyad rnam gsum*),[250] the first two of which I received in the context of great-accomplishment ceremonies, and the third—the *Naturally Arising Wrathful Deities of the Eight Heruka Sadhanas* (*bka' brgyad drag po rang byung rang shar*)—for which I received only the empowerment;
- *Gathering of the Great Assembly*, for which I received both the Kham and central Tibetan lineages;[251]
- Longsel Nyingpo's *Vajra Essence*, for which I twice received the empowerments;
- *Collected Revelations* (*gter chos*) of Düdül Dorje, for which I received the complete empowerments and reading transmissions;
- Jamgön Kongtrul's *Great Treasury of Precious Revelations, Treasury of Knowledge, and Treasury of Precious Instructions* (*gdams ngag mdzod*);
- *The Kalachakra Tantra*, for which I received the higher and highest empowerments from both the Jonang and Butön traditions;[252]
- all the extant texts of the Jonang and Shalu traditions;
- Dampa Deshek Rinpoche's *Trio of the Peaceful and Wrathful Deities and Vajrakila* (*zhi khro phur gsum*); *Uncommon Exorcism of the Vitality of the Matarah* (*ma mo'i srog gtad thun min*); and *Uncommon Exorcism of the Vitality of the Seven Classes of Mamo in the Retinue of Omniscient Ekajati* (*kun mkhyen sde bdun gyi srog gtod thun min*);
- Venerable Jamyang Khyentse Wangpo's *Tsasum Ösel Nyingtik, "Three Roots' Heart Essence of Luminosity,"*[253] and *Drubtop Nyingtik, "Heart Essence of the Accomplished Master,"*[254] for which I received the empowerments and precious instructions;
- Jamgön Kongtrul's commentaries on the *Profound Inner Meaning* (*zab mo nang don*); the *Unsurpassed Continuum of the Mahayana* (*rgyud bla ma*); and the *Two-Chaptered Tantra of Hevajra* (*brtags gnyis*);
- Jamgön Rinpoche's *Collection of Clear Vajrakilaya Commentaries* (*phur tik bum nag*);[255]
- his *Explanation of the Rays of the Sun* (*nyi ma'i 'od zer gyi rnam bshad*);
- Lama Mipam's explanation of Padmasambhava's *Secret Commentary on Vishuddha Heruka* (*yang dag grub pa'i gsang 'grel*);
- Rongtön's *Commentary on the Prajnaparamita, Meditation Stages*

in the Five Treatises of Maitreya and *Meditation Stages in the Exposition of Valid Cognition;*

▸ Yaktön Sangye Pel's *Commentary on the Prajnaparamita;*

▸ the Dharma Lord Dampa Deshek's *Commentary on the Guhyagarbha Entitled Words Spoken at Chimpu* (*gsang 'grel bka' mchims phu ma*), which was redacted in the form of a guidebook by Tsangtönpa;

▸ the *Annotated Commentary on the General Sutra That Gathers All Wisdom Intentions* (*spyi mdo'i mchan 'grel*), along with Dampa Deshek Rinpoche's *Commentary on the Difficult Points and Its Topical Outline* (*spyi mdo dgongs pa 'dus pa'i dka' 'grel rdo rje'i tha ram 'byed pa'i lde'u mig*);

▸ the *Annotated Commentary on the Sutra of All-Inclusive Awareness* (*kun 'dus rig pa'i mdo'i mchan 'grel*);

▸ Tsangtönpa's *Commentary on the Lamp for the Eye of Concentration* (*bsam gtan mig sgron khrid*);[256]

▸ Dong Jadralwa's *Detailed Instructions on the Mind Class of the Great Perfection* (*sems sde'i pra khrid*);

▸ Yeshe Gyaltsen's *Commentary on the Explanation That Binds All the Vehicles Entitled Rays of the Sun* (*theg pa spyi chings kyi 'grel pa [nyi ma'i 'od zer]*) and Shakya Dorje's *Commentary on Difficult Points in the Explanation That Binds All the Vehicles* (*theg pa spyi chings kyi dka' 'grel*);

▸ Commentaries on the *Guhyagarbha Tantra* by Venerable Konchok Tsultrim of Zurtso, the Mantrin Namkha Rinchen, Zurmo Gendun Bum, and Menlungpa Mikyö Dorje;

▸ Buddhaguhya's *Extensive and Short Stages of the Path of the Magical Net* (*lam rim che chung*);

▸ Namkha Gyaltsen's *Annotated Commentary on Buddhaguhya's Innermost Essence of the Mind* (*thugs thigs mchan 'grel*);

▸ Namkha Pel's *Commentary on the Short Path of the Magical Net* (*lam chung 'grel*);

▸ Lilavajra's *Clarification of Samaya* (*dam tshig gsal bkra*) and *Subtle Unfolding of Samaya* (*dam tshig phra rgyas*) with their annotated commentaries;

▸ Dampa Deshek's *Exalted Meanings of the Same Wording* (*'dra mthun don 'phags*);

▸ Situ Rinpoche's own *Concise Summary of Jamgön Mipam's Venomous*

Snake (dug sbrul gyi stong thun); *Concise Summary of Jamgön Mipam's Sword of Insight (ral gri'i stong thun)*; and *Concise Summary of Jamgön Mipam's Ashoka Tree, Entitled Pebble Commentary on the Root Tantra (ljong shing stong thun)*;

▸ King Ja's *Array of the Path of the Magical Net (lam rnam bkod)*;

▸ the empowerment of the *Black Wrathful Mother Krodhakali (khros ma nag mo)*;

▸ the empowerment of the *Tantra of the Litany of Manjushri's Names* according to the Marpa tradition, and its commentaries by Chöying Tobden Dorje of Rongpo and Vimalamitra;

▸ guidance on the *Tantra of the Great Elucidation of Freedom from Constructs (spros bral don gsal chen po'i rgyud)*, combined with the *Buddhasamayoga (sangs rgyas mnyam sbyor)*, which were both revealed by Guru Chöwang and interpreted according to the Great Perfection in the later treasure-teachings of Guru Tseten Gyaltsen;

▸ guidance on Dorje Lingpa's *Blazing Clear Expanse (klong gsal 'bar ma)*;

▸ the *Commentary on the Threefold Razor Tantras (spu gri'i rnam gsum gyi rgyud 'grel)*;[257]

▸ Nyangrel's explanations of the *Eight Heruka Sadhanas* entitled *Storehouse of Secret Mantra Scriptures (gsang sngags lung gi bang mdzod)*; *Wild Cogongrass (tha ram)*; and *Key to the Commands of the Transmitted Teachings (dka' bsgo lde mig)*;

▸ the *Perfection of the Seats of the Five Stages (rim lnga gdan rdzogs)*, which is an annotated commentary on the *Tantra of the Secret Assembly* from Guru Chöwang's *Eight Heruka Sadhanas: Consummation of All Secrets (bka' brgyad gsang ba yongs rdzogs)*;

▸ Rigdzin Godemchen's *Essential Guidance of the Sky-Faced One (gnam zhal don khrid)*;[258]

▸ the essential guidance on the *Eight Heruka Sadhanas* according to Longsel Nyingpo;

▸ the reading transmission of the *Father and Son Teachings of the Kadam School (bka' gdams pha chos bu chos)*;

▸ guidance on the channels and energies according to Sherab Özer's *Vital Nucleus of Liberation (grol thig)*;

▸ the preliminary practices of Rigdzin Godemchen's *Northern Treasures* entitled *Five Nails (zer lnga)*; and

▸ guidance on the channels and energies according to the teachings of Longsel Nyingpo.

From the precious master Öntrul, I received:

- reading transmissions for the nine-volume recension of Nyangrel's *Eight Heruka Sadhanas;*
- the thirteen-volume recension of Sangye Lingpa's *Embodiment of the Master's Realization;*
- the nine volumes of Düdül Dorje's *Collected Revelations;*
- the single volume containing the *Miscellaneous Writings of Dampa Deshek and His Spiritual Heir Tsangtönpa (dam pa yab sras gsung 'thor bu);*
- the *Miscellaneous Writings* of Trulshik Wangdrak Gyatso;
- Karma Chakme's *Oral Instructions for Mountain Retreat (ri chos);* and
- Longsel Nyingpo's *Unlabelled Cycle (them med skor).*

From Lingtsang Khenpo I received:

- the *Four Medical Tantras (rgyud bzhi),* with the four-volume edition of Sangye Gyatso's commentary entitled *Blue Beryl (bai dur sngon po);*
- *Sealed Supplement of the Pith Instructional Tantra (man gnag bka' rgya lhan thabs);*
- Darmo Menrampa's *Sealed Instructions on Medical Science (man ngag bka' rgya ma);*
- Mipam's *Commentary on Pulses and Urinalysis (rtsa chu'i 'grel pa);*
- his *Pebble Commentary on the Root Tantra (rtsa rgyud rde'u 'grel);* and
- his *Practical Instructions on Herbal Medications (sngo sman lag khrid).*

From Khenpo Gyaltsen Özer, I received:

- the guidance on the *Khandro Yangtik* entitled *Cloudbanks of the Ocean of Profound Meaning;*
- pointing-out guidance on the *Essence of Ultimate Meaning;*
- *Demonstration of the Vajra Path of Secret Conduct;*
- *Trilogy of Essential Guidance from the Lama Yangtik (bla ma yang tig gi don khrid skor gsum);*
- essential guidance on the *Trilogy of Whispered-Lineage Instructions*

from the Lama Yangtik and the *Trilogy of Natural Liberation* (*rang grol skor gsum*);

► the complete empowerments and reading transmissions for the *Thirteen Offering Liturgies of the Nyingma Transmitted Teachings* (*bka' ma'i mchod khag bcu gsum*); and

► the guidance on *Sadanana* (*gdong drug*).

When Khenpo Kunpel returned to Katok, he gave me practical guidance (*lag khrid*) on controlling the channels and energies according to the *Longchen Nyingtik*.

From Lama Trinley of Bhutan, I received the *Cycle of Sealed Guidance* (*bka' rgya can gyi khrid skor*) and the *Cycle of Minor Manuscripts* (*yig cha phran bu'i skor*), composed by Alak Namkha Gyatso, a direct disciple of Dodrub Jigme Trinley Özer.

From Golok Sonam Palden, I received:

► Je Tsongkhapa's *Extensive and Concise Stages of the Path to Enlightenment* (*byang chub lam rim che chung*);

► his *Stages of the Path of the Secret Mantra* (*gsang sngags lam rim*) and the *Guidance on the Five Stages* (*rim lnga'i khrid*), which comprise this tradition's Whispered Lineage;

► Gyaltsab Dharma Rinchen's *Commentary on the Way of the Bodhisattva;*

► his *Ornament of the Essence of Explanation of the Prajnaparamita* (*phar phyin rnam bshad snying rgyan*);

► Je Tsongkhapa's *Commentary on the Introduction to the Middle Way* (*'jug tik*);

► his *Commentary on the Chapter of the Prajnaparamita* (*shes tik*); and

► his *Ocean of Reasoning* (*rigs pa'i rgya mthso*), which is a great commentary on Nagarjuna's *Fundamental Stanzas of the Middle Way, Entitled Insight.*

From Pema Norbu, the supreme tulku from Palyul, I received the reading transmissions for:

► the restricted section of the *Treasury of Precious Revelations,* which comprises three volumes;

► the *Collected Revelations of Namchö Mingyur Dorje* (*nam chos pod bcu gsum*) in thirteen volumes, supplemented by his own wisdom mind-treasures (*dgongs gter*), totaling eighteen volumes;

▸ all the extant guidance on the *Collected Revelations of Namchö Mingyur Dorje;*

▸ the *Collected Revelations of Ratna Lingpa* (*ratna gling pa gter chos pod bcu gsum*), with their supplement, totaling thirteen volumes;

▸ the *Collected Revelations of the Northern Treasures* (*byang gter pod drug*) in six volumes;

▸ the *Collected Revelations of Minling Terchen* (*smin gter pod drug*) in six volumes;

▸ the *Collected Revelations of Jatsön Nyingpo* ('*ja' tshon pod drug*);

▸ the *Vital Nucleus of Liberation*, in two volumes;

▸ the *Texts on the Protector Sage Loktri* (*loktri'i gzhung*) in one volume; and

▸ Guru Chöwang's *Vajrakila: The Supremely Secret Razor* (*yang gsang spu gri*), in one volume.

Je Öntrul Rinpoche and I exchanged what we had of the textual cycles belonging to the *Nyingma Transmitted Teachings,* and I received an additional twenty-six volumes, along with the *Eight Heruka Sadhanas' Fortress and Ravine* (*bka' brgyad rdzong 'phrang*) commentaries by four Indian and Tibetan scholars,[259] and some minor empowerments from the *Embodiment of the Master's Realization.*

From the Lord Refuge, Situ Rinpoche, I also received Yeshe Gyaltsen's *Ocean of Mahamudra Pith Instructions* (*phyag chen man ngag rgya mtsho*) and Dong Chadralwa's *Four Stages of Yoga* (*rnal 'byor bzhi rim*), with Bartröpa Tashi Rinchen's *Guidance* on the latter.

From the great treasure-revealer Drime Ösel Lingpa, I received:

▸ both revelations of *Yamantaka Lord of Life* (*gshin rje tshe bdag lcags sdig*), which are respectively entitled *Imitation Meteorite* and *Meteorite Scorpion,* comprising four volumes;

▸ the *Pearl Garland* (*mu tig phreng ba*) empowerment liturgy for the *General Sutra That Gathers All Wisdom Intentions,* according to the Nub tradition;

▸ Nelpa Delek Pel's *Empowerment Liturgy of the Transmitted Teachings Entitled Jewel Rosary* (*dbang bka' rin po che'i phreng ba*), which is usually reserved for the consecration of stupas, but which I requested because there is also a tradition of conferring it on students; and

▸ the texts and volumes of Guru Chöwang's *Quintessential Embodiment of the Great Compassionate One* (*thugs rje chen po yang snying 'dus pa*).

Again, from Situ Rinpoche I received the single-volume *Wrathful Black Mother Khrodikali,* according to the revealed treasures of Nyang-rel Nyima Özer, and some sections of the *Tantra of the Ocean of Dakinis* (*mkha' 'gro rgya mtsho*).

From Tsangpa Lama, I received *Khechari according to the Sakya Tradition* (*sa lugs mkha' spyod*), in one volume, along with the empowerments, guidance, and the blessing that directly reveals reality (*chos nyid dngos bstan gyi byin rlabs*).[260]

I have mentioned the above merely as a rough summary of the enormous number of teachings I received, which are listed in detail in my record of received teachings.

VISIONS

The following is a brief description of the pure visions I had during this period.[261]

I had long harbored a wish to visit the holy place of Reting in Jang, and one night in a dream vision, I found myself there. It did not look like a monastery, but rather like a large protruding rock, upon which was what I assumed was the bodhisattva Dromtönpa's residence. I arrived on the eastern side, and a woman came to welcome me. "What is a woman doing at a great seat of the Kadampas?" I thought to myself.

"Who are you?" I asked. "Can you introduce me to the bodhisattva Dromtönpa?"

Smiling gently, she said, "I am Arya Tara, who has blessed you throughout all your lifetimes. You don't recognize me? Let's go inside."

She showed me the way, and we entered a house-like cave hermitage, whose translucent walls were made of six-syllable mantras, stacked like stones, in the colors of all the cardinal directions, with a blue ceiling and a white floor.[262] She showed me an empty throne, also made of six-syllable mantras.

"This is the throne of the bodhisattva Dromtönpa, so prostrate and go receive a blessing. He is staying in Tushita Heaven right now," she explained.

I prostrated and went to receive a blessing, thinking to myself, "How can it be that I have such feeble merit that I cannot meet the lama?" Besieged with suffering, I felt as if my heart had been torn from my chest. Aloud I said, "Victorious Father and Son, residing up in Tushita, think of me with compassion and grant your blessings that I may be inseparable from you!" With that supplication, I wept.

The woman showed me a small flat stone upon which four tiny insects were moving in the four directions, and one was walking around them, making a total of five. She pointed at each one saying, "Meditate on this one with loving-kindness, this one with compassion, this one with sympathetic joy, this one with equanimity, and this one with bodhichitta." I meditated accordingly, and the four immeasurables and bodhichitta arose instantaneously.

"That's it!" the woman said. "Even if you were to meet the bodhisattva Dromtönpa in person, he would have no other wisdom realization than this. You are equal to the bodhisattva himself, so here, take this hat that he was given when the Precious Jowo Atisha enthroned him as his regent."

From her robe pocket she brought forth a pandita hat with flaps that were not very long, the whole hat no more than a cubit high, with a spiraling, conch-like design embroidered on it in gold thread. She handed it to me, and I remembered my previous life as Pandita Kshitigarbha.

At that moment many people gathered, and the woman said, "You are no different than Dromtönpa, so give these people a teaching."

With that, everyone chanted the verse that begins, "According to the wishes of beings . . ."[263]

I thought to myself, "If I put on this hat and they discover that a woman gave it to me, it will be embarrassing! But I can't give teachings without wearing a hat. And maybe this really is the Precious Jowo Atisha's hat!" I thought for a moment.

Then without hesitation, I donned the hat, and the *Jewel Rosary of the Bodhisattva's Former Lives* arose vividly in my mind. I gave an extensive teaching on this, at the end of which the woman recited the dedication that begins, "By this merit . . ." and the entire assembly dispersed.[264]

Knowing for certain that the woman was indeed Arya Tara, I requested a blessing of the four patron deities of the Kadampas.

"The earlier proceedings were the blessings of the four deities," she said. "I don't know of any four-deity blessing other than this."

I returned the hat, but she refused it, saying, "It's yours, so you may keep it."

Then I woke up. On that occasion, I composed a supplication and a prayer of aspiration to the Victorious Father Atisha and his three spiritual sons, as well as their lineage.[265]

On another occasion, I undertook morning and evening sessions of recitation practice for *Wrathful Guru with the Fiery Hayagriva and Garuda* (*bla ma drag po rta khyung 'bar ba*) in accordance with the following prophecy:

> In the years of the Fire Hare and the Water Ox,
> His wisdom intention will be perfectly fulfilled.
> The mantrin born in the Tiger or Hare year
> Will survive the Fire Monkey and Iron Tiger,
> If he engages the key point of his meditative commitment
> (*thugs dam*).[266]

I was busy teaching during the day, but I maintained the clear visualization of the deity and the mental recitation of the mantra without cease for nine months. One night, I fell into an extremely deep sleep. When I arose from that state, in a clear vision, I heard what sounded like many small bells tinkling. I looked and saw four white-clad women holding the ends of four silken ribbons, which were tied in the four directions to a rainbow disk that looked like a drum stand, decorated with symbols of the five buddha families.

"Have a seat," they said.

"Where are we going?" I asked.

"We're going to Monkha Nering Senge Dzong and Taktsang Senge Samdrub. The Guru Couple (Padmasambhava and Yeshe Tsogyal) are staying there, so you had better go."

"No, I can't possibly walk that far. I am never apart from Guru Rinpoche," I protested.

"Why walk? You can ride on this carpet," they said.

The cubit-long carpet then became as broad as a house. As soon as I sat down, we flew up into the sky and set off into space heading west. On the ground below, I saw inconceivable countries and lands.

"What are those places?" I inquired.

"They are most likely places in Tibet," they answered.

After we had gone some distance, we came to a place where there were numerous lands below. The dakinis appeared to be resting in the sky, and from a bowl they helped themselves to copious quantities of raw meat and beer, offering me some as well. As they ate, they pointed out the places below and told me many stories about how their kings, ministers, monks, geshes, men, women, and so forth had greatly benefited the teachings and beings through the power of their past aspirations.

I assumed that the meat they offered me was human flesh, so I declined to partake.

They knew it and said, "This is not human flesh, it is lotus petals! If you don't drink beer, we'll serve you celestial beer!" They offered me something that looked like mercury, which I drank. I ate the meat, which did look like lotus petals but smelled like beer and tasted sour.

"We have more wonderful things to tell you," they said, and they danced and sang melodious praises of women and what sounded like numerous prophecies.

"Prophecies are the downfall of treasure-revealers. I have no idea what you're singing," I said. "Let's go."

"Yes, yes, celestial individuals like you have no need for them, but they are necessary for people of middling and inferior capacities," they explained.

"Well then, what about all the disgraceful people we see nowadays who beguile others with claims that they are following prophecies?" I asked.

"That's not exactly the case. It's just that there are few who know when to enact them," they replied.

"So why are prophecies revealed at the wrong time and not revealed at the right time?" I asked.

"Heh, heh! Prophecies are revealed at the right time, but there is no one to fulfill them. What to do?" They sighed and proceeded onward.

The mountain of Taktsang was craggy with brilliant blue and white rocks, with a densely forested canyon below and a rocky cliff shaped like a white lotus petal above, projecting upward to a great height on three sides. We arrived at the base of a grand mansion, many stories high, situated below the south face, and I was set upon the ground. The women flew vigorously up the rock face like birds.

I took hold of the energies of space and effortlessly went up after them. The earth, sky, and all of space resounded with the spontaneous sound of Vajrakila, like a roll of thunder. At the same time, a loud paean—"VICTORY TO THE DIVINE!"—boomed down from the sky.

One of my companions said, "This time we are victorious over the battle of obstacles!"

There, facing the slope of a wide steppe on the northern side of the mountain was a Tiger's Den Cave, just big enough for a human being. Above the opening, I saw the syllables KI LA YA, seemingly spontaneously formed. Each syllable was about human height, vibrating and spontaneously emitting its sound.

"Guru Rinpoche is there in person," I thought, and I supplicated him with the *Seven Vajra Verses*. The syllables merged and instantly transformed into the dark-blue wrathful Vajrakila and the maroon wrathful Vajrakila, indistinguishable from each other like a butter lamp and its shadow. Seeing them, I received an empowerment for the expressive power of self-awareness and recited the following verses:

> OM! Great glorious Dorje Drowolö,
> According to your great pledge (*thugs dam*) of the past,
> We are nondual in the space of reality,
> Our buddha body, speech, and mind united!

I tossed a flower of awareness (*rig pa'i me tog*), and from the deity's form, a second dark-blue wrathful Vajrakila emerged.[267] Like one butter lamp lighting another, it dissolved into me, causing my own body to transform into the actual form of Dorje Drollö.

One of the aforementioned dakinis transformed into a tigress, while another dakini instructed me to mount her. As I did so, I roared the sound of HUM, shattering the three planes of existence. We immediately headed south toward India and arrived at what I thought was the great charnel ground of Sitavana. There, inside what looked like a hide tent, was the Guru Couple, as well as Nyang Nyima Özer and many other treasure-revealers, some of whose names I had heard, and others I had not. A human corpse had been placed on top of a mandala.

"What are they doing?" I inquired.

Nyang replied, "They are preparing to give the great empowerment of the *Eight Heruka Sadhanas.*"

At that moment, the tigress suddenly ripped apart the corpse, and from inside its trunk the hosts of deities of the *Eight Heruka Sadhanas* rose up, filling all of space. The assembly beat drums and recited a deity visualization practice. Some mantrins held up what appeared to be a jug of beer on a tray and said to me, "This is known as the brown leather box of empowerment. You should take its accomplishments."

I looked inside and took a big gulp of what tasted like sour beer. "Why does this beer have so little flavor?" I asked.

"It is fantastic that it has any flavor at all! The lamas from Tibet have churned it so much that the beer has lost its potency," they explained.

"Do you have any of the flavorful beer left?" I asked.

"There used to be some with flavor and potency reserved for you in an iron casket in the naga-spirit Tiparaja's throat, but you disregarded it and threw it away," they replied.

The tigress sprang away again, and we traversed most of the regions of India and roamed through many charnel grounds. We encountered many yogins dressed in tantric loincloths, wielding hand drums, bells, and tridents, or holding birds, fish, or weapons. Each time the tigress roared, they shrank in fear.

In each of the eight great charnel grounds, there was one of the Indian vidyadharas of the Sadhana Sections alongside one of the corresponding Tibetan vidyadharas serving as retreat attendant.[268] They were engaged in discussion about the many general and specific sections contained in the *Eight Heruka Sadhanas*, so it seemed to me that there was no way to identify which of the *Eight Heruka Sadhanas* they were discussing with absolute certainty.

Then, off in the far distance, I saw a stupa so large that it soared up through the clouds in the sky. It looked like it was made of smoke. Recognizing it as the Glorious Intangible Stupa, the palace of the dakinis, I thought, "I should request some tantra texts there," and I headed toward the dome's eastern entrance.[269] Many young girls with their hair covering most of the fronts and backs of their bodies came to welcome me, and I entered the dome. An ancient crone of ashen complexion, blind, deaf, and without a single tooth in her mouth, sat wrapped in a wretched, ragged garment.

"She looks like a true wisdom dakini," I thought, "so I will request the empowerments of Chakrasamvara, Hevajra, and Guhyasamaja."

When I supplicated her, she acted as if she couldn't hear me. "What? What?"

I repeated my request, and she replied, "You may not have all three. I will give you the Guhyasamaja." From the top of her tongue she took a blue vajra, its four prongs marked with the four seed-syllables E WAM MA YA, and placed it in my hand.

"It pains me to give this away," she said and vanished.

I went back out through the main entrance, and a man was standing there scowling.

"What is wrong?" I asked.

"We have had so many things stolen from this room in the past. Now even more has been lost, carried off by you!"

"What is there to take from any empty room that has never had anything substantially existent in it? The possessions of emptiness have been entrusted to you, so guard them carefully. Heh, heh!" I teased.

"I am the guardian of this room. I am not unhappy about what you have taken. I am unhappy that you have no worthy disciples to whom to give it."

He instantly transformed into the Four-Armed Mahakala and said, "If you would like to go to Shri Parvata, I will help you."

He led the way, and we arrived at Shri Parvata in south India, though we did not meet Nagarjuna or Aryadeva. There were many women playing and laughing, and I went over to them. They looked like ordinary women. They were using five-colored dice, their six sides marked with the terms "isolation of body," "isolation of speech," "isolation of mind," "luminosity," "illusory body," and "unity."[270]

"Sit down and play dice with us," they told me, placing in my hand a set of six dice with syllables written on them.

"If 'isolation of body' and 'isolation of speech' are combined, that leaves only five," I said.

"Nonsense! We are adept at this game. Now throw your dice!" they said.

I tossed one and it landed on "illusory body." They said nothing. I tossed another and it landed on "unity."

"Unity without luminosity is meaningless, so how can you win?" they chided. After offering me a drink of beer, they sent me on my way.

I roamed through most regions of India and came to the border of India and Nepal, where I met the great Lhatsün Namkha Jigme on the snowy peak of Kanchenjunga Mountain. I offered him a mandala of my experiences and realization, and he seemed very pleased.

I said to him, "You have stated that the Dagpo Kagyü masters regard thoughts as the dharmakaya, but that you do not.[271] However, Dagpo Rinpoche Gampopa said:

> The innate nature of mind is the dharmakaya.
> Innate appearances are the dharmakaya's light.

"I think that he is implying that the nature of mind is the abiding nature of thoughts rather than asserting that thoughts are the dharmakaya."

"Your previous life as Ngamdzong Tönpa makes you very attached to the Kagyü tradition," he explained. "However, I did not say that Gampopa regarded thoughts as the dharmakaya. Nowadays, some lamas are introducing students to the stillness, movement, and observation of mind, and claiming that these are the nature of mind, but they are none other than concepts. It is important to know the dividing line between deviation and nondeviation."

At that moment, the clear vision vanished and I awoke. Even now, whenever the image of the sacred Kanchenjunga region arises in my mind, the image of the Great Lhatsün arises with it.

The night after I received the empowerment of the *Kalachakra Tantra,* I dreamed of the body and speech mandalas of the *Kalachakra,* drawn in colored sand inside the stupa of Shri Dhanyakanaka. The places reserved for the mind and power mandalas were filled entirely with blue Rahu vital nuclei.[272] However, when I received the *Kalachakra* empowerment according to the Shalu tradition, I dreamed that the mind mandala and the power mandala of great bliss were vividly present.[273]

Another time, after a period in which I had accumulated one hundred thousand recitations per meditation session of the *Aiming at Loving-Kindness* (*dmigs brtse ma*), from an extraordinary guru yoga practice in Panchen Lobzang Chökyi Gyaltsen's *Hundred Deities of Tushita* (*dga' ldan lha brgya ma*), I dreamed that I journeyed to the sacred place of Sumanadhar-madhara.[274] There I met the Venerable Lord Tsongkhapa and his two spiritual sons,[275] with the Buddha's regent, Lord Maitreya, above them, and Jowo Atisha and his spiritual son Dromtönpa to their left. I asked the Venerable Tsongkhapa about the philosophical position of his opponent Jayananda, which is rebutted in the chapter on Higher Insight from the *Great Treatise on the Stages of the Path* (*lam rim chen mo*), as well as the methods for resolving doubts. He gave some clarification regarding these topics and said, "I can lend you Khedrup Je as your spiritual mentor for twenty-five years, but then you need to give him back to me."

I calculated that I would be in my early sixties at that point, and I wondered if that would be the duration of my life, though I was not sure.[276] He turned Khedrup Je into a divine child and gave him to me, and I tucked him inside my robe. On my way home, I looked in at him, and he had transformed into a long, thin volume of scripture that contained an explanation in fifty chapters, beginning with the topics of monastic discipline and phenomenology and ending with the *Kalachakra Tantra.*

That particular event brought about a level of intellectual engagement with every aspect of Venerable Tsongkhapa's works that far surpassed what I had experienced previously, and I gained confidence in his blessings. I then composed *Notes on the Guidance of the Five Stages* (*rim lnga'i khrid kyi brjed byang*); *Notes on the Kalachakra Tantra* (*dus 'khor gyi brjed byang*); *Notes on the Essential Chapters on the Provisional and Ultimate Meanings* (*drang nges snying po'i skabs kyi brjed byang*); the *Guide to the Valid Cognition of the Prasangika Tradition* (*thal 'gyur lugs kyi tshad ma'i zin bris*); the *Structural Presentation of the Refutations of Valid Cognition* (*tshad ma'i ldog pa'i rnam bzhag*); and a large number of other short tracts.

After that, while undertaking the recitation practice of Longsel Nyingpo's *Blazing Wisdom* (*ye shes rab 'bar*) for the second time, I went to attend the vow-restoration ceremony (*gso sbyong*) in the assembly hall of Katok Monastery. The statue of Longsel Nyingpo inside the hall smiled, and the image of Amitabha inside the turban on his head recited the six-syllable mantra three times.

I undertook extensive recitation practice for *Eight Heruka Sadhanas, Embodiment of the Master's Realization,* and the *Kalachakra Tantra.* During the recitation practice of the *Kalachakra* in particular, I had a vision of the Kalachakra deity without consort, standing upon the powerful mandala of great bliss, and received his blessings, which was a clear indication of successful practice. During the recitation practice of the *Embodiment of the Master's Realization,* I dreamed of the protectors Gongtsen and Shaza Khamochey, petitioning me to teach and study the *Embodiment of the Master's Realization.*[277]

While I was engaged in the recitation practice of Jamyang Khyentse Wangpo's *Whispered-Lineage Dakinis according to Tangtong Gyalpo* (*thang rgyal snyen brgyud mkha' 'gro*), the Lord Mahasiddha Tangtong Gyalpo himself took me into his following and conferred blessings at the Indian charnel ground of Rameshvara.

Another time, I contracted a terrible illness that appeared to be an epidemic contagion, and I came very close to death. As a healing ritual, the Lord Refuge Situ performed one hundred thousand Vajrasattva fire-offerings, and it was most likely due to his compassion that one night in my visionary experience, the Lord Mahasiddha Tangtong Gyalpo came in person and said, "I need to bathe you with the streaming waters of compassion and beat you with the stick of insight."

He stripped off my clothes and bathed me from head to toe with what looked like milky water from a ceremonial vase, so that both my mind and body were restored to well-being. He then took a bamboo walking stick and beat my whole upper and lower body, whereupon my grasping onto true existence was liberated into emptiness, and my mind was left with nothing more to do.

When I awoke, my health had greatly improved. That same night, Situ Rinpoche himself dreamed that the Venerable Lord Jamyang Khyentse Wangpo came and conferred upon me an elaborate long-life empowerment of Tangtong Gyalpo, which meant that this illness would be of no harm, he told me.

During my illness, I dreamed that Palden Lhamo gave me a myrobalan fruit, and her donkey steed licked my body with its tongue. The Sole Mother Palden Lhamo is a deity worthy of offerings from all the lineage holders of glorious Katok.

Another time, many women who resembled drummer-spirits (*rnga ging*) appeared and handed me a drum. We mounted our skull-drums and rode away to a place in the west that I did not recognize, filled with clusters of red flowers that radiated such brilliant light that the sky turned red. A web of rainbow light spread in all directions, and there stood the Lord Mahasiddha Tangtong Gyalpo, his form as high as a mountain. Before him was a round, red mandala with nine sectors, each one with a different sadhana, which he then gave to me. In the northeastern sector, he gave me the complete empowerments and precious instructions for the extremely profound and condensed cycle on wrathful sorcery entitled *Revolving Vajra Wheel That Averts Pollution* (*rdo rje dme log bskor ba'i 'khor lo*).[278] I recalled them when I awoke, but I have since forgotten.

Another time, in preparation for what would be a terrible period of war and fighting in many different regions, the Lord Refuge Situ wished to perform the *Thread-Cross of Mahakali and Mahakala That Averts Worldly Battles* (*ma mgon gyul mdos*),[279] and he asked me to contribute by undertaking the recitation practice of Mahakala and Mahakali in the Dampa Deshek Temple. Following his request, I undertook the recitation practice, and one night in a clear vision, a monk gave me a black horse saddled with a human corpse. When I mounted, he handed me an iron bow and arrow.

The instant I held them in my hands, I transformed into the glorious Maning Nakpo, wearing a black brocade cloak and a garland of skulls, my four limbs adorned with eyes, and my mane of venomous snakes streaming upward in a thick swarm. I became so wrathful, ferocious, terrifying, and awesome that a powerful pride rose up in me, and I thought, "I am the sovereign of all life throughout the three planes of existence!" I galloped off to a kingdom, in the lower reaches of which I saw what looked to be many wild yaks. With my enormous pride, I bellowed out a thunderous war cry, and the yaks, as if struck by a gale, transformed into the myriad Dharma protectors of the Ancient and New traditions, bowing meekly.

Among them was the Oath-Bound Dharmaraja, who launched an attack in the form of a black man brandishing a sword. I pierced his heart with an arrow, rupturing his heart and lungs, the shreds of which stuck to the arrow feather. He toppled over and lay there dead. Overcome with desperate compassion for him, I transformed into a fully ordained monk. The thought arose that had I not given rise to such strong compassion, my energy and power could easily have been unrivaled throughout Tibet.

Once, during the summer rains' retreat at Katok, the conch-shell call to prayer awakened me, and when I lifted my head I perceived myself to be Sangdak Trinley Lhündrub at Dargye Chöling. Close by were four children of various ages with heads of black hair, who I knew to be my sons. Some were sleeping, and one was standing. This clear vision, in which I was unable to even recall that I was at Katok, lasted until the second conch-shell call had nearly ended.

While I was teaching in the assembly hall, some of my students saw a beam of white rainbow light radiate from the image of a white-robed man-trin in an old mural in the skylight gallery, which depicted many historical lamas, and penetrate the crown of my head. Later, when I went to check which image it was, I discovered that it was the image of Sangdak Trinley Lhündrub. I realized it was a sign that this great vidyadhara was looking after me with compassion. From then on, I was able to comprehend tantric liturgies, the rubrics of ritual activities, and the stages of ripening empowerments and liberating instructions, merely upon seeing them.

On another occasion, I went with some of my students to walk the outer circuit of the monastery. As I was washing in the holy water of the Manjushri power place,[280] several of my companions saw a fine beam of rainbow light connecting me to the sacred mountain. It was filled with DHI syllables, shining forth and reconverging. I learned that others on that same day had observed a dragon emerging from the cliff at that sacred place and soaring up into the sky.

From Choktrül Chökyi Langpo, I received Karma Chakme's *Concise Guidance on the Namchö Revelations* (*gnam chos khrid chung*); guidance on Ratna Lingpa's *Longsel Nyingtik, "Heart Essence of the Clear Expanse"* (*klong gsal snying thig*); reading transmissions for the former's *Oral Instructions for Mountain Retreat* and the *Unlabelled Cycle;* along with the restricted permissory initiations for both Jambhala and the female deity Kurukulle from the *Unlabelled Cycle,* and so forth.

One night, while I was engaged in the recitation practice of Kurukulle, I had a clear vision in which I remembered how the learned and accomplished Karma Chakme Rinpoche had magnetized nearly all the human and non-human students from Mongolia on the shores of Lake Kokonor near Ziling using the gnostic mantra (*rigs sngags*) of the Sublime Lady Kurukulle. I also clearly remembered him binding under vajra oath the naga-king Migön Karpo from the Markham region, and so on.

Since my early childhood, I have naturally felt that the Noble Great Compassionate One Avalokitesvara was my yidam deity, and special faith in him, as well as great compassion, have emerged spontaneously within me.

At one point, the Lord Refuge Situ Rinpoche, sovereign of all Buddhist teachings, suggested we establish a small branch monastery here at Jönpalung. Earlier, before he had founded the tantric college at Katok, the Venerable Lord Situ had dreamed of a great lotus flower surrounded by five identical lotuses, each with a fine sword adorning its center. Light rays streamed forth, and each lotus further emanated five identical lotuses. He interpreted this as an auspicious indication that the tantric college at Katok would give rise to five more such colleges. Inspired by such excellent signs, the newly constructed forty-pillar temple here at Jönpalung—complete with sacred representations of buddha body, speech, and mind—was established without hindrance.[281] I know that this was due to the power of the Lord Refuge Situ Rinpoche's blessings and compassion.

The prophetic inventory to Moktsa Drubtop's *Vajravarahi* states:

> When frog and snake dispute the vajra cross,
> One bearing the name "Ngak" will appear from the east.
> Not attached to the palm-sized mirror of light,
> If he dwells in the direction of Katok,
> His enlightened activities and deeds will ultimately flourish.

Accordingly, the most auspicious circumstances for my principal seat would be in unknown lands; the middling circumstances would be at Katok; and the least auspicious would be here in Jönpalung. Of these, I ended up with the middling and least auspicious circumstances.

Next, I went to Palyul to establish a monastic college. There, to a gathering of about thirty, I taught several minor texts, including *Melody of*

Inexhaustible Auspiciousness (*bkra shis mi zad pa'i sgra dbyangs*), which is a work by the Dharma Lord Jamgön Mipam, concerning Shangkarapati's *Praise to He Who Surpasses the Gods* (*lha las phul byung*); Mudgaragomin's *Praise to the Exalted One* (*khyad par 'phags bstod*); and Jinaputra's *Commentary on the Recollection of the Three Jewels* (*dkon mchog rjes dran 'grel*). Along with these, I gave an explanation of Shantideva's *Way of the Bodhisattva.* Since then, the school has flourished and vastly expanded, and it has produced many learned scholars.

Also, a prophetic inventory of Orgyen Sang-ngak Lingpa states:

> The retreat hermitage and monastic college at Palyul will flourish. Many scriptures never seen before will be propagated.

That prophecy has indeed come to fruition.

Once, while I was staying at Palyul Monastery, I had a vision of the Dharma Lord Patrul Rinpoche, in which I received his explanation of the fourth chapter of the *Way of the Bodhisattva,* along with the bodhichitta vow. Afterward, he said, "You will be of greater service to the Buddhist teachings if you found a school than if you strive for your own inner peace. The light of the Buddha's precious teachings depends on the manifestly pure application of the three foundations of monastic discipline, as well as whether or not the scriptures of the Sutra and Mantra are being taught and studied. Therefore, the application of monastic discipline, as well as teaching and studying, are of utmost importance. The many individuals who claim to be highly realized yet know absolutely nothing are a sign of the corruption of the teachings. All these many urban yogins resemble the proverbial 'fox with so many cubs that a single den is not enough.' Likewise, there are many ramshackle Nyingma monasteries, but none of them is functional."

Then, in the year of Hemalambha,[282] at the repeated behest of Chaktsa Choktrül Rinpoche, the fifth incarnation of Katok Ngedön Wangpo, I traveled to Dayul and settled in the monastic residence at Dralak Shedrub Ling. In preparation for offering the empowerments and reading transmissions of the *Great Treasury of Precious Revelations* to a large gathering of students from Golok and Serta, I held a nine-day Vajrasattva great-accomplishment ceremony to remove obstacles, with an outer mandala of colored sand.

Right after that, to open the door of blessings at the outset, I conferred the four circular empowerments and the torma empowerment from the *Secret Embodiment of the Guru* (*bla ma gsang 'dus*), and for seven days we practiced the synoptic inventory (*mdo byang*) for the *Embodiment of the Sugatas of the Eight Heruka Sadhanas*.

Proceeding in this manner, I sequentially conferred the empowerments and reading transmissions for the *Treasury*, starting from the beginning. As for the guidance, nowadays there is no tradition of conferral except in the case of the brief guidance indicated in the index. However, the Lord Refuge Situ Rinpoche does maintain the guidance transmission, and most recitation-practice manuals do have oral traditions of guidance that had been received by Jamgön Kongtrul Rinpoche, Khenpo Tashi Özer, and Thubten Gyaltsen Özer. I taught all of their guidance traditions, which I too had received.

Thus, for a period of six months, I taught the practical application methods according to the vidyadharas' lineage, without skipping over or belittling even the subtlest aspects for the sake of convenience. I conferred the empowerments in conjunction with the sadhana ritual arrangements, exactly as they are listed in the liturgical manuals and the index. I conferred the ritual arrangements in tandem with practical techniques, which inspired confidence and faith, a far cry from today's coarse methods. I feel that by this alone I have rendered great service to the teachings of the Early Translation school, which represents the tradition of the Victorious Lord Padmasambhava.

From the time the empowerments and reading transmissions began until their conclusion, a group of seven, comprising a vajra master and six students who were selected from the monastic body on account of their excellence, performed the Vajrasattva sadhana each morning. This they did with the elaborate self- and frontal-visualizations, complete with five great amendment ceremonies and feast offerings.[283] They concluded by making select-portion amendment offerings (*mchod pa phud skong*) and amendment offerings for the sake of living creatures (*srog chags rgyu'i skong*), turn by turn, as well as by performing the general dharmapala offering liturgy of the Mindroling tradition. Whenever we completed a section of the Three Roots' empowerments and reading transmissions, groups of eight lamas would take turns performing a feast offering, during which they would make offerings worth at least four ounces of Chinese silver.

Proceeding in this manner, the empowerments, reading transmissions, and guidance were completed without obstacle. We opened the outer boundaries,[284] and over the next five days, I gave the following teachings to a gathering of visiting laypeople:

- Guru Chöwang's *Quintessential Embodiment of the Great Compassionate One,* in conjunction with an empowerment of the Thousand Buddhas;[285]
- Ratna Lingpa's *Great Compassionate One,* in conjunction with an empowerment of the Thousand Buddhas;
- Garwang Shikpo Lingpa's *Great Compassionate One* in conjunction with an empowerment of the Thousand Buddhas;
- Karma Lingpa's *Peaceful and Wrathful Deities: Natural Liberation through Encountering the Four Empowerments (zhi khro dbang bzhi phrad tshad rang grol)*; and
- Jatsön Nyingpo's *Peaceful and Wrathful Deities ('ja' tshon zhi khro).*

I undertook the preparations for these empowerments in the mornings and bestowed them in the afternoons. The assembly was so enormous that I was forced to remain in the monastery until sunset each evening, which was extremely trying. But motivated by the thought of others' welfare, I gave it my best effort.[286]

During this period, I gave some concise explanations of the benefits of reciting the supreme six-syllable mantra, and without prompting, over seven hundred people pledged to recite the MANI mantra one hundred million times. Moreover, many people from each tribal group vowed to engage in positive actions and give up negative ones: stop thieving, banditry, hunting, fishing, killing insects, harvesting wild turnips, mustard, cordyceps, and so on.[287]

At the same time, there was a nonhuman being who was enduring a cruel rebirth as an anguished spirit, the result of his negative past actions.[288] He was thought to be extremely powerful, but with great compassion I was able to summon and decisively bind him to an oath. In doing so, I was able to bring vast benefit for beings directly and indirectly connected to me.

I received individual invitations from various leaders and well-meaning people in the Golok region, but the political upheavals that summer destroyed whatever auspicious connections we may have had.

During that period, and also at Jang Monastery and elsewhere, I received copious material offerings. However, the life of a spiritual mentor should be concerned solely with honoring and serving the Buddha's precious teachings through teaching, debate, and composition, which naturally benefit others. Biographies that refer to the magnificence of amassed wealth are clearly the deceit of imposters. There is no point in writing about that here.

In fact, whenever I received material goods, however small or grand, I dedicated the roots of virtue to others' welfare and to the attainment of perfect enlightenment, doing so completely free from the three dualistic concepts (of subject, object, and their interaction).[289] Nearly all the items I received were used to fund the construction of sacred representations of buddha body, speech, and mind, and I let nothing go to waste.

Next, I moved my camp to the upper reaches of the Nyichu Valley, where I established a teaching encampment. I gave the empowerments and reading transmissions of the *Four Nyingtik Mother-and-Child Cycles* and the *Longchen Nyingtik,* and I taught the preliminary practices and guidance on *Yeshe Lama* to a vast assembly.

Namochey in Nyi is a sacred place blessed by Vajravarahi, so when we first arrived many paranormal events took place. A short time later, a beautiful young woman miraculously appeared and offered me yogurt and a leg of wild ass. She vowed to accomplish whatever activities I commanded of her and then departed.

Then I received a letter requesting me to come immediately to Katok, where the Lord Refuge Situ Rinpoche had decided to assemble a thousand monks for a special ceremony. That night, I dreamed of a big empty city with a wretched old woman weeping inside its desolate remains.

"What happened to you?" I asked.

"There is no one to look after this city," she lamented.

"Why, you are suffering from hoping that something composite and by nature impermanent will last permanently!" I replied.

"What are you saying?" she retorted. "The Buddha's teachings are about to disappear, and all these books are going to go to waste."

I looked and saw countless beautiful volumes of scripture without covers stacked inside the walls of a large palace. She extracted a volume from above the eastern entrance and handed it to me. I opened it and looked inside. It was entitled the *Tantra of the Wheel of Lightning,* which I recognized as the text given to me long ago by the great master Garab Dorje. "What should I do with this?" I asked.

"It is yours, so take good care of it. Don't spread its secrets to others, and don't propagate it. Now we have to go," she said.

"Where are we going?" I asked.

"We are going to Sumanadharmadhara," she replied, and for a moment I found myself in some other place. Then I awoke.

When I arrived at Katok, I went before Rinpoche and made prostrations, asked after his health, and presented him with offerings. Even at that time, he appeared terribly ill. The first thing we did, with a thousand monks in attendance, was to perform a great-accomplishment ceremony of the *Quintessential Embodiment of the Great Compassionate One*. When we reviewed the accomplishments, I directly perceived the ritual vase as Mahakarunika—the Great Compassionate One—in union with consort, and I mentally took the empowerment of the profound inner path. This greatly enhanced my bodhichitta.

Right after that, we continued with the ritual sadhana of Jatsön Nyingpo's *Blazing Lotus Light* (*pad ma 'od 'bar*) and undertook a siddhi-mantra vase attainment. Rinpoche's condition had worsened to the point where for several days he was unable to lead the assembly.

A few days later, during the invocation of blessings in the ritual sadhana of the *Secret Embodiment of the Guru,* multitudes of dakinis in the form of drummer-spirits filled the air in the assembly hall, singing and dancing.

I was thinking to myself that I should ask them if the Lord Refuge Situ Rinpoche's life was in danger, when a dakini named Rinchen Seldrön danced from among them and sang in melodious tones:

> The rays of the setting sun have struck the peaks of the eastern
> mountains;
> The waxing third-day moon is rising on the ridge of the eastern
> mountains.
> The wax and wane of the teachings depend on the past actions of
> trainees;
> This gathering of dakinis may well be a reception party.[290]

Realizing that the Lord Refuge's lotus feet would not remain firmly in the world for much longer, I was stricken with grief, as if my heart had been ripped from my chest. As soon as the ceremony was over, I focused on prolonging Rinpoche's life, performing Rigdzin Jigme Lingpa's rituals entitled *Reversing the Reception Party of the Dakinis* (*mkha' 'gro'i sun bzlog*); Tekchen Drodön Tarchin's *Banishing King Spirits through the Wrathful Guru* (*gur drag rgyal rdzongs*); and *One Thousand Vajrakila Reversals* (*phur pa stong bzlog*).

One day, Situ Rinpoche summoned me and said, "At this point, given the nature of my illness, it is unlikely that further longevity rituals will do any good. Although from my perspective I have not committed any major transgressions of the basic and branch commitments,[291] from the time I was young until now I have propagated the profound paths of Vajrayana's ripening empowerments and liberating guidance to everyone indiscriminately, whether or not they were suitable recipients. So, there is a great danger that the faults of "associate transgressions" (*zlas nyams*) and "incidental transgressions" (*zhor nyams*) may cause obscurations impeding my attainment of the bodhisattva levels and paths. Therefore, I would like you to perform the fire offering of the *Black Wrathful Mother Krodhakali* according to the treasure revelations of Nyang-rel Nyima Özer, which is entitled *Fusing the Vitality of the Vidyadharas* (*rig 'dzin srog mthud*). Do it out on my roof terrace so I can hear you. I will undertake as much of the recitation practice as I can. You need to do the chanting and instrumentation loudly. I do not know if you and I will have another chance in this lifetime to join together in the tantric mandala."

According to his wishes, I offered one hundred thousand *Krodhakali* fire offerings over several days, out on the roof terrace on top of his house. Right afterward, I went to see him.

"That was excellent," he said. "Though I myself was unable to undertake the ritual sadhana, I accumulated the fire-offering recitation one hundred thousand times and got clear signs and indications that my transgressions have been purified. Now there's no need to bother with any more longevity rituals."

I implored him to keep his lotus feet planted firmly in the world for a long time, but he replied, "No one wishes to die, but this time I don't think that's going to help."

"What should I do after you leave us?" I asked.

"I have worked hard for these tulkus at Katok, and at great cost, so they themselves should surely figure out what they need to do," he said. He sat staring into space with a fixed gaze.

The next morning, the array of his physical body dissolved into the space of reality, and he departed for the palace of Sumanadharmadhara.[292] After five days, I offered my services by preparing the precious body and arranging an array of offerings. Privately, I made offerings to his holy body (*gdung mchod*), recited supplications, took the four empowerments, merged my mind with his buddha mind, and so forth, until I was fully contented.

Beyond that, since there was no one who could assign me any tasks, there was nothing else I could do for the teachings except follow the proverbial example of "the old lady with a kind heart."[293]

The following year [1926], I went to Lingshi Jangkar Monastery and conferred the empowerments and reading transmissions for the *Great Treasury of Precious Revelations*. A multitude of lamas, tulkus, and monks came from the surrounding monasteries, and there were also lamas and monks representing many different traditions—Nyingma, Kagyü, Sakya, and others—who said they had journeyed for over three months to get there, from as far away as Mili in China. Large numbers of laymen and laywomen came as well. All told, there were well over three or four thousand people in attendance. To them, I conferred the empowerments in combination with the guidance over a period of five months, completing them without hindrance.

Needless to say, I did not undertake this merely to amass offerings for my own purposes. Earlier, the Lord Refuge Situ Rinpoche had said that the *Treasury of Precious Revelations* represented the enlightened activity of both Jamgön Kongtrül Lodrö Taye and Jamyang Khyentse Wangpo, and that I, as well, needed to deliver the *Treasury* three times. I kept this in mind, and it has been with the sole intention of preserving the Buddha's precious teachings that I took on this responsibility.

Owing solely to that empowering condition, Choktrül Mingyur Rinpoche and his brother Lhündrub collected all the editions of the *Great Treasury of Precious Revelations* and commissioned deity cards and mandala paintings (*tsakli dkyil thang*), after which Choktrül Mingyur Rinpoche himself conferred the empowerments and reading transmissions of the *Treasury* about two times in the Tsawarong region.

Of the lamas and monks present, one thousand six hundred pledged to undertake the recitation practice of the Three Roots, three hundred pledged to recite each of the Three Roots mantras a hundred million times, two hundred pledged to undertake the approach practices of Vajrakila and Vajrapani, and others who ransomed the lives of three thousand five hundred animals. The laypeople, as well, as their situations allowed, pledged to accomplish positive actions and give up negative ones, stop hunting and fishing, and to refrain from robbing and plundering pilgrims at Khawa Karpo. I also bound under oath an evil king-spirit (*rgyal po*) from that region.

Thereafter, I received multiple invitations to places such as Pungri and Drakholri, but as it was summertime, I feared the heat of such lowlands and postponed going. On my way back to my encampment, I went to Yaso

Monastery and consecrated the reliquary of the learned and accomplished master Lama Yönten Rinpoche, a student of the Venerable Lord Jamyang Khyentse Wangpo.

After that, I went to Tsophu Monastery, where Tulku Lodrö Gyalpo of Yaso Monastery arranged for me to confer upon an assembly of 150 people the empowerments, reading transmissions, and most of the guidance of the *Longchen Nyingtik,* as well as the complete empowerments and reading transmissions for Terdak Lingpa's *Excellent Wish-Fulfilling Vase,* over a period of one month.

During that time, there were about sixty people who, for the sake of my long life, pledged to recite the hundred-syllable mantra 1.5 million times, ransom the lives of numerous animals, and recite the full number of Three Roots mantras according to the *Longchen Nyingtik.* Sixty others pledged to undertake the recitation practice of *Vajrasattva according to the Mindroling Tradition* and maintain it as a daily heart practice (*rgyun gyi thugs dam*), and to recite the six-syllable mantra 100 million times. On the way from Lingshi Jangkar Monastery to this place (Tsophu Monastery), more than three hundred people pledged to recite 100 million six-syllable mantras.[294]

The Lord Refuge Situ Rinpoche indicated that I would have obstacles in my forty-ninth year [1927], so heeding his warning I remained at my abode and entered strict retreat. I practiced continually day and night, undertaking most of the recitation practices for the Three Roots contained in the *Treasury of Precious Revelations.*

I began with the king of all guru sadhanas, *Secret Embodiment of the Guru,* undertaking the approach, accomplishment, and ritual activity practices according to the traditional methods (*phyag bzhes*). At one point, I dreamed that I was Guru Chöwang, in a plain near the Layak Guru Lhakhang in Lhodrak. My attendant, who was Guru Chöwang's son, Pema Wangchen, and I went out for a walk. I saw an Indian acharya descending from the upper reaches of a distant plain, wrapped in a white shawl and carrying a large sack.

He approached me and bowed respectfully. "Guru Rinpoche sent me to give you this command. Please be seated for a moment."

We sat down, and he opened his bag and took out many things that looked like Chinese-style bound books. He gave them to me, and one of them held a document entitled *Main Verses of the Guru's Instruction,* which contained advice on what I needed to do in my lifetime as well as several prophecies. At the end was a fivefold admonition to me: (1) do not go to faraway places,

(2) give away your possessions as offerings or charitable donations, without attachment, (3) have irreversible devotion to Guru Rinpoche, (4) know that the object of your accumulation of merit is the Lama, and (5) perform the Tenth-Day offering ceremony every month without fail.[295]

In another, I saw an elucidation of the twenty-five incarnations of Guru Chöwang. The text described the extent of his benefit to beings, how vast his enlightened activity was, and how many students he had in each of the twenty-five lifetimes. I was number nineteen in the succession. It appeared that I myself would not have many students, while the scope of the other twenty-four incarnations' benefit and enlightened activities was immense.

Soon after that, since at Katok I had previously completed the recitation practice of Sangye Lingpa's *Embodiment of the Master's Realization* based on the ritual sadhana *Sunset Heat* (*las byang tsha ba dmar thag*), on this occasion I opted to perform the recitation practice of the ritual sadhana *Beautiful Flower Garland* (*las byang me tog 'phreng mdzes*). At one point, I had a vision of the nine principal deities of the *Embodiment of the Master's Realization* that lasted continuously throughout the day and night, and the guardian deities Gongtsen and Shaza Khamochey repeatedly exhorted me to propagate the teaching of the *Embodiment of the Master's Realization*.

Next, I undertook the recitation practice of Akshobhya, according to the teachings of Longsel Nyingpo's *Vajra Essence,* and I beheld the entire eastern direction as a buddha realm, just as it is described in the *Sutra of the Array of Buddha Akshobhya's Pure Realm* (*sangs rgyas mi 'khrugs pa'i zhing gi bkod pa'i mdo*). Rays of blue light radiated from Buddha Akshobhya's body and completely permeated all the three realms, until the lower realms of existence were virtually purged and everything arose as the array of Akshobhya.

From the lips of the Tathagata I received the following prophetic declaration: "Besides the obvious benefits of properly performing the ritual described in the *Sutra of the Array of Buddha Akshobhya's Pure Realm,* merely touching the sand consecrated by the secret mantra, reciting the incantation of Akshobhya, and hearing its sound, the door to rebirth in the lower realms will be blocked, and you will be born in the pure realm of Buddha Akshobhya." From then on, my body was no longer afflicted by inner and outer parasites,[296] and from time to time the vision of the pure realm and Buddha Akshobhya would arise. A strong compassion spontaneously emerged toward helpless beings that had gone astray in the lower realms, and I mastered the perfection of patience.[297]

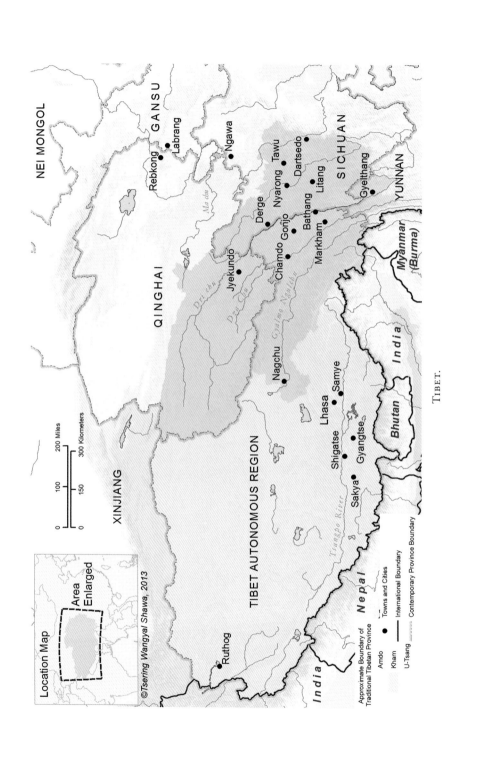

TIBET.

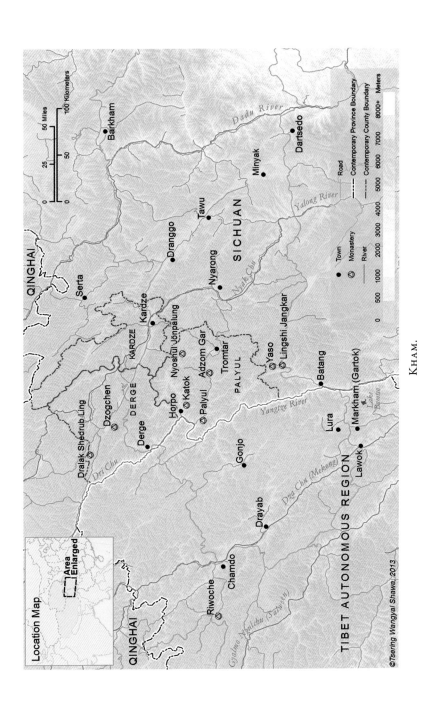

Location Map

Area
Enlarged

QINGHAI

QINGHAI

Dralak Shédrub Ling ⊘

Dzogchen ⊘

Derge ●

DERGE

Dri Chu

Serta ●

Kardze ●

KARDZE

Horpo ●
Katok ⊘

Palyul ⊘

Nyoshul Jonpalung ⊘

Adzom Gar ●

PALYUL

Gonjo ●

Tromtar ●

Drangg o ●

Tawu ●

Nyarong ●

Nyak Chu

SICHUAN

Yaso ⊘
Lingshi Jangkar ⊘

Batang ●

Yangtze River

Barkham ●

Dadu River

Minyak ●

Dartsedo ●

Yalong River

Lura ●

Markham (Gartok) ⚹

Tibet

Dza Chu (Mekong)

Burntso

Lawok ●

Drayab ●

Riwoche ⊘

Chamdo ●

Gyalmo Ngulchu (Salween)

TIBET AUTONOMOUS REGION

0   500   1000   2000   3000   4000   5000   6000   7000   8000+   Meters

●   Town
⊘   Monastery
⚹
──   River
──   Road
──── Contemporary Province Boundary
┄┄┄ Contemporary County Boundary

0   25   50   50 Miles

0   50   100 Kilometers

QINGHAI

©Tsering Wangyal Shawa, 2013

KHAM.

ROCK CAIRN MARKING THE BIRTHPLACE OF KHENPO NGAKCHUNG
IN TRODA NYAKSHAR.

MIKCHE LAKHA, WHERE KHENPO NGAKCHUNG LEFT THE VOLUME HE
RECEIVED FROM CHANDRAKIRTI AS A CHILD.

SHUGUSHAR, WHERE NYOSHUL LUNGTOK MEDITATED ON BODHICHITTA.

LOCATION ABOVE DZOGCHEN MONASTERY WHERE PATRUL RINPOCHE
INTRODUCED NYOSHUL LUNGTOK TENPEY NYIMA
TO THE NATURE OF MIND.

Nyoshul Jonpalung. The monastery is on the mountainside in the center.

GOLDEN VALLEY, THE LOCATION OF KHENPO NGAKCHUNG'S DREAM
OF OMNISCIENT LONGCHENPA.

SHRI SINGHA BUDDHIST COLLEGE AT DZOGCHEN MONASTERY,
WHERE KHENPO NGAKCHUNG COMPLETED HIS STUDIES
(RECONSTRUCTION, 2004).

KATOK MONASTERY, 1920.

KATOK MONASTERY, WHERE KHENPO NGAKCHUNG SERVED AS KHENPO
FOR THIRTEEN YEARS. PHOTO BY JANN RONIS.

SANGYE TSERING RINPOCHE'S PRIVATE RESIDENCE AT NYOSHUL JONPALUNG,
WITH A ROCK FACE WHERE KHENPO NGAKCHUNG IMPRINTED SYLLABLES
AND IMAGES.

SYLLABLE AH DRAWN BY KHENPO NGAKCHUNG WITH HIS FINGER
ON THE ROCK FACE AT NYOSHUL JONPALUNG.

LOCATION OF KHENPO NGAKCHUNG'S RETREAT CAVE
IN NYOSHUL JONPALUNG.

KHENPO NGAKCHUNG'S RETREAT CAVE AT NYOSHUL JONPALUNG.

STATUE OF KATOK SITU CHOKYI GYATSO INSIDE THE TEMPLE
AT NYOSHUL JONPALUNG.

STATUE OF NYOSHUL LUNGTOK TENPAI NYIMA IN FRONT OF A STONE
WITH NATURALLY APPEARING AH RA PA TSA NA DHI MANTRA.

VIEW OF NYOSHUL JONPALUNG MONASTERY, WHICH IS THE MAIN TEMPLE UP TO THE LEFT. PHOTO TAKEN IN 2004.

After that, I undertook the recitation practices of the *Embodiment of the Sugatas of the Eight Heruka Sadhanas* and Rigdzin Godemchen's *Naturally Arising Wrathful Deities of the Eight Heruka Sadhanas* just long enough to make them efficacious.[298] Then I undertook the recitation practice of Sangye Lingpa's *Mind Quintessence of the Kila Sadhana* (*phur sgrub thugs kyi nying khu*); the *Three Razor Scriptures,* comprising Guru Chöwang's *Vajrakila: The Supremely Secret Razor,* Pema Lingpa's *Vajrakila Razor,* and the *Vajrakila Razor according to the Northern Treasures,* as well as Ratna Lingpa's *Vajrakila: The Unsurpassedly Supreme Secret;* Nyangrel's treasure revelation entitled the *Black Wrathful Mother Krodhakali;* Venerable Jamyang Khyentse Wangpo's reconcealed treasure entitled *Gathering of All the Dakinis' Secrets;* and Rashak Sonam Dorje's *Peak Arising of the Matarah* (*ma mo sgang shar*).

During this period, I experienced extremely disturbing spiritual eruptions, such as seeing numerous women in actual physical form congregate around me and call me by name, and hearing various sounds and voices. These visions were largely experienced by others as well.

As I had previously completed both the peaceful and wrathful recitation practices of Yamantaka Lord of Life numerous times, on this occasion I opted for the recitation practice of *Red and Black Indestructible Yamari* (*gshin rje king kang dmar nag*), as well as the *Reversal of Imminent Events* (*'char ka yang bzlog*), based on the ritual arrangement of the Great Fifth Dalai Lama. At the end, in a vision, I met the Great Fifth Dalai Lama in the Potala Palace. "Well done!" he said, inspiring me with his joyful words. Then he gave me an edict, impressing a seal on the side of a large crystal vase. The seal carried the inscription "Powerful Adept of Charismatic and Joyous Enlightened Activity." This was a definite sign that I had been liberated from the pitfalls of this life.[299]

After that, during the latter half of all my nighttime sessions, I chanted the three syllables (OM AH HUM) in vajra resonance by way of purification, and I experienced the extraordinary signs of all the energies arising, entering, and abiding within the central channel, whereby I achieved a state of certainty.

During that time, I had a vision of the Dharma King Vyakaranavajra. He combined the *Array of the Path of the Magical Net* with Padmasambhava's *Wish-Fulfilling Gem: Scrolls of the Whispered Lineage of the Great Perfection's Longchen Nyingtik,* which he bestowed, along with nineteen fine vajras and bells, and he then appointed me as a "Lord of the Buddhist

Teachings." Based on this experience, I composed two manuals: an *Explanation of Yogic Inner Heat* and a *Manual on Yogic Exercises,* both according to the *Nyingtik.*

When I undertook the recitation practice of Sangye Lingpa's *Longevity Sadhana: Sealed with the Sun and Moon,* and Ratna Lingpa's *Longevity Sadhana,* my room was permeated by a sweet scent, the tormas melted into nectar, and I beheld the visage of Amitayus above the long-life vase.

While I was reciting the mantra of Rigdzin Jigme Lingpa's *Guru Sadhana Sealed with a Vital Nucleus,* I beheld the form of the Great Omniscient Longchenpa, who said, "If you were to compose a treatise elucidating the key points of the philosophy of the Great Perfection, that would fulfill the prophecy that you will benefit as many beings as there are grains of sand in a stupa. There is therefore a need for a text that extracts the key points of the Great Perfection."

At his command, I composed *Light of the Sun: A Commentary on the Inner Writings of Both Trekchö and Tögal according to the Lama Yangtik,* as well as *Commentary on the Buddha Mind of Samantabhadra: A Key to the Mother-and-Child Cycles of the Great Perfection* (*rdzogs pa chen po [ye shes bla ma'i spyi don snying thig] ma bu'i lde'u mig kun bzang kyi thugs kyi ti ka*), and the *Heart-Drop of the Dakinis: Guide to the Whispered Lineage of All-Surpassing Realization: Unwritten Pith Instructions That Are the Ornament of the Wisdom Mind of Samantabhadra* (*thod rgal snyan brgyud kyi zin bris kun tu bzang po'i dgongs rgyan yig med u pa de sha*). As soon as these were finished, I ended my retreat.

I then departed for Katok, having received a council petition requesting me to preside over their monastic assembly. Once there, I held a great-accomplishment ceremony of Sangye Lingpa's *Embodiment of the Master's Realization,* and when the time came to receive the accomplishments, my ordinary perceptions merged into reality, and for a while my awareness lingered in a state free of thoughts. Then, reemerging from that state, I beheld, as an outwardly clear vision, Guru Rinpoche in times gone by, conferring the complete and essential empowerments, tantras, transmissions, and pith instructions of the *Embodiment of the Master's Realization* at Chimpu Hermitage in Glorious Samye to the group of twenty-five disciples, headed by King Trisong Detsen, during their final assembly. The other thirteen lamas attending the ceremony, who were offering the accomplishment substances, all appeared as dakinis, their number representing the thirteen volumes of the *Embodiment of the Master's Realization.* I received the inner empowerment from them, after which no other visions arose. From this, I understood that the *Embodiment of the Master's Realization* has an extraordinary descent of blessings. Simultaneously, I clearly perceived myself as Chökyi Lodrö, the lama of Sangye Lingpa.

When the monastic assembly broke up, I returned to my mountain hermitage. It took a day's journey to reach the sacred place called Rakye Shel. That night, in a clear vision, the precious Nubchen Sangye Yeshe, who is known as the second recipient of the descent of the oral teachings,[300] the threefold Sutra, Magical Net, and Mind series, took me into his following and bestowed upon me the *Prophetic Declaration,* which was King Ja's commentary on the *General Sutra That Gathers All Wisdom Intentions,* along with the tantra of the *Sutra That Gathers All Wisdom Intentions,* and the *Lamp for the Eye of Concentration* (*bsam gtan mig sgron*) according to the Great Perfection. Based on this, I composed *Guru Sadhana of Nubchen* and a concise guide to that practice. I know that whatever rough understanding I have of the meaning of tantra has come about solely through Nubchen's blessings.

When the time arrived for my life to be in peril in my forty-ninth year, I did indeed meet with a formidable obstacle. However, Penor Rinpoche of Palyul Monastery led his congregation in prayer, and they recited the entire *Kangyur* three times, the *Prajnaparamita in Eight Thousand Lines* three hundred times, the Vajrakila mantra three hundred million times, the Amitayus mantra three hundred million times, and the Simhavaktra mantra one hundred million times. They performed one hundred thousand feast offerings according to the *Eight Heruka Sadhanas,* in conjunction with the ritual activities for purging the mark of impending death,[301] and reversing the reception party of the dakinis (*bka' rgyad khram phyis sun bzlog*). They also prepared Rigdzin Jigme Lingpa's *Threadcross of Mahakali and Mahakala That Averts Battles,* Jampa Trinley's *Threadcross of Tara That Averts Battles,* and Mati Ratna's *Ten Thousand Reversals of Simhavaktra.*

Individual students from Golok, Drango, Powo, Nyarong, and Palyul districts ransomed the lives of thirty-one thousand animals, and accumulated ten million recitations of the *Seven-Line Prayer,* and a group of twenty individuals undertook the recitation practice of Ratna Lingpa's *Longevity Sadhana* to support my long life.

Chaktsa Choktrül Rinpoche of Dralak Monastery erected a prayer wheel containing one hundred million imprints of the hundred-syllable mantra, dedicated to my health and long life. His congregation also recited the whole

Kangyur three times and the Vajrakila mantra three hundred million times, the Vajra Guru and the Simhavaktra mantras one hundred million times each, and one hundred thousand recitations each of *Spontaneous Fulfillment of Wishes* (*bsam pa lhun grub ma*) and *Dispelling of Obstacles from the Path* (*bar chad lam sel*). They performed *Purging of the Mark of Impending Death* from the *Eight Heruka Sadhanas* and one hundred thousand feast offerings of the Three Roots. There were many individual students from various regions who offered the recitation practice of the Three Roots and the longevity sadhana, and the laypeople from the upper and lower reaches of Dzachukha (Dayul) collectively accumulated three hundred million recitations of the Amitayus mantra and ransomed the lives of three thousand animals.

The people of the Absey Dila tribal group recited the Amitayus mantra one hundred million times, ransomed the lives of three hundred animals, made one hundred thousand terra-cotta imprints,[302] and offered one hundred thousand statues of Guru Rinpoche in support of my health and longevity. Also, in accordance with Chaktsa Choktrül Rinpoche's command to the different districts of Golok and Serta, I received letters from each of the local chieftains of that region, stating that the lives of five thousand animals had been saved.

Indeed, it was through the power of the truth of these actions that I was released for a time from the perilous defile of obstacles.

At my mountain retreat in Jönpalung, I erected a statue of the wrathful Achala,[303] according to one of the *Sixteenfold Vital Nuclei Empowerments of the Kadam Tradition,* as a representation of buddha body, and as a representation of buddha speech I had the corresponding tantra text carved in stone five times.[304] Once, while I was reciting the mantra of Achala, I had a vision of Jowo Atisha and his spiritual son Dromtönpa, and heard their speech. They gave me direct explanations of how the nuclei empowerments were not to be applied separately, but were to be conjoined in clusters of four. One should experience them in clusters of four, with the vital nucleus containing the inconceivable dharmakaya practice at the heart center of the visualized wrathful deity Achala, who is within the vital nucleus of the bodhisattva Dromtönpa's heart, in the vital nucleus of the Uru region of central Tibet, situated, in turn, on the ground of the pure Jambu continent. Accordingly, I also composed a text on the proper way to perform this recitation practice.

In the Snake year, when I was fifty-one years old [1929], I journeyed to Gartok in Markham, in response to numerous invitations I had received over the years from the Markham area, primarily from the son of the Ümda Shelling family and the son of the Pangda family.[305] On the way, reception parties arrived one after another, with welcoming food and horses. When we arrived at Gartok, I rested for several days.

As the fruit of many aeons of pure virtuous actions, my hosts and their kin made a fervent request that I inaugurate the *Great Treasury of Precious Revelations* there. In Gartok itself, the atmosphere was constrained due to the strong military presence of Tibetan government forces, so it was inconvenient to erect the cairns of the great guardian kings and so forth in great-accomplishment style. So, in order to fulfill their wishes, we moved to the Sangpu Lura assembly hall, where I offered the empowerments, reading transmissions, and elaborate retreat guidance for the *Longchen Nyingtik*. In between sessions, those attending the later empowerments and reading transmissions practiced as many of the preliminary trainings as they could.

Then I offered the empowerments and reading transmissions for the *Four Nyingtik Mother-and-Child Cycles;* the reading transmissions for the Omniscient Longchen Rabjampa's *Seven Treasuries* and his *Miscellaneous Writings;* and guidance on the *Trilogy of Resting,* headed by *Resting in the Nature of Mind,* in the context of which I gave guidance on the main practice and on *Yeshe Lama.* When these were finished, in order to eliminate obstacles in the preparatory phase of the *Treasury of Precious Revelations* empowerments, we recited the entire *Kangyur,* and we did numerous recitations of the *Prajnaparamita in Eight Thousand Lines.* During this period, we also accumulated more than ten million recitations of the hundred-syllable mantra.

Right after that, those who had gathered from the surrounding area to receive the empowerments and reading transmissions of the *Treasury of Precious Revelations* assembled, and we began with the great-accomplishment ceremony of glorious Vajrasattva, sovereign lord of the hundred buddha families. The cairns of the Great Guardian Kings were erected, and the entire assembly gathered within their boundaries. When we had properly accomplished the preliminaries, such as subjugating the oath-transgressing demons (*dam sri*)[306] and hanging the inner and outer sign boards,[307] we arranged the ornaments and ritual implements, principally the accomplishment vase (*sgrub bum*), upon a mandala of colored sand. Then we performed the main accomplishment ceremony within the seven-day format.

Then, combining the inner sadhana with the empowerments, I conferred the empowerment of the *Secret Embodiment of the Guru,* linked with

Vajrasattva. We drew the mandala of the main deity, Vajrasattva, in colored sand and painted the mandalas of the other deities on canvas. With these, I offered all the empowerments and guidance exactly according to the practical techniques of the lineage. The reading transmissions were given by Tulku Gyurme Dorje, and we finished within five months.

The first day of the ceremony was graced with a canopy of rainbow light, an earth tremor, and other signs. In fact, on all three occasions over the years when I have given the empowerments for the *Treasury of Precious Revelations,* earth tremors and many other wondrous signs have occurred.

At one point, while we were taking a break between teaching sessions, we held a vast torma feast offering. When we had correctly performed the regular liturgies (*gsol ka*) of the manifold classes of actual protectors and their entourages, and threw the offering torma into the incense offering (*bsang*), everyone in the assembly saw a canopy of conjoined rainbow spheres spread across the sky, from which numerous rainbows shaped like king's and queen's earrings,[308] silk streamers, parasols, victory banners, and other ritual objects arched down and pierced the earth. Clouds shaped like humans and horses raced back and forth on the upper rainbow canopy. These visions were the talk of the region, and the whole population was wonder struck. As a result, the gathering at the empowerments was enormous. What's more, braid-like flowers grew from the tormas, butter lamps burned for days, the amrita boiled, and numerous other events occurred.

When the empowerments and reading transmissions were about one-third finished, on the evening of the tenth day of the fifth lunar month, I had a vision in which the dakini Pema Nyugu Dewatsel appeared from the south of the mandala, her clothing worn and her body frail.

"Why have you come here looking like that?" I asked.

"Because you and your students have been making such meager feast offerings and amendments during the *Treasury of Precious Revelations,*" she replied. "Your mother sent me to tell you that she needs to see you now."

When she said that, I was filled with longing to see my mother. "Where is my mother?" I asked.

"She is far from here," she said.

In those days I had such bad gout in my legs that I could hardly walk, and even in my dreams, the imprint was so strong that I wondered what to do when it came time to walk somewhere.

"You don't need to walk," she said. "You can travel like this." She transformed into an eagle and soared into space. I did so as well and instantly flew off through the sky. Crossing over Bhutan and India, we alighted on a mountain plateau, as smooth and flat as a ruler, at the border between India and the western land of Oddiyana. At the center of the western land of Oddiyana, which was infinitely vast, I saw what looked like a royal palace with multiple stories, its rooftop adorned with glazed tiles, victory banners, silk pendants, and parasols.

"Who is the king of that great kingdom and palace down there?" I asked.

"That is called the Assembly Palace of the Dakinis in the western kingdom of Oddiyana," she explained.

"Then you have tricked me, haven't you! I am not even halfway through giving the empowerments and guidance. I am right in the middle of giving guidance on the Great Perfection to some destined and fortunate disciples, so for the time being I cannot go," I said.

She looked extremely disappointed. "Well then, if you do not wish to go this time, so be it. But before long, you need to come." She turned herself back into an eagle and flew off with all her might toward the great palace. Then the vision vanished.

The next day we held an elaborate feast offering and amendment. Over the course of the empowerments and reading transmissions, we did our best to hold elaborate feast offerings with what seemed to us like lavish material offerings, but it is difficult to please the assembly of dakinis. I doubt it would do any good to recite the verse, "All real and imagined offerings . . ." thousands or even tens of thousands of times if all you offered was a little pellet of dough. As it is said:

> In the presence of the venerable lamas,
> I confess my meager supplies and material offerings!

Indeed, feast offerings and the like can in turn become the cause of degeneration. As Nyang Rinpoche says, "Inviting many guests to a meager meal will only cause displeasure." From now on, I thought, rather than relying merely on offerings emanated through absorption, I need to make sumptuous material offerings.

When the empowerments and reading transmissions were complete, there was a lavish thanksgiving feast offering, and I was presented with huge quantities of gifts in gratitude, including many kinds of precious gems and metals, silk brocades, bricks of tea, horses and mules, various kinds of fruits, and so on.

Right after that, I received an invitation from the bursar of Lawok. I set out in that direction, and many people greeted me along the way with food and silken scarves. When the brilliant red cliff that is the palatial abode of Tsenchen Trobar came into view,[309] I made an incense offering. My whole body went numb, and for a short while I was left suspended in a state free from the fluctuations of dualistic grasping. In the vision that followed, a procession of hunting spirits (*btsan*) wearing leather armor and helmets, carrying military banners and riding red mounts, ascended from the direction of the Trobar's palatial abode to welcome me. I was so absorbed in the spectacle that I neglected to drink the tea they served me.

The chieftain of Lawok, Gönpo, came before me and asked, "Rinpoche, have you fallen ill?"

"Not at all," I said.

"Did you have a vision?" he asked.

"No, nothing of the sort," I replied.

Then we arrived at his estate. They provided bountiful provisions and facilities for the hundred or so people who had come to receive teachings. The chieftain requested that I teach the *Four Nyingtik Mother-and-Child Cycles* and the *Seven Treasuries,* along with some empowerments and reading transmissions from the *Northern Treasures.* According to his wishes, I offered the empowerments and reading transmissions one after another.

One night I felt a strong urge to visit the land of Oddiyana. Assuming the illusory body, I departed for Oddiyana, the realm of the dakinis. Manifold dakinis of various buddha families came to welcome me. Dancing and playing flutes, they sang a fervent song of the vidyadharas (*rig 'dzin gdung glu*) in unison:

LEY SHAK, Vidyadhara, LEY SHAK!
LEY SHAK, Pema Ledreltsel, LEY SHAK![310]

Inserting the above as the refrain, they sang:

O Son, with whom we all shared common aspirations
In the Gegong Cavern of Samye Chimpu,
At the feet of Pema Tötreng,
Have you neglected the armor of your former aspirations?
It has taken you so long
To join our dakini assembly!
We beg you to be our friend in times of parting and sadness.

There in the land of Oddiyana, in a building shaped like a barley grain that did not touch the ground, had no ceiling, and was fringed by a waist-deep border of five-colored light, I saw variegated dakas and dakinis of the five families wearing yogic shorts and silken ribbons. An assembly of dakinis was clustered around the principal daka, and an assembly of dakas was clustered around the principal dakini. Every direction was filled with intermingled members of the buddha families, such that there was no telling where they ended, and they were all amusing themselves by singing, dancing, playing music, and enjoying meat, beer, and assorted fruits.

In the center was a stupa-shaped palace, and at its lion-throne podium were four gates. In front of the eastern gate was the White Lady of Pacification, who was bathing in a pool. "This gate is the entrance for those on the Path of Accumulating, so you need not enter here," she said.

"What are you doing?" I asked.

"I am on the Path of Accumulating, so I am purifying the negativity of my mind through ablution," she explained.

At the southern gate was the Yellow Lady of Enrichment, who sat pounding a large amount of rice in a big stone mortar.

"What are you doing?" I asked.

"This is the entrance for those on the Path of Joining, so you need not enter here. I am on the Path of Joining, so I am differentiating the subtle conceptions of true existence," she explained.

Before the western gate, in the middle of a large flagstone floor, was a lotus seat one-and-a-half cubits high. When I arrived, the Red Lady of Magnetizing, Pema Nyugu Dewatsel, emerged from the western gate to welcome me, adorned with myriad jewels and silken ribbons. In her right hand she held a bouquet of crocuses, and in her left, a crystal vase filled with beer. She said:

Upon the lotus seat that transcends
The Paths of Accumulating and Joining
Are the flowers and incense of the seven branches of enlightenment,
And the nectar-like beer of the eightfold path.
To partake of these, come here to the Path of No-More-Learning.

Then she seated me upon the lotus and handed me the vase of beer, which I drank down to the last drop.

"Should I enter through the northern gate?" I asked.

"No need," she replied. "You have drunk the beer of the eightfold noble path, which is sufficient. This gate is the gate of subjugation, supreme delight, so entering here is greatly auspicious. Have you not understood that you are the lord of the lotus-family dakinis?"

In a flash, she opened the western gate, which was adorned with precious gems and a latticework of silk, and she passed through it. I followed her inside and found myself in a celestial mansion of jewels, bedecked with gems and red lotuses. There was a square courtyard with four corridors, above which were eight-petaled lotuses of body, speech, and mind—white, red, and blue respectively—stacked one on top of the other. Above them was a four-petaled variegated lotus, at the center of which was a dharmodaya triangle pointing downward.[311] Above that were the dakas and dakinis of the five buddha families and the twenty-four lands, surrounding their principal dakini. I sat down before her on a lotus seat draped with a tiger skin, and made this supplication:

> OM. Your timeless, vast, and sacred samaya,
> At one with every conqueror,
> Where death is merging with the Dharmakaya,
> The bardo is to manifest Sambhogakaya,
> And taking birth is pure Nirmanakaya.
> Confer on me this great empowerment!

The Vajra Dakini of the East dipped her curved knife into a skull-cup of nectar and raised it, saying:[312]

> OM. In the celestial mansion, within the vase of emptiness and
>   clarity,
> The mandala of the dakinis of phenomenal existence arises.
> Emptiness, naturally devoid of inherent existence,
> And great bliss, identified with the five wisdoms,
> Are perfected in the symbolic seal of those divine forms,
> Which are a unity of bliss and emptiness.
> Primordially indivisible from oneself,
> Bewilderment and false conceptions are purified
> Through coarse and subtle kinds of absorption.
> With regard to the former, from the subtle vital nuclei
> At the lower end of the central channel,
> One-tenth the size of a white mustard seed,
> The wisdom of great bliss emerges.
> Kalasha![313]

So saying, she sprinkled nectar and conferred the empowerment.
Likewise, the Karma Dakini said:

> AH. Visualize that the three syllables arise from the sacred places
> Of all the buddhas of the three times;
> That the red and white vital nuclei are indivisible,
> And that their movement is a vajra melody.
> Through the stages of inducing,
> Retaining and dissolving the vital nuclei,
> The three, two, and six knots of the central channel,
> Which are hard for anyone to discern, are unraveled.
> Through these outer and inner immediate causes,
> The lower orifice is opened by adopting and then rejecting,
> So that luminosity arises.
> Without fabrication, this magical illusion is naturally perfect within.

Likewise, the Dakini of the West said:

> HRIH. The Samvara mandala of the dakinis
> Accords with the divisions of the five buddha families,
> Where body, speech, and mind are devoid
> Of incorrect clinging to true existence.
> Uniting skillful means and insight,
> The five energies merge,
> And through this auspicious circumstance, all thoughts cease,
> And wisdom itself increases.
> The luminosity of the three appearances,
> And the accompanying five-colored energies,
> Then arise as the actual wisdom dakinis.
> Without relying on a lineal sequence of future rebirths,
> The fruit will be obtained in this lifetime.

Likewise, the Dakini of the South said:

> TVAM. Mudras and vitality yoga (*srog rtsol*) are skillful means,
> Which, on further examination,
> Are elaborate or unelaborate.
> The vidyadhara who has received these empowerments,
> By means of inducing, retaining, and dissolving the vital nuclei

Will cause innate wisdom to arise.
Then, if the energy that rides upon it,
Does not stray from that inner identity,
And one succeeds in reversing the flow,
The Samvara mandala of all the dakinis, without exception,
And the deities within it,
Will actually manifest at the crown center or heart center,
As forms of emptiness, and the flow will become an elixir of
   immortality.

Then the principal Dakini of the Center said:

OM. Since the aforementioned paths
Do not abandon the two stains,[314]
They may not bring about the maturation of buddha mind
And buddha body, exactly as they should.
Therefore, here at the outset of this uncorrupted path,
You should perfect the accumulations of merit and wisdom.
In this unity of genuine luminosity
And nonconceptual emptiness,
The movements of the dualistic mind are actually obstructed.
Through this sublime wisdom
The potency of the twofold obscuration will be thoroughly
   destroyed,
And you will thereby reach the level of No-More-Learning.
So it is that, distinct from those three kinds of practice
That engage in summoning and union
Respectively with consorts of the devi, nagini, and inferior class,
The four outer and inner awakenings
Will bring about the accomplishment of Mahamudra,
Which itself is supreme wisdom.
In this way, fundamental ignorance and dissonant mental states will
   be destroyed.
Therefore, if you remain in equipoise,
That bodiless body, supreme among bodies,
Will be the illusory body that subsequently emerges.
Once again, by remaining in equipoise,
In the unity of luminosity and emptiness,
Both appearances and the emptiness of inherent existence

Will coalesce indivisibly—
This will leave nothing whatsoever to be learned.

With that, the principal dakini snapped her fingers, and the dakinis of the four buddha families dissolved into her. She in turn melted into a vital nucleus of blue light, which settled upon the central seat, and sounded of its own accord the following verses:

All things are naturally empty.
They neither arise, nor do they cease.
A vast sea of wakefulness, so free,
Is suchness, pristinely pure.

The vital nucleus then transformed into a thumb-sized turquoise mirror, adorned with a symbolic white syllable AH indicative of the nonarising nature, which sounded of its own accord the following verses:

Exemplified by the mirrorlike insight,
Phenomena are understood to be illusory.
All-pervasive enlightened mind
Manifests everywhere as great capacity.[315]

As those words echoed, the syllables HA RI NI SA roared forth of their own accord, and simultaneously, the following verses resounded:

The auspicious connection of this wondrous and marvelous teaching
Is naturally unobstructed.
The Samvara mandala of the dakinis
Arises and manifests everywhere.

Consequently, in the hearts of the five lotuses, which were in the center and the four cardinal directions, in the middles of the dharmodaya triangles, each the color of its particular buddha family, there arose three hundred and sixty buddha-dakinis in union with consort in the central lotus; thirty-two vajra-dakinis in union with consort in the east; sixteen ratna-dakinis in union with consort in the south; sixty-four lotus-dakinis in union with consort in the west; and twenty-eight karma-dakinis in union with consort in the north.

Surrounding them, on the eight lotuses indicative of buddha mind, there were eight sacred abodes starting with Purimalaya, where the yoginis of buddha mind were in union with their consorts, headed by the daka Khandakapala and the yogini Chandali. Surrounding them were lotuses representing the eight sacred abodes of buddha speech, starting with Kamarupa, where the eight yoginis of buddha speech were in union with their male consorts, headed by the daka Angura and his female consort Erava. Surrounding them, on eight-petaled wheels indicative of buddha body, there were the eight sacred abodes starting with Pretapuri,[316] where the yoginis of buddha body were in union with their male consorts, headed by the daka Mahabalachakra and the female consort Vegadhari.

In the corners and the projecting bays were eight Matarah, headed by Gauri, and in the courtyard were eight Pishachi, headed by Simhamukhi, and the twenty-eight Ishvari.[317] In addition, there were hundreds of thousands of dakinis, such as the Great Dark-Blue dakini and the Great Dark-Yellow dakini, along with the four great spirit-dancers at the four gates. Offering goddesses stood on the platforms outside the mandala palace in the manner of servers with enticing forms and voices, delighting all those within it with their sumptuous offerings.

The female deity Dhatvishvari, who represents the natural purity of objects of touch, then said:[318]

The sixteenfold delight is the wine of space.
Enjoy the offering of the supreme delight of evenness.
As you fall into a drunken sleep, appearances dissolve into
luminosity.

The moment I heard that, my mind and its dualistic thoughts dissolved through the progression of appearance, increase, and attainment, and merged into the space of luminosity.[319] Sense objects merged into emptiness—the space of reality—and for a long time I remained in a state in which all the movements of mind and its energies ceased.[320]

When the energies once again began to stir, I experienced the progression to "near attainment" in reverse sequence.[321] After that, with the three appearances serving as the primary cause and the five-colored light rays of the energies riding upon them serving as the secondary cause, an illusion-like clear vision arose in my heart center, where the Mahasamvara mandala of the dakinis appeared, complete with its celestial mansion and deities, but without subjective apprehension or objective recognition of emptiness.

Then my perception grew coarser and my consciousness reawakened to sense objects. Simultaneously, I awoke in my bed.

Another day I again had an urge to visit that sacred land, and in a vision I arrived in a delightful grove in Oddiyana, encircled by magical trees, medicinal trees, and fruit trees, and adorned with many kinds of flowers. There I saw numerous dakinis of the lotus family, such as Pema Nyugu Dewatsel, who were engaged in esoteric yogic exercises. With pleasure, they each offered me a garland of red flowers and served me various offerings to delight the senses, singing:

> From now until the heart of enlightenment,
> We are committed to you as your inseparable companions—
> understand this!
> Stay here and maintain your feast offerings.
> Is this agreeable to you, child of noble heritage?

Then the principal dakini sang:

> At this point it is not advisable to stay;
> The action of a bodhisattva
> Is purely to benefit others,
> So I request you to look after those left to be trained.

She offered me beer and many kinds of fruits, explaining that these were longevity substances, and she spoke for what seemed a very long time. Afterward, she said, "Let's go to the palace of the dakinis at Lake Bamtso, where there will be wonderful conversation." She was still speaking when I woke up from the vision.

Then I left Lawok and went to the bursar's estate. For several days, I performed prayer rituals for his long life and offered him whatever teachings he requested. He asked me to consecrate a statue of Trobar on his rooftop, which I did as well. On that occasion, one of the monks was immediately possessed by the deity, and from that evening onward there were signs such as nonhuman beings gathering on the roof and the sounds of various indistinct syllables, which continued for several days. All were astonished. At that same time, the protectress Singmo Takcham Marmo offered me a ceremonial scarf and asked after my health.

After that, I went to the home of Rushipa Ku-ngo Kalzang. For several days, I offered the prayer rituals he requested, including a long-life empowerment and so forth, and then I moved to an encampment on the Pangda estates. There I rested for a while. Later, I gave some reading transmissions and guidance on Patrul Rinpoche's *Collected Works,* as well as his *Commentarial Explanation of the Ornament of Emergent Realization* and the *Prajnaparamita.*

Earlier, when I had given the empowerments for the *Treasury of Precious Revelations,* the principal deity of that estate's protector chapel, Dorje Drakden,[322] had said to me, "Anoint my face with gold and perform my liturgies like this, and all will be well!" Then I perceived him receiving some of the empowerments. On this occasion, as well, he was immensely pleased with my explanation of the *Prajnaparamita* and attended the teachings. I realized that it was quite possible that the reason my students and I incurred no obstacles at all, from the moment I began the empowerments of the *Treasury of Precious Revelations* until their completion, was the enlightened activity of that great Dharma protector.

Then I went to see the Lhadün Vairochana rock image and performed an elaborate hundred-thousandfold offering. Based upon Rigdzin Jigme Lingpa's fourfold mandala-offering ritual entitled *Ornament of Nagendra's Wisdom Mind (klu dbang dgongs rgyan),* I accumulated one thousand recitations of the *Praise to the Twenty-One Taras,* rather than emphasizing the accumulation of the dharani mantra and so on. I kept in mind the fact that the *Praise to the Twenty-One Taras* was spoken by the Tathagata Vairochana himself, and kept the benefit and well-being of the teachings and beings as my focus.

During that period, I received so many donations that I had difficulty finding containers for all the butter and sieving all the flour for torma offerings. I used the excess clarified butter to fill and offer numerous lamps made of stone and copper.

There are two legends as to the origins of this particular image of Buddha Vairochana and his entourage: that they were hidden treasures revealed by Kongjo or that they were fashioned by miraculous means. Regardless, they comprise natural stone images of Vairochana, one story high, and the Eight Close Sons, each higher than human height, along with the Buddhist king Songtsen Gampo, and wrathful gatekeepers. For the duration of the day, I witnessed the hair and eyebrows on the peaceful face of the Lord of Secrets Vajrapani assume a wrathful expression, such that his countenance manifested various semiwrathful forms, bluish sparks flared out from the swirling mountain of flames that blazed around his hair and eyebrows, his eyes moved, his lips smiled, and so on.

Then I went to the shores of Bamtso Lake. This particular lake is shaped like the body of Vajravarahi, and in the center of the lake one can even see two small hillocks symbolizing Vajravarahi's breasts. On the side of her left shoulder, near her face, I offered prayer flags to the lake, powdered sacred substances, three gemstone pills, gold, silver, and numerous kinds of precious gems and metals. I set up camp next to her left hip and made a vast feast offering, which caused a heavy rain to fall. As soon as it cleared, rainbows of various colors filled the space between the large and small hills, joining the two. I remained there for three days making feast offerings.

When I struck camp on the evening of the following day, I heard many women with beautiful voices singing and dancing on the two hills. I came to know that the nomads throughout that vast area talked of seeing rainbows stretching between my tent and the sacred lake for three whole days. Whatever the case, the blessings of that sacred place cleared the physical elements that had been disturbing me for a long time, and from then on not a trace of illness remained.

After that, I returned to Pangda and did whatever prayer rituals they needed, along with Longsel Nyingpo's *Glorious Shri Devi's Prosperity Sadhana with Prosperity Pledges and Vows (dpal chen mo'i gyang sgrub gyang gta' sdom pa bcas)*. They offered enormous amounts of material wealth and riches.

Then once again I traveled to Gartok in Markham, where, for the entire military encampment of the Tibetan central government, I conferred a long-life empowerment, along with rituals to enhance the glory of the luck element or wind-horse (*rlung rta dpal bskyed*),[323] a testimonial paean to the vitality element of the warrior spirits, and a consecration of their armor.

General Shelsey had renovated the sacred images, books, and stupas of Özer Monastery, so for a period of three days I consecrated them, as well as the town and the sacred artifacts of that place, utilizing Terdak Lingpa's *Inspection of the Wishing Cow of Excellent Virtue (dge legs 'dod 'jo dngos lta)*. They offered a mandala of copious material riches. I distributed monetary offerings to all the monks and sponsored tea at all the Sakya and Geluk monasteries in that area, and then departed.

Various officials escorted me one day's journey, until we reached the outpost of Chubum. I was told that the upper and lower reaches of Markham had been stricken with poor harvests for many years, but that year the entire area, particularly in and surrounding Chubum and Gartok, experienced bountiful harvests. The winter fodder fields that had been planted for the horses, as well, produced excellent grains. These events were considered wondrous. The villagers within a day's journey from there also made offerings, which were lavish given their economic condition, and many came to request blessings for good harvests in the future. Later, I learned that for three years afterward the harvests were abundant.

Then, stopping along the way at Drugudo, I made a pilgrimage to the sacred site of Dorje Drollö in Tsangshi, the renown of which is unparalleled throughout lower Dokham. It is described as a sacred abode of buddha mind in the revelations of Rigdzin Düdül Dorje and in the *Chronicles of Tsogyal* (*mtho rgyal bka' thang*) discovered by the treasure-revealer Takshampa Nüden Dorje. It is one of the three "tiger dens" blessed by the inseparable union of Guru Rinpoche's body, speech, and mind.

I settled into Neygo Monastery. There, I sponsored a thirteen-day ceremony for my *Attainment of Medicinal Nectar: The Great Secret Swift Path* (*bdud rtsi sman sgrub gsang chen myur lam*), utilizing the structure of a sadhana based on my *Manifold Display of Great Bliss: A Ritual Purification from the Eight Heruka Sadhanas* (*bka' brgyad las byang bde chen rnam rol*). The ritual was performed by those who lived at the monastery, plus more than a hundred lamas and monks from the surrounding area. We performed the preparation, main practice, and concluding ritual activities precisely according to the practical method of the lineage of vidyadharas.

At the end, while conferring the empowerment for that accomplishment ceremony, I made vast numbers of connections through teachings and the distribution of sacred medicine. I offered four silver coins each to those assembled and made proportionate offerings of thirty, twenty-five, twenty, fifteen, and at the very least ten silver coins to the lamas and tulkus, but that was merely a token. From start to finish, according to calculations done in Chinese currency, the accomplishment ceremony cost over three thousand silver coins, the virtue of which I dedicated to perfect enlightenment and sealed with the *Prayer of Good Conduct*.

Inside a cave at that sacred abode, there is a spontaneously arisen stone statue of Dorje Drollö, the principal deity of the site, as well as two consecrated hand-carved images to his right and left of Düdül Dorje and Takshampa. There are also images of the Three Roots, a facial likeness of Dorje Drollö, and so on. The night before I planned to leave, light blazed inside the cave and the offering-shrine shook. Earlier, several birds never seen before alighted and stayed for a whole day at that sacred place. These and many other wondrous omens appeared, according to the caretaker of the temple.

The following day I went inside the sacred cave. I had amassed forty bags of white barley flour, eight bags of wheat flour, seven bags of butter, three bags of dried cheese, five bags of assorted fruits, and three dzo carcasses, with the intention of performing a hundred-thousandfold feast offering. I exerted myself in making as many feast offerings as I could, based on Düdül Dorje's *Dorje Drollö* treasure-teaching, as well as incense offerings (*bsang*) and burnt offerings (*bsur*), in an effort to please the four types of guests.

At that point, I received a letter from a messenger saying that I needed to come for the enthronement of Gyalse Rinpoche's reincarnation. Although I had not yet completed one hundred thousand recitations of the sadhana, I had already offered several hundred thousand of the actual feast offerings. The caretaker of the temple seemed amazed, saying that never before had such elaborate feast offerings been made during a hundred-thousandfold feast-offering ceremony. I also offered a capital endowment for butter lamps to burn continuously day and night.

During that period, when I first invited the deity at the outset of the practice, the spontaneously arisen stone image of Dorje Drollö had moved and bluish sparks flared out, causing my awareness to be suspended in the nature of reality for an entire day. I knew this was an indication that this supreme deity had granted his blessings. I revitalized the site and performed Rigdzin Godemchen's consecration entitled *Showering Blessings on Great Sacred Places* (*gnas chen byin 'bebs rab gnas*). I later heard that virtue and auspiciousness ensued in the surrounding regions.

Then I went to Gyalse Monastery and settled into a mountain hermitage. On the morning of the twenty-second day of the ninth lunar month, the anniversary of Buddha's Descent from the Heavens[324] when the planets and stars were in excellent alignment, we performed an elaborate sadhana, including self- and frontal-visualizations, based on Rigdzin Longsel's treasure teaching entitled *Blazing Lotus Light*,[325] combined with the *Longevity Sadhana: Unexcelled Supreme Secret* (*tshe sgrub yang gsang bla med*). Most importantly, the precious reincarnation was enthroned.

First, I performed a ritual ablution and supplication to purify any inauspicious hindrances or misfortunes, and then I visualized the mighty king of the conquerors, Pema Öbar, "Blazing Lotus Light," the sovereign of all mandalas, and invited him to come, whereby the wisdom deity dissolved inseparably into the commitment deity. I made inner and outer offerings, performed the consecration and enthronement, and conducted the ceremony up to the beginning of the mandala offering. Then the actual mandala offering was introduced with delightful and eloquent speeches.

Each of the monastic institutions, headed by Katok, made celebratory offerings, while the inventory of these offerings was read aloud. We concluded the ceremony with an auspicious benediction and a longevity empowerment. That day, the Sakyapa Gona Trichen Tulku and his entourage came, as well as numerous lamas and monks from the surrounding area. I offered them the great empowerment of Sangye Lingpa's *Embodiment of the Master's Realization,* the great empowerment of Nyangrel's *Embodiment of the Sugatas of the Eight Heruka Sadhanas,* the empowerment of Karma Lingpa's *Peaceful and Wrathful Deities,* Düdül Dorje's *Vajrakila* and his *Blazing Lotus Light,* Longsel Nyingpo's *Red Lion-Faced Dakini (seng ha dmar mo),* along with his *Peaceful and Wrathful Deities,* and his *Great Compassionate One,* and so on, as well as the empowerments and reading transmissions of the *Four Nyingtik Mother-and-Child Cycles.*

Afterward, I was invited to Gona Monastery. I traveled there, and for two days I offered connections through empowerments and teachings, and consecrated the assembly hall and the rest of the monastic compound. I received copious gifts from each of the monastic communities in the surrounding areas as well.

Once again, I returned to Gyalse Monastery and established connections with the monastic community and the locale at large through empowerments and teachings. The general public and private individuals made mountainous offerings.

Then I went to Serding Monastery, where I offered empowerments and teachings to an audience composed of the monastic community and the general public. Inside Serding Rinpoche's private room, with my focus on the reincarnation, I performed a Guru Drakpo feast offering and cast lots to determine the circumstances of the reincarnation.[326] That day, even though it was still winter, the local people spoke of seeing summer rainbows pervading every direction around the monastery. The investigation revealed the reincarnation to be the young son of Lingshi Tertön Karma's son and heir, Palden Gyatso. However, the auspicious conditions were disrupted, and I heard that the reincarnation did not live very long.

Then I departed, accompanied by a party from the Maryön Pön family and many people from the monastery who came to see me off. Along the way, we passed a place called Menchukha, where the Chinese Princess Wencheng long ago washed her hair, and pine trees grew where the water droplets fell. The site is renowned as the dwelling place of the twenty-eight Ishvaris. As we drew near, a heavenly fragrance of medicinal incense wafted throughout, whereupon my body and mind were pervaded by blissful absorption and my awareness was suspended in the state of nonconceptual reality.

A moment later in a clear vision, Her Majesty Kongjo, the Princess Wencheng, appeared in the sky before me, dressed in the garb of a Chinese girl. She was tall and slender, with fair skin and rosy cheeks. From time to time she transformed, and in her hands, which were red like lotus petals, she held a single volume of scripture. It was the *Tantra of Tara's Manifold Activities (sgrol ma las sna tshogs pa'i rgyud)*, and as she recited it, from the beginning, she emanated in forms corresponding to the context and bestowed the empowerments, along with an explanation of the tantra. The vision lasted until we reached the perimeter of the sacred site of Ri Pemachen, "Lotus Mountain."

Then I went to the Marpön estate and gave some ripening empowerments and liberating teachings, according to their wishes.

Then, after striking camp, I arrived in the nomadic tribal area of Lhatok.[327] I visited Tsam Chumik Karmo and the spontaneously arisen six-syllable mantra of the Tsangshi grasslands. The naga king Migön Dzalung Karpo told me that he had a share of wealth in Dzalung Karpo that belonged to me, which he intended to give to me, but as I had little need for it, I let it be.

Then I arrived in Gönjo District. I received invitations from the surrounding monasteries and individual chieftains, but because the winter cold was harsh and it was snowing heavily, I stayed in Upper and Lower Dodruk and the Pala District, where I collected alms. I gathered nearly 160 bags of grain, which I then donated for a newly constructed Shakyamuni statue at Katok.

Along the way, I stopped briefly at seven or so Gönjo principalities, and eight or nine monasteries. I received invitations from Lapak Monastery, Lhasung, Khora, and Duri in Drayab County, but I postponed going. Then I made my way gradually down the main road until I arrived at the home of the chieftain Samdrup. I rested there for a few days and then performed prayer rituals privately for the chieftain and for the general public.

I went briefly to Nyakla Jangchub Dorje's encampment, as well, and gave novice and full ordination to sixty-four monks. They made offerings that were free of the three concepts of giver, receiver, and object given.

Between Markham and that place, I ordained nearly three hundred monks, gave guidance on the Great Perfection to more than a thousand, guidance on the channels and energies to about forty, and guidance on the *Yeshe Lama* to about one hundred. This was not merely pompous guidance for the pretentious or wordy guidance for intellectuals; it was pith instruction of the Great Perfection according to the oral transmission of the lineage of the vidyadharas. As such, I gave introductions to awareness in the context of Trekchö and to the four lamps in the context of Tögal, so effectively that even old realized yogins were compelled to say that they had never heard such Great Perfection guidance before. People came in enormous numbers to offer me their realization and resolve their doubts. During that period, I gave guidance to groups of thirty or forty at once, rather than teaching students individually, so the methodology seemed a bit crude. However, the assemblies were exceedingly large, so I had little choice.

From the moment I left Markham, I constantly perceived the protectors Trobar and especially Singmo Takcham Marmo escorting me. The latter had said she would turn back once we reached the area under the administration of Samdrup, as I would no longer need an escort at that point, but since Mahakala and Mahakali and the other guardians of Katok had not yet arrived to welcome me, she said she needed to escort me until they came. She was clearly a guardian adhering to past samaya.

Then, with no mishaps along the way, I arrived at Katok. I made token offerings to the monastic community in general and to Choktrül Rinpoche in particular. I contributed the remaining gold and silver I had received, equivalent to 10,300 Chinese silver coins, to the restoration of the gilding of the great three-dimensional mandala of the Zangdok Pelri Temple.

Once again, I returned to my home and made as many teaching connections as I could with those who had gathered there from the surrounding areas. At the beginning of the Monkey year [1932],[328] a request came from Chaktrül Rinpoche asking me to come preside over the establishment of a new Buddhist college at Dralak Monastery, and I agreed to go. At New Year, I went to the place where the treasure-revealer Drime Rinpoche had passed away. I made offerings and cremated his precious remains.

I had arranged to go to Dralak Monastery at the beginning of the second lunar month, but Drubwang Pema Norbu of Palyul fell gravely ill, and I was transported there in a palanquin. After the passing of the Lord Refuge Situ Rinpoche, I knew for certain there was none greater than Penor Rinpoche to fulfill my hopes of bringing some small benefit to the Nyingma school. With a pure heart, I performed many healing prayer rituals, but they brought little benefit. I requested permission to take leave briefly and departed for Dralak, planning to return before long.

On the way, after a day's journey, I stopped for the night and had a clear vision of the saintly and venerable Lord Tsongkhapa, alongside the venerable Dharma Lord Mipam Rinpoche and my own gracious lama Lungtok Rinpoche. The former two were engaged in a question-and-answer session of logical refutation concerning Shri Chandrakirti's Prasangika presentation of the Madhyamaka.[329] In particular, Je Tsongkhapa and Lama Mipam were holding an animated debate about the subjective, and whether or not common perceptions exist.[330] Listening to them, I could tell there was much to be learned, but gracious Lama Lungtok said, "Show me the several guidance commentaries on the Great Perfection that you have composed." I showed him, and with great joy and delight, he exclaimed, "Well done!" When I analyzed the signs in the dream, I had the thought that a fine Buddhist college would be established at Dralak Monastery.

Then I stopped for the night at a place near Dralak Shedrub Ling. The next morning, many welcoming parties from near and far arrived on horseback. When I reached the monastery I stayed in Chaktrül Rinpoche's home. To some forty bright students, I gave:

▸ the permissory initiation and explanatory transmission of Jamyang Khyentse Wangpo's *Praise and Sadhana of Manjushri* to increase their intelligence;

▸ the permissory initiation of Pandita Mati's *White Manjushri* and the reading transmission of its sadhana;

▸ Mipam's *Commentary on the Recollection of the Three Jewels Sutra Entitled Melody of Inexhaustible Auspiciousness;*

▸ detailed explanations of Bodhisattva Shantideva's *Way of the Bodhisattva* based on the commentary by Tokmey Zangpo; and of

▸ Jamgön Mipam's *Commentary on the Insight Chapter Entitled Water-Purifying Gem (sher 'grel ke ta ka).*

In addition, to some people who had gathered from the surrounding areas, I taught:

▸ *Words of My Perfect Teacher;*

▸ guidance on *Yeshe Lama;*

- ▸ essential guidance on *Trilogy of Natural Liberation;* and
- ▸ essential guidance on the three places and the three virtues according to *Resting in the Nature of Mind.*

At one point toward the end of my stay, in a dream vision, I came to know that the supreme emanation Penor Rinpoche was departing for another realm. Assuming the array of the illusory body, I traveled to see him. When I inquired after his health, he said, "It seems that this illness has contaminated virtually all of my vital organs and innards, and I no longer wish to remain in this illusory form. I am preparing to leave."

"I can assist you in going to whichever pure realm you wish," I offered.

"I have mastered the instructions on consciousness borne on the energies, so I can go to any realm I choose. In particular, I have recited the six-syllable mantra, the quintessence of the Noble Great Compassionate One, over one hundred million times. I have reached nearly that number of recitations of Palchen Düpa mantras from Rigdzin Jigme Lingpa's *Sadhana of Buddha Mind: Embodiment of the Great Glorious Heruka*, as well. I have frequent visions of Guru Rinpoche, so it will be easy for me to go to either Potala or the Glorious Copper-Colored Mountain. However, I have not had time to be of much service to your teachings on the *Ösel Nyingtik,* so I have great hopes of returning to help you with that. I make the strong aspiration to be reborn at your feet," he said.

"For the time being, that will not help. Karma Chakme Rinpoche wrote in his *Stallion for Selecting a Pure Realm (zhing khams 'dam pa'i rta pho)* that Sukhavati (Dewachen) is best.[331] That's true. Indeed, you can go there for a while and then take whatever emanated form you wish," I suggested.

"Well, for now I will go to Lotus Light.[332] Later, I would greatly appreciate your support for the fulfillment of my wishes," he replied.

Several days later, a messenger arrived to tell me that the illness had become extremely grave and I needed to come. I rushed back, but when I arrived it had been five days since his passing. I released him from his postdeath absorption *(thugs dam)* and made aspirational prayers for the swift arrival of his reincarnation. I prepared his precious mortal remains and arranged the offerings. Karma Yangsi of Palyul and his students also arrived. We performed the funeral ceremonies for about three days. Adzom Drukpa's sons Gyurme Dorje and Kalzang Tendzin both came.

As soon as we had finished the preparations for the cremation, we held the cremation ceremony based on four mandalas, principally the *Gather-*

ing of the Great Assembly and Nyang-rel's *Embodiment of the Sugatas of the Eight Heruka Sadhanas.* On that occasion, there was a strong earth tremor, flat cymbals and bell cymbals spontaneously resounded, the fragrance of incense wafted throughout, and a canopy of five-colored rainbow light interlaced with rainbow spheres pervaded all of space. These and many other wondrous signs filled the minds of his students with awe and inspiration.

Then, after I identified and collected the bone relics, rinsed them and so on, I was invited to Palyul. As a farewell ceremony, we made offerings for about three weeks. Afterward, I gave teachings, along with the empowerments and reading transmissions of the *Four Nyingtik Mother-and-Child Cycles,* to an assembly of fortunate students. When I conferred the empowerments for Rigdzin Jigme Lingpa's *Vajrakila according to the Tantra Tradition (phur pa rgyud lugs),* flames blazed out of the torma during the empowerment of the Vajrakila protector deities, and sparks flew. Several disciples heard the howls and barks of wolves, foxes, and wild dogs.

At one point, I received a letter asking me to come for the enthronement of the Lord Refuge Situ Rinpoche's reincarnation, so I departed for Katok.[333] Khyentse Yangsi Rinpoche, Jamyang Lodrö Gyatso, requested that I preside over the enthronement as vajra master, which I then did. In the past, during the enthronement of Tsangyang Gyatso (the reincarnation of the Great Fifth Dalai Lama), the Great Regent of Tibet, Sangye Gyatso, had asked Minling Terchen for advice, and per his response, he had conferred the bodhisattva empowerment from the *Gathering of the Great Assembly.* Likewise, on this occasion we enthroned Situ Rinpoche's reincarnation as the sovereign lord of the buddha families and their infinite mandalas.

In the autumn of my forty-fifth year, I had dreamed that Tsarchen Losal Gyatso and Jamyang Khyentse Wangchuk of Nesar were with me and my students, such that I could not distinguish whether we were identical to them or separate from them. We were walking along with a white mule loaded down with scriptures. We stopped somewhere for the night and gathered water and firewood. While we were boiling tea, a cluster of three yellow flowers bloomed to the right of the hearth. To the left, a cluster of seven red flowers bloomed. I asked Tsarchen Rinpoche what they meant.

"The three yellow ones are a sign that I will need to take three future rebirths as a fully ordained monk in order to fortify the foundation of the Buddha's teachings. The red ones indicate that you will need to take seven future rebirths as an extraordinary ngakpa," he explained.

"What is this place?" I asked.

"Isn't this Dekyi Khangsarma, near Buchu Temple in Kongpo?" he replied.[334]

When I was fifty-five [1933/4], I entered strict retreat to dispel obstacles and undertook the recitation practice of *Vajrakila: The Unsurpassedly Supreme Secret,* which is a revelation discovered by the great treasure-revealer Ratna Lingpa. I did so because it is an extraordinarily profound and sublime treasure, the core teaching (*mnog chos*) of Guru Rinpoche's buddha mind, which he imparted to Khandro Yeshe Tsogyal, without adding or omitting, augmenting or diminishing anything.

Once in a dream vision, I perceived myself going to Monkha Nering Senge Dzong in Bhutan. At the head of a stream, I arrived at a delightful place by a rocky overhang. There, upon a mandala, inside a triangular Vajrakila treasure chest, I saw a kila fashioned of meteorite and wrapped in blue silk, shaking and spitting flashing sparks. I supplicated it with devotion, and it transformed into Yeshe Tsogyal. Before her, I saw Atsara Saley, her vigilant spiritual consort, who had been bequeathed by Guru Rinpoche, seated in the form of her retreat attendant. With fierce devotion, I sang:

Arising from the space of vajra reality,
Whose very nature is the wisdom body of all the buddhas,
In the treasure trove of your body, blazing with unbearable wrath,[335]
May I be born as your son!

When I made that supplication, the blazing dark-blue triangular kila stand in front of Tsogyal gradually expanded, like ripples in a pond when a stone is tossed. In the center was the blazing dark-blue triangular abode of the principal deity, Vajrakila, rimmed by a fence, outside of which were the abodes of his supreme sons, in the form of a four-spoked wheel of meteorite.[336] Outside of that, in the cardinal and intermediate directions, were the abodes of the eight wrathful kings in the form of an eight-spoked wheel. Above the skylight in the celestial mansion was a solar cushion, in the abode of the wrathful king of the zenith. The seat of the principal deity was in the form of a hollow triangle, its downward-facing three-sided point facing in the direction of the courtyard. In place of the front gate was the seat of the wrathful king of the nadir.

Tsogyal then recited what sounded like the *Root Tantra of Vajrakila.* Kilas, fashioned of meteorite, emanated one after another from her heart center and assumed the triangular form of a Vajrakila treasure chest in each of the abodes of the deities. These further transformed and arose with vivid clarity as the three basic mandalas. With Atsara Saley acting as the ritual officiant, she then conferred the exact empowerment that is contained in her *Collection of Clear Vajrakilaya Commentaries.*

At its conclusion, the ritual officiant began the empowerment of the oath-bound protectors with a long whistling tune.[337] Simultaneously, in an instant, the twelve oath-bound Matarah mother goddesses and the four female gatekeepers arrived in a crowd and conferred a life-force empowerment in the form of a command. Although I supplicated her to bestow *Answers to Tsogyal's Questions,* a treasure revealed by Ratna Lingpa, she replied, "I received this *Commentary on Vajrajkila* from Guru Rinpoche. It is the wisdom mind of the three masters (Padmasambhava, Vimalamitra, and Shilamanju), and I need to teach it to you." So saying, she gave it to me.

Then the three basic mandalas dissolved into Yeshe Tsogyal, and the mandala of the oath-bound protectors dissolved into Atsara Saley. Tsogyal transformed into a nine-pronged meteorite vajra, marked with the blue syllable HUM, and the spontaneous sound of HUM resounded with a whir. That, as well, vanished like a rainbow in the sky, and my awareness, the kila of wisdom, dissolved into the field of unborn reality. I was left for a while without thoughts, in the space where dualistic constructs come to rest.

In another vision, I met Jamgön Kongtrül Lodrö Taye, who looked extremely frail and aged, wearing a single dark-maroon brocade robe. He expressed great joy at the three conferrals of the empowerments and reading transmissions of the *Treasury of Precious Revelations,* which I had given previously. "My revealed treasure, the *Yumka Khandrö Sangtik,* is your inheritance, so I need to bestow the empowerment," he said, and he gave me the empowerment as well as a wonderful dakini tantra.

"In these modern times," he continued, "it has fallen to you to ensure the spiritual and temporal well-being of the Buddhist teachings and beings. However, it is a great loss that you have devoted yourself to such a simple lifestyle."

He delivered numerous other prophecies, but they are not important, so I have not written them down.

Conclusion

Nowadays, in this final era of five hundred years,[338]
Nations and times are base, so the guides of beings are corrupt.

With my feeble faith, diligence, intelligence, and insight,
How could I set forth an authentic, detailed autobiography?
Yet a few learned and accomplished spiritual mentors
Took me into their following,
And so, with strenuous effort and diligence,
I studied, contemplated, and meditated upon
The profound and vast repository of the teachings.
Because of this, my mind is slightly tamed,
And that is due to the kindness of saintly beings.
I have no poetic compositions to gladden myriad scholars.
As for direct realization obtained through spiritual practice,
What have I achieved?
Nevertheless, I have abandoned
The extremes of exaggeration and deprecation,
And I have not kept my ways secret but have spoken honestly.
For those with the karmic destiny to follow me,
The wisdom intent of this lineage
Maintains not one but manifold pith instructions,
Free from pretension, hypocrisy, omissions, and additions.
They are uncorrupted, and I have written of them to inspire confidence.
From the time of the genuinely perfect Buddha
Down to today, the words have remained uncorrupted,
And the wisdom realization of their meaning
Has been handed down from one to the next,
Like goods passed from hand to hand, or like a royal edict.
Indeed, the ultimate lineage of blessings remains unbroken.
The scriptural lineage and the lineage of oral instructions are unbroken
    as well.
Their truth, ungraspable through mental analysis,
Is the ultimate transmission of the supreme secret.[339]
This is a source of confidence for fortunate beings
Who have accumulated merit.
Through the power of composing this shining array of words and
    meanings,
May the delusion in beings' minds be wholly dispelled,
May they experience the truth of the Great Perfection,
And may the two aims be gloriously fulfilled!

Over the years, numerous holders of the three pitakas have urged me to write this autobiography, principally Choktrül Gyurme Dorje, the precious Khenpo Lekshey Jorden, Khenpo Nüden, Tulku Könchok Drakpa, and others. To honor the oft-repeated requests of these awareness-professing spiritual mentors, I, Pema Ledreltsel, composed this at my home in Jönpalung. May it be the cause for perceiving the lama as the Buddha and thereby realizing the level of self-awareness, Samantabhadra!

May virtue prevail! May virtue prevail! May virtue prevail!

Note: Khenpo Ngakchung's autobiography ends in 1933 when he was fifty-five years old. He died in 1941 at the age of sixty-three (sixty-two according to Western calculations), so there are eight years of his life unaccounted for in this volume. These later years, as well as his parinirvana, are detailed in Khenpo Sonam Tenpa's *Elixir That Restores and Increases Faith.* (See appendix 1.)

Appendix 1: Elixir That Restores and Increases Faith

*A Compendium of Miscellaneous Biographical Writings
about the Omniscient Lama Ngakgi Wangpo*

By Khenpo Sonam Tenpa

Indestructible Dharmakaya, wholly free of the extremes of eternalism
and nihilism,
Uncreated Sambhogakaya, by nature devoid of birth and death,
Nirmanakaya emanation beyond the two extremes, taming beings with
unfathomable skillful means,
Indivisible Svabhavikakaya, Omniscient Lama Ngakgi Wangpo, I bow
before you.

The vast ocean of the liberated story of your three secrets,
Is indeed incomprehensible to someone as feebleminded as I.
Yet, with thoughtful analysis, I voice the melody of pure primordial sound
As a cloud of offerings to delight the faithful.

WITH THIS INVITATION, I shall discuss the following. Generally
speaking, noble bodhisattvas abiding on the bodhisattva levels are
unsullied by the marks of birth and death and have actualized the immortal, unchanging vajra body, yet in response to the varying needs of their
students, they reveal themselves in manifold ways. The *Unsurpassed Continuum* states:

So that we may see reality exactly as it is,
Although they have transcended birth and so forth,

The great compassionate ones exhibit birth,
Death, old age, and sickness.

Likewise, these manifestations are simply the expressions of enlightened activity and are not to be construed otherwise. In particular, the Omniscient Lama Ngakgi Wangpo, who is indeed completely inseparable from the ultimate Vajradhara and has attained manifest enlightenment in primordial space, returns again and again in infinite miraculous manifestations to train beings. Here is a brief summary of twenty-five of his incarnations: he manifested three times as prophesied by the Buddha, three times as Indian scholars, three times as powerful yogins, three times as Tibetan translators, three times as great Dharma kings, three times as Tibetan scholars, three times as vidyadhara treasure-revealers, three times as renunciate yogins, and so forth. In particular, his exalted name, Omniscient Lama Ngawang Palzang, also known as Ösel Rinchen Nyingpo Pema Ledreltsel, was renowned throughout the world. He states in his autobiography, *Wondrous Dance of Illusion*—which describes the perfect liberation of his body, speech, and mind—that he is wholly inseparable from the Great Pandita Vimalamitra and the King of the Victorious Ones, Drime Özer (Longchenpa). In this present composition, I have written down a collection of stories told by some of his close disciples, without any exaggeration or omission, and not in any particular order.

The Great Pandita Vimalamitra promised that during the period when the Nyingtik doctrine becomes adulterated by mental speculation, one of his incarnations would come every hundred years. Accordingly, beginning with Dangma Lhündrub Gyaltsen, he has returned every hundred years to dispel the corruptions that have infiltrated the Ösel Nyingtik teachings during the degenerate era. Coming once again for the purpose of clarifying the Nyingtik teachings, he appeared as our own omniscient Lama Ngawang Palzang, an unmistakable emanation of Vimalamitra. His root lama, Lama Lungtok Tenpey Nyima Rinpoche, attended Patrul Orgyen Jigme Chökyi Wangpo for twenty-eight years, relying upon him without separation like a wick and its flame. Finally, when the time came for Lama Lungtok to leave Dzachu Mamo Kamdo and return to his homeland, as per Patrul Rinpoche's orders, Abu caressed Lungtok's head with both his hands and said, "Dear Lungtok, there is no need for you to be sad. Though indeed I myself did not meet the Great Omniscient Longchenpa, before you die you will meet him—there is no doubt about that."

Lungtok, who could not bear to leave, wept as he turned away. After a few steps, he came back and leaned his head against Abu Rinpoche's heart, weeping. Again, caressing his head, Abu Rinpoche repeated what he had said about meeting the Omniscient One. Lungtok thrice returned to Abu, and each time Abu comforted him in the same way.

Lama Lungtok then spent three years in the Jangsem Cave at Katok Monastery, and afterward he roamed at random to mountain hermitages. Once, while he was staying at Dodrub Gar, he announced, "I need to go home. I have dreamed repeatedly of a golden stupa lying on its side in the lower Sershung Valley, at the base of the mountain just east of Nyoshul Jönpalung. I am right on the verge of erecting it each time the dream ends. The time has come for me to teach."

On a plateau near Yel-le Gar, Lama Lungtok established a mountain hermitage called Pema Rito Gar, where he resided permanently. Before many hundreds of students who had gathered around him, Lama Lungtok repeated what Kind Abu Rinpoche had said. Pointing to Khenpo Ngakchung, he said, "If this child is not the Omniscient One, then I shall not have met him in this lifetime. That is for certain. After all, while in general it is difficult to accurately identify the emanations of the Great Omniscient One, the hundred-year period during which Vimalamitra's emanation is to appear is about to end. Moreover, this child recited the Vajrakila mantra when he was only three days old, he ejected the consciousness of a dzo calf, his body bears the natural markings of the hand emblems of the five buddha families, and there is an AH on the tip of his nose. The expressive power of insight and loving compassion spontaneously arose within him. From every vantage point, there is no doubt that he is an emanation of the Great Omniscient One."

He thereby recognized Khenpo Ngakchung and sang his praises. Thus, the emanation of the inseparable three secrets of the Omniscient Dharma King Drime Özer was none other than the Omniscient Lama Ngawang Palzang, the banner of whose renown is exalted throughout the world.

Once when he was young, he went with his sister, Kharli, to herd the sheep. At noon, while he and his sister were playing, he ran off and returned with several unusual, fist-sized gold statues. He arranged them on a shelf and set out offerings in front of them. That night they left the statues there, but the next day when they returned, only the shelf remained. There was not a single statue in sight.

Another time, when he and his sister went to herd their sheep, a ewe got stuck on the side of a steep, rocky cliff and was unable to get down. Khenpo Ngakchung put a stone in his slingshot and shot it, breaking the ewe's leg. Now the ewe was even more helpless, so Khenpo climbed up the rock face and pushed her off. She tumbled down three stories to the ground and lay writhing on the verge of death. Khenpo and his sister left her there while they went to retrieve the rest of the flock. Khenpo's sister, wondering what they should do and fearing the scolding they would get from their parents, sat down to drink some tea. When she looked again, she saw that the ewe had rejoined the herd and had no signs of injury whatsoever! Overjoyed, she told her brother. He just smiled.

Another time, when the two siblings went to herd cattle in the hills above Jönpalung, Khenpo's sister, Kharli, saw an enormous monastery complete with assembly hall in the place where the actual monastery stands today. When she told Khenpo Ngakchung, he replied, "That is a sign that a large monastery will be built there in the future." This prophecy and the other stories were recounted by his sister, Kharli.

Khenpo Ngakchung spent a total of six years attending the lotus feet of his karmic lama of lifetimes, Lungtok Rinpoche, without separation. He received the Great Perfection *Longchen Nyingtik* preliminaries and main practices in their entirety, and through the transference of the blessings of the true transmission of wisdom realization, the minds of guru and disciple became one.

In accordance with his lama's orders, Khenpo Ngakchung went to study at Dzogchen Monastery and spent three years at Shri Singha College.[340] He listened to, contemplated, and mastered the sutras and tantras, as well as the five sciences, thereby wholly perfecting the expressive power of his insight. Word of his brilliant scholarship spread far and wide.

Then, in the year of the Male Earth Monkey [1908], when Khenpo Ngak-chung was thirty years old, based on the unanimous prophetic commands of Lama Lungtok, the great treasure-revealer Ngawang Tendzin, and the Dharma Lord Mipam Rinpoche, as well as the admonitions of the Sole Mother Palden Lhamo, and in accordance with the wishes of the Sovereign Lord of the Teachings, Situ Chökyi Gyatso, Khenpo Ngakchung spent a total of thirteen years serving as abbot of the Shedrub Norbü Lhünpo Tantric College at Glorious Katok Monastery. His work for the benefit of beings was as vast as the sky. He had over thirty students who were able to teach, debate, and write without effort or hindrance, and who were definitely capable of working for others' welfare.

One day during that period, his attendant, Yönga, finished preparing

Khenpo Ngakchung's noontime meal and waited, but Khenpo did not come. Another monk wondered if he should go call Khenpo, but he eventually turned up late that afternoon. When presented with his meal, Khenpo said, "I'm not hungry, but I'm extremely thirsty. Today the great treasure-revealer Nyoshul Ngawang Tendzin's mother passed away. They asked me to oversee the distribution of her corpse to the birds, so I could not refuse them. But when I went there, people were eating so much meat that I was overcome with nausea, and now my mouth tastes like vomit. I need to drink some tea." That day was the new moon of the fourth lunar month. When they checked later, Lama Palgyey learned that the great treasure-revealer's mother had indeed passed away on that very day.

Once, an old man named Dratruk went crazy and began running around naked. His friends caught him, got him dressed, and took him before Khenpo Ngakchung. The mere sight of Khenpo's face restored the man's sanity, and he blurted out, "I have to cover up my penis!" Everyone burst out laughing. Khenpo Gyaltsen Özer told me these stories.

One time, when the dzomos and cows in Horpo District had stopped producing milk, Khenpo said to the animals, "If you don't produce milk, there's a good chance you'll be slaughtered, so you had better start producing nicely!" As soon as the animals heard this news, they began producing milk, and everyone gained faith in the Khenpo.

Another time, in the Tantric College, a monk named Nyakla Neykyab was stricken with an ear infection that caused him continual, unbearable pain, day and night. He went to Khenpo to ask for a blessing. With an angry look on his face, Khenpo shouted, "Who are you, you ill-fated wretch?" and boxed him in the ear. Terrified, the monk fled, but as soon as he reached his room, his ear was cured.

Another monk named Tashi got liver disease, and when he was on the verge of death, Khenpo gave him a lump of his leftover tsampa. The monk ate it right away, and he immediately recovered from his illness.

Also, in the Nyingön Retreat Center at Katok, there was a lama from Gyarong who served as session master.[341] Once, when it was time to break for lunch, he failed to blow the conch to signal the end of the session, and they ran overtime. The retreatants eventually found the lama lying motionless on his bed. Thinking him dead, they went to call Khenpo. "He's not dead, he's in a coma. Say HIK in his ear and he'll get up," Khenpo instructed. They did as they were told and sure enough, the lama came to and reached for his teacup to finish his tea, which made everyone laugh.

One time, Khenpo went to the town of Horpo Ley and from there looked up at the extremely high mountain peak to the left of the town of Eyjung. "There used to be a Bönpo monastery up there. Two lifetimes ago, I was head of that monastery," he remarked casually. Later, several people went to the top of the mountain to confirm this, and indeed they found an old abandoned monastery. This immeasurably increased their faith.

One time, Kyabje Katok Situ Chökyi Gyatso dreamed of a big lake with a lotus in the middle, adorned with a volume of scripture and a sword, surrounded by four lotuses in the four cardinal directions, which multiplied infinitely.[342] He said that the eastern lotus with scripture and sword was Jönpalung, and commanded that a new monastery be built there. According to this dream, and also based on the fact that Jönpalung was the principal seat of Lama Lungtok Rinpoche and the landscape is naturally endowed with the fourfold features of the supremely sacred Glorious Copper-Colored Mountain, a new monastery was built without hindrance in the year of the Male Water Dog [1922]. The monastery contains representations of buddha body, speech, and mind, such as a Guru Rinpoche statue handmade by the great treasure-revealer Vidyadhara Longsal Nyingpo, which liberates upon seeing. Khenpo Ngakchung says the successful construction of the monastery was due to the kindness and compassion of Kyabje Katok Situ Rinpoche.

During the latter half of his life, Khenpo Ngakchung resided permanently at this monastery in Jönpalung, satiating his students with the nectar of vast and profound Dharma. In particular, by means of the innermost secret Great Perfection *Longchen Nyingtik* preliminaries, the vital-essence pith instructions of the Whispered Lineage from the Omniscient Great Vidyadhara Jigme Lingpa, and direct introductions to reality in all its nakedness, free of mental analysis, many of his students became supremely realized and perfected the insight of the four visions. Today, his disciples and granddisciples and so forth span the globe.

Once, while Khenpo was staying at the monastery in Jönpalung, everyone saw him carrying fresh butter in his hands, which he then used to write the six syllables of spontaneous liberation (A AH SHA SA MA HA) on the mountainside above the monastery, and the letters remained miraculously manifest on the rock. On that same rock face, he drew an elephant just for fun, as well as the twelve syllables of the vajra guru mantra all mixed up. These one can plainly see even today.

One day, Khenpo said to a group of his students, including his bursar,

Bikli Sonam, "To the north of this monastery, behind the nearby Khamdo mountainside, there is a boulder the size of a storeroom. It is in an inauspicious geomantic position for our monastery, and it needs to be destroyed." They used hatchets and heat from fires, and finally a yak-sized rock broke off, revealing three paper-thin frogs that were experiencing the torments of an ephemeral hell realm. When they fell to the ground, they grew until they were the size of normal frogs. The students put them in a bag and took them to Khenpo. When they arrived, one frog had mysteriously disappeared. They placed the other two frogs in front of him.

"When the Nyoshul settlement was first being established," Khenpo explained, "an official and his wife came and demanded a great deal of money in taxes, beat people, and so forth—hence this rebirth. At the time, they made a small connection with me, so I am now able to guide them. The other one had no connection with me, so I'm unable to guide him at this point. But before long, he will attain liberation and will no longer have to experience suffering."

When he performed the transference of consciousness using a Vajrasattva ablution ritual, the frogs stared straight into Khenpo's face and died.

In Kham and various other parts of Tibet, noxious local spirits intent on harming beings, who no one else could tame, surrendered themselves to Khenpo's protection, overwhelmed by the power of his genuine compassion. They offered him their life and heart, promising to fulfill his every command. Khenpo bound them under oath to accomplish his enlightened activities, as well as those of his retinue and his reincarnations, and he assigned them abodes in each of the directions around the Jönpalung monastery. They included Norbu Yulgyal, Yönten Ritra, Yungdrung Taktsey, Tingdzin Gyalmo, and so on. When they first appeared before Khenpo, some of them offered blacksmith tables, and others offered rosebush cutting—hence the large rosebushes one sees here today.

In accordance with Katok Situ Rinpoche's orders, Khenpo held annual great-accomplishment ceremonies based on Troröl (*khro rol*) practices of the Mindroling Eight Heruka Sadhanas tradition to consecrate amrita medicine. From the medicinal powder inside the mandala, an actual image of the Great Glorious Mahottara Heruka with three faces and six hands emerged. When they showed it to Khenpo, he said, "What is this? It looks like a scorpion. Mix it in with the blessed medicine and make pills."

The following year, an image emerged of Vajradhara seated in vajra posture. Some of the students said, "Last year we just mixed the Great Glorious Heruka image into the medicine, so this year let's not bother asking Khenpo. Let's just mix it in with the medicine."

Later, they told Khenpo what they had done. "Oh, you're worthless! You were supposed to keep that image for the curse prayer!" he scolded.

Another time, the sand mandala became completely covered with small black myrobalan fruits. They were mixed in with the medicine, which then became liberating upon tasting and was renowned as the Sacred Black Medicine.

Also, in the fifth lunar month of the Iron Dragon year, during the Troröl Eight Heruka Sadhana great-accomplishment ceremony for consecrating medicine, inside the mandala, a great fire blazed out from beneath the main daka skull-cup. When flames spread outside the assembly hall skylight, everyone screamed. Even throwing water could not quell the fire.

A moment later when the fire had died down, Khenpo, who was leading the ceremony, asked, "What was all the hullabaloo?"

They explained what had happened.

"You unlucky fools. When wisdom fire blazes, how can ordinary water possibly put it out?" Khenpo replied.

That batch of medicine became known as Sacred Fire Medicine.

On that occasion, Khenpo Münsel was seated in the assembly row, and he was the one who described this to me. I heard about it from Tsering Gyatso and many of Khenpo's other close disciples as well.

On another occasion, at Glorious Katok, Khenpo was conferring the *Nyingtik Mother-and-Child* ripening empowerments to Dechab Choktrül Jamyang Losel Dorje and others. During the expressive-power-of-awareness empowerment, Khenpo opened his shirt and revealed a bright, sparkly, eight-inch-tall blue HUM syllable at his heart center, as well as a white AH syllable on the tip of his nose, which looked as if it were about to drop off. Dechab Choktrül Jamyang Losel Dorje saw them and said to me, "He really and truly is Vimalamitra."

One time, when Dechab Choktrül Jamyang Losel Dorje went to see the Khenpo, Khenpo said, "Jamyang, do you want to go see the Lhasa Jowo?"

"What need is there for anything beyond the teachings of Chödrub?" Lama Jamyang asked.

"That's exactly right," Khenpo replied. "Whether the matter is large or small, one must consult one's lama. Generally speaking, nowadays everyone, regardless of how much study and reflection they have done, consults only the Sarma scriptures and then becomes an adherent of the Sarma schools.[343] However, Khenpo Sonam Chödrub, despite spending many years studying the Sarma scriptures at Dza Sershul Monastery, became a strict adherent of the Nyingma. Chödrub Rinpoche is currently the only person who embraces the unerring philosophy taught by Lama Mipam Rinpoche. Staying at Katok won't help you a bit. Go and see Chödrub Rinpoche."

This I heard directly from Lama Jamyang.

The vast majority of Khenpo's students clearly perceived the AH syllable on the tip of his nose. It was especially distinct whenever he displayed a wrathful expression. On his body, he had the images of the hand emblems of the five buddha families in full color, and his secret sign, like the king of horses, the "all-knowing horse," was withdrawn within its sheath.[344] He had these and various other marks and signs of a Vimalamitra incarnation.

One time, the Kardzey Khangsar chieftain invited Khenpo to visit. As they were preparing to enter a hot spring, Khenpo addressed his close disciples, Khen Aghey, Asang, and so forth, and said, "You've missed out. I have a mark that makes them claim I'm an emanation of Vimalamitra." He showed them a prominent, thumb-sized mole, half-white and half-black, on his right inner thigh. That particular mark is mentioned in the *Khandro Nyingtik:*

> On the inside of the right thigh,
> There is a mole like a dakini's eye.

Likewise, the many marks of buddha body, speech, and mind described in the Great Perfection tantras were all clearly perceptible.

One time, Chaktrül Pema Trinley Gyatso and his disciples went to Lhasa. When they got to the top of the eastern snowy mountain pass, one of their pack mules, which was loaded down with bags, tumbled down the steep glacial face of the mountainside and crashed all the way down to the valley floor. Chaktrül Rinpoche, not knowing what else to do, cried out in anguish, "Omniscient Ngakgi Wangpo, think of me! Omniscient Ngakgi Wangpo, think of me!" Instantly, clear as day, he beheld the Omniscient Lama in front of him, smiling radiantly. Chaktrül was overcome with such immense faith and devotion that he wept until his heart was eased. The pack mule and its bags were utterly unharmed, and this he knew was due to the Lama's compassion.

On his way home, he went to see the precious Katok Khenpo Ngakgi

Wangpo. As soon as he saw him, Khenpo said, "Did you hear about the old pack mule that fell off the eastern snowy mountain pass, and the faint-hearted young monk who was so sad that he sat there and cried?"

Chaktrül put his head on Khenpo's knee and said through tears, "You saved his life!"

One time, a lama named Nyakla Ata, who taught at Gyüdey Monastery, went outside to relieve himself in the middle of the night. It was pitch-dark and he had no lantern, so he lost his way. He saw a flash of light, and just as he was about to step off the ledge of the temple skylight, someone grabbed him from behind and prevented him from falling. The next day he went to see Khenpo Ngakchung, who said, "Goodness, if I hadn't been there last night, you would have died!" He knew then that the Khenpo had saved his life.

When the time came, Khenpo went to Katok and gave extensive ripening empowerments and liberating instructions, such as the *Four Nyingtik Mother-and-Child Cycles* and Dampa Deshek Rinpoche's *Trio of the Peaceful and Wrathful Deities and Vajrakilaya,* but I won't go into that here.

One morning in the year of the Female Water Pig [1923], during the ninth lunar month, Khenpo said, "I dreamed that Lama Yönten and I were in the main assembly hall of Jönpalung Monastery tying an auspicious good-day scarf on the Avalokitesvara Kasharpani statue. I wonder what it means . . . "

That day, Yönten brought Dorje Chökyong, then four years old, to receive a blessing. Khenpo recognized him as the reincarnation of Lama Lungtok, and he seated the boy upon his own seat before the warmth had left it and enthroned him. Khenpo, Khen Dorli, and the others prostrated themselves before the boy and performed the enthronement benediction.

Another time, in the year of the Wood Rat [1924], when Khenpo was in Dralak conferring the *Treasury of Precious Revelations* with its supporting ripening empowerments and liberating instructions, a white flower with a hundred petals bloomed in the temple corridor inside the assembly hall. It did not wilt until the empowerments were complete. This and many other wondrous signs occurred.

Once during that period, the leftover rice in the Khenpo's jade bowl was divided among the students, including Chaktrül and some others. Khenpo asked the monk Gönten to distribute it. He did so, but there wasn't enough rice to go around. At the time, a monk named Lodrö Zangpo scoffed, "Boy, is that Derge lama ever full of himself, serving us his leftovers—even to Chaktrül Rinpoche!"

A short time later, a terrible plague of bloody dysentery broke out, and those who had the chance to eat Khenpo's leftover rice were not sick at all. The others fell very ill, and in particular the monk with misconceptions of the Khenpo came very close to death. This restored and increased everyone's faith.

There was also a monk named Lalo who was afflicted with a kind of insanity, and none of the medicines, ablutions, or Chöd rituals that Khenpo offered him helped. One day, when Lalo went to see Khenpo, Khenpo picked up a sharp knife that was lying on a plate of mutton in front of him and plunged it into Lalo's back, between the spine and shoulder blade, sinking the knife in all the way up to its hilt. Fresh red blood spurted out, and Khenpo, angered by the blood in his room, ordered him to leave. He left, and a moment later when Khenpo's anger had cooled, he called to the monk, "Lalo, you poor thing, come here." The other monks were terrified and rushed to Lalo's side to support him. They brought him before the Khenpo, who gently rubbed the wound with his hand. Khenpo put some of his saliva on the wound, and instantly the blood stopped flowing and the wound healed. The illness, too, was completely cured from that moment on.

Later, Khenpo Ngakchung's reincarnation said that Lalo had told him he still had a scar on his back.

There was a monk from the Getsey Horama Monastery, who was from the Gönten family. They were terribly poor and owned only eight dri (female yaks) and about fifteen sheep. One day, the monk and his brother decided to slaughter a ewe and invite the Khenpo to visit. Planning to offer him their best dri when he came, they set off to see the Khenpo. They offered him a large chunk of mutton and invited him to visit them.

"Very well, you go home and cook the ewe's head whole, without cutting the meat off the bones, and I'll come," Khenpo said.

When Khenpo arrived at their home, he ate all the head meat and all the broth, as well as a big chunk of meat, six bowls of yogurt, and about five bowls of Tibetan sweet potatoes (dro ma) with clarified butter, down to the last bite.

"We would like to offer you the best of our eight dri. You have been so kind. Please accept it," they said.

"I am wealthier than you are, but in order to complete your accumulations of merit and wisdom, I will accept your dri. Soon you will grow rich," Khenpo replied.

Years later, when Khenpo's reincarnation came to Dralak, they invited him to visit.

"We now have over two hundred head of cattle and just as many sheep, plus money and riches. All this sumptuous wealth is thanks to Khenpo's kindness," they said, and they showered the reincarnation with gifts.

When the great Khenpo Ngakchung went to the nomadic settlements on an alms round, Domna Lama Gönpo Tendzin thought to himself, "This lama looks so splendid, and from every perspective he seems just like Marpa the Translator, the wellspring of Kagyü protectors in the Land of Snows. And I am just like his disciple, Milarepa!"

Instantly, Khenpo looked down from his horse with imposing majesty and said, "Even if I were to come in Lord Marpa's stead, would you really be able to endure hardships like Milarepa?"

Another time, after Khenpo had finished giving the empowerments for the *Treasury of Precious Revelations,* he gave the reading transmission of his autobiography. When he came to the part about his reincarnation being reborn in Kongpo, Chaktrül promised to be in charge of the reincarnation, and Khenpo expressed great happiness. During the empowerment commitments, Khenpo ordered that Chaktrül Rinpoche should grant both the empowerments and reading transmissions for the *Treasury of Precious Revelations* to Khenpo's reincarnation, and Chaktrül Rinpoche promised that he would.

In the year of the Wood Ox [1925], Khenpo went to Katok to preside over a special ceremony with a thousand monks in attendance. Situ Rinpoche passed away, and Khenpo performed all the concluding rituals. To those assembled, he conferred the empowerments and reading transmissions for the *Four Nyingtik Mother-and-Child Cycles,* the two root volumes of the *Longchen Nyingtik,* and so forth.

In the year of the Dog, after transmitting the *Treasury of Precious Revelations,* he returned home to Jönpalung. To Tulku Arik (Rigdzin Wangchuk), Dongtok Tulku, and some others, he taught the *Four Branches of the Nyingtik* (*Nyingtik Yabshi*), the two *Longchen Nyingtik* root volumes, the preliminary *Words of My Perfect Teacher* and *A Guide to the Words of My Perfect Teacher,* the *Guhyagarbha Tantra,* the *Kalachakra Tantra,* the *Seven Treasuries* along with miscellaneous teachings of Longchenpa, Kedrup Je's *Essential Exposition, Opening the Eyes of the Fortunate,* the *Generation and Completion Stages of the Peaceful and Wrathful Deities,* the *Whispered-Lineage Cycle,* and *Unimpeded Realization of the Great Perfection.*

In the year of the Iron Sheep [1931], to lamas including Katok Khenchen Gyaltsen Özer, Khenpo Orgyen Rigdzin, Khenpo Norko, Gyamda Tulku, and Tulku Orgyen Dorje, Khenpo taught works such as the *Nyingtik Yabshi* and the *Longchen Nyingtik* root volumes, the *Seventeen Tantras Whispered-Lineage Cycle,* the preliminary *Words of My Perfect Teacher* and *A Guide to the Words of My Perfect Teacher,* the guidance text *Yeshe Lama,* his own commentary on *Entering the Middle Way,* and Jigme Lingpa's *Collected Works.*

When Palyul Drubwang Rinpoche fell seriously ill, Khenpo went to Palyul and performed extensive healing rituals. Then he went to Dralak to establish a new Buddhist college and returned home to give elaborate guidance on the preliminaries, main practices, and the *Longchen Nyingtik* channels-and-energies practices to Chaktrül, Tulku Gyurlo, Khenpo Gyaltsen Özer, and others.

In the year of the Wood Dog [1934], to Drakmar Khenpo, Lama Palden Yeshe, Khenpo Kalzang, Jang Tsultrim Zangpo, and others, Khenpo taught works such as the restricted sections of the *Treasury of Precious Revelations, Yeshe Lama, Yumka, The Excellent Wish-Fulfilling Vase,* Kongtrül Rinpoche's *Embodiment of the Wisdom Mind of the Three Roots* (*rtsa gsum dgongs 'dus*),[345] and teachings from the *Nyingma Transmitted Teachings.*

That year, Tersey Chimey went to see the Khenpo, but the Tromchu River was flooded and his packhorse could not cross. Without hesitation, he plunged in and tried to cross, but he was swept downstream and submerged up to his neck. Terrified, he called out, "Omniscient Lama Ngakgi Wangpo, think of me!" and instantly, right in front of him, he vividly beheld the master. Immediately, as if waking from a dream, he found himself on the other side of the river.

That day, the great Khenpo Ngakchung announced that a welcome party should be sent to receive Tersey Chimey, who had come to visit. They set out, and as soon as Tersey Chimey arrived, Khenpo said, "Heh heh, aren't you embarrassed? Today when you were crossing that little creek, you got so scared you hollered for my help!"

He bestowed many profound teachings upon Tersey Chimey, such as the Whispered Lineage cycle, the preliminary and main practices, and so forth. He also gave him the wooden kila that he had used as a child to reverse the stream.

In the year of the Wood Dog [1934],[346] when the Chinese army invaded Tibet, he performed extensive rituals, such as *Wrathful Guru Blazing Wisdom* and the *Eight Heruka Sadhanas Wrathful Torma Exorcism.*

He conferred many profound teachings upon the great treasure-revealer

Ngawang Tendzin's son, Bhadi, as well as Apey, Atrin, Akal, and others, and he took a kila known as the "Lang Kila" down from the mandala and blessed them with it.

In the year of the Earth Hare in the sixteenth sixty-year cycle [1939],[347] Khenpo entered a strict Vajrakilaya retreat. The following year, he went to Katok and gave numerous empowerments and reading transmissions, including the Great Perfection scriptures of the threefold Sutra, Magical Net, and Mind series, Dampa Deshek's *Trio of Peaceful and Wrathful Deities and Vajrakilaya,* the *Nyingtik Yabshi,* and the *Longchen Nyingtik* root volumes.

In the year of the Iron Dragon [1940], in accordance with Kyabje Katok Situ Rinpoche's prosphesied aims, Khenpo established a new tantric college called Kunkhyen Do-Ngag Shedrub Chöling, "Dharma Center of Omniscient Sutra and Tantra Teaching and Practice." When the foundation was being laid, a wondrous, gem-shaped stone was found—the one that is currently on display—naturally marked with the syllables A RA PA TSA NA, the essence-syllables DHI and HRI, and a white conch.

Also, at that time, Khenpo gave many teachings to Khenpo Münsel and others who were gathered there, including the preliminary and main practices, *Yeshe Lama,* the *Whispered-Lineage Cycle, Imitation Meteorite,* and *Meteorite Scorpion.*

One of the walls in the college assembly hall was leaning dangerously to one side, on the verge of collapse, and the monks had no idea what to do. Khenpo Münsel said to the Khenpo, "The college assembly-hall wall is going to fall down. What should we do?"

"Oh, if an Indian pandita were here, that would be easy. Without one, there's nothing that can be done," Khenpo replied.

The next morning, sure that the wall had collapsed, Khenpo Münsel went to look. The wall had been completely restored and was now perfectly erect, as straight as if someone had drawn a line with a ruler. Khenpo Münsel, in the midst of a gathering of hundreds of students, declared, "My Lama is really and truly the Great Pandita Vimalamitra in person."

One day, Khenpo declared, "Khenpo Münsel will definitely benefit the Buddhist teachings in a vast way, both generally and specifically, so we should enthrone him today." The whole community of students and the great Khenpo Lama Ngakchung himself constructed a sod throne, upon which Khenpo Münsel was enthroned. In general, Khenpo Münsel infinitely spread the Nyingtik teachings, and specifically, by accepting Lhasey

Shedrub Tendzin Nyima, the reincarnation of Lama Lungtok, as his disciple, his benefit to beings at places such as the monastic seat in Jönpalung is unmistakable.

Again, to Sögyal of the Yönru family, Kholri Tulku, and others, Khenpo Ngakchung taught the preliminary and main practices, including the *Four Branches of the Nyingtik,* the *Seven Treasuries, Vajrakilaya according to the Tantra Section,* the *Whispered-Lineage Cycle, Peaceful and Wrathful Mayajala,* the *Samdhisamgraha Sutra,* sections of Chöd empowerments, and *Wrathful Guru Blazing Wisdom.*

In the middle of the valley below the monastery, there was a small hillock with a multi-storied stone structure built upon it that contained the remains of the king of Tromtar. Some of the students asked if they could dismantle the ruins. Khenpo replied, "No, that would not be good. The place is haunted by nonhumans, gods, and ghosts. But if we were to destroy it, your ability to do so would be nothing compared to mine. Back when I took rebirth as Chökyong Bernak of Gadeh, a kinsman of Gesar of Ling, I was so skilled with the catapult that I still haven't forgotten it. With a rock and a catapult, I could smash that structure to smithereens in an instant. But there is no need."

One day, Khenpo Ngakchung climbed up the hill behind his monastic residence at Jönpalung. Displaying a wrathful expression, he seized an enormous boulder with his right hand and miraculously hurled it into space. It grazed the trunk of a big pine tree, snapping it in two, and continued with a roar for nearly three leagues [13.5 miles]. It is the very one we see today over there in Kyilko, lying like a ball of butter on a plate.

At one point, when Khenpo was traveling toward Markham, he stopped along the road and told Bikli Sonam and the rest of his monk retinue, "Back when I was fighting with a bow and arrow and a catapult in the Battle between the Kingdoms of Hor and Ling,[348] I wore an ivory ring on my thumb, but it was uncomfortable, so I buried it. I need to look for it now." He dug a hole and extracted a bowl-sized, ivory thumb-ring that sparkled brightly. Everyone saw it. He started to take it with him but then ordered, "The time is not right. I cannot take it. Put it back where it was and bury it." The students, who had no choice but to do as he said, were very much disappointed. I have heard this story told numerous times.

One time, while Khenpo was staying in the Markham area, a man disturbed by a jealous spirit offered Khenpo a poisoned dish. Aware of this, Khenpo ate all of the food so as to fulfill the man's wishes. For those with ordinary perception, he displayed signs of illness, and Khenpo's attendants were miserable. In a vision, Khenpo journeyed to the Glorious Mountain Lotus Light pure realm and visited his mother.

"What are you doing here?" his mother asked.

"I came because I was poisoned," Khenpo replied.

"What? Getting poisoned is no excuse. You still haven't finished benefiting the teachings and beings, so don't come here," she scolded.

With renewed determination, Khenpo promised he would work hard for the teachings and beings, and he returned to his body. Following that, all signs of illness vanished.

Another time, when Khenpo was returning home from Katok, at a very narrow point in the path along a steep mountainside in the Rakchab region, a large fallen pine tree was blocking the way. Seeing no other option, Khenpo, with an expression of extreme, unbearable wrath, lifted the towering tree in his hands and hurled it to the valley floor.

Later, while they were taking their noon tea along the path, his companions sat whispering among themselves.

"What are you talking about?" Khenpo asked.

"The way you threw that tree," they answered.

"That might have happened because I had a vision of myself hurling a big tree that blocked the way back when I was with the Ling warriors . . ." Khenpo mused.

He thereby acknowledged that he was an emanation of Gadey, and he brought forth the *Secret Sadhana of Gesar Entitled Vajra Fortress* (*ge sar gyi gsang sgrub rdo rje'i rdzong mkhar*).[349]

Another time, Khenpo erected a clay statue of the wrathful Achala in Jönpalung. While he was reciting the *Vajrakilaya Ritual of Demon Suppression* (*phur pa sri mnan*), he grew wrathful and began beating the shrine attendant, Shasang, with his book stand. The shrine attendant and the others were terrified and put their heads on the floor. Once his anger had cooled a bit, they peeked up at him and directly beheld the great Khenpo as Vajrakilaya, with nine heads and eighteen arms, his body filling all of space and absorbing wisdom flames. On that occasion, my uncle Rabjor was seated with the statue-makers, and I heard this story directly from him.

Likewise, many have seen Khenpo manifest himself in deity form during the consummation of the three aspects of objective perception in the generation stage of sadhana practice.

One time, a lama named Draktrül encountered Khenpo Ngakchung on the road near a nomad camp in Nyarong Absey. Draktrül thought to himself, "This Khenpo is famous . . . today I'll put him to the test and see for myself what he's like."

The moment Draktrül saw the Khenpo, he perceived him as the great king Vaishravana, guardian of the northern direction, golden in color, hands and face blazing with dazzling light rays. Instantly, all his thoughts stopped and he fell to the ground unconscious. When he came to, he touched his head to the Khenpo's feet with fervent yearning born of faith and devotion, and became his disciple.

To Lord Khyentse Chökyi Lodrö, Katok Getse Gyurme Tenpa Namgyal, Tulku Kunzang Nyendrak, and others, Khenpo Ngakchung taught the *Four Branches of the Nyingtik* and *Yeshe Lama,* and to the great Khenpo in particular, he gave detailed guidance on the extraordinary Whispered Lineage of the *Khandro Yangtik* contained in the guidance text *Cloudbanks of the Ocean of Profound Meaning.*

When Khenpo Orgyen requested a divination regarding the rebirth of his late mother, Khenpo told him she had been reborn as a bird in the bamboo forests of a buddha realm. At a later point, he said, "Your mother, who was reborn as a bird in the bamboo forest, was eaten whole by a poisonous snake, but now she'll take rebirth as an authentic, fully ordained monk in the region of Kham and will gradually be liberated from samsara."

Once, during a Dharma teaching to a large assembly at Katok, Khenpo exclaimed, "Oh no, the monk Yangpel, who stole a large amount of money and belongings from Katok Situ Rinpoche, has been reborn as an enormous fish, his body as big as Ösel Dong Mountain to the left of Nyin Monastery! The poor thing!"

Another time, Khenpo was on his way to Dago Lhari Ösel Ling near Palyul Monastery and stopped to rest along the road. He said to his students, "I need to make a torma. See if you can find some clay."

His students Sangten and Angyur found an already-formed lump of clay the size of a teapot and brought it to the Khenpo.

When Khenpo broke it open with his hands, he found an eight-inch, liberation-upon-seeing statue of Guru Rinpoche, made of precious materials. "Oh, this is wonderful," he said. "Although I am a pure monk in this life, I will be an authentic mantrin with a wife and children in my next life, and this gold statue will dispel obstacles to that rebirth. Bursar Bikli Sonam, don't lose this."

Later, before Khenpo's reincarnation was born, Tulku Ado [the reincarnation of Lama Lungtok] gave the gold statue to Khenpo's future mother.

Another time, Khenpo performed a healing ransom ritual at a family's home in Markham. Simply directing his attention at the sheep effigy in front of him caused it to spin around in circles. When he imparted guidance to his students, simply by focusing his attention on them, they were directly introduced to naked awareness. When he conferred empowerments and taught the Whispered Lineage teachings, many students experienced indications of the wisdom deity descending, such as their bodies bouncing, swaying, and dancing, their voices uttering various sounds and words, and their minds experiencing faith, renunciation, and the nonconceptual union of bliss and clarity. Jamyang Losel Dorje, Khenpo Gyaltsen Özer, and others have much to say about this, but because many are suspicious of such things, I have not written it down.

At one point, Khenpo gave his old lotus crown to Tulku Ado, the holy reincarnation of Lungtok Tenpey Nyima, and placing the reincarnation upon his bed, Khenpo enthroned him as his regent. He sang his praises, and having entrusted him with all his material belongings, both inside and outside of the monastic residence, Khenpo appointed Tulku Ado as his representative at his monastic seat.

In the twelfth month of the Iron Dragon year [January 1941], at the behest of the king of Derge, Khenpo went to Lhündrup Teng, "Palace of Spontaneous Perfection,"³⁵⁰ and performed the *Thread-Cross of Mahakala and Mahakali That Averts Worldly Battles* and taught *Commissioning Protection from Local Guardian Spirits* (*sa bdag gtad srung*).

"On this occasion, we need to set out sumptuous offerings and recite elaborate supplications and aspirations. Generally speaking, since these are times of spiritual degeneration, this printing house, the Great Treasury of Dharma, is of inestimable value. It is like the essence of the Buddhist teachings. Also, this old monk needs to make himself useful regarding sickness and death." Khenpo then performed healing rituals for many days, during which time fire and smoke emerged from the tormas, and the wick stick spontaneously caught fire, its smoke curling around the mountain and over the pass to the back of the mountain.³⁵¹ Everyone heard a roaring sound.

In the third lunar month of the Iron Snake year [April 1941], Khenpo traveled to Glorious Katok and announced that he needed to offer the Düdül Longsel empowerments and reading transmissions to the reincarnations of Katok Situ, Moktsa, and Önpo. He then conferred all the ripening empowerments and liberating instructions in their entirety to an assembly of over three hundred monks and lamas, including Tulku Apey, Khenpo Jamyang Gyaltsen, and Khenpo Ah-sher.

At that point, Khenpo displayed signs of a strange illness, with a small trickle of blood emerging from each nostril. The people of Horpo Ley Township carried him by palanquin back to Jönpalung.

In the fourth lunar month [May 1941], the following long-life rituals were performed on Khenpo's behalf: a hundred thousand Vajra Vidarana[352] and Ucchusmakhroda recitations,[353] the *Further Reversal of the Lord of Death* (*gshin rje yang bzlog*); *Reversing the Reception Party of the Dakinis; Thread-Cross of Mahakala and Mahakali That Averts Worldly Battles, Banishing King Spirits;* the *Buddhist Canon* (the Kangyur and Tengyur); and so forth. Students and people in each of the local villages gave up hunting, saved lives, and so forth. The khenpos, tulkus, and the rest of the monastic community at Glorious Katok performed a nearly unfathomable number of long-life rituals, including *Guru Drakpo* and *Banishing King Spirits* rituals to reverse the reception party of the dakinis, one hundred thousand feast offerings, Vajra Vidarana and Ucchusmakhroda, the hundred-syllable mantra, and so forth. The monastic communities in Dralak, Markham, Palyul, and the Nyarong region each offered elaborate healing rituals.

As these long-life rituals were going on, signs of the exhaustion of his life seemed to increase. The *Root Tantra* (*rtsa ba'i rgyud*) states:

As for the vision of the exhaustion of phenomena in reality,
Once visionary experiences have been exhausted,
The body is exhausted, and sense objects are also exhausted.
Once one has been freed from confused thoughts,
One is devoid of words, the basis of expression.

Accordingly, all the indications that Khenpo's body, speech, and mind had reached the level of the exhaustion of phenomena in reality manifested as described in the tantras. Khenpo's younger brother, Hali, peeked through a nail hole in the door, and he said that at times the Khenpo's body had completely disappeared from his bed. At other times he saw a mass of rainbow light. At night, in the lamplight, Khenpo's body cast no shadow at all. Others present saw exactly what the brother saw. Outside Khenpo's monastic residence, as well, onlookers saw his room completely surrounded with light at night.

When his attendants said, "Please eat this, please drink this," Khenpo replied, "Please eat this, please drink this." When they asked, "Are you feeling well today?" Khenpo replied, "Are you feeling well today?" Aside from repeating what was said, Khenpo said nothing at all. All his utterances had become echoes.

Years before, when the great Khenpo was thirty-eight years old and was exerting himself in the *Hundred Deities of Tushita* guru yoga practice at Katok,[354] he had a visionary experience in which Je Tsongkhapa Rinpoche said, "I can lend you Khedrup Je as your spiritual mentor for twenty-five years, but then you need to give him back to me." In Khenpo's autobiography, having calculated that he would then be in his early sixties, he writes, "I wondered if that would be the duration of my life, though I wasn't sure." Since the time coincided exactly with that prophecy, his students were sure that nothing could be done to prolong the Khenpo's life. They were besieged with grief.

At the age of sixty-three, on the seventeenth day of the fifth lunar month in the year of the Female Iron Snake [ca. July 14, 1941], Khenpo Ngakchung's physical manifestation dissolved into the expanse of the youthful vase body, the sphere of inner luminosity, the original ground of the primordially pure dharmakaya.

For seven days and nights, the precious body was kept hidden and undisturbed. When this period was over and his attendants entered the room, they discovered that a nectar-like liquid that looked, smelled, and tasted like honey was flowing from all the pores of the precious body. The nectar neither spoiled in the summer nor dried up in the winter. They collected two or three teapots full, and in subsequent years when it came time to make sacred medicine, they added a bowlful to each batch. All who tasted it were liberated from the sufferings of samsara and set upon the path to liberation.

The precious body was prepared and adorned, and for twenty-one days everyone was welcome to pay their respects. An indescribable number of people vowed to accomplish positive actions and renounce negative ones. Khenpo's main students from the surrounding areas, such as Yishin Tulku Arik, as well as khenpos and reincarnations belonging to Khenpo's home monastery and from elsewhere, made vast offerings to the reliquary. Tulku Ado Rinpoche performed all the requisite outer and inner tasks, and the renown of his worldly and spiritual abilities spread far and wide.

When Chaktrül Rinpoche came before the reliquary, he fell unconscious for a spell. When he came to, he spoke to the precious body, and many of the students heard Chaktrül Rinpoche and the body conversing as if they were having an actual conversation.

They built a structure on the stone-tiled area in front of the assembly hall to house the reliquary, and they performed the cremation based on the fire offering with the four activity-rituals. Khenpo's horse, Norbu Tikgya, who had been standing nearby, whinnied and ran around the reliquary three times. He then stood in front of it with his head hanging down. Everyone was overcome with sadness.

All the indications of the attainment of Buddhahood manifested in the shared perception of the students, just as described in the Great Perfection tantras. The *Tantra of the Heart Mirror of Vajrasattva* states:[355]

> As for parinirvana, there are two types: genuinely complete Buddhahood and manifestly complete Buddhahood.

Various signs of the latter occurred, including lights, sounds, forms, and earth tremors, and in particular, numerous indestructible, five-colored relic pills, both pea-sized and mustard-seed-sized, were found among the ashes. Many individual students constructed reliquaries made of precious materials to house one or more of the relics.

Nyakla Kasung asked Tulku Ado Rinpoche for some precious ashes and subsequently discovered two relic pills. I heard these accounts personally.

As the *Blazing Relics of Buddha-Body Tantra* states:[356]

> When the child of a noble family passes into parinirvana,
> And the defiled bodily remains
> Are cleansed through cremation,
> Relics of all the buddhas will emerge.
> According to the buddha family distinctions,
> Five kinds of relic will emerge.

The great Khenpo was just such an emanated spiritual master, and during his lifetime he revealed himself directly to Reting Tulku and taught him *A Guide to the Words of My Perfect Teacher,* as well as the main practices in their entirety. Also, he appeared to the Chakgong-gö Tersey Dodra in wisdom form, accepted him as his disciple, and conferred the Whispered Lineage of the Great Perfection, along with the scriptural transmission that is currently held by his two sons, Nyinda and Dampa.

Later, after the great Khenpo Ngakchung had passed away, Khenpo

Münsel Rinpoche, while in prison, beheld him in a vision, in which Khenpo assured him that the time had come for him to benefit beings by spreading the Whispered Lineage.

While Khenpo Aghey was staying in strict retreat practicing the Omniscient Longchenpa's *Guru Sadhana Sealed with a Vital Nucleus,* he had a vision of Khenpo and the Great Omniscient One as one inseparable being, who conferred a five-page verse text containing the preliminaries and main practices. Khenpo Aghey's awareness became deeply immersed in the state of reality. This is one of many instances when Khenpo's direct disciples experienced him in pure visions.

All the outer and inner posthumous tasks, such as constructing the reliquary and gathering the college students for prayer and providing food, were performed by Tulku Ado Rinpoche, and the Khenpo's monastic seat expanded like a summer lake.

A brief summary of Khenpo Ngakchung's students follows:

The four main disciples who were like four great pillars in the four directions were Drubwang Palchen Düpa, Chaktrül Pema Trinley Gyatso, Yishin Tulku Arik, and Lungtok Tulku Rinpoche Dorje Chökyong [a.k.a. Tulku Ado].

The eight who were like roof beams were Getrul, Khenpo Jorden, Khenpo Gyaltsen Özer, Khenpo Münsel, Rongta Tulku Jamyang Losal Dorje, Chatral Sangye Dorje, Golok Tulku Gyurme, and Tersey Chimey.

The thirteen "rosary strings" were Khyentrül Chökyi Lodrö, Khenpo Shenga, Pomi Khenchen, Tertön Rinchen Lingpa, Tulku Mingyur, Tangöd Tulku, Lama Palden Yeshe, Jang Gyurme Dorje, Khenpo Peyjik, Khenpo Orgyen Tendzin, Khenpo Akyi, Goji Tertön Yeshe Jungney, and Khenpo Gedün Rabgyey. These I copied from Tulku Ado's writings.

In addition, there were many khenpos, such as Khen Rinpoche Nüden, Orgyen Tenpel, Sonam, Kalzang Chönyi, Oten, Drimey, Pendey Özer, Otrin, Jamyang Gyaltsen, and Hasa Khenpo. Reincarnations included Kunzang Nyendrak, Serden Tulku, Gyada Tulku, Gyalsey Tulku, Apey, Karma Yangsö, Moktsa Tulku, Situ Tulku, Wön Tulku, Dartok Zenkar Tulku, Razi Tulku, Tsamshu, Drakmar, Apey, Bhadhi, Atrin, Akel, Draktrül, Palchen Dorje, Tendzin Norbu, Shakya, Tubzang, Wönpo, Kölri Tulku, Döntok, Yönrü Tulku, Könchok Drakpa, Lishi Lhündrup, Orgyen Chemchok, Lodrö Gyalpo, Naktar Tulku, and Tulku Orgyen Dorje. Others include Tsokha Apey, Drolma Tsering, Adi, Peyjung, Sangye Gönpo, Yönrü Tersey Sögyal, Samten, Tenga, Asang, Drakyab Lodrö Rabpel, Tutop Lingpa's daughter Samten Drolma, and Jetsün Chöying Wangmo. Devout chieftains included Jagö Tobden, Lakar Pön, Shelkar, Pomda, and Degey. Those from other traditions—Sakya, Kagyü, and so forth—who received connections to Khenpo Ngakchung through empowerments and teachings are so numerous that I could never list them all.

In the Great Khenpo's *Cycle of Prophecies,* he writes:

Eight great beams and four pillars,
A constellation of outer students and inner attendants;
Thirteen rosary strings are the waxing moon
Through outer and inner auspicious connections and numerous
    skillful means,
The pillars, in full number, are the succession of abbots,
The beams, in full number, shall uphold monastic seats.
The rafter-like assembly of students
Will turn the vajra wheel with a powerful wind,
Completing the teachings of the castle fortress.
HA HA

The legacy of treatises inherited by Khenpo's followers totals thirteen volumes, equal in number to the thirteenth bodhisattva level, "Holder of the Vajra." Khenpo's *Collected Works* comprise four cycles: the sutra cycle, which contains commentaries on the *Introduction to the Middle Way, Four Hundred Stanzas on the Middle Way,* and so on; the sadhana cycle, which contains Whispered Lineage sadhanas such as Vajrakilaya and Dorje Drollö; the general cycle on the three divisions of the Vajrayana, which contains writings on the generation and completion stages, the path of skillful means, and so on; and the specific cycle of innermost secret unsurpassed extraordinary teachings, which contains *Heart Drop of Samantabhadra* and so forth.

With the ripening of his bodhichitta aspirations, Tulku Shedrub Tendzin Rinpoche compiled all the writings and distributed them widely.

On the vast sacred path of marvelous bodhichitta,
Having brought forth the sun of this spiritual autobiography
With the great offering-lotus of my faithful heart,
In whichever pure realm you dwell shall be the delight of offerings.
By the virtue of this endeavor, may the essence of the teachings

Of the Omniscient Father and Son spread impartially through all
realms,
May the aims and aspirations of the holy ones be swiftly realized,
And may we merge inseparably with the three secrets.

The incomparably kind sole refuge, Tulku Lhasey Shedrub Tendzin,
requested that these stories about the Omniscient Lama Ngakgi Wangpo's
life be compiled, and the golden vajra of his command descended upon
my crown. Furthermore, Khenpo Tsering Gyatso, whose intentions for
the teachings of the Luminous Nyingtik are exceedingly pure, and who
possesses the elixir of sublime motivation and action, repeatedly asked me
to write this compendium. So as not to disappoint them, Nyarong Sonam
Tenpa, the itinerant monk of the Shakya lineage, wrote this without exaggeration based upon the records of Tulku Ado Rinpoche and adorned with
stories recounted by my elders. I composed this at the Katok Dorje Den
monastic college, Shedrub Norbü Lhünpo, while teaching the *Exposition
of Valid Cognition*.
    May virtue and excellence prevail!

Appendix 2: Time Line

Part One

1879 (Age 1)   Born in Washul Village
1880 (Age 2)   Taken to Lungtok Rinpoche by father
1881 (Age 3)   Performs the transference of consciousness for a
                 dying calf
1883 (Age 5)   Reverses the water at Ringmo Dilgyuk,
                 near Jönpalung
                 Meets Lungtok Rinpoche
1885 (Age 7)   Begins to learn to read

Part Two

1887 (Age 9)   Meets Chomden Dorje and receives *All-Pervasive
                 Natural Liberation* preliminary teaching
1888 (Age 10)   Studies Manjushri commentary and teaches it at
                 Dzongkar near Ta and Trom
1889 (Age 11)   Blessing by Manjushri that enables Khenpo
                 Ngakchung to read swiftly
1890 (Age 12)   Receives a wish-fulfilling gem from a naga
1891 (Age 13)   Discovers a text on medicine, but returns it to the
                 treasure guardians
1892 (Age 14)   Receives and completes Longsel Nyingpo
                 preliminaries under the guidance of Jigdral Tutop
                 Lingpa, Ngawang Tendzin

1893 (Age 15)	Receives complete transmission of the *Longsel Nyingpo* cycle and has auspicious and extraordinary signs
1894 (Age 16)	Novice ordination
1895 (Age 17)	Extraordinary experience of insight following a reading of the extensive *Prajnaparamita*.
1896 (Age 18)	Lungtok leaves Drubchen Gar and settles at Pema Ritrö; Khenpo Ngakchung receives *Words of My Perfect Teacher* from him; practices preliminaries; and encounters Longchenpa in a dream
1897 (Age 19)	Bodhisattva vow; mind training; and *Resting in the Nature of Mind*
1898 (Age 20)	Full ordination given by Lama Atob (Katok Khenpo Tashi Özer)
1899 (Age 21)	Begins main practice teachings with Lama Lungtok
1900 (Age 22)	Goes to Dzogchen Monastery; numerous studies
1901 (Age 23)	Studies with Jamgön Mipam Rinpoche; Lama Lungtok passes away
1902 (Age 24)	Khandro Nyingtik empowerment from Drukpa Kuchen; Three-month retreat on Vajrakilaya
1903 (Age 25)	Khandro Yangtik retreat at Kyilko
1907 (Age 29)	Vision of Yeshe Tsogyal Mother passes away Receives *Nyingma Transmitted Teachings* from Tertön Ngawang Tendzin Visit to Dzogchen Monastery; numerous teachings with great masters including Khenpo Shenga; composes a praise to Manjushri; turns down the position of khenpo at Dzogchen Writes a great-accomplishment ceremony arrangement for Karma Lingpa's *Peaceful and Wrathful Deities* Year-long retreat on Rinchen Lingpa's treasure
1908 (Age 30)	Arrives in Katok

Part Three

1909–22 (Ages 31–44) Khenpo of Katok
1923 (Age 45) Vision of Tsarchen Losal Gyatso and Nesar
Khyentse Wangchuk, predicting his future lives
1925 (Age 47) Katok Situ Chokyi Gyatso passes into
parinirvana, oversees all posthumous rituals
1926 (Age 48) Transmission of *Great Treasury of Precious
Revelations* at Lingshi Jangkar Monastery in
Batang
Consecration of Lama Yönten Rinpoche's stupa
at Yaso Gön, a branch of Katok
Transmission of *Longchen Nyingtik* and
Excellent Wish-Fulfilling Vase at Tsophu Gön in
Batang
1927 (Age 49) Retreat practice at his residence of most of the
Great Treasury of Precious Revelations
Composes Great Perfection treatises at the
visionary behest of Longchenpa
Briefly visits Katok for *Embodiment of the
Master's Realization* practice
Vision of Nubchen Sangye Yeshe
Extensive ceremonies performed to remove
obstacles to Khenpo Ngakchung's life
1928 (Age 50) Erected statue at his hermitage at Jönpalung
Vision of Atisha and Dromtönpa; composes
manual for the *Sixteenfold Vital Nuclei
Empowerments of the Kadam Tradition*
1929–31 (Age 51–53) Journeys to Gartok in Markham
Ancillary visits to nearby Lawok
Visit to Bamtso Lake, sacred to Vajravarahi
Travels to other places in Markham including
Chubum, Drugudo, Tsangshi, and Neygo Gön
Travels to Menchukha and Pema Richen with
visions of Tara as Princess Wencheng on the way;
Lhatok, Gönjo, and the encampment of Nyakla
Jangchub Dorje
Return to Katok and visit to his own region near
Jönpalung

1932 (Age 52)   New Year visit to the location of Tertön Drime's passing
                 Attending to Penor Rinpoche at Palyul Monastery
                 Visit to Dralak Gön
                 Cremation of Penor Rinpoche at Palyul
                 Enthronement of Situ Yangsi
1935 (Age 55)   Vajrakilaya retreat; visions of Yeshe Tsogyal and Jamgön
                 Kongtrül Lodrö Taye
                 The autobiography ends here
1941 (Age 63)   Passes into parinirvana

Khenpo Ngawang Palzang's Twenty-Five Incarnations

1. Genyen Litsawi (Vimalakirti, *dge bsnyen li tswa bi*)
2. Gelong Lochang (*dge slong blo 'chang*)
3. Acharya Manjushrimitra (*slob dpon 'jam dpal bshes gnyen*)
4. Arya Nagarjuna (*'phags pa klu grub*)
5. Lobpön Lodrö Tenpa (Sthiramati, *slob dpon blo gros brtan pa*)
6. Shri Chandrakirti (*dpal ldan zla ba grags pa*)
7. Acharya Dharmakirti (*slob dpon chos kyi grags pa*)
8. Drubpey Wangchuk Norbu Goleb (*grub pa'i dbang phyug nor bu go leb*)
9. Lobpön Vimalamitra (*slob dpon bi ma la mi tra*)
10. Lotsawa Nagadhadza (*na ga da+ha dza*)
11. Nyangben Tingdzin Zangpo (*nyang ban ting 'dzin bzang po*)
12. Gelong Namkhai Nyingpo (*dge slong nam kha'i snying po*)
13. King Nyima Nampar Nön (*rgyal po nyi ma rnam par gnon*)
14. King Lha'i Metok (*'dzam gling rgyal po lhai me thog*)
15. Omniscient Longchen Rabjampa (*kun mkhyen klong chen rab 'byams*)
16. U-öd Yeshe Bumpa (*dbu 'od ye shes bum pa*)
17. Chetsün Senge Wangchuk (*lce btsun seng ge dbang phyug*)
18. Nyang Nyima Özer (*nyang nyi ma 'od zer*)
19. Pema Ledreltsel (*pad+ma las 'brel rtsal*)
20. Tertön Karma Lingpa (*gter ston kar+ma gling pa*)
21. Omniscient Sonam Senge (*kun mkhyen bsod nams seng ge*)
22. Gelong Rinchen Lodrö (*dge slong rin chen blo gros*)
23. Khedrup Karma Chakme (*mkhas grub kar+ma chags med*)
24. Dharma King Tenpa Tsering (*chos rgyal bstan pa tshe ring*)
25. Dorje Zijitsel [a.k.a. Khenpo Ngawang Palzang] (*rdo rje gzi brjid rtsal, mkhan po ngag dbang dpal bzang*)

Appendix 3: Liturgies by Khenpo Ngawang Palzang

༄༅། །བརྒྱུད་གསུམ་རིག་འཛིན་བླ་མའི་གསོལ་འདེབས་སྨོན་ལམ་དང་བཅས་པ་བཞུགས་སོ།།

Supplication and Aspiration Prayer to the Vidyadharas of the Three Lineages

ཨེ་མ་ཧོཿ ཆོས་སྐུ་ཀུན་བཟང་ལོངས་སྐུ་རྡོ་རྗེ་འཆང་། །མངོན་རྫོགས་དགོངས་བརྒྱུད་སྟོན་པ་བཅུ་གཉིས་དང་། །དགའ་རྡོར་ལ་སོགས་བརྡ་བརྒྱུད་རིག་འཛིན་ལྔ། །ཉིང་འཛིན་བཟང་པོ་ལྷུང་མ་ལྷུན་རྒྱལ་སོགས། །སྙན་བརྒྱུད་རིག་འཛིན་བླ་མ་དགོངས་སུ་གསོལ། །ཁྱད་པར་རྒྱལ་བ་ཀློང་ཆེན་རབ་འབྱམས་པ། །སྨོན་ལམ་འདི་ལ་མགོན་པོས་དབང་མཛོད་ཅིག །

Emaho! How wonderful!
Dharmakaya Samantabhadra, Sambhogakaya Vajradhara,
The Twelve Teachers of the Mind Lineage, such as the Truly Perfected King,[357]
Five Vidyadharas of the Symbol Lineage—Garab Dorje and the rest,

Tingdzin Zangpo, Dangma Lhüngyal, and the others–
Masters of the Whispered Lineage of Vidyadharas, please look upon me!
In particular, Victorious Longchen Rabjampa,
Bear protective witness to this prayer.

བདག་གྱུང་དེ་ནས་ཚེ་རབས་ཐམས་ཅད་དུ། །འོད་གསལ་སྙིང་པོའི་ཡང་ཞུན་
བཅུ་བདུན་རྒྱུད། །མཛོད་ཆེན་བདུན་དང་ཡང་ཐིག་རྣམ་པ་གསུམ། །ཁྲབ་དང་རྒྱ་
ཆེ་གསང་བའི་གནས་རྣམས་ཀུན། །མི་བརྗེད་གཟུངས་ཀྱིས་ཚིག་དོན་སེམས་ལ་
ཤར། །སྤོབས་པ་རྒྱ་མཚོས་འགྲོ་ལ་ཆོས་སྒོ་འབྱེད། །ཆོས་ཉིད་དགོངས་པ་བར་
མཆམས་མེད་པར་ཤོག

Henceforth and throughout all my lifetimes,
May the ultra-refined essence of the Luminous Great Perfection—the
    Seventeen Tantras,
The *Seven Great Treasuries*, and the three *Yangtik* teachings,
And all the secret topics of the vast and profound traditions—
May their words and meanings dawn in my mind through the power of
    unforgetting retention!
With infinite confidence, may I open the door of the Dharma for beings,
And may my realization of reality be uninterrupted.

བི་མ་མི་ཏྲ་མེད་འོད་ཟེར་གྱིས། །མངོན་སུམ་ཡེ་ཤེས་སྐུ་ཡིས་རྗེས་བཟུང་ནས། །
དོན་བརྒྱུད་དགོངས་པའི་དགོངས་པ་བདག་ལ་འཕོས། །ཀུན་མཁྱེན་བླ་མ་ཁྱེད་བཞིན་
འགྱུར་བར་ཤོག །

Vimalamitra and Drime Özer,
Please accept me with your actually manifest wisdom body
And transfer the wisdom realization of the ultimate lineage;
Omniscient Lama, may I become like you!

ཞིང་འདིར་བསྟན་པའི་འཕེལ་འགྲིབ་རྫོགས་པ་དང་། །བསྟན་པའི་བཅས་གསུམ་
མཛེས་ལྡན་བཀོད་པར་འབེབས། །ཞིང་ཁམས་དེ་རུ་བདག་གིས་ཐོས་བསམ་ཞིང་།
།བསྒོམ་པས་གསང་ཆེན་བསྟན་པ་འཛིན་པ་དང་། །འགྲོ་ལ་ཆོས་ཀྱི་སྒོ་འབྱར་འབྱེད་
གྱུར་ཅིག །

Here in this realm, when the wax and wane of the teachings is complete,
The Three Sources of the Teachings will come to the pure realm Beautiful
    Array.[358]
In that pure realm, by studying, reflecting and meditating,
May I become a holder of the Great Secret teachings,
And open the door to the Dharma for beings.

དེ་ནས་བྱང་ཕྱོགས་ཡངས་པ་སྐྱོབ་པའི་ཞིང་། །སངས་རྒྱས་ཨུཏྤལ་མེ་ཏོག་མཛེས་
པའི་དྲུང་། །འཁོར་གྱི་ཐོག་མར་བདག་ཉིད་སྐྱེ་བར་ཤོག །བདེ་བར་གཤེགས་
པ་ཚུལ་བཞིན་བསྟེན་པ་དང་། །སྨིན་གྲོལ་ཟབ་མོའི་བདུད་རྩི་རབ་ཏུ་མྱོང་།
སངས་རྒྱས་བསྟན་ལ་བྱ་བ་བྱེད་པར་ཤོག །

Then, in the northern pure realm, Spacious Shelter,
Before the Buddha Beautiful Utpala Flower,
May I be born foremost among his retinue.
Properly attending this *sugata*,
And savoring the amrita of the profound ripening empowerments and
    liberating instructions,
May I serve the Buddhist doctrine.

དེ་ནས་བསྟན་པའི་བཅས་གསུམ་ནུབ་ཕྱོགས་འཕར། །གཚུག་ཕུད་དྲུངས་ཞེས་བྱ་
བའི་འཛིན་རྟེན་འབེབས། །

སངས་རྒྱས་འཁོར་བ་འཇིག་གིས་བཟུང་ནས་ལོ། །འབུམ་ཕྲག་བདུན་དུ་བསྟན་པ་
གནས་པ་ལ། །བདག་ཉིད་དང་པོ་སྲས་ཀྱི་ཐུ་བོ་དང་། །བར་དུ་རྒྱལ་བའི་རྒྱལ་
ཚབ་ཉིད་དུ་གྱུར། །ཐམ་གདལ་བུའི་ཕྲག་མ་མ་ལུས་པ། །བདག་ཉིད་གཅིག་
པུས་ཐམས་ཅད་སྨིན་གྲོལ་ལ། །བཀོད་ནས་ཐར་པ་དམ་པའི་གྲིང་བགྲོད་ཤོག །

When the Three Sources of the Teachings leap to the West,
They will come to the realm of Tsukpü Yang.
Buddha Samsara-Destroyer, having accepted me,[359]
During the seven hundred thousand years the teachings remain extant,
May I first be the primary heir,
Then the Buddha's regent,
And finally, may I single-handedly lead
All remaining beings without exception
To maturation and liberation, and reach the holy land of liberation.

སྐྱེ་བ་འདི་ནས་ཚེ་རབས་ཐམས་ཅད་དུ། །གཟུངས་དང་བློ་གྲོས་སྤོབས་པར་དབང་
འབྱོར་ནས། །གསང་བའི་གསང་བ་འོད་གསལ་བཅུ་བདུན་རྒྱུད། །རང་ཤར་
རང་གྲོལ་རྒྱུད་དང་ཡི་གེ་མེད། །རྒྱུད་ཀྱི་སྙིང་པོ་རྗེ་འབངས་འཛོམ་པ་ལྟའི། །
མ་ནོར་གཟུངས་ཀྱིས་རྒྱུད་ལ་འཛིན་པ་དང་། །སྤོབས་པས་འགྲོ་ལ་ཆོས་ཆར་
འབེབས་པར་ཤོག །

Now and throughout all my lifetimes,
Attaining mastery of perfect recall, discerning intelligence, and
    courageous eloquence,
May the extremely secret *Luminous Seventeen Tantras*—
The tantras of *Self-Manifest Awareness, Self-Liberated Awareness* and
    No Letters,
Just as a king and his subjects converge, may these essence tantras
Be retained in my being through unerring perfect recall,
And with courageous eloquence, may I shower Dharma upon beings.

ནོར་བུ་ཕྲ་བཀོད་ཕྲུགས་ཀྱི་མེ་ལོང་དང་། །རྗེ་རྗེ་སེམས་དཔའ་སྙིང་གི་མེ་ལོང་
གསུམ། །མ་ནོར་གཟུངས་ཀྱིས་རྒྱུད་ལ་འཛིན་པ་དང་། །སྤོབས་པས་འགྲོ་ལ་
ཆོས་ཆར་འབེབས་པར་ཤོག །

May the three vital-essence tantras that perfectly illumine—*Studded
Jewels, Heart Mirror of Samantabhadra*, and *Mind Mirror
of Vajrasattva*,
Be retained in my being through unerring perfect recall,
And with courageous eloquence, may I shower Dharma upon beings.

མུ་ཏིག་ཕྲེང་བ་སེང་གེ་རྩལ་རྫོགས་རྒྱུད། །བཀྲ་ཤིས་མཛེས་ལྡན་རྒྱུད་ཀྱི་མེ་ཏོག
གསུམ། །མ་ནོར་གཟུངས་ཀྱིས་རྒྱུད་ལ་འཛིན་པ་དང་། །སྤོབས་པས་འགྲོ་ལ་
ཆོས་ཆར་འབེབས་པར་ཤོག །

May the three flowering tantras—*Pearl Garland, Perfected Lion*,
And *Graceful Auspiciousness*,
Be retained in my being through unerring perfect recall,
And with courageous eloquence, may I shower Dharma upon beings.

རྫོགས་པ་རང་བྱུང་རྒྱུད་ཀྱི་སྤོམ་གཅིག་པུ། །དེ་སྤྲོད་སྤྲོས་པ་སྤྲང་བ་གཏིང་ནས་རྫོགས། །
ཨེ་ཤེས་གསལ་བ་བསྒྲིག་ཅི་ཟླ་སྤྱོར་རྒྱུད། །མ་ཆད་ཁ་སྐོང་རིན་ཆེན་སྤུངས་པ་དང་། །
སྐུ་གདུང་འབར་བ་རྒྱུད་ཀྱི་ཡན་ལག་གཅིས། །མ་ནོར་གཟུངས་ཀྱིས་རྒྱུད་ལ་འཛིན་པ་
དང་། །སྤོབས་པས་འགྲོ་ལ་ཆོས་ཆར་འབེབས་པར་ཤོག །

May the *Self-Existing Perfection Tantra*, which alone summarizes all
tantras,
The *Tantra of Pointing-Out Instruction*s that perfects perception from
the depths,

The *Union of the Sun and Moon*, whose wisdom averts the battles of
  unawareness,
And the two amendment branches—*Piled Gems* and *Shining Relics*,
Be retained in my being through unerring perfect recall,
And with courageous eloquence, may I shower Dharma upon beings.

རྣམ་པར་གྲོལ་བ་སྒྲོན་མ་འབར་བའི་རྒྱུད། །སྙིང་དང་འདྲ་བ་ཀློང་དྲུག་རྒྱུད་དང་ནི།
རང་གནུང་གསང་བ་ཐལ་འགྱུར་རྩ་བའི་རྒྱུད། །ཞག་མོ་ཁྲོས་མ་འགགལ་བྱེད་བརྣག་
པའི་རྒྱུད། །མ་ནོར་གཟུངས་ཀྱིས་རྒྱུད་ལ་འཛིན་པ་དང་། །སྤོབས་པས་འགྲོ་ལ་
ཆོས་ཆར་འབེབས་པར་ཤོག །

May the perfectly liberating *Blazing Lamp Tantra*
The heart-like *Six Spheres Tantra*,
The secret root text—the *Talgyur Root Tantra*,
And the *Tantra of the Black Wrathful Goddess* that annihilates
  obstructers,
Be retained in my being through unerring perfect recall,
And with courageous eloquence, may I shower Dharma upon beings.

རྒྱས་པར་སྟོན་པ་གསང་བ་མཛོད་ཆེན་བདུན། །ཁབ་མོའི་མན་ངག་སྙིང་ཐིག་མ་བུ
བཞི། །གསང་ཆེན་རྡོ་རྗེ་སྙིང་པོའི་བསྟན་པ་དང་། །ཚེ་རབས་འདི་ནས་
ཚེ་རབས་ཐམས་ཅད་དུ། །མི་འབྲལ་དགའ་ཅན་མཁའ་འགྲོས་རྗེས་གཟུང་དང་།
ཀུན་མཁྱེན་བླ་མས་མཛོད་སྤྱམ་འཛོམས་པར་ཤོག །

The secret *Seven Treasuries* reveal the teachings in elaborate form;
The profound pith instructional teaching is the fourfold *Nyingtik
  Mother-and-Child*.
May I never be separate from these Great Secret Vajra Essence teachings
Now and throughout all my lifetimes;

May the oath-bound guardians and dakinis grant their permission
  blessings,
And may the Omniscient Master instruct me directly.

རྒྱུད་དང་མན་ངག་ཐབས་མོ་རབ་འབྱེད་པའི། །མཐའ་དྲུག་ཚུལ་བཞིའི་བློ་གྲོས་སྣང་

བ་ཐོབ། །དྱང་གསུམ་དག་པའི་ཤེས་རབ་མིག་རྙེད་ཅིང་། །ཚུལ་གསུམ་ཚང་

བའི་རིགས་པར་དབང་འབྱོར་ནས། །ཇི་མེད་འོད་ཟེར་ཁྱོད་ཀྱི་ལྟ་དགོངས་དང་། །

ཏིང་འཛིན་སྤྱོད་པ་ཇི་བཞིན་བདག་གྱུར་ནས། །འགྲོ་བའི་ཕན་བདེའི་བདག་གིས་

འགྲུབ་པར་ཤོག །

May I gain lucid understanding of the six limits and the four modes[360]
That perfectly illuminate the tantras and the profound pith instructions.
Having attained the eye of knowledge of threefold pure scrutiny,
And mastered all three aspects of logic,
May my enlightened view, absorption, and action
Become just like yours, Drime Özer,
That I may bring benefit and happiness to beings.

ཅེས་ཀུན་མཁྱེན་བླ་མ་ལ་གསོལ་བ་སྟེང་ནས་འདེབས་པ་འདིའང་རང་གིས་འདི་ལྟར་ཡུན་རིང་དུ་སྨོན་ལམ་བཏབ་

ཅིང་སྐྱལ་བ་མཆམས་པའི་ཏྲེགས་པའི་སྐྱེ་བོ་རེ་ཟུང་གིས་བཏོན་ནའང་ཕན་ཡོན་རྒྱ་ཆེར་འབྱུང་སྲམ་པའི་བློ་ནས་འོད་

གསལ་རིན་ཆེན་སྙིང་པོ་པདྨ་ལས་འབྲེལ་རྩལ་གྱིས་བྲིས་པ་དགེའོ། །

*This heartfelt supplication to the Omniscient Master Longchenpa is something
that I myself have prayed for a long time. Thinking that it might bring vast
benefit even if only a handful of people with a similar fate in these dark ages
were to recite it, I, Ösel Rinchen Nyingpo Pema Ledreltsel, wrote it down.
May it bring benefit!*

༄༅། །ཀུ་རུའི་སྒྲུབ་པ་བྱིན་རླབས་ཆར་འབེབས་ཞེས་བྱ་བ་བཞུགས་སོ། །

Guru Sadhana: Bringing Down a Rain of Blessings

དང་པོ་སྐྱབས་འགྲོ་སེམས་བསྐྱེད་སྟོན་དུ་སོང་ནས། ཨ༔ གཞི་ལུས་ཐ་མལ་འཛིན་པ་བྲལ་
བ་ལས། །ཟུང་འཇུག་རིག་པ་གཉེར་ཏོགས་ཡེ་ཤེས་ཉིད། །ཐ་མལ་ཉམས་
ཀྱི་འཛིན་སྟངས་ཞིག་པ་ལས། །རིག་འཛིན་གཙོ་མཆོག་རྡོ་རྗེ་ཐོད་ཕྲེང་རྩལ། །
མཐིང་ནག་བརྗིད་པ་ཞི་ཁྲོ་ཡི་ཉམས། །ཞལ་གཅིག་ཕྱག་གཉིས་རྡོ་རྗེ་ཕུར་
པ་འཛིན། །རྐྱལ་འགྱུར་སྐུག་ཕྱམས་རུས་པའི་རྒྱན་གྱིས་བརྒྱན། །དུ་སྐྲ
ཐོར་ཚུགས་དར་དཔུངས་རིན་ཆེན་མཛེས། །ཡུམ་མཆོག་མཚོ་རྒྱལ་དཀར་མོ་གྲི
ཐོད་འཛིན། །གཅེར་བུ་སྐྱ་གྲོལ་རིན་ཆེན་རུས་པས་བརྒྱན། །ཕྱི་གཙུག་ཐག
ཞལ་ནག་མོ་དང་སྐུ་སྒྲོགས། མེ་ཏོག་མནྡ་ར་བའི་རྒྱན་པོ་འཕྱང་། །བདེ་ཆེན
ཉམས་ཀྱི་ལྡང་ཙོ་འབར་བའི་སྐུ། །ཐབས་མཆོག་ཡབ་ཀྱི་སྐུ་ལ་གཉིས་མེད་འཁྱིལ། །
ཙ་གསུམ་རྒྱལ་བཞི་དང་ཁྲོ་བོ་དང་། །གནས་ཡུལ་དུར་ཁྲོ་མ་སྙིང་མཁའ་འགྲོ
བཅས། །སྣང་ལ་རང་བཞིན་མེད་པ་སྟོང་པ་ཉིད། །གསལ་ལ་རེ་འཛིན་བྲལ་བ
ཡེ་ཤེས་རྩལ། །སྣང་སྟོང་སྒྱུ་མ་འཛའ་ཡི་རྒྱལ་དུ་གསལ། །ཨོཾ་ཨཱཿཧཱུྃ།

AH
Freed of clinging to the ordinary body,
Unity awareness, wisdom itself, fundamentally perfect,
Destroys the ordinary mode of apprehending experience:
I arise as the supreme lord of vidyadharas, Powerful Vajra Skull Garland,[361]
Blue-black, resplendent, with a semi-wrathful expression,
One face, two hands holding vajra and kila,

Wearing a yogin's tiger-skin skirt, adorned with bone ornaments,
Hair in a topknot, embellished with silken ribbons and precious gems.
Supreme consort Tsogyal, red, holding hooked knife and skull,
Naked with hair flowing, adorned with gems and bones.
Upon her crown a sow's head, black and squealing.
Draped with a garland of mandarava flowers,
Body ablaze with youthful beauty and great bliss,
Inseparably entwined with the male body of supreme skillful means.
Surrounded by the victorious peaceful and wrathful Three Roots,
And the mother and sister dakinis of the sacred places, countries and
   charnel grounds.[362]
Visualize this like a rainbow, an empty and illusory appearance,
Emptiness that is apparent yet without true existence—
The expressive power of wisdom, vivid and free of fixation.
OM AH HUM

ཧཱུྂ༔ དཔལ་རི་པད྄མ་འོད་ཀྱི་ཕོ་བྲང་ནས། །རིག་འཛིན་གཙོ་མཆོག་རྡོ་རྗེ་ཐོད་ཕྲེང་
རྩལ། །འཁོར་དུ་རྩ་གསུམ་རྒྱལ་བའི་དཀྱིལ་འཁོར་བཅས། །སྤྲུལ་མཆོག་
བདག་ལ་བྱིན་རློབས་དབང་བསྐུར་ཕྱིར། །གནས་མཆོག་ཉམས་དགའ་འདི་རུ་
གཤེགས་སུ་གསོལ། །སྤྲུལ་མཆོག་བདག་ལ་དགོངས་ཏེ་གཤེགས་སུ་གསོལ། །
སྤྲུལ་པའི་དཀྱིལ་འཁོར་འདི་ལ་བྱིན་གྱིས་རློབས། །སྐལ་ལྡན་བོས་པའི་བུ་ལ་
དབང་བཞི་བསྐུར། །རྫས་འབྱོར་ལུས་ངག་ཡིད་གསུམ་བྱིན་གྱིས་རློབས། །ཡེ་
ནས་རང་དངུ་འབྲལ་མེད་པ་ཡི། །གཉིས་སུ་མེད་པ་ལེ་ཤེས་ཆེན་པོའི་ངང་། །
ཆོས་ཉིད་མཉམ་པ་ཆེན་པོར་བཤགས་ནས་སྐྱང་། །བདག་ལ་དུས་འདི་ནས་བཟུང་
བྱང་ཆུབ་བར། །ཕྱོགས་རྗེས་དགོངས་ལ་བྱིན་གྱིས་བསྒྲུབ་ཏུ་གསོལ། །

HUM
From the Glorious Mountain Palace of Lotus Light,
Supreme Lord Vidyadhara, Powerful Vajra Skull-Garland,

Surrounded by the mandala of the victorious Three Roots:
To bless and empower me, a supreme practitioner,
Come here to this supreme delightful place, I pray.
Think of me, a supreme practitioner, and come, I pray.
Bless this practice mandala.
Grant the four empowerments to your fortunate, devoted child.
Bless this yogin's body, speech and mind.
Originally inseparable from me,
In the state of great nondual wisdom,
Although you dwell in the great evenness of reality,
Fom this moment until my enlightenment.
Pray, look upon me with compassion and grant your blessings!

རང་གྲུ་རིན་པོ་ཆེ་གསལ་བའི་ཐུགས་རིན་པོ་ཆེ་མཆོང་གུར་ཕུབ་པ་ལྟ་བུའི་དབུས་སུ་པད་དང་ཉི་མའི་གདན་ལ་
གསེར་གྱི་རྡོ་རྗེ་རྩེ་ལྔ་པའི་ལྟེ་བར་ཧཱུྃ་མཐིང་གའི་མཐའ་བསྐོར་དུ་རྡོ་རྗེའི་ཚིག་གི་ཕྲེང་བ་རྣམས་ལུ་གུ་རྒྱུད་བར་མ་
ཆད་པར་གྱི་ལྡི་ལི་འཁོར་བའི་འོད་དང་སྒྲ་དང་ཟེར་ལས་རྒྱལ་བ་ཐམས་ཅད་དང་ཁྱད་པར་དུ་གུ་རུ་མཚོ་སྐྱེས་རྡོ་རྗེའི་
ཐུགས་རྒྱུད་བསྐུལ། མཁྱེན་བརྩེ་ནུས་པའི་ཡོན་ཏན་ཐམས་ཅད་འོད་ཟེར་དཀར་དམར་མཐིང་གའི་རྣམ་པར་
བདག་ལ་ཐིམ་པར་བསམ་ལ།

Visualize yourself as Guru Rinpoche. In the core of your heart, like a canopy of precious gems, is a lotus and a sun seat, upon which is a five-pronged gold vajra. At the vajra's center is a blue hum, encircled by a rosary of vajra syllables, strung together like a chain and spinning continuously. Its light, sounds and rays invoke the enlightened minds of all buddhas and in particular that of the Guru Lake-Born Vajra. Imagine that all the qualities of their discerning awareness, love and power dissolve into you in the form of white, red and blue light rays. Recite:

ཧཱུྃ། ཨོཾ་རྒྱན་ཡུལ་གྱི་ནུབ་བྱང་མཚམས། །པདྨ་གེ་སར་སྡོང་པོ་ལ། །ཨ་
མཚན་མཆོག་གི་དངོས་གྲུབ་བརྙེས། །པདྨ་འབྱུང་གནས་ཞེས་སུ་གྲགས། །
འཁོར་དུ་མཁའ་འགྲོ་མང་པོས་བསྐོར། །ཁྱེད་ཀྱི་རྗེས་སུ་བདག་བསྒྲུབ་ཀྱི།

ཐེན་ཐྱིས་རྩོབ་ཕྱིར་གཤེགས་སུ་གསོལ། །གུ་རུ་པདྨ་སིདྡྷི་ཧཱུཾ། ཞེས་པ་ཛབ་ཀྱི་ཚུལ་དུ་བ
ཟློས། །

HUM
On the northwest border of the land of Oddiyana,
On a lotus, pistil-cup and stem,
You attained supreme, wondrous accomplishments.
Renowned as the Lotus Born,
You are surrounded by a retinue of many dakinis.
Following in your footsteps, I practice.
Pray, come and grant your blessings!
GURU PADMA SIDDHI HUM

Recite this as a mantra.

སླར་ཡང་འོད་ཟེར་འཕྲོས་པས་སྣང་སྲིད་དག་པར་སྦྱངས་ཏེ། །སྲིད་བཅུད་ཐམས་ཅད་མེ་མེ་ཁྱོག་ཁྱོག་ཞིག་
ཞིག་ཏུ་འགུལ་བས་ལྷ་ཀླུ་བདུད་བཙན་མ་མོ་སོགས་ཡེ་ཤེས་དང་འཇིག་རྟེན་པའི་རྟགས་པ་གཏེར་གྱི་སྲུང་མ་ཐམས་
ཅད་དང་། །རིན་པོ་ཆེ་ས་ཡི་གཏེར་ཐམས་ཅད་གནས་ནས་འགུལ་ཏེ་གུ་རུ་རིན་པོ་ཆེའི་གསང་བ་གསུམ་དུ་
བཞེངས་ནས་བདག་ལ་ཐིམ་པར་བསྒོམ་ལ། །ཚིག་བདུན་གསོལ་འདེབས་ཁོ་ན་ལ་བརྩོན་པར་བྱུ། མཐར།

Once more, light rays stream forth, purifying phenomenal existence. The entire universe and all its beings quake, shiver, tremble and shake, causing both wisdom beings and worldly spirits, such as gods, nagas, demons, tsen spirits and mamos, all treasure-guardians, and all precious earth-treasures to jolt out of their places. Meditate that they emerge from Guru Rinpoche's three secret centers and dissolve into you. Exert yourself exclusively in reciting the Seven-Line Prayer. Finally, recite:

ཨྃཿ གནས་དང་སྐྱེང་བ་ཐམས་ཅད་ཀུན། །ཡེ་ནས་ཡེ་ཤེས་རོལ་པའི་དང་། །
རང་ཐལ་རིག་པ་རྗེན་པའི་གློང་། །ཁྲོ་འདུས་ཚོགས་སྐུའི་རང་ཞལ་བལྟ། །ཨྃཿ

AH
All situations and appearances
Are the primordial display of wisdom.
The expanse of unimpeded naked awareness—
Dharmakaya beyond thought: behold my own true nature!
AH

Thus, sustain the stream of wisdom mind.

ཞེས་དགོངས་པའི་རྒྱན་བསྐུང་དོ། །ཞེས་པ་འདང་བླ་མ་དམ་པ་ཚུལ་ཁྲིམས་རྒྱ་མཚོས་བསྐུལ་དོར་སྤྲགས་བཙུན་ ལས་འབྲེལ་རྩལ་གྱི་བློ་མཚོ་དྭངས་པ་ལས་བྱུང་བ་དགེའོ།། །།

At the behest of the holy Lama Tsultrim Gyatso, this emerged from the clear mind-lake of the tantric monk Ledreltsel. May it be of benefit!

༄༅། །པཚ་ལས་འབྲེལ་གྱིས་མཛད་པའི་སྡོམ་གསུམ་སྤྱི་བཤགས་བཞུགས་སོ། །

General Confession Prayer for the Three Levels of Vows
By Pema Ledrel

ཨོཾ། རིག་འཛིན་བླ་མ་བདེ་གཤེགས་ཞི་ཁྲོ་དང་། །དཔའ་བོ་མཁའ་འགྲོ་ཆོས་
སྲུང་དམ་ཅན་ཚ། །དཔང་འགྱུར་མགོན་པོ་ཡེ་ཤེས་སྤྱན་མངའ་བ། །ཀུན་
མཁྱེན་གསལ་བའི་དགོངས་པ་བླ་ན་མེད། །ཐུགས་རྗེ་དངོས་གྲུབ་བྱིན་རླབས་རྒྱ་
མཚོའི་བདག །བདག་གི་ནོངས་པ་འཆགས་ལ་དགོངས་སུ་གསོལ། །

OM
Vidyadhara masters, peaceful and wrathful *sugatas*,
Dakas, dakinis, oath-bound Dharma guardians,
Protectors who bear witness with eyes of wisdom,
Your omniscient clear realization unsurpassed,
Sovereigns of the ocean of compassion, accomplishments and blessings:
Please heed my confession of errors, I pray.

དང་ཉིད་ཡེ་ནས་སངས་རྒྱས་ཡིན་མོད་ཀྱང་། །རྟོག་པའི་དབང་གིས་འཁོར་བ
འདིར་འཁྱམས་ནས། །ལས་དང་ཉོན་མོངས་བཟོད་དཀའས་ཡུན་རིང་མནར། །
རྒྱུན་རིང་ཤུགས་དྲག་རྟོག་པའི་རྦ་རླབས་གཡོས། །སྲོག་བསྲུལ་སྤུ་ཚོགས་དབང་
གིས་ཉམས་རེ་ཐག །འདི་ལ་བསྒྲུབ་དང་སྤྱོད་པར་མཛད་དུ་གསོལ། །

My reality has indeed always been buddha.
Yet under the influence of discursive thoughts, I wander here in the cycle
      of miseries,
Long tormented by unbearable karma and emotions,
Long pounded by violent waves of thoughts.

Myriad sufferings have rendered me so miserable!
Please guard and protect me, I pray.

བདག་ནི་ཐོག་མ་མེད་ནས་ད་ལྟའི་བར། །ཉོན་མོངས་འདོད་ཆགས་ཞེ་སྡང་
གཏི་མུག་དང་། །རྒྱལ་ཕྲག་དོག་འཁྲུལ་པས་ཀུན་བསླང་ནས། །སྲོག་གཅོད་
མ་བྱིན་བླངས་དང་མི་ཚངས་སྤྱོད། །རྫུན་ཚིག་ཕྲ་མ་ཚིག་རྩུབ་ངག་འཁྱལ་དང་། །བརྣབ་སེམས་གནོད་སེམས་ལོག་པར་ལྟ་བ་དང་། །མཚམས་མེད་ལྔ་དང་དེ་དང་ཉེ་
བ་ལྔ། །ལྕི་བཞི་ལོག་བརྒྱད་ཁ་ན་མ་ཐོ་བའི། །སྡིག་པ་བགྱིས་དང་བཅུག་སྐུལ་
ཡི་རང་བའི། །རང་བཞིན་མི་དགེ་སྡིག་པ་ཅི་མཆིས་པ། །སྐྱབས་གནས་རྒྱ་
མཚོའི་སྤྱན་སྔར་མཐོལ་ལོ་བཤགས། །མི་གསང་མི་སྦེད་གནོང་འགྱོད་དྲག་པོས་
བཤགས། །

From beginningless time until now,
I have been driven by delusion, and through the disturbing emotions of
    desire, anger, ignorance, pride and jealousy,
I have killed, taken what is not given, engaged in sexual misconduct,
Lied, slandered, spoken cruelly, and chattered pointlessly,
Coveted, thought malicious thoughts, and harbored flawed views.
I have committed the five heinous crimes, their five associated crimes,
The four "heavies," the eight "wrongs," and the "unmentionable" negative
    actions.
Whatever naturally non-virtuous negative actions I have done, asked
    others to do, or celebrated,
I openly acknowledge and confess before the infinite refuge.
Concealing nothing, I confess with deep regret and sorrow.

ཕྱིན་ཆད་སྲོག་ལ་བབ་ཀྱང་མི་བགྱིད་དོ། །ཕམ་པ་བཞི་དང་ལྷག་མ་བཅུ་གསུམ་
དང་། །སྤང་ལྟུང་སུམ་ཅུ་ལྟུང་བྱེད་དགུ་བཅུ་དང་། །སོར་བཤགས་བཞི་དང་
ཉེས་བྱས་བརྒྱ་བཅུ་གཉིས། །དཀར་ནག་ཆོས་བརྒྱད་བླང་དོར་ཉམས་པ་དང་།
རྟ་བའི་ལྟུང་བ་བཞི་དང་ཡན་ལག་གི། །ཉེས་བྱས་བཞི་བཅུ་ཞེ་དྲུག་ལ་སོགས་པའི།
རྒྱལ་སྲས་བྱང་ཆུབ་སེམས་དཔའི་གནང་བཀག་གི། །མཚམས་ལས་འགལ་བའི་
ཉེས་ལྟུང་ཅི་མཆིས་པ། །མི་གསང་མི་སྦེད་གནང་འགྱོད་དྲག་པོས་བཤགས། །

Henceforth, even at the cost of my life, I shall not repeat such actions.
The four "defeats," the additional thirteen,
The thirty renunciation downfalls, the ninety transgressions,
The four food offenses, the 112 misdeeds,
The eight right and wrong dharmas,
The corrupted moral practices of acceptance and rejection,
The four root downfalls,
The 46 branch misdeeds and so forth—
Whatever faults and downfalls I have committed,
That contradict the bodhisattva's permissions and prohibitions,
I confess with deep regret and sorrow, concealing nothing.

བཏུལ་ཞུགས་ཉེར་ལྔ་རྩ་ལྟུང་བཅུ་བཞི་དང་། །ཡན་ལག་སྦོམ་པོའི་ལྟུང་བ་རྣམས་པ་
བརྒྱད། །ཁྱད་པར་རྟོགས་པ་ཅན་པོའི་ངན་ཚིག་ནི། །ཉི་ཤུ་རྩ་བདུན་རྩ་བའི་ལྟུང་
བ་དང་། །ཡན་ལག་ངམ་ཚིག་ཉི་ཤུ་ལྔ་དང་། །ལྷག་པའི་ངམ་ཚིག་ཆེན་པོ་
ཉི་ཤུ་སྟེ། །བསྒྲུབས་རྣམ་འགྱུར་བ་རྣ་མེད་པ་ཡི། །ངམ་ཚིག་རྣམས་ཆག་མི་དགེ
སྒྲིབ་པའི་ཚོགས། །གནང་འགྱུར་དྲག་པོས་མཐོལ་བཤགས་བཟོད་པར་སྩོལ། །
བདག་ནི་སེམས་ཅན་འཁྲུལ་པའི་རང་བཞིན་ལགས། །མི་ཤེས་དབང་གིས་ཉེས་པ་
ཅི་མཆིས་པ། །ཐོན་དམ་ཡེ་ཤེས་མཐའ་བའི་ལྷ་ལ་བཤགས། །

The twenty-five yogic disciplines, the fourteen root downfalls,
The eight serious branch downfalls,
And especially the samayas of the Great Perfection—
The twenty-seven root downfalls,
The twenty-five branch samayas,
And the twenty additional great samayas—
The mass of non-virtuous negative actions and corrupt samayas
Of Kriya, Upa and Yoga tantra, the action of Annutarayoga,
I confess with deep regret and sorrow, and beg forgiveness.
I am indeed a deluded sentient being.
Whatever faults I have committed due to ignorance,
I confess to the divine ones who possess ultimate wisdom.

བརྩེ་བའི་དབང་གིས་བཟོད་པ་དང་དུ་བཞེས། །དག་ཅིང་ཚངས་པ་དགྱེས་པའི་ ཞལ་རས་སྟོན། །ཕྱིན་ཆད་མི་བགྱིད་དམ་བཅའ་ཁྱོད་ལ་འབུལ། །རྩ་གསུམ་ རྒྱ་མཚོའི་བྱིན་རླབས་རྣ་དབྱུང་གིས། །བདག་རྒྱུད་ཡོངས་སུ་དག་པར་བྱིན་གྱིས་ རློབས། །

Through the power of love, forgive and accept me.
Reveal your pure and noble faces of delight!
Henceforth I shall not commit misdeeds; I offer you this promise.
That the sublime blessings of the infinite Three Roots
May completely purify my being, grant your blessings!

ཅེས་པའདི་ནི་གུ་ཎའི་མིང་གིས་བསྐུལ་བའི་ངོར། དུག་ལྔའི་མེ་ལྕེ་དབྱིངས་སུ་འཁྱིལ་བའི་ཆོ་ཟེར་ཅན་སྔགས་ཀྱི་ རྣལ་འབྱོར་པ་ལས་འབྲེལ་རྩལ་གྱིས་བྲིས་པ་དགོའི།། །།

At the behest of one named Guna, this was composed by the tantric yogin
Ledreltsel, for whom the sun of the five poisons blazes into the space of reality.
May it bring benefit!

༄༅། །སྐྱེས་རབས་བསྡུས་པ་ནི།

Prayer to Khenpo Ngawang Palzang with Brief Summary of his Previous Lives

ཕྱི་ལྟར་སློབ་དཔོན་འཇམ་དཔལ་བཤེས་གཉེན་དང་། །ནང་ལྟར་རིག་འཛིན་ཆེན་པོ་ ཧཱུྃ་ཀ་ར། །གསང་བ་པཉྩ་ཆེན་པོ་བི་མ་མི་ཏྲའི་ཞབས། །ཡང་གསང་ཆོས་ཀྱི་རྒྱལ་པོ་ ཀློང་ཆེན་པ། །རྡོ་རྗེ་གཟི་བརྗིད་རྩལ་ལ་གསོལ་བ་འདེབས། །

Outwardly, you are Acharya Manjushrimitra.
Inwardly, you are the Great Vidyadhara Humkara.
Secretly, you are the venerable Mahapandita Vimalamitra.
Most secretly, you are the Sovereign of Dharma, Longchenpa.
Dorje Zijitsel, to you I pray.

ཤེས་རབ་ཆེན་པོས་ཆོས་ཀྱི་དེ་ཉིད་གཟིགས། །སྙིང་རྗེ་ཆེན་པོས་འགྲོ་རྣམས་རྗེས་ སུ་འཛིན། །དཔལ་ལྡན་བླ་མས་རྗེས་བཟུང་མཁྱེན་བརྩེའི་གཏེར། །ངག་གི་ དབང་པོའི་ཞབས་ལ་གསོལ་བ་འདེབས། །

Through great discerning awareness, you beheld the true nature of
    phenomena.
Through great compassion, you cared for beings.
Trained by glorious lamas, you are a treasury of wisdom and love.
Ngakgi Wangpo, at your feet I pray.

འདི་དང་ཕྱི་མ་བར་དོ་ཐམས་ཅད་དུ། །འབྲལ་མེད་བརྩེ་བས་རྗེས་བཟུང་སྨིན་གྲོལ་ གྱི། །གསང་ཆེན་བདུད་རྩི་ཐོབ་ནས་འགྲོ་ཀུན་གྱི། །ཐུག་ཏུ་ཕན་བདེ་འབྱུང་བར་ བྱིན་གྱིས་རློབས། །

In this life, in the bardo, and in all my future lives,
Care for me lovingly, without separation.
Grant your blessings that I may obtain the great secret elixir
Of the ripening empowerments and liberating instructions,
And can forever accomplish the benefit and happiness of beings.

ཞེས་པ་འདི་ནི་གཏེར་ཆེན་རིན་པོ་ཆེའི་ཞལ་སྲུ་ནས་འཇམ་དཔལ་དགྱེས་པ་ཟིལ་གནོན་ངག་གི་དབང་པོའམ།

རྡོ་རྗེ་གཟི་བརྗིད་རྩལ་དུ་མིང་གི་ཆོད་པན་གནང་བའི་སྙོམས་ལས་པ་དེས་གང་དྲན་ཧྲ་ཧྲ་ལྟར་བྲིས་པའོ།།

At the behest of Terchen Rinpoche, the lazy one crowned with the name Jampal Gyepa Zilnön Ngakgi Wangpo—aka Dorje Zijitsel—wrote down whatever spontaneously came to mind.

Short Devotional Supplications

ༀ རིགས་བརྒྱའི་ཁྱབ་བདག་དཔལ་ལྡན་རྡོ་རྗེ་སེམས། །ལྔ་བརྒྱའི་གཙུག །
རྒྱན་པཎ་ཆེན་བི་མ་ལའི། །ཨེ་ཤེས་སྒྱུ་མའི་རྣམ་རོལ་ངག་གི་དབང་། །རྡོ་རྗེ་
གཟི་བརྗིད་རྩལ་ལ་གསོལ་བ་འདེབས། །

Sovereign lord of the hundreds of buddha families—Glorious Vajrasattva,
Crown jewel of five hundred great Indian scholars—Mahapandita
    Vimalamitra,
Illusory wisdom emanation—Ngakgi Wangpo,
Dorje Zijitsel, to you I pray.

ཞེས་པའང་དད་ལྡན་ཡིད་ལྷུང་དར་རྒྱས་དོར་བཙུན་པ་ཚུལ་ཁྲིམས་རྒྱ་མཚོས་སོ།། ༎

*This was written for the faithful Li-Lhung Dargyey by the noble monk Tsul-
trim Gyatso.*

ༀ ས་མཆོག་དགྱིལ་འཁོར་མཆོན་གྱུར་བི་མ་ལ། །ཀུན་བཟང་ཆོས་སྐུའི་སྟོན །
པ་ཀློང་ཆེན་པ། །ལྔ་ལྡན་ལོངས་སྐུ་རྡོ་རྗེ་གགས་པ་ལས་འཕེལ་རྩལ། །དབྱེར་མེད །
ངག་གི་དབང་པོར་གསོལ་བ་འདེབས། །

Manifestation of the supreme level mandala—Vimalamitra,
Teacher of dharmakaya Samantabhadra—Longchenpa,
Fivefold sambhogakaya—Ledreltsel,
To their indivisible union—Ngakgi Wangpo, I pray.

དོན་བརྒྱུད་དགོངས་པའི་བྱིན་རླབས་སེམས་ལ་ཕོབས། །སེམས་ཉིད་རིག་སྟོང །
རྗེན་པའི་རང་ཞལ་སྟོན། །རང་བབ་དགོངས་པའི་དོན་ཆོས་བརྗེས་པ་དང་། །ཕར །
གྲོལ་དུས་མཉམ་སྟོང་པས་བོགས་དབྱུང་ཤོག །

Shower the wisdom blessings of the ultimate lineage upon my mind!
Reveal my true face, the nature of mind—naked empty awareness.
May I discover the wisdom of naturalness, just as it is,
And progress by embracing liberation upon arising.

ཅེས་པའང་རི་གསལ་པར་སྐྱ་བ་དབང་ཕྱུག་རྡོ་རྗེའི་ངོར་པདྨ་ལས་འབྲེལ་རྩལ་གྱིས་སྦྱར་བ་དགོ།

This was composed for the learned Wangchuk Dorje, by Pema Ledreltsel.

Appendix 4: Key to Translations

English	Tibetan
absorption	ting nge 'dzin
awareness	rig pa
beings	sems can / 'gro ba
buddha body, buddha speech, buddha mind	sku gsung thugs
channels, energies, vital nuclei	rtsa rlung thig le
clear vision	gsal snang
completion stage	rdzogs rim
concentration	bsam gtan
conquerors	rgyal ba
constructs	spros pa
defilement	zag pa
dependent arising / auspicious connections	rten 'brel
Dharma	chos
Dharmakaya	chos sku
disturbing emotions	nyon mongs

equipoise	mnyams bzhags
essence	snying po
expanse	klong
expressive power / dynamism	rtsal
familiarization	goms pa
generation stage	bskyed rim
Great Perfection	rdzogs chen
guidance	khrid
illusion	sgyu ma
insight	shes rab
instructions	gdams pa
levels and paths	sa dang lam
logical argument	gtan tshigs
luminosity	'od gsal
Middle Way / Madhyamaka	dbu ma
Mind Lineage	dgongs brgyud
mind-treasure	dgongs gter
nirmanakaya	sprul sku
Nyingtik	snying thig
pith instructions	man ngag
precious instructions	gdams ngag
pure vision	dag snang
qualities	yon tan
reality	chos nyid

relative truth	kun rdzob kyi bden pa
samaya / oath	dam tshig
Sambhogakaya	longs sku
samsara	'khor ba
self-awareness	rang rig
self-cognizant awareness	rang shes rig pa
space	dbyings
space of reality	chos kyi dbyings
spiritual practice / heart practice / pledge	thugs dam
students / beings to be benefited	'dul bya
study, reflection, and meditation	thos bsam sgom
Symbol Lineage	brda brgyud
three planes of existence	sa gsum
three realms	khams gsum
Tögal	thod rgal
Trekchö	khregs chod
ultimate truth	don dam gyi bden pa
unawareness	ma rig pa
valid cognition	tshad ma
vidyadhara	rig 'dzin
vital nucleus / nuclei	thig le
vital-essence	dwangs ma / dwangs bcud

Whispered Lineage	snyan brgyud
wisdom mind / wisdom realization / wisdom intent	dgongs pa
wisdom / wakefulness	ye shes
yogic discipline	brtul zhugs
yogic inner heat	gtum mo

Appendix 5: Khenpo Ngawang Palzang's Name Variants

Primary Name: Ngawang Palzang

Primary Titles: Katok Khenpo Ngawang Palzang, Dzogchen Khenpo Ngakchung, Palyul Khenrab Ngawang Palzang

Personal Names: Khenpo Ngaga, Khenpo Ngakchung, Ngakgi Wangpo, Shönnu Pema Lekdrub, Tsultrim Gyatso, Tenpa Rabpel, Dorje Zijitsel, Khenpo Ngaklu, Jampal Gyepa Zilnön

Secret Initiatory Name: Pema Ledreltsel

Pen Name: Ösel Rinchen Nyingpo, Jampal Gyepa Zilnön

NOTES

1. This name was bestowed upon Khenpo Ngakchung by a dakini in a pure dream-vision during his retreat at Kyilko.
2. See Tulku Thondup, *Masters of Meditation*, 266, and Nyoshul Khenpo, *Marvelous Garland*, 247.
3. *zhal gdams* by Khenpo Ngakchung. *Collected Works* 2:142.
4. Tulku Thondup, *Masters of Meditation*, 222, and Nyoshul Khenpo, *Marvelous Garland*, 238.
5. *drang srong skyo glu nyes pa'i mtshangs 'don* by Khenpo Ngakchung. *Collected Works* 2:232–34.
6. Khenpo Ngakchung's *Collected Works* are available in nine volumes from the Tibetan Buddhist Resource Center (TBRC).
7. Email communication, September 2012.
8. Patrul Rinpoche, *Words of My Perfect Teacher*, 311–12.
9. Dilgo Khyentse, *Brilliant Moon*, xxvii.
10. Smith, *Among Tibetan Texts*, 27.
11. *snyan brgyud.* Literally "aural lineage"; sometimes translated as "oral lineage." This is the mouth-to-ear transmission of sacred teachings passed from master to disciple. While the teachings are not necessarily "whispered," we chose this translation to indicate the preciousness and secrecy of the teachings transmitted in this way.
12. *sgyu ma'i nor.* Illusory wealth; a metaphor for the lack of permanence and stability.
13. Profound View is the Mahayana tradition promulgated by Arya Nagarjuna with emphasis on the profound view of Madyamaka, and the Vast Action tradition of Arya Asanga is the Yogacharya tradition that expounds on buddha nature.
14. *rgyal ba'i sras* is an epithet of tenth-level bodhisattvas.
15. A single emanation body (*nirmanakaya*) who fully reestablishes the Buddhist teachings is endowed with ninety-six qualities of enlightened activity. For more on this, see Jamgön Kongtrül, *Treasury of Knowledge: Buddhism's Journey*, 107–8; also Dudjom Rinpoche, *Nyingma School*, 22, 137.

16. The era of spiritual degeneration refers to the fourth age of this aeon, which is characterized by five spiritual degenerations. See glossary of enumerations.

17. *mkha' 'gro'i snying thig.* This is a treasure cycle transmitted by Guru Padmasambhava to Princess Pemasel, daughter of the Tibetan king Trisong Detsen. She later took rebirth as the treasure-revealer Pema Ledrel Tsel, who established the teaching. Pema Ledrel Tsel's subsequent rebirth was Longchen Rabjam (1308–64), who included the *Khandro Nyingtik* in his profound collection of Dzogchen practices, the *Four Nyingtik Mother-and-Child Cycles* (*snying thig ya bzhi*). This particular prophecy refers to the successive incarnations of Vimalamitra, the eighth-century lineage holder of Mahayoga and the Great Perfection. Khenpo Ngakchung is revered as one of these incarnations.

18. The *rab byung* (sexagenary cycle) comprises sixty years, according to the Tibetan calendar, the first of which began in 1027 C.E. We are currently in the seventeenth such cycle, which began on February 28, 1987.

19. *gtum mo* (Skt. *chandali*) is the name of a subtle energy channel, and by extension the name of a yogic exercise belonging to the completion stage of meditation (*rdzogs rim*). Success in the practice is marked by an ability to generate an unusual degree of physical heat, enabling practitioners to withstand severe cold.

20. This refers to the Tibetan system of recognizing reincarnations of deceased spiritual masters, in which students of a previous master follow indications to determine the location of the lama's rebirth, often arriving unannounced at a family's home and identifying their child as the reincarnation. The family is then obliged to give the child to the search party, and the child is then taken back to their former monastery for spiritual training.

21. These are the names of two charnel grounds in India or the Nepalese Terai, where Vimalamitra trained in tantra. Here Khenpo Ngakchung is implying that he is a bona fide reincarnation of Vimalamitra.

22. *ging.* A sword-wielding class of protective acolyte (*las mkhan*), sometimes assuming dancing skeletal forms, which may pass freely through space. See de Nebesky-Wojkowitz, *Oracles and Demons,* 278–80.

23. PAT (Tib. *phat*). Frequently pronounced as "pey" or "poy," this is the sound uttered during the practice of consciousness transference (*'pho ba*). This is an essential practice of the completion stage of meditation, which is to be applied at the time of death either by the dying person or by one who is adept at making this transference of consciousness on behalf of others.

24. This is the mantra of the bodhisattva of great compassion, Avalokiteshvara, the recitation of which is said to purify the sufferings of the six classes of beings and prevent rebirth in the lower realms.

25. The kila (*phur ba*) is a three-sided peg, stake, knife, dagger, or nail-like ritual implement traditionally associated with Indo-Tibetan Buddhism, Bön, and Indian Vedic traditions.

26. The verses associated with the seven branches (homage, offering, confession, rejoicing, requesting teachers to turn the Wheel of Dharma, requesting them

not to pass into nirvana, and dedication of merit) comprise the first twelve four-line stanzas of this popular aspirational prayer.

27. *btags grol.* A text comprising complex Sanskrit mantra recitations, which may be printed as a diagram and worn close to the body on account of its power to liberate upon tactile contact.

28. Since Khenpo Ngakchung was known as a reincarnation of Vimalamitra, the *Liberation by Wearing* text and diagram derived from the *Vima Nyingtik* (*bi ma snying thig*), entitled *btags pas grol bar bstan pa bug cig gig sang 'grel,* was in fact introduced to Tibet by Vimalamitra.

29. This refers to the practice of reciting entire Tibetan texts by chanting the letters, syllables, and final pronunciation of each word in a rapid, rhythmic manner, as a way of training young children to read.

30. *pad ma bka' yi thang yig.* Also translated as *The Lotus Chronicles,* this treasure text is perhaps the most popular biographical account of Guru Padmasambhava, revealed from the Crystal Cave (*shel brag ma*) by Tertön Orgyen Lingpa in the fourteenth century.

31. *tshig bdun ma'i gsol 'debs* is the title of the renowned seven-line prayer dedicated to Guru Padmasambhava, the multiple meanings of which are expounded in Jamgön Mipam's *tshig bdun rnam bshad padma dkar po* (NK, vol. 119) and translated in Jamgön Mipam. *White Lotus.* OM AH HUM VAJRA GURU PADMA SIDDHI HUM is the primary mantra of Guru Padmasambhava.

32. Several classic texts mention that wherever there is a Buddha teaching the causal vehicles of the sutras, there will also be a Guru Padmasambhava teaching the resultant vehicle of the tantras. See Tarthang Tulku, *Kum Nye Tibetan Yoga,* 13.

33. These are two of the Eight Medicine Buddhas, known respectively in Tibetan as *legs par yongs sgrags dpal gyi rgyal po* and *chos bsgrags rgya mtsho'i dbyangs.*

34. This is part of the ritual of taking refuge in the Buddhist tradition, in which a strand of the student's hair is cut by the refuge master.

35. *kun rig (rnam par snang mdzad).* This is the primordial buddha according to the *Sarvadurgatiparisodhanatantra,* a class of Yoga Tantra popular in the Sakya tradition.

36. This is a reference to the section in the *Heart Sutra of Insight* that describes the ultimate nature, beyond the scope of the five senses.

37. *mdo* (Skt. *sutra*) and *sngags* (Skt. *mantra*) respectively refer to the causal teachings expounded in the aforementioned three vehicles and the resultant vehicles of the tantras, also known as the vehicles of vajra reality (*vajrayana*). On the latter, see e.g., Dudjom Rinpoche, *Nyingma School,* 346–72.

38. Mulasarvastivada is the tradition of monastic ordination that survives within the various Tibetan traditions. On the eighteen distinct Vinaya schools, see Lamotte, *History of Indian Buddhism,* 571–606.

39. This means that the spiritual lineage of Patrul Rinpoche would have been broken.

40. This refers to the metaphor in which the transmission of a lama's knowledge and qualities to a disciple and future lineage holder is likened to pouring all the contents of one vase (the lama) into another vase (the disciple).

41. The *Sangwa Nyingtik, "Secret Heart Essence"* (*gsang ba snying thig*), is generally identical to the Pith Instructional Class (*man ngag sde*) of the Great Perfection, on which see Dudjom Rinpoche, *Nyingma School*, 329–45. More specifically, it refers to the *Seventeen Tantras* of the unsurpassedly secret cycle (*yang gsang bla na med pa'i snying thig gi skor*), which form the fourth and highest cycle of the Pith Instructional Class according to the arrangement of Shri Singha. All lineages of this *Sangwa Nyingtik* passed from Shri Singha and continued in Tibet through his close disciples, Padmasambhava and Vimalamitra. In the fourteenth century these two lineages fell to Rangjung Dorje, the Third Karmapa, and his close associate Longchen Rabjam (1308–63), the latter of whom systematized these teachings in his great body of writings. Longchen Rabjam is revered as an incarnation of Princess Pemasel, the daughter of King Trisong Detsen, and of Pema Ledrel Tsel, who were both earlier recipients of the *Khandro Nyingtik* (*mkha 'gro snying thig*).

42. For a detailed description of these two practices, see Glossary of Enumerations under "twofold path of the luminous Great Perfection."

43. "Abu" is an affectionate epithet of Patrul Rinpoche

44. Translated into English under the title *Kindly Bent to Ease Us.*

45. These are most likely in the vicinity of Jönpalung and Tromtar.

46. *nges pa don gyi rdo rje 'chang chen po.* This is a title of great respect given to unsurpassed spiritual masters and lineage holders within the tradition of the Buddhist tantras. The definitive meaning (Tib. *nges don*, Skt. *nitartha*) is contrasted with the expedient or provisional meaning (Tib. *drang don*, Skt. *neyartha*), and all Buddhist teachings may be categorized in terms of these distinctions.

47. *'bog tho.* This refers to the round yellow felt hat, trimmed with fur, which was formerly worn by Tibetan government officials.

48. Because the butter was offered to Lungtok by his mother with such powerful faith and love, Abu Rinpoche felt that he would be misusing offerings made by the faithful (*dkor*) were he to accept it.

49. This is a quintessential Mahayana teaching and meditation for generating bodhichitta, the altruistic aspiration to attain Buddhahood for the sake of all beings. The steps of this meditation involve recognizing all beings as having been one's mother (*mar shes*) in previous lifetimes; remembering the kindness of motherly love (*drin dran*); repaying the kindness of motherly love (*drin gso*); and so forth. The practice is known as the *Sevenfold Pith Instruction on Cause and Effect* (*rgyu 'bras man ngag bdun*) and constitutes one of the main methods for generating bodhichitta.

50. This is an edible white-colored variety of azalea (*sur dkar*). (Oral communication: Tulku Pema Wangyal.)

51. It is an ancient Indian and Tibetan tradition to welcome highly honored guests by waving incense.

52. In this context, the New Treasure tradition might refer to Rigdzin Jigme Lingpa's revelations contained in the *Longchen Nyingtik*, or alternatively to the new treasures discovered by the somewhat controversial treasure-revealer Rinchen Lingpa of Yel-le Gar.

53. The descent of the actual wisdom deity (Skt. *jnanasattva*) into the visualized commitment deity (Skt. *samayasattva*), which is the body of the recipient participating in the empowerment ceremony, is often said to induce spontaneous and effortless song and dance. Such events are recounted in, for example, the biography of Longchen Rabjampa. See Dudjom Rinpoche, *Nyingma School,* 580–88.

54. This refers to the activity of the treasure-revealers (*gter ston*), who may unearth spiritual revelations (*gter ma*) concealed in the form of ritual objects that had been invisibly sealed inside rocks and so forth by Padmasambhava and others in the past. See Dudjom Rinpoche, *Nyingma School,* 743–49.

55. Lerab Lingpa's fame derives from his association with the Thirteenth Dalai Lama. Bronze-alloy (*li ma*) is a highly valued indigenous Tibetan alloy of bronze and other metals, including meteorite.

56. The Great Perfection (*rdzogs pa chen po*) is a synonym of Atiyoga, the highest of all the nine vehicles of the Buddhist teachings according to the Nyingma tradition. On its content, see Dudjom Rinpoche, *Nyingma School,* 294–345; on its transmission in ancient India, ibid., 490–501; and in Tibet, ibid., 538–96. Despite the contemporary fascination with the Great Perfection outside Tibet, within the Tibetan tradition it is even now regarded as an esoteric system of practices, suitable only for the most advanced recipients of the Buddhist teachings.

57. Gracious One (*bka' drin can*) is the intimate and respectful title by which Khenpo Ngakchung often refers to his lama, Nyoshul Lungtok.

58. This line is an apparent contradiction to an earlier statement that he was five years old when he first met Lungtok Rinpoche.

59. When young reincarnate lamas are recognized, their families are urged to keep them in clean conditions to prevent defilement and illness.

60. *gang gi blo gros ma.* This is a famous twelve-stanza prayer in praise of the bodhisattva Manjushri that begins with the words "You whose intelligence . . . ."

61. On the traditional preparation of paper, see Jamgön Kongtrül's detailed explanation in Dorje, *Treasury of Knowledge.*

62. The mantra of Manjushri, the bodhisattva associated with transcendent insight and intelligence, is OM AH RA PA TSA NA DHI. The mantra is frequently recited by children to improve their speech and speed their learning process, or by anyone wishing to enhance his or her skills in debate, memorization, composition, and comprehension.

63. Female nagas or naginis (*klu mo*) are powerful, long-lived, serpent-like beings who inhabit water and often guard great treasures. Said to partake equally of

the animal and god realms, they generally assume the form of snakes, but they may change into human form.

64. This is probably the Second Drime Shingkyong, Jigme Rigdzin Gönpo (fl. 18th to 19th centuries), but it could possibly refer to the Third Drime Shingkyong, Jigme Yonten Gönpo, who passed away around 1898. However, it cannot be, as our text suggests, the Fourth Drime Shingkyong, Dechen Dorje, who was only born in 1899.

65. This refers to the meditative process of recognizing one's inherent buddha nature by first visualizing oneself as a yidam deity. This is known as the commitment aspect of the deity (Tib. *dam tshig sems dpa'*, Skt. *samayasattva*), which is contrasted with the wisdom deity (Tib. *ye shes sems dpa'*, Skt. *jnanasattva*). When the latter dissolves into the visualized form, this purifies notions of ordinariness and gives rise to the experience of divine pride, the conviction that one is in fact the actual wisdom deity. See Trungpa, *Journey Without Goal*.

66. The karmic body is the body we have from birth to death, in which all kinds of suffering and happiness resulting from past negative and positive actions come to full fruition.

67. This refers not to ordinary pride, but to the unshakable confidence that results in complete identification with the deity and the certainty of uniting with the deity's primordial nature.

68. The vows of the novitiate consist of ten basic precepts. These can be extended to thirty-six precepts, which are normally maintained for the duration of one's life. The basic ten are to abandon: killing, taking what is not given, sexual intercourse, lying, intoxicants, singing / dancing / playing music, self-beautification (perfume, ornaments, cosmetics, etc.), sitting on high or expensive beds or thrones, eating after midday, and touching gold, silver or precious objects (including money). By contrast, fully ordained monks hold 253 vows, and fully ordained nuns hold 364 vows. The three phases of conferral (*tshig gsum rim nod*) refer to the preparation, the actual conferral of ordination, and the subsequent advice that is imparted. See Nyima, *Encyclopaedic Tibetan-English Dictionary*, 601. Alternatively, it has been suggested that this expression might refer to the gradual receipt of the vows of the three levels of ordination: laity, novitiate, and full-fledged ordination.

69. Fully ordained monks are required to keep their formal monastic cloaks with them at all times.

70. One of the enumerations of the sixteen aspects of emptiness—namely, the emptiness of emptiness (*stong pa'i stong pa nyid*)—refers to the lack of substantiality of emptiness. This means that emptiness is not an absolute that one might assume, leading to the unwanted establishment of nihilism as ultimate truth. Khenpo Ngakchung here indicates the delight in finding freedom from such an extreme. See Huntington, *Emptiness of Emptiness*.

71. The culmination of awareness (*rig pa tshad phebs*) is the third of the four visions experienced in the Tögal (*thod rgal*) practice of the Great Perfection.

72. The full discernment of phenomena (Tib. *chos rab tu rnam 'byed,* Skt. *dhar-mapravicaya*) is one of the seven branches of enlightenment, the others being stability, mindfulness, diligence, rejoicing, pliancy, and impartiality.

73. This is a poetic way of saying that he gave a direct introduction to the nature of mind to each practitioner, and with the warmth of the precious instructions and sustained practice, each one, like an egg, would hatch into Buddhahood. (Oral communication: Lobpon Jigme Rinpoche.)

74. "Ngakli" is a nickname for Khenpo Ngakchung.

75. The celebration of Guru Padmasambhava's birthday, when vast feast offerings are made, usually falls in July.

76. Feast offerings (Tib. *tshogs kyi 'khor lo,* Skt. *ganacakra*) are a unique tantric method for conferring accomplishment and pacifying obstacles. In general, feast-offering ceremonies are frequently held to commemorate important events in the Buddhist calendar, such as the Tenth-Day feast offering, dedicated to Padmasambhava. The overall purpose is to distribute merit and wisdom in the context of a specific tantric ritual.

77. The mandala offering is a skillful means of cultivating detachment, while accumulating merit (*bsod nams*) and wisdom (*ye shes*), by mentally and symbolically offering the entire universe to one's spiritual teacher and the Three Jewels (Buddha, Dharma, and Sangha). The universe is symbolized by a mandala plate, upon which are heaped all the wealth and glory of the universe, symbolized by various grains, jewels, medicines, and so forth. See Patrul Rinpoche, *Words of My Perfect Teacher,* 281–95.

78. For a further explanation, see ibid., 221–22.

79. *'bum lnga.* The preliminary practices consist of accumulating one hundred thousand repetitions of each of five different practices, on which see ibid. 169–347.

80. The hundred-syllable mantra of Vajrasattva (*yig brgya*) may be literally translated as follows: "OM Vajrasattva. Protect my commitments. Vajrasattva. Let them be firm. Let me be steadfast. Let me be satisfied. Let me be nourished. Let me be loved. Bestow all accomplishments upon me. With regard to all my past actions, make my mind virtuous. HUM [seed-syllable of buddha-mind] HA [four immeasurable aspirations] HA [four empowerments] HA [four delights] HA [four buddha-bodies] HO [joyous laughter]. Transcendent One, Vajra Reality of all the Tathagatas! Do not forsake me! Make me into vajra reality! Great Being of Commitment, AH [nondual union]." The recitation of this mantra, in conjunction with the visualization of Vajrasattva and the confession of negativity, is an essential component of the preliminary practices (*sngon 'gro*).

81. See "four supports" in glossary of enumerations.

82. The Path of Accumulating (*tshogs lam*) and the Path of Joining (*sbyor lam*) are the first two of the five bodhisattva paths outlined in the Mahayana tradition, the other three being the paths of Seeing, Meditation, and No-More-Learning. Specifically, on the Path of Accumulating, bodhisattvas generate

both aspirational and engaged bodhichitta, and make a concerted effort to accumulate merit. The Path of Joining is so named because it links the Path of Accumulating with nonconceptual wisdom on the Path of Seeing. See Patrul Rinpoche, *Collected Works*, 4:173–86 and *Brief Guide*.

83. *bka' gdams mchod rten*. This refers to a distinctive bulbous or bell-shaped style of stupa, which was introduced to Tibet by Atisha, progenitor of the Kadampa lineage.

84. These are the superior, middling, and inferior scopes discussed in works such as Tsongkhapa's *Great Treatise on the Stages of the Path* (*lam rim chen mo*).

85. Incense from Mindroling Monastery in southern Tibet is even now made from a special recipe and esteemed for its purity.

86. Four dry measures amounts to some 56 kg of grain. The unit of dry measure (*khal*), so called because it is equivalent to one side-load carried by a pack animal, comprises twenty-eight *rgya ma* (14 kg).

87. This mandala-offering prayer reads: "OM AH HUM. To offer to the Buddhas in all buddhafields the entire cosmos of a billion worlds, replete with everything that could be desired, will perfect the wisdom of the buddhas." See Patrul Rinpoche, *Words of My Perfect Teacher*, 284.

88. The amendment refers to an additional accumulation of 11,111 repetitions that are offered to make up for any deficiencies in the initial series of 100,000, bringing the total requirement to 111,111. The second verse mentioned here is as follows:

The ground is sprinkled with scented water and strewn with flowers.
Adorned with Mount Meru, the four continents, and the sun and moon.
Thinking of it as a blessed buddhafield, I offer it
So that all beings may enjoy the happiness of the perfectly pure buddhafields.
IDAM RATNA MANDALA KAM NIRYÄTA YAMI

89. "Words of truth" (*bden tshig*) is a power that has been achieved by many great accomplished masters. This means that whatever they say will happen or be realized. (Oral communication: Tulku Thondup.)

90. This popular Tibetan folk saying means that just as a dog will find a lung (which Tibetans do not consider meat) and wolf it down without checking to see if it is good meat or not, so will certain imprudent individuals apprentice themselves to spiritual teachers without first examining them for proper qualifications. This can result in later losing faith and breaking samaya. (Email communication: Tulku Thondup.)

91. These verses are cited from the *Treasury of Songs of Realization* (*do ha'i mdzod*). Although ultimate innate wisdom is naturally present in all beings, it can only be realized under these conditions.

92. The common mandala offering refers to the accumulation of merit with concepts, and the uncommon mandala offering refers to the accumulation of wisdom beyond concepts.

93. The *Beggar's Accumulation* (*ku sa li'i tshogs*) is made by hermits and renunciates

who, lacking any other possessions, use their own bodies as offerings. Because we cherish our bodies more than any other possession, the body-offering practice is a very powerful way to generate merit. See Patrul Rinpoche, *Words of My Perfect Teacher*, 296–307.

94. These three phases comprise the arising (*lhongs*) of terrifying paranormal phenomena known as spiritual eruptions; their eradication (*tshar*); and their settlement or resolution (*chod*).

95. *sems bskyed sdom chog*. A bodhisattva is one who, motivated by great compassion, has generated bodhichitta, the spontaneous wish to attain Buddhahood for the benefit of all beings. In Mahayana Buddhism, bodhisattvas vow to remain for as long as samsara endures in order to liberate all beings and lead them to enlightenment. With this motivation, the bodhisattva then promises to engage in the practice of the six or ten transcendent perfections.

96. The mistaken conflation of the Nyingma tradition with Bön owes much to the polemics of certain sectarian scholars of the eighteenth and nineteenth centuries. The specific reference here is to the inherent contradiction in lofty views that are intermingled with corrupt actions. On the Bön tradition and its evolution, see e.g., Kvaerne, *Bon Religion of Tibet;*, Baumer, *Bon;*, and Namkhai Norbu, *Dzogchen*.

97. This he did in his famous treatise entitled *Treasury of Precious Qualities* (*yon tan mdzod*), in which he expounds the entire Buddhist path, from the Shravakayana teachings up to the Great Perfection.

98. On the four concentrations (*bsam gtan bzhi*) and their association with the hierarchical abodes within the world of form, see Jamgön Kongtrül's presentation in the *Treasury of Knowledge* (*shes bya klun khyab mdzod*), book 6, part 1, translated in Dorje, *Treasury of Knowledge*.

99. Awareness (Tib. *rig pa*, Skt. *vidya*) is the gateway through which practitioners of the Great Perfection approach the wisdom (Tib. *ye shes*, Skt. *jnana*) of buddha mind. See Karma Lingpa's *Introduction to Awareness: Natural Liberation through Naked Perception* (*rig pa'i ngo sprod gcer mthong rang grol*) in Dorje, Coleman, and Jinpa, *Tibetan Book of the Dead*, 35–57.

100. Mahamudra, the "Great Seal" (Tib. *phyag chen*, Skt. *mahamudra*), is regarded as the highest esoteric or pith instruction according to the New Translation schools, corresponding in its status to the Great Perfection within the Nyingma school. There are both sutra- and tantra-based transmissions of Mahamudra, on which see Konchok Gyaltsen, *Garland of Mahamudra Practices;* Drigung Kyapgön Chetsang, *Practice of Mahamudra*.

101. He trained his mind according to Rigdzin Jigme Lingpa's revelation entitled *Seven Mind Trainings in the Longchen Nyingtik* (*sems sbyong rnam bdun gyi don khrid thar pa'i them skas*).

102. The alaya or universal substratum (Tib. *kun gzhi*, Skt. *alaya*) is the ground of all ordinary experience: a karmically neutral state resulting from the nonrecognition of awareness, which functions as the ground of all samsara.

103. Khenpo Jigme Samten is unidentified. Possibly either Khenchen Jigme Lodrö (Tendzin Lungtok Nyima: 455–57) or Khenchen Jigme Tamdrin Yonten Gönpo (ibid., 466–69).

104. *srid zhi.* This expression encompasses the extremes of samsara and nirvana. For the bodhisattva, dwelling in the extreme of nirvana is as undesirable as dwelling in samsara, because it entails abandoning miserable beings. Also, from an ontological perspective, both are equally nonexistent.

105. On the truth of cessation (*'gog pa'i bden pa*) and the truth of the path (*lam gyi bden pa*) through which it is attained, see the presentation in Jamgön Kongtrül's *Treasury of Knowledge* (*shes bya kun khyab mdzod*), book 6, part 3, which is translated in Jamgön Kongtrül, *Treasury of Knowledge: Frameworks,* 111–22.

106. This is his famous *A Guide to the Words of My Perfect Teacher* (Translated in Ngawang Palzang, *Guide to the Words of My Perfect Teacher.*)

107. Presumably, "Terchen" here is Tertön Sögyal (Lerab Lingpa), in which case the new treasure (*gter gsar*) referred to here will be those texts and cycles contained in his seventeen-volume *Collected Visionary Revelations and Textual Discoveries.*

108. The *Longchen Nyingtik* was published in two volumes in eastern Tibet, although nowadays it frequently can be seen in three volumes or even more.

109. Recitation or approach practice (Tib. *bsnyen pa,* Skt. *seva*) is one of the four phases of approach and accomplishment practice (Tib. *bsnyen sgrub yan lag bzhi*), by which a yidam deity is propitiated or "approached," and accomplishments are consequently attained. Specifically, recitation or approach practice employs three techniques: visualization, mantra recitation, and stability, and it is usually undertaken in strict closed retreat.

110. Among the ten bodhisattva levels, the attainments of the first seven are considered reversible, owing to the persistence of subtle pride, whereas those of the highest three levels are deemed to be irreversible.

111. These are the practices of the completion stage with characteristics from the *snying thig rtsa pod.*

112. There is a distinction between the impure illusory body (*ma dag pa'i sgyu lus*) and the illustrative luminosity (*dpe'i 'od gsal*), which are so called because they have to be cultivated by the meditator, and the pure illusory body (*dag pa'i sgyu lus*) and the genuine luminosity (*don gyi 'od gsal*), which are fruitional and uncultivated. See Padmasambhava, *Natural Wisdom.*

113. The siddhi mantra is the primary mantra of Guru Padmasambhava: OM AH HUM VAJRA GURU PADMA SIDDHI HUM.

114. When referring to his lama's belt, Khenpo Ngakchung used the ordinary term for "strap" or "tail" as opposed to the honorific term, which would indicate respect in the Tibetan language.

115. These verses are quoted from the *Diamond Cutter Sutra* (*Vajracchedika,* T 16).

116. Early Translations (*snga 'gyur*) is a synonym for the teachings of the Nyingma tradition, which were largely translated during the earlier phase of Buddhist

dissemination in Tibet, during the Tibetan Imperial Age, and are therefore contrasted with the New schools (*gsar ma*) of the later phase of dissemination (*phyi dar*).

117. The text reads "fifth chapter."

118. The logical argument of the three purities (*dag pa gsum*) comprises purity of the universe, its inhabitants, and the mindstream. The logical argument of the four modes of evenness (*mnyam pa bzhi*) comprises emptiness, the unity of appearances and emptiness, freedom from constructs, and evenness itself. The logical argument of Great Identity (*bdag nyid chen po*) establishes all phenomena as being atemporally present in the nature of mind. See Dorje, *Guhyagarbhatantra*, 116, 932. Several commentaries expound on these logical arguments of Mahayoga, including Jamgön Mipam's *Overview of the Guhyagarbha Entitled Luminous Essence* (*gsang snying spyi don 'od gsal snying po*) (published under the title *Luminous Essence*) and Dodrub Tenpey Nyima's *Overview of the Guhyagarbha* (*gsang snying spyi don*).

119. For an interpretation of the logical argument of these four kinds of realization (*rtogs pa bzhi'i gtan tshig*), see Dorje, *Guhyagarbhatantra*, 115–16; also 890–96.

120. The Vehicle of Definitive Characteristics (*mtshan nyid theg pa*) is synonymous with the sutra-based vehicles. Specifically, within the Madhyamaka school of the Mahayana there are two modes of establishing the view of emptiness: through consequential reasoning (Skt. *prasanga*), which relies on reductio ad absurdum, while positing no distinct arguments; and through the employment of independent syllogisms (Skt. *svatantra*).

121. The Mind Only (Tib. *sems tsam*, Skt. *cittamatra*) represents a distinctive stand of Mahayana philosophy, largely distinct from the Madhyamaka perspective. See e.g., Jamgön Kongtrül, *Treasury of Knowledge: Frameworks*, 175–93.

122. Buddhapalita (*sangs rgyas bskyang*) and Bhavaviveka (*legs ldan*) were two of the greatest interpreters of Nagarjuna's Madhyamaka in ancient India. Later authorities like Chandrakirti consider them to have respectively founded the Prasangika and Svatantrika systems of the Madhyamaka school. The latter was also an original systematizer of Indian philosophical schools and views. On Buddhapalita, see e.g., Reugg, *Literature of the Madhyamaka School*, 60–61, and on Bhavaviveka, see ibid., p. 61–66.

123. Ultimate truth is distinguished by whether or not it can be expressed in words (*rnams grangs dang rnam grangs min pa'i don dam*). On this distinction, see Dudjom Rinpoche, *Nyingma School*, 206–9. Alternatively, the conventions used in the Padmakara Translation Group's translation of Mipam Rinpoche's commentary on Shantarakshita's *Ornament of the Middle Way* (see Shantarakshita and Jamgön Mipam, *Adornment of the Middle Way*, 108–13) are "approximate ultimate" and "actual ultimate in itself."

124. For a detailed explanation of this view that sees the unity of the entire Mahayana, see Mipam Rinpoche's *Madhyamakalamkara* (*dbu ma brgyan*), translated in English as *The Adornment of the Middle Way*.

125. This refers to the meticulous Tibetan practice of carving mantras or entire prayers onto stone or rock surfaces.

126. *gcig du bral ba.* This dialectical argument, the reasoning of discerning the absence of both the singular and the plural, is praised as the "king of Madhyamaka reasoning." It was originally presented by Shantarakshita in his *Ornament of the Middle Way* (*Madhyamakalamkara*), on which see Blumenthal, *Ornament of the Middle Way;* and Shantarakshita and Jamgön Mipam, *Adornment of the Middle Way.*

127. From form to omniscience (*gzugs nas rnam mkhyen gyi bar*). This Buddhist epistemological term denotes all phenomena, starting from the coarsest material forms and extending as far as the subtlest omniscience of the buddhas.

128. This reasoning presented here is the logical basis for the Vajrayana view of pure perception (*dag snang*), and establishes how wisdom sees all conventional phenomena without subjective confusion, validly recognizing all appearances as innately pure.

129. These words echo Karma Lingpa's *Tibetan Book of the Dead* (*bar do thos grol chen mo*), ch. 11. See Dorje, Coleman, and Jinpa, *Tibetan Book of the Dead,* 233 passim.

130. For a detailed explanation, see Padmasambhava and Jamgön Kongtrul, *Light of Wisdom: Vol. II,* p. 107.

131. The vajra guru approach mantra is the primary mantra, OM AH HUM VAJRA GURU PADMA SIDDHI HUM. The Vidyadhara accomplishment mantra is OM AH HUM VAJRA MAHA GURU SARVA SIDDHI HUM.

132. These enlightened activities, referred to as the "four karmas" (*las bzhi*), bring benefit on an ordinary level. They are pacification, enrichment, magnetizing, and subjugation.

133. The isolation or withdrawal of speech (*ngag dben*) is the second of the three modes of isolation according to the completion stage of meditation.

134. *skad cig dran rdzogs.* In this advanced mode of the development stage, the visual image of the deity is perfected in a single moment of recollection. This practice is more frequently mentioned in connection with Anuyoga. See e.g., Dudjom Rinpoche, *Nyingma School,* 287.

135. Yughanaddha, the unified state of Vajradhara, in which duality is eliminated and all aspects of appearance and emptiness are realized as unity.

136. In consequence of which he wrote *Definitive Structure of the Commitments: Taking Others as One's Own Child and Taking Oneself as Another's Child* (*bdag sras gzhan sras dam tshig rnam gzhag*).

137. For an English translation, see Lingpa, Patrul Rinpoche, and Mahapandita, *Deity, Mantra, and Wisdom.*

138. Name mantras (*mtshan sngags*) include the mantras of any given deity, when the visualization is awakened merely by saying the mantra of the deity in question.

139. Here the mantra-garland is visualized as swinging around and around inside the bodies of the male and female buddha consorts like a swing (Skt. *dola*).

This term may also refer to a bamboo pole that supports two pannier baskets at either end, and to the bamboo shoulder poles used to support a palanquin or stretcher.

140. Dharmavajra (*chos kyi rdo rje*) is the name of one of the sixteen offering goddesses, whose mantra is the space of reality (Skt. *dharmadhatu*). (Oral communication: Tulku Thondup.)

141. The Vinaya specifies that the province of Magadha in India is the central region of Buddhist culture, and that ten fully ordained monks are required for the bestowal of full ordination. The Vinaya also states that in outlying regions, only five fully ordained monks are required to be present. Here Nyoshul Lungtok insists that they abide by the standards of the central region and have ten monks present.

142. Monks are required to possess certain articles, such as monastic robes, begging bowls, and so on, or at least symbolic representations of these objects. These objects must be blessed by the preceptor or another monk.

143. Revulsion (*zhen log*) is a synonym for renunciation. When one has understood the consequences of negative actions and the futility of ordinary pursuits, one feels a natural disgust for samsara, just as a jaundiced person feels when presented with a meal of greasy food.

144. That is, in the refuge section of the preliminary practices, according to the *Longchen Nyingtik*.

145. The intermingling of white and red vital nuclei with the vital energies of the subtle body occurs at the moment of conception. White vital nuclei or fluids produce bone tissue, bone marrow, semen, and breast milk, while red vital nuclei or fluids produce blood, flesh, and skin. See Dorje, Coleman, and Jinpa, *Tibetan Book of the Dead*, 474; also Parfionovitch, Dorje, and Meyer, *Tibetan Medical Paintings*.

146. This means that despite the excellent indications of success in practice that Khenpo Ngakchung experienced, he did not entertain any thoughts of prideful expectations or attempt to hold on to the experiences.

147. Entry, abiding, and absorption are the three phases of mastering the energies within the central channel of the subtle body.

148. This expression (*ey shi re*) indicates a serious resolve or intent, meaning, "Even if it kills me, I will do this!" or "Even at the expense of my own life, I won't do this!" (Oral communication: Tulku Thondup.)

149. The nightingale (*'jol mo*) has a mournful call that Tibetans say sounds like weeping about impermanence and suffering. The onomatopoeic sounds of its call in Tibetan are "*khyö kyi-hü, nga kyi-hü.*"

150. A water torma (*chu gtor*) is an offering and dedication ritual whereby a liquid mixture of water and milk with balls of dough and popped barley grains added is poured into a copper or other type of vessel.

151. Rigdzin Jigme Lingpa lived in the southern and central parts of Tibet.

152. Here Lungtok Rinpoche is suggesting that while it is not permissible to write

down the secret teachings of the Whispered Lineage, it would be even more catastrophic if the Whispered Lineage were lost entirely.

153. These are Khenpo Ngakchung's two secret restricted (*bka' rgya ma*) teachings: *gzhi khregs chod skabs kyi zin bris bstan pa'i nyi ma'i zhal lung snyan rgyud chu bo'i bcud 'dus* and *shin tug sang ba chen po thod rgal snyan brgyud kyi zin bris kun tu bzang po'i dgongs rgyan yig med ud pa de sha mkha'i 'gro'i thugs kyi ti la ka.* They constitute volume 9 of his *Collected Works*.

154. This small bell-like chime (*ting shag*) is generally sounded when making dough-ball offerings to anguished spirits (*yi dvags*), in order to relieve their sufferings.

155. The body of transformation (Skt. *samkrantikaya,* Tib. *'pho sku*), otherwise known as the "great transformation into the rainbow body," is the ultimate result of Atiyoga practice. See Dudjom Rinpoche, *Nyingma School,* 342, 501.

156. Short-term aims (*blo sna thung ba*) are appropriate when one has understood the truth of impermanence. Knowing that death could come at any moment, one focuses on the present moment rather than investing energy in long-term future plans.

157. The path of sudden or one-step realization (*gcig char ba*) is discussed in Nubchen Sangye Yeshe's *Lamp for the Eye of Concentration* (*bsam gtan mig sgron*), and contrasted with the path of gradual realization (*rim gyis pa*). See NK, vol. 104.

158. When students have spiritual insights or experiences, they offer a description of their realization (*rtogs 'bul*) to their lamas, who may then identify these insights in the context of the path.

159. The Mönpa are an indigenous race belonging to the Indo-Tibetan borderlands. They have maintained a traditional slash-and-burn method of agriculture. See Stanley, Roy, and Dorje, *Buddhist Response,* 866, 869.

160. The fourth of the four visions (*snang ba bzhi*) in Dzogchen practice: manifest reality (*chos nyid mngon sum*); increasing experience (*nyams snang gong 'phel*); awareness reaching its full measure (*rig pa tshad phebs*); and exhaustion of phenomena in reality (*chos nyid zad pa*). On this fourth realization (*chos zad / chos nyid du zad pa*), see Dudjom Rinpoche, *Nyingma School,* 339.

161. This protuberance (*gtsug tor*) is one of the thirty-two major marks of a nirmanakaya.

162. A chaitya is a Buddhist or Jain shrine or temple containing a stupa. In modern texts on Indian architecture, the term "chaityagrha" is often used to denote an assembly or prayer hall that houses a stupa.

163. Lungtok Rinpoche later explained that this dream foretold the destruction of the doctrine in the East and its spread to the West. (Patrul Rinpoche, *Guide to the Words of My Perfect Teacher,* xxv.)

164. *rig pa'i rtsal dbang.* On its conferral, see Dudjom Rinpoche, *Nyingma School,* 370, 673–74, 763–64.

165. This expression (*rdzogs chen rang gi brgyud pa gsum*) could refer either to the three general modes of transmission of the tantras, namely: the Mind Lineage of the Conquerors (*rgyal ba dgongs brgyud*); the Symbol Lineage of the

Vidyadharas (*rig 'dzin brda brgyud*); and the Whispered Lineage of Ordinary Individuals (*gang zag snyan brgyud*) (See Dudjom Rinpoche, *Nyingma School,* 447–57). It could also refer to the historical transmissions of the three classes of the Great Perfection, on which see ibid., 490–501, 538–96.

166. It was Prahevajra's foremost student, Manjushrimitra, who classified all the tantras of the Great Perfection into the three classes: mind class (*sems sde*); space class (*klong sde*); and pith instructional class (*man ngag sde*). Respectively, these focus on the nature of mind, the space of reality, and their integration. See Dudjom Rinpoche, *Nyingma School,* 490–94.

167. Embellic myrobalan (Tib. *skyu ru ra,* Latin: *Emblica officinalis*) is a round yellow fruit with vertical white lines, related to the gooseberry, which becomes transparent when wet, so one can clearly see what is inside. This sacred medicinal fruit is depicted in the hand of the central Medicine Buddha and is used as a panacea in Tibetan medicine.

168. For a fuller description of the origin of the *Longchen Nyingtik,* refer to Dilgo Khyentse, *Wish-Fulfilling Jewel,* 4–8.

169. Tantra (*rgyud*) means "continuum" in the context of the ground (*gzhi*); the path (*lam*); and the result (*'bras bu*) of spiritual practice. On these distinctions, see Dudjom Rinpoche, *Nyingma School,* 263–67. The tantra texts form their literary expression. Among these three, the continuum of the path, through which the continuum of the ground is manifestly transformed into the result, entails the continuous application of body, speech, and mind in respect of empowerments and practice.

170. On the superiority of the higher tantras over the outer tantras, see Dudjom Rinpoche, *Nyingma School,* 268–74 and 346–72.

171. The twenty-one techniques of mental focusing (*sems 'dzin*) are expounded in Longchenpa's *Resting in the Nature of Mind* (*sems nyid ngal gso*) and in his *Treasury of the Supreme Vehicle* (*theg mchog mdzod*). See Namkhai Norbu, *Dream Yoga,* 23–75.

172. See Khenpo Ngakchung's own *Light of the Sun: A Commentary on the Inner Writings of Both Trekchö and Tögal according to the Lama Yangtik* (*bla ma yang tig gi gnyis ka'i yang yig gi 'grel pa nyi ma'i snang ba*), p. 19.

173. *byung gnas 'gro gsum.* This contemplative process undermines the ingrained deluded assumption that mind truly exists; the process consists of investigating whether or not mind actually has an origin (*'byung sa*), or a dwelling place (*gnas sa*), or a destination (*'gro sa*).

174. This topic is considered uncommon because the investigation into the actual nature of the subjective mind is superior to the previous two: mind and the view of subjective phenomena.

175. As opposed to the action of yogic discipline, the action of harmonious skillful means is in harmony with ordinary conventional behavior.

176. *'od gsal sbubs 'jug.* See Padmasambhava, *Natural Wisdom,* 235–55; also Dorje, Coleman, and Jinpa, *Tibetan Book of the Dead,* 225–72

177. *grong 'pho grong 'jug gi 'pho ba.* See Patrul Rinpoche, *Words of My Perfect*

Teacher, 351–65; also Padmasambhava, *Natural Wisdom,* 195–233; and Dorje, Coleman, and Jinpa, *Tibetan Book of the Dead,* 197–224.

178. *rnam rmin srid pa bar do.* This is the final of the three intermediate states after death, and the one that precedes a new rebirth. See Padmasambhava, *Natural Wisdom,* 257–73.

179. *rnam shes rlung zhon.* This refers to the dying process when the red and white vital nuclei dissolve and the deceased's consciousness rides the subtle energies, exiting from the body at a particular aperture, which may determine the realm of rebirth. See Dorje, Coleman, and Jinpa, *Tibetan Book of the Dead,* ch. 9, 173–81, and ch. 11; also Beer, *Encyclopedia of Tibetan Symbols,* 141.

180. According to Tulku Thondup, visionary experiences (*snang nyams*) are experiences that can be perceived, and cognitive experiences (*shes nyams*) are experiences that can be realized. Cognitive experiences are transitional experiences—such as bliss, clarity, and nonthought (*bde gsal mi rtog gsum*)—which are experienced during the unfolding of the four visions (*snang ba bzhi*) in Tögal practice. Visual experiences in Tögal practice enable practitioners to directly encounter the true nature of awareness (*rig pa*).

181. According to Tulku Thondup, this means that losing one's recollection of mind can easily be misconstrued as perfecting the power of insight, in which there is no dualistic perception that sees and understands.

182. The higher are based upon the lower vehicles, so the basic principles of the lower vehicles are inherent in the higher vehicles. See Dudjom Rinpoche, *Nyingma School,* 80–87.

183. This is his *Heart-Drop of the Dakinis: Guide to the Whispered Lineage of All-Surpassing Realization: Unwritten Pith Instructions That Are the Ornament of the Wisdom Mind of Samantabhadra (thod rgal snyan brgyud kyi zin bris kun tu bzang po'i dgongs rgyan yig med u pa de sha).*

184. Vishuddha Heruka (*yang dag he ru ka*) and Vajrakila (*rdo rje phur ba*) are two of the deities of the *Eight Heruka Sadhanas (sgrub pa bka' brgyad),* respectively representing buddha mind and buddha activities. See Dudjom Rinpoche, *Nyingma School,* 283, 476–77, and 481–82. For the various transmissions in Tibet, see ibid., 710–16.

185. *ma gshin phur gsum.* Yamantaka and Matarah are two further deities among the *Eight Heruka Sadhanas,* the former specifically representing the buddha body and the latter being one of the three mundane deities within the group. See Dudjom Rinpoche, *Nyingma School,* 283; also 477–79 on Yamantaka and 483 on Matarah.

186. The *Three Razor Scriptures (spu gri rnam gsum)* are listed separately in the bibliography of texts referenced by the author under Guru Chöwang, Pema Lingpa, and Nyang-rel Nyima Özer.

187. *lcags 'dra lcags sdig gnyis.* These are contained in the revelations of Dumpa Gya Shangtrom and Chokgyur Dechen Lingpa. In the ninth century, Nubchen Sangye Yeshe received a teaching from the Nepalese king Vasudhara entitled

the *Meteorite Scorpion Teaching* (*nam lcags sdig pa'i chos sde*). King Vasudhara would not allow Nubchen to immediately bring this teaching to Tibet, but he agreed to compose a similar teaching for temporary purposes. This was the *Imitation Meteorite* (*lcags 'dra*), which Nubchen brought with him. Through this wrathful practice, Nubchen was able to repel the terror of King Langdarma. (Oral communication: Orgyen Topgyal.) See also Dudjom Rinpoche, *Nyingma School*, vol. 1, pp. 607–14, and vol. 2, p. 249.

188. The Geluk tradition places great importance on establishing the correct view through a dialectically based approach. The curriculum, which centers on philosophical and logical enquiry, may last twelve to twenty years, after which one of four levels of academic degree is awarded from the monastic university.

189. Varuna (*chu lha*), who is the Vedic god of the heavens and of water, and one of the guardians of the ten directions. Varuna presides over the dark half of the sky, or the "dark side" of the sun as it seems to travel from west to east during the night. This is therefore a poetic way of saying that the sun is setting.

190. This would have been the Second Katok Situ Chökyi Lodrö (1820–79?).

191. For the history of the Kham lineage of these transmitted oral teachings, see Dudjom Rinpoche, *Nyingma School*, 688–702.

192. Specifically, as far as the Gyarong River below Dartsedo, which marks the traditional Sino-Tibetan frontier.

193. The rainbow body ('*ja' lus*), also known as the body of great transformation, is the culminating result of the Great Perfection, in which even the physical body dissolves into rainbow light (the essence of the five elements) at the time of death, sometimes leaving only hair and nails behind. See Dudjom Rinpoche, *Nyingma School*, 259 passim.

194. *gso sbyong* (Skt. *posadha*). This is a ritual performed on certain days of every month, during which novices and fully ordained monks confess their downfalls and restore their monastic vows, while the laity guard their commitments, restore their virtue, and confess their negative actions.

195. Insight (Tib. *shes rab*, Skt. *prajna*) is said to arise through study, reflection, and meditation.

196. This is a Tibetan expression meaning: "You are now free to do as you please; your life is in your own hands." When the nose-rope that is used to lead a yak is wrapped around the yak's head, the yak is free to go where it pleases.

197. According to Buddhist cosmology, over the course of each intermediate aeon (Skt. *antarakalpa*), the human life span gradually decreases from eighty thousand years to ten years as crimes and evils increase. Our present age is placed toward the end of the first intermediate aeon, when the human life span is less than one hundred years. The remainder of this intermediate aeon is prophesied to be miserable, as life spans continue to decrease and all the evil tendencies of the past reach their ultimate in destructiveness. Eventually, people will live no longer than ten years, and they will marry at the age of five, food will be poor and tasteless, and no form of morality will be acknowledged. The most

contemptuous and hateful people will become the rulers. Incest will be rampant. Hatred between people, even members of the same family, will grow until people think of each other as hunters do their prey. Eventually, a great war will ensue, which will mark the end of the first intermediate aeon.

198. A synonym for the texts contained in the *Vima Nyingtik*.

199. *nyin mo bde legs*. Referred to as "nyinmo delek" (good day), these very long silken scarves carry inscriptions wishing the recipient "good day and good night."

200. On the thirteenth or buddha level, named "Holder of the Vajra" (*bcu gsum rdo rje 'dzin pa*), see Dudjom Rinpoche, *Nyingma School*, 254 and 462.

201. *gang du skye ba ma*. This is a well-known dedication prayer by Longchen Rabjampa, found in the *Longchen Nyingtik*.

202. This is the protector of Samye Monastery, who is also the protector of Shri Singha College. See de Nebesky-Wojkowitz, *Oracles and Demons*, 166–176.

203. *seng ge mjing bsnol*. This is a symbol of a fully defended, protected position: two lions seated with their necks entwined, such that they are facing in opposite directions and no one can harm them from either direction. This serves as a metaphor for Mipam Rinpoche's way of establishing the view: by entwining the two lions of the Madhyamaka and Pramana (Valid Cognition; *dbu tshad seng ge mjing bsnol*). See Shantarakshita and Jamgön Mipam, *Adornment of the Middle Way*, 119; Phuntsho, Karma, *Mipham's Dialectics*, 18 and 101; and Duckworth, *Mipam on Buddha-Nature*, xvi.

204. *tshul gnyis*. These refer to the two truths—relative and ultimate. (Oral communication: Tulku Thondup.) This quote derives from the *Ornament of the Middle Way*.

205. Primal matter (Tib. *gtso bo*, Skt. *pradhana*) is the source of the twenty-five categories expounded in the Samkhya philosophy, representing the view of eternalistic pluralism. Almighty god (Tib. *dbang phyug*, Skt. *isvara*) is an omnipotent being posited by the Aisvarya as a substitute for the natural efficacy of past actions.

206. See Padmakara, *The Root Stanzas of the Middle Way*, p. 26.

207. Here Khenpo Ngakchung explains that his understanding is derived from the integration of the two truths: dependent arising as the relative truth, and the lack of inherent existence of dependently arisen phenomena as the ultimate truth.

208. Patrul's works on astrology, including the five planetary aspects (*gza' lnga*) and the fivefold calculation (*lnga bsdus*), are contained in his *Collected Works*, 2:1–123. His writings on prosody (*sdeb sbyor*) are contained in his *Collected Works*, 1:383–95.

209. The first volume includes texts on the generation stage of meditation, and the second covers the completion stage.

210. The tradition of Profound View and the tradition of Vast Action are Nagarjuna's and Asanga's traditions of bestowing the bodhisattva vows, respectively.

211. *skyor dpon.* This term denotes a monk overseeing a monastic school where students learn to recite texts from memory.

212. The text misreads "Shakyamitra."

213. This was the Fifth Dzogchen Rinpoche, Tubten Chökyi Dorje (1872–1935).

214. A geshe (*dge bshes*) is a holder of the Tibetan academic degree for monks, principally in the Geluk school, but also in the Sakya and Bön traditions. The curriculum of study emphasizes textual memorization and ritualized debate, representing an adaptation of the subjects studied at medieval Indian Buddhist universities, and lasts between twelve to twenty years. There are four categories of geshe degree: Dorampa, Lingtse, Tsorampa, and Lharampa, which is the highest.

215. This is the first line of the *Treasury of Abhidharma,* on which see Lamotte, *Karmasiddhi Prakarana,* 55.

216. It seems that at Dzogchen Monastery, Gyalse Shenpen Taye was the only teacher known by the honorific title "Kusho" (*sku zhabs*), so it may well mean that Khenpo Ngakchung borrowed the text from his residence. (Oral communication: Tulku Thondup.)

217. Cancer (Tib. *skar ma rgyal,* Skt. *pusya*) is an auspicious constellation, corresponding to the sixth lunar mansion in Indian astrology. Many people traditionally buy gold during this month.

218. Jamgön Mipam alludes to his nervous disorder (*rtsa dkar nad*) elsewhere. See Dudjom Rinpoche, *Nyingma School,* 878.

219. A permissory initiation or blessing (*rjes gnang*) confers authorization to meditate on a particular deity, and study and teach the practice.

220. *grub dbang rdzogs chen pa* is a formal title of the successive Dzogchen rinpoches.

221. On the signs of approaching death (*'chi ltas*), see Parfionovitch, Dorje, and Meyer, *Tibetan Medical Paintings;* also Dorje, Coleman, and Jinpa, *Tibetan Book of the Dead,* ch. 8 and 9, on the ritual deception of death (*'chi bslu*). Traditionally, great lamas are escorted from the human realm to a realm of the dakinis at the time of their passing. To placate the dakinis and prolong a lama's life, the ritual deception of death is performed utilizing an effigy in the likeness of the lama, surrounded by his or her possessions, and these are offered to the dakinis as a substitute.

222. This may refer to the new treasures of Rinchen Lingpa.

223. Although Nyoshul falls within present-day Palyul County, it is geographically closer to Nyarong, on which see Stanley, Roy, and Dorje, *Buddhist Response,* 644–46. While historical references do not mention any specific disturbances in Nyarong during the years 1900–2, which is the time period referred to here by Khenpo Ngakchung, it seems that discontent was rife for many years in the wake of the death of the ruthless Khampa warrior Gonpo Namgyal, who had taken control of Kham in the early nineteenth century and was later defeated by Lhasa in 1865. Following the fall of Gonpo Namgyal, local tribesmen continued to revolt from time to time, as in 1894 when Nyarong tribesman

rebelled and attacked the neighboring kingdom of Chakla. It was not until 1903 that the Qing government in Beijing appointed General Zhao Erfeng "Army Commander of Tibet" to integrate Tibet into China, which led to the 1905 Tibetan Rebellion. For further reading, see Gruschke, *Cultural Monuments: Kham.*

224. *gtsang btsan chen po rdo rje legs pa,* on whom see de Nebesky-Wojkowitz, *Oracles and Demons,* 154–59.

225. The heart-mantra of dependent arising (*rten 'brel snying po*) is YE DHARMA HETUPRABHAVA HETUN TESAM TATHAGATO BHAVAT AHA TESAM CA YO NIRODHO EVAM VADI MAHASRAMANAH YE SVAHA, which may be translated as "All phenomena arise from a cause, the Tathagata has told the cause thereof, and the great virtuous ascetic also has taught their cessation as well."

226. *mkha' 'gro'i gsang ba snying thig.* This is an alternative title for the Khandro Nyingtik.

227. Shenpa Sokdrub (*shan pa srog sgrub*) is an important protector of the Nyingtik tradition.

228. Khenpo Ngakchung would later sign his compositions, including this autobiography, with this name.

229. This is the Sanskrit equivalent of "Tashi delek," meaning "Let there be glorious fortune and auspiciousness!"

230. An important protectress of the *Nyingtik,* Durtrö Lhamo (*dur khrod lha mo*), who presides over charnel grounds.

231. Longchen Rabjampa and Khenpo Ngakchung both shared the personal name "Ngakgi Wangpo."

232. The so-called Ali-Kali mantra, which comprises the sacred vowels and consonants of the Sanskrit alphabet, is revered as the pure essence of all speech.

233. An aspect of Mahakala, on whom see de Nebesky-Wojkowitz, *Oracles and Demons,* 46, 53; Tsewang Rigzin, *Story of the Vajra Dharmapalas,* 3–19, and Jigme Chökyi Dorje, *nang bstan,* 985–1007.

234. The hide of the spotted antelope (Skt. *krsnasara*), symbolizing the attainment of Buddhahood, is a garment worn by Avalokiteshvara.

235. This was in Khenpo Ngakchung's former existence as Longchen Rabjampa.

236. This is a poetic way of stating that the source of the lineage is authentic and traces back to the ancient Buddhist masters.

237. Since Khenpo Ngakchung's mother was by all appearances a simple nomad woman, Tibetans would not expect such a person to display signs of high realization at the time of death.

238. The *Sutra That Gathers All Wisdom Intentions,* the *Tantra of the Magical Net,* and the *Mind Class of the Great Perfection,* which are the oral teachings of the Early Translation school.

239. Remati is a wrathful or semiwrathful aspect of the protectress Shri Devi (*dpal ldan lha mo*).

240. The tenth or highest bodhisattva level, Cloud of Dharma (Skt. *dharmamegha*), is known in Anuyoga as "Riding on Perfection" (*rdzogs pa ci chibs kyi sa*). It is

the gateway to the attainment of the buddha levels. See Dudjom Rinpoche, *Nyingma School,* 288.

241. Orgyen Topgyal (oral communication) comments that while treasure-revealers are indeed known to lie, this is for the sake of concealing and guarding the teachings.

242. The tenth day of the sixth lunar month is honored as the birthday of Guru Rinpoche and is marked by great festivities at Katok Monastery every summer. The ceremony is described in Stanley, Roy, and Dorje, *Buddhist Response,* 579.

243. Guru Vidyadhara (*bla ma rig 'dzin*), in certain revelatory traditions, sometimes substitutes for one of the deities of the *Eight Heruka Sadhanas,* or else Guru Vidyadhara may appear alongside the other eight, forming a single mandala of nine clusters. The main scripture is the *Root Tantra of the Assembly of Vidyadharas* (*rig 'dzin 'dus pa rtsa ba'i rgyud*), which is the fifteenth tantra of Nyangrel's revelation, *Embodiment of the Sugatas of the Eight Heruka Sadhanas.*

244. *sman rag.* Offerings symbolic of skillful means and insight.

245. This stick (*mig thur*) is a ritual implement used for removing the strips of red cloth that cover the eyes of recipients during an empowerment ceremony.

246. These are contained in his *Ascertainment of the Three Vows.* See bibliography of texts referenced by the author.

247. *Path and Fruit* (*lam 'bras*) constitute the main pith instructions of the Sakya school, on which see *dpal ldan sa skya pa'i gsung,* vols. 20a and 20b.

248. The *Masters' Explanation of the Pith Instructions* (*man ngag slob bshad*) comprises the esoteric oral teachings of the Path and Its Fruit, which were originally passed down from Do-ring Kunpangpa to Tsarchen Losal Gyatso, and then from him to Jamyang Khyentse Wangchuk and Mangtö Ludrub Gyatso.

249. This may have been linked to the assault on eastern Tibet the following year (1910) by the Chinese warlord Zhao Erfeng, who sought to carve out a distinct Chinese province that he would name Xikang.

250. The *Three Cycles of the Eight Heruka Sadhanas* (*bka' brgyad rnam gsum*) are listed separately in the bibliography of texts referenced by the author under their respective revealers: Guru Chöwang, Nyang-rel Nyima Özer, and Rigdzin Godemchen.

251. The Khampa and central Tibetan transmissions of *Gathering of the Great Assembly* (*tshogs chen 'dus pa*) are outlined in Dudjom Rinpoche, *Nyingma School,* 700–1 and 717–32 respectively.

252. These are the traditions associated with Butön Rinchen Drub of Shalu and Dolpopa Sherab Gyaltsen of Jonang.

253. According to Dilgo Khyentse Rinpoche (Oral communication, 1981), in Jamyang Khyentse Wangpo's previous life as Rigdzin Jigme Lingpa, he received five yellow parchments in a vision, three of which he deciphered and propagated as the *Longchen Nyingtik.* Then in his subsequent life as Jamyang Khyentse Wangpo, he propagated the last two parchments as the *Tsasum Ösel Nyingtik,* "*Three Roots' Heart Essence of Luminosity.*"

254. A terma cycle that focuses on the great Tibetan mahasiddha Tangtong Gyalpo.

255. Explanation on a Vajrakilaya commentary from the *Nyingma Kama* that combines the instructions given to Yeshe Tsogyal by the three masters Padmasambhava, Vimalamitra, and Srila Manzu.

256. *bsam gtan mig sgron* (alt: *rnal 'byor mig gi bsam gtan*). This esoteric instruction for the Great Perfection was composed by Nubchen Sangye Yeshe (ninth century c.e.), one of the twenty-five disciples of Guru Rinpoche. The text distinguishes the respective views and practices of the Gradual Vehicle (chapter 1), the Sudden Vehicle of Bodhisattvas as found in Ch'an or Zen Buddhism (chapter 2), Mahayoga (chapter 3), and Atiyoga (chapter 4). It was discovered among the Dunhuang texts in 1908. Khenchen Palden Sherab wrote a commentary on the *Samten Migdrön* entitled *Opening the Eyes of Wisdom* (*gnubs chen sangs rgyas ye shes kyi bsam gtan mig sgron le'u rnams kyi spyi bshad mdor bsdus shes rab mig 'byed*).

257. These three principal Phurba practices from the terma tradition are Guru Chöwang's *Supremely Secret Razor* (*phur ba yang gsang spu gri*); Pema Lingpa's *Most Secret Razor of Life* (*phur pa yang gsang srog gi spu gri*); and Rigdzin Godemchen's *Supremely Secret Razor* (*phur ba yang gsang spu gri*).

258. The Sky-Faced One, Namshelma (*gnam zhal ma*), is the consort of Kalden Drendzey, one of the manifestations of Guru Padmasambhava. On the life of Rigdzin Godemchen (1337–1409), see Dudjom Rinpoche, *Nyingma School*, 780–83.

259. These commentaries on the fortress of the view (*lta ba'i rdzong*—i.e., the recognition of awareness) and the ravine of meditation (*sgom pa'i 'phrang*—i.e., the visualization manifesting as undistracted awareness display) were written by Guru Rinpoche and Vimalamitra of India, and Namkhai Nyingpo and Vairochana of Tibet.

260. The "blessing that directly reveals reality" (*chos nyid dngos bstan gyi byin rlabs*) is Sakya terminology for the introduction to the nature of mind.

261. Pure visions (*dag pa'i snang ba*) arising from wisdom of sublime beings are free from confusion, in contrast to "impure visions," which would include the confused projections or hallucinations of ordinary beings.

262. The colors of the four cardinal directions are as follows: the east white, the south yellow, the west red, and the north green.

263. A famous verse for requesting teachings:
According to the wishes of beings
And their individual capacities,
Please turn the Wheel of Dharma
Of the Greater, Lesser and Common Vehicles!

264. A very common verse of dedication:
By this merit, may I attain omniscience
And defeat the enemies of wrongdoing.
From the ocean of existence,
Buffeted by waves of birth, old age, sickness, and death.
May I liberate all beings!

265. Atisha's three spiritual sons (*sras sku mched gsum*) were Khutön Tsöndrü Yudrung (*khu ston brtson 'grus gyung grung*); Ngok Lekpey Sherab (*rngog legs pa'i shes rab*); and Dromtönpa Gyalwey Jungney (*'brom ston pa rgyal ba'i 'byung nas*).

266. The positive and negative relationships between the five elements and twelve animal signs are examined in the context of Elemental Divination (*'byung rtsis*), on which see Dorje, *Tibetan Elemental Divination Paintings*.

267. A symbolic paper "flower of awareness" (*rig pa'i me tog*) is tossed during an empowerment ceremony, indicating by the way it alights the particular affinity the recipient will have with the practice in question. Tossing the "flower of awareness" also means abandoning dualistic fixations of good and bad with respect to self-visualization and frontal-visualization, or with respect to the visualized deity of meditative commitment and the actual wisdom deity.

268. That is, the Indian Vidyadhara of the Vishuddhi Mind Sadhana would have been Hungkara, and would have been attended by Namkha Nyingpo.

269. On the legends found in the literature of the New Translation schools concerning this stupa in southwest India, see Situ Chökyi Jungney's *Inventory to the Likeness of the Intangible Stupa of Paramadya, Entitled Wish-Fulfilling Rain of Good Auspices* (*dpal mchog reg pa med pa'i mchod rten gyi snang brnyan dge legs 'dod dgu'i char 'bebs kyi dkar chags utpala'i phreng ba*), contained in his *Collected Works*, vol. PA, 727–28.

270. *lus dben, ngag dben, sems dben, 'od gsal, sgyu lus, zung 'jug*. These are the six phases of the completion stage, according to the Guhyasamaja system of Highest Yoga Tantra.

271. Dagpo Kagyü (*dvags po bka' brgyud*) is the name of the lineage that Marpa Chökyi Lodrö passed down through Milarepa to Gampopa. It is named after Gampopa (1079–1153), whose full name is Dagpo Lhaje Sonam Rinchen (*dvags po lha rje bsod nams rin chen*).

272. The *Kalachakra Tantra* altogether comprises four successive mandalas: those of buddha body, speech, mind, and power. See Dalai Lama, *Kalachakra Tantra*; and Bryant, *Wheel of Time Sand Mandala*. Rahu (*sgra can*) is the "eclipser" in Indo-Tibetan astrology.

273. *bde chen nus ma'i dkyil 'khor*. "Shalu" here indicates the tradition of Butön Rinchen Drup.

274. *Aiming at Loving-Kindness* (*dmigs brtse ma*) is a five-line prayer to Je Tsongkhapa.

275. Gyaltsab Dharma Rinchen (*rgyal tshab dar ma rin chen*, 1364–1432), who was the first throne-holder of Ganden Monastery after Tsongkhapa, and Khedrub Gelek Palzang (*mkhas grub dge legs dpal bzang*, 1385–1438), who was retrospectively recognized as the First Panchen Lama.

276. In fact, Khenpo Ngakchung lived to be sixty-two (sixty-three according to Tibetan calculation).

277. Gongtsen (*dgongs btsan*) and Shaza Khamochey (*sha za kha mo che*) are the specific protectors associated with Sangye Lingpa's revelation. (Oral communication: Tulku Thondup).

278. *rdo rje dme log bskor ba'i 'khor lo.* "Pollution" here denotes obscurations resulting from acts of murder or violent quarrels that provoke schisms within a religious community.

279. *mdos.* An exorcist ritual in which negative forces are trapped within a framework of wooden sticks, entwined with colored yarn.

280. A sacred spring on the circuit around Katok Monastery.

281. Tibetan temples are measured by the number of interior pillars required to support their exterior structures. A temple requiring forty interior pillars is fairly large. The monastery at Jönpalung was completed in 1922, the year of the Male Water Dog.

282. Hemalambha (*gser 'phyang*), which is equivalent to the Fire Bird year within the sixty-year cycle. Note that the paragraphs that follow in the Sichuan edition (p. 152, line 13–p. 158, line 5) are found out of sequence in the Jönpalung woodblock edition (249ff., line 6 to 259ff., line 1).

283. These are two techniques of the generation stage of meditation: self-visualization (*bdag bskyed*), implying that the meditator visualizes him or herself as the deity, and front-visualization (*mdun bskyed*), implying that the meditator visualizes the deity in front of and therefore separate from him or herself.

284. This indicates that Khenpo Ngakchung transmitted the *Great Treasury of Precious Revelations* in a closed retreat setting, for which the boundaries were initially sealed, and then opened only when all the empowerments had been completed.

285. *sangs rgyas stong dbang.* The empowerment of the thousand buddhas of this auspicious aeon.

286. During the conferral of an empowerment, the lama sometimes blesses each recipient individually, making the process very time-consuming in large gatherings.

287. According to some traditional Tibetan beliefs, harvesting these items wild from the mountains harms the local mountain deities, depletes the essence of the soil, and causes merit to degenerate. (Oral communication: Minyak Khenpo Tashi, May 2006.)

288. Anguished spirits (Tib. *yi dvags,* Skt. *preta*), also translated as "hungry ghosts," comprise one of the six classes of samsaric beings. They are born in this realm due to miserliness and unfulfilled self-centered ambition in their past actions, and they suffer from insatiable hunger, thirst, and craving.

289. The hallmark of an accomplished sage is the absence of clinging to these three. A beginner on the path will inevitably think "I, the subject (1), have offered this object (2), to that recipient (3)," and he or she will be attached to the thought of such virtue and unable to let go of the fixation on self, other, and action. While this deluded positing of self and other is natural for sentient beings, it is an artificial construct that leads to suffering. Such duality is gradually eliminated on the path through the realization of nondual wisdom.

290. A reception party of the dakinis is an indication that the master is on the verge

of being carried off to be received in another realm. In other words, this heralds the imminent passing of a master from this world.

291. On the Nyingma classifications of basic and branch commitments (Tib. *dam tshig*, Skt. *samaya*), see Dudjom Rinpoche, *Nyingma School*, 71–95.

292. The Third Katok Situ Rinpoche passed away in 1925.

293. Here Khenpo Ngakchung is saying that beyond his ordinary, pure intentions, he had no special or extraordinary powers to help.

294. The Jönpalung woodblock edition at this point mistakenly adds a sentence: "The next year, as previously mentioned, I went to Lingshi and bestowed the *Treasury of Precious Revelations* and many other teachings. Then I returned to my own mountain hermitage." This refers to the interpolated passage, on which see note 282.

295. *tshe bcu'i dus mchod*. The ritual feast-offering ceremony held on the tenth lunar day of each month in commemoration of Guru Rinpoche.

296. These would include inner parasites, such as worms and animalcules, and outer parasites, such as body and hair lice. (Oral communication: Tulku Thondup.)

297. Here, patient endurance (*bzod pa*) also implies confidence in the ultimate truth. (Oral communication: Tulku Thondup.)

298. This means that Khenpo Ngakchung didn't necessarily accomplish high attainments through these practices, but he did enough of the practices so that he was able to teach them and perform the relevant ceremonies. (Oral communication: Tulku Thondup.)

299. This means that a major obstacle to Khenpo Ngakchung's life had been cleared away.

300. *bka' babs bar ma*. The first recipient was Nyak Jnanakumara and the third was Zurpoche Sakya Jungne. See Dudjom Rinpoche, *Nyingma School*, 601–49.

301. This refers to the ritual of erasing the notch on the tally stick of the Lord of Death (*khram phyis*) and his henchmen. See e.g., Dorje, Coleman, and Jinpa, *Tibetan Book of the Dead*, 322.

302. *tshva tshva*. Small terra-cotta votive images stamped from a mold.

303. Achala (*mi gyo ba*) is a sword-wielding aspect of the gatekeeper Vajrapani.

304. This would be the *Tantra of Achala* (*acalakalpatantraraja*, T 432).

305. On the military adventures of the Pangda family, who sought to mark out an independent Kham Province, distinct from Tibet and China, see Gruschke, *Cultural Monuments: Kham*.

306. *dam sri*. Compare with the famous incident from the life of Longchen Rabjampa, when he subjugated the oath-transgressing demons at Zha Lhakhang. Dudjom Rinpoche, *Nyingma School*, 589.

307. *sgo byang phyi nang*. These are the notice boards indicating the areas that are off-limits to outsiders and to peripheral recipients during the empowerment ceremonies.

308. The king's earrings (*rgyal po'i rna cha*) and queen's earrings (*rgyal mo'i rna cha*) comprise two of the seven well-known motifs known as the seven aspects of

royal wealth (*nor bu cha bdun*). See glossary of enumerations.

309. This is the red-walled canyon of the Mekong Gorge at Troting Gang (*khro mthil sgang*), the abode of the local protector and *btsan* spirit, Trobar (*khro 'bar*).

310. *lyai shak* intentionally represents a secret or encoded word that requires a key to understand it. (Oral communication: Tulku Thondup.)

311. Tib. *chos 'byung*, Skt. *dharmodaya*. For a description of this symbol, which represents the real source from which visualized deities arise, see Beer, *Handbook of Tibetan Buddhist Symbols*, 209–11.

312. The verses that follow contain esoteric instructions pertaining to the path of skillful means. They are presented in symbolic and poetic language that require further clarification from a qualified master in the context of the pith instructions. (Oral communication: Tulku Tubzang of Palyul.)

313. That is, vase, indicating the conferral of the vase empowerment.

314. The path of skillful means (*thabs lam*) purifies the stains or obscurations of disturbing emotions and mistaken views about phenomena onto the path, transforming them without abandoning them.

315. The compassionate motivation on the basis of which the nirmanakaya appears in the world is an unfolding of emanational spirituality. Hence, the Tibetan term *thugs rje*, in the context of *ngo bo rang bzhi thugs rje*, is to be understood in that fruitional sense rather than in the causal sense of the compassion cultivated by aspiring bodhisattvas.

316. The twenty-four sacred lands of ancient India and the Himalayan world are subdivided into three groups of eight, respectively, on the basis of their association with buddha mind, speech, and body. See Nordrang Orgyan, *Chos rnam kun btus*, 3195–96. Among them, Purimalaya, first in the list of places associated with buddha mind, is a well-known pilgrimage destination in Orissa. Kamarupa, first in the list of places associated with buddha speech, is a renowned power place in Assam. Pretapuri or Tirthaburi, first in the list of places associated with buddha body, is actually located in the upper Sutlej Valley of Ngari in far-west Tibet.

317. On the Matarah group of wrathful female deities, who appear among the fifty-eight wrathful deities of the *Magical Net*, see Dorje, Coleman, and Jinpa, *Tibetan Book of the Dead*, 105–6 and 397–98. On the Pishachi group of wrathful animal-headed female deities, who appear among the fifty-eight wrathful deities of the *Magical Net*, see ibid., 106–7 and 398–99. On the peripheral Ishvari group of twenty-eight female acolytes, who also appear among the fifty-eight wrathful deities of the *Magical Net*, see ibid., 110–12 and 401–2.

318. The central female buddha in the assembly of peaceful deities, on whom see ibid., 98 and 389.

319. When the appearance of "whiteness" dissolves into "increase," there are forty thought patterns originating from attachment that cease. When the increase of "redness" then dissolves into the subtle mind of "attainment," there are thirty-three thought patterns originating from aversion that cease.

320. Mind and its energies (*rlung sems*) refer to the energies within the subtle body and the ordinary dualizing consciousness that rides upon them.

321. See Dorje, Coleman, and Jinpa, *Tibetan Book of the Dead*, 175. When the subtle mind of "attainment" dissolves into the subtle mind of "near attainment" through the reverse flow of the energies, there are seven thought patterns originating from delusion that cease.

322. On Dorje Drakden, the protector most closely associated with the state oracle of Nechung, see de Nebesky-Wojkowitz, *Oracles and Demons*, 123–27 passim.

323. The "wind-horse" motif symbolizes good luck, according to elemental divination (*'byung rtsis*). Rituals are performed to generate prosperity by energizing the "wind-horse of good luck" (*rlung rta / klungs rta dpal bskyed*), thereby enhancing the prospects of success, brilliance, charisma, and so forth.

324. The anniversary of Buddha's Descent from the Heavens (*lha babs dus chen*) commemorates Buddha Shakyamuni's descent from Tushita Heaven, where he had gone to teach his deceased mother.

325. *pad ma od 'bar*. This is actually a treasure revelation of Rigdzin Düdül Dorje. See bibliography of texts referenced by the author.

326. *brtags bsgril 'phang pa*. Here, Khenpo Ngakchung performed rituals in search of the reincarnation of Serding Rinpoche by writing names on paper, rolling the paper inside balls of barley dough, placing the balls in a bowl, and shaking the bowl until one of the balls fell out.

327. It is clear that Khenpo Ngakchung climbed from the Yangzte riverbank areas of eastern Gonjo back into the southern grasslands around Lhatok, on which see Stanley, Roy, and Dorje, *Buddhist Response*, 574–75. This is the locale of Takmo Gön, a branch of Katok in the Tsangshi grasslands, which had been founded by the predecessor of the late Lodrö Jampa Taye in the early twentieth century.

328. Khenpo Ngakchung was fifty-three years old at this point.

329. This refers to the refutations made by Chandrakirti against the objections raised by Bhavaviveka on the interpretations of the Madhyamaka by Buddhapalita (Oral communication: Tulku Thondup.)

330. *chos can mthun snang yod med*. On this topic found in the discussions of Great Madhyamaka, see Dudjom Rinpoche, *Nyingma School*, 210.

331. The paradise or pure land of Amitabha Buddha.

332. *padma'i 'od*. This is the place of lotus light on the summit of Zangdok Pelri.

333. This would have been the Fourth Katok Situ Chökyi Nyima.

334. Dekyi Khangsarma was the place of Khenpo Ngakchung's subsequent rebirth, nearby the geomantic temple of Buchu Tergyi Lhakhang in Kongpo.

335. That is, the form of Vajrakila.

336. The four supreme sons (*sras mchog bzhi*) are the four aspects of Vajrakila, surrounding the central form. See Boord, *Bolt of Lightning*, 193–203.

337. On the oath-bound protectors (*dam can*) of Vajrakila, see ibid., 98–99 passim.

338. *lnga brgya'i tha ma*. According to Buddhist calculations, the duration of Shakyamuni Buddha's teaching is five thousand years, which is divided into ten

periods of five hundred years each. The tenth and final period is called the Age of Convention or symbols, because at this point the actual practice of the path will be lost, and only conventional tokens of the renunciate ordination (Skt. *pravajya*) will remain. See Dudjom Rinpoche, *Nyingma School*, 2:94–95n1349.

339. This refers to the Great Perfection's Trekchö and Tögal as meaning rather than words, and indicates that primordial purity and spontaneous presence are indivisible.

340. In fact, he stayed there for a total of only twenty-four months, a period that spanned three years.

341. The person who blows the conch shell to announce the beginning and end of practice sessions in retreat centers.

342. Note that in the autobiography, Khenpo Ngakchung describes this dream slightly differently. See page 191 of the main translation.

343. *gsar ma.* The Sarma schools, or "New schools," are the schools of Tibetan Buddhism that were established from the eleventh century onward, namely the Kagyü, Sakya, and Geluk, as well as Shijey and Chö, Jordruk, Shangpa Kagyü, and Nyendrub (the Kalachakra system).

344. *cang shes kyi rta.* The all-knowing horse, which is clairvoyant and swiftly encircles everything in a moment.

345. The re-revealed (*yang gter*) *Konchok Chidü* (*dkon mchog spyi 'dus*), established jointly by Jamgön Kongtrul and Jamyang Khyentse Wangpo.

346. The text misreads "Fire Dog."

347. The text misreads "tenth."

348. This refers to the most famous war in the legend of King Gesar of Ling. Stein, *Recherches sur l'épopée et le Barde au Tibet*, 188–89, indicates that "Hor" was an ethnonym that originally referred to the Uyghurs, and from the twelfth-century C.E. to the Mongols.

349. This mind-treasure brought forth by Khenpo Ngakchung is contained in his *Collected Works*, vol. 3.

350. *lhun grub steng.* The "Palace of Spontaneous Perfection" in Derge was founded by Tangtong Gyalpo (1361–1485), but since then it has been used as the main temple for the Derge kings. It houses the famous Derge printing house, known as the "Great Treasury of Dharma," which was built by the king of Derge according to the instructions of the Second Dzogchen Rinpoche, Gyurme Tekchok Tendzin (1699–1757).

351. Wick stick (*dug me*). A slender stick wrapped with wick cotton that is lit and waved in the air by the vajra master, who chants prayers and then uses the wick stick to set alight a burnt offering (*byin sreg*) or other ritual fire.

352. *rdo rje rnam par 'joms pa.* The Vajra Subjugator. One of the lords of the Vajra buddha family, Vajra Vidarana's sadhana is practiced for the removal of contamination and negativity.

353. Trowo Metsek (*khro bo sme brtseg*). The wrathful aspect of the meditational deity Hayagriva.

354. *dga' ldan lha brgya.* A guru yoga of Tsongkhapa, by the Fifth Dalai Lama.

355. *rdo rje sems dpa' snying gi me long gi rgyud.* One of the eighteen Great Perfection tantras.

356. *sku gdung 'bar ba.* One of the eighteen Great Perfection tantras.

357. *mngon rdzogs rgyal po.* Truly Perfected King, the eleventh of the twelve Great Perfection teachers.

358. The Three Sources of the Teachings (*bstan pa'i ntsas gsum*) denotes the three great sources of the teachings of buddha body, speech, and mind (*sku gsum bstan pa'i btsas chen po*), which are described in the Dzogchen tradition of Longchenpa. These comprise the hand-sized vajra representing the Dharmakaya (*chos kyi sku*), the four-digit-size book representing the Sambhogakaya (*long spyod rdzogs pa'i sku*), and the image fashioned of gemstones, equal in size to the physical body of beings, representing the Nirmanakaya (*sprul pa'i sku*). See Jamgön Kongtrul's *Myriad Worlds*; and Jamgön Kongtrül, *Treasury of Knowledge: Buddhism's Journey,* 108–12; also Dudjom Rinpoche, *Nyingma School,* 134–35. (E-mail communication: Alak Zenkar Rinpoche via Gyurme Dorje, Jan. 2013.)

359. Tib. *sangs rgyas 'khor ba 'jig,* Skt. *buddha krakucchanda.* The fourth buddha of the 1,002 buddhas of this aeon.

360. Six limits and four modes. The indispensable keys for unlocking the meaning of the tantras. See glossary of enumerations.

361. Dorje Tötreng Tsal, one of Guru Rinpoche Padmasambhava's names.

362. These refer to the twenty-four major places, the thirty-two major countries, and the eight charnel grounds. In total, there are sixty-four places and countries.

GLOSSARY OF PLACE NAMES

Adzom Gar (*a 'dzom sgar*). The seat of **Adzom Drukpa,** on the Dzing River in Tromtar, Kham. *See* Stanley, Roy, and Dorje, *Buddhist Response,* 581.

Chikchar (*cig char*). Sacred site in Old Tsari (*tsa ri rnying ma*) on Pure Crystal Mountain (*dag pa shel ri*), one of the three main holy mountains of Tibet.

Chimpu (a.k.a. Samye Chimpu, *bsam yas chim phu*). Mountain retreat above **Samye Monastery.**

Derge (*sde rge*). Former seat of the Derge kings; important religious, industrial, and political center in eastern Tibet, famous for its three-story printing house.

Do Ari Forest (*rdo a ris nags*). Famous hermitage in the Do Valley of **Golok** (*mgo log*), near the present Dodrubchen Monastery.

Drubchen encampment (*grub chen gar*). Site of Dodrubchen Monastery, founded by the second Dodrubchen Jigme Püntsok Jungney. In the Do Chi Valley of southern **Golok.**

Dzatö (*rdza stod*). The region surrounding the source of the Yalong River (*rdza chu*) and **Dza Patrul Rinpoche's** birthplace. In Sershul County.

Dzogchen Gangtrö Hermitage (*rdzogs chen gangs khrod*). Cave hermitage of **Dodrubchen Jigme Trinley Özer, Dza Patrul Rinpoche, Jamgön Mipam,** and **Nyoshul Lungtok.** In the mountains above **Dzogchen Monastery.**

Dzogchen Monastery (*rdzogs chen dgon pa*). Founded in 1685 by Dzogchen Pema Rigdzin. In Dzachukha region of Derge County.

Four Rivers and the Six Ranges (*chu bzhi sgang drug*). The Four Rivers are the Yangtze (*'bri chu*); Yellow (*rma chu*); Salween (*rgyal mo rngul chu*); and Mekong (*zla chu*).

The Six Ranges are the Drida Zelmo Gang (*zla mo sgang*); Tsawagang (*tsha ba sgang*); Markhamgang (*smar khams sgang*); Poborgang (*spo 'bor sgang*); Mardzagang (*dmar rdza sgang*); and Minyak Rabgang (*mi nyag rab sgang*).

Ganden Monastery (*dga 'ldan dgon pa*). Founded in 1409 by Je **Tsongkhapa** (*rje tsong kha pa*). One of the "great three" Gelugpa monasteries of Ganden, Sera, and Drepung. In Taktse County near Lhasa.

Gemang Monastery (*dge mang dgon pa*). A branch of **Dzogchen Monastery**. In Dzachukha region of Derge County. Monastic seat of the successive **Gemang** rinpoches.

Golok (*mgo log*). Region near the upper reaches of the Yellow River in present-day Qinghai Province.

Gorum Temple (*sgo rum*). The original temple at Sakya Monastery, founded in 1073 by Khön Könchok Gyalpo. On the Tromchu River in Tsang.

Gyarong Tsakho (*gyal rong tsha kho*). In the Marchu Gorge, Barkham County.

Jang (*'jang*). Homeland of the indigenous Naxi people, to the southeast of Gyeltang.

Jönpalung. *See* Nyoshul Jönpalung.

Kanchenjunga Mountain (*gangs can mdzod lnga*). The world's third highest mountain. On the border of Nepal and Sikkim.

Katok Dorje Den Monastery (*ka thog rdo rje'i gdan dgon pa*). One of the six major Nyingma monasteries and the oldest Nyingma monastery in eastern Tibet. Founded in 1159 by Katok Dampa Deshek.

Khyungpo (*khyung po*). Region of Kham corresponding to Tengchen County.

Ku-sey (*ku se*). On the west bank of the Yangtze, opposite **Palyul**.

Kyilko (*'khyil ko*). In the **Tromtar**, Kham area, near **Jönpalung**.

Labrang Tashikyil Monastery (*bla brang bkra shis 'khyil dgon pa*). Founded in 1709 by Jamyang Sheypa. In Amdo, southwest of Lanzhou.

Lhari Yerpa Cliff (*lha ri yer pa*). Also known as Drak Yerpa (*brag yer pa*), an area of many cave hermitages. Related to the enlightened speech activity of Padmasambhava. Near Lhasa.

Markham (*smar khams*). In the Chamdo Prefecture in the Tibetan Autonomous Region, between the Mekong and Yangtze Rivers.

Mindroling Monastery (*smin grol gling dgon pa*). One of the six main Nyingma monasteries. Founded in 1676 by Rigdzin Terdak Lingpa. In Drachi Valley of southern Tibet.

Minyak Lautang (*me nyak lau' thang*). Near Nakdren Township, Tawu County.

Monkha Nering Senge Dzong (*mon kha ne ring seng ge rdzong*). An important cave hermitage in the northern Lhüntse District in eastern Bhutan. Related to the enlightened activity aspect of Padmasambhava.

Nakchungma Hermitage. Forest hermitage behind **Dzogchen Monastery,** near the Pematang and the upper Rudam Gangtrö hermitages.

Nangchen. Nangchen County occupies the upper reaches of the Ngom-chu and Dza-chu headwaters of the Mekong, in Yushul Tibetan Autonomous Prefecture of Qinghai Province.

Nyoshul Jönpalung. The monastic seat and hermitage of Khenpo Ngakchung.

Palyul Monastery (*dpal yul dgon*). One of the six main Nyingma monasteries. Founded in 1665 by Rigdzin Kunzang Sherab. The monastic seat of the successive Penor incarnations. Near **Derge.**

Pekar Kordzö Ling (*pe dkar dkor mdzod gling*). A satellite temple on the north side of **Samye Monastery.**

Pema Rito (*pad ma ri khrod*). The hermitage of **Lungtok Tenpey Nyima,** between Jönpalung and **Yel-le Gar.**

Penpo Nalanda Monastery (*'phan po na lendra*). This is an important Sakya institution, originally founded in the Penpo District of central Tibet in 1425 by **Rongtön Sheja Kunrig** (1367–1459).

Reting Monastery (*rwa sgreng dgon pa*). Founded in 1056 by **Dromtönpa Gyalwe Jungne.** In the Jang region of central Tibet.

Ringmo Dilgyuk. A small valley halfway between Khenpo Ngakchung's birthplace and **Jönpalung.**

Riwoche (*ri bo che*). Riwoche County is located in the Chamdo Prefecture of the

Tibet Autonomous Region, southwest of **Nangchen**. Also the name of the village in Riwoche County, home to the famous Riwoche Tragyelma Temple, a great center of the Taklung Kagyü and Nyingma traditions, and the seat of the successive Pakchok and Jedrung incarnations.

Saljey Gang (*gsal rje gangs*). Name of a hilly region near **Nyoshul Jönpalung**, in present-day **Palyul** County.

Samye Monastery (*bsam yas dgon*). The first Buddhist monastery built in Tibet, constructed ca. 775–79 C.E. under the patronage of King Trisong Detsen.

Serta (*gser thal*). Serta (also Sertal) County corresponds to the headwaters and gorge of the Serchu, above Gyarong. Home to the famous Khenpo Jigme Püntsok (1933–2004), founder of the Serta Buddhist Institute, a.k.a. Larung Gar, in Gogentang.

Shitavana (*gsil ba'i tshal*). One of the eight great charnel grounds of ancient India, where Guru Padmasambhava and the eight vidyadharas received the *Eight Heruka Sadhanas*. Near Bodhgaya, India.

Shri Parvata (*dpal gyi ri*). The mountain abode of Saraha, where **Nagarjuna** is said to have spent his last days. In south India.

Shri Singha College (*shri seng ha bshad grva*). The famous shedra at **Dzogchen Monastery**, founded in 1842 by **Gyalse Shenpen Taye**, which produced many of the finest scholars in Tibet.

Takhokma (*rta khog ma*). Khenpo Ngakchung's home region, near **Jönpalung**.

Taktsang Senge Samdrub (*stag tshang seng ge bsam 'grub*). One of thirteen power-places in Tibet and Bhutan known as "Tiger's Den." This one is Paro Taktsang, where Guru Padmasambhava manifested as Dorje Drollö. On the east side of Paro Valley in western Bhutan.

Tromtar (*khrom thar*). Small town in Kham near **Adzom Gar** where the road forks northeast toward Kardze and southeast to Nyarong.

Tsari (*tsa ri*). One of the three most important sacred mountains of Tibet, along with Mount Kailash (*gang dkar ti se*) and Lapchi (*la phyi*). On the border of Tibet and Arunchal Pradesh, India.

Upper Dzachukha. A region in modern Sershul County.

Yartö Shampo Snow Range (*yar stod shams po gangs kyi ra ba*). A mountain range south of the Yarlung Valley, in southern Tibet.

Yel-le Gar (*ye le sgar*). The seat of **Rinchen Lingpa,** now an academy for Buddhist studies.

Yi-Lhung (*yid lhung*). A nomadic grassland region near Manigango, in Derge County.

GLOSSARY OF PERSONAL NAMES

Abu Rinpoche. *See* Dza Patrul Rinpoche.

Adzom Drukpa Drodül Pawo Dorje (*a 'dzom 'brug pa 'gro 'dul dpa' bo rdo rje,* 1842–1924). A.k.a. Natsok Rangdrol. Famous *Longchen Nyingtik* master who founded Adzom Gar in 1886. Student of Jamyang Khyentse Wangpo and Jamgön Mipam Rinpoche.

Alak Kalden Gyatso (*a lag skal ldan rgya mtsho,* 1607–77). Born in Rongpo Gonchen in Repkong. His sixth incarnation was a contemporary of Khenpo Ngakchung.

Alak Namkha Gyatso. Disciple of Dodrubchen Jigme Trinley Özer.

Alak Rigdra (*a lag rigs grwa*). Khenpo Ngakchung's previous incarnation. Scholar and tantric practitioner from Labrang Tashikyil Monastery.

Asanga (*thogs med,* fl. 4th century). Indian master and brother of Vasubandhu. Author of Abhidharma and Yogacharya texts, recipient of *Five Treatises of Maitreya.* Nagarjuna and Asanga are called the Twin Chariots of Mahayana.

Bhavaviveka (*legs ldan 'byed,* ca. 500–78). Critic of Buddhapalita, founder of the Svatantrika Madyamaka tradition. Author of key Svatantrika commentary on Nagarjuna's *Root Verses of the Middle Way.*

Buddhaguhya (*sangs rgyas gsang ba,* fl. 7th–8th century). Indian Mahayoga master, teacher of Vimalamitra.

Buddhapalita (*sangs rgyas bskyang,* 470–550). Indian commentator on Nagarjuna and Aryadeva, founder of Prasangika Madyamaka tradition.

Chandrakirti (*zla ba grags pa,* ca. 570–640). Abbot of Nalanda, defender of Buddhapalita. Author of Prasangika commentaries on Nagarjuna's *Root Verses of the Middle Way.*

Chapa Chöseng (*phywa pa chos kyi seng ge,* 1109–69). Kadampa commentator on Dignaga and Dharmakirti.

Chöying Tobden Dorje (*chos dbyings stobs ldan rdo rje,* 1785–1848). Dzogchen master, author of the *Treasury of Sutras and Tantras,* disciple of Dodrubchen Jigme Trinley Özer.

Dampa Deshek (*dam pa bde gshegs,* 1122–92). Founder of Katok Dorje Den Monastery in 1159. Younger brother of Pagmo Drupa Dorje Gyalpo.

Dharmapala (*slob dpon chos skyong,* fl. 6th century). Abbot of Nalanda. Later known as Virupa, one of the Eighty-Four Mahasiddhas, originator of the Lamdre lineage.

Do Khyentse Yeshe Dorje (*mdo mkhyen brtse ye shes rdo rje,* 1800–66). Meditation master, treasure-revealer, reincarnation of Rigdzin Jigme Lingpa. Student of Dodrubchen Jigme Trinley Özer and teacher of Dza Patrul Rinpoche.

Dodrubchen Jigme Trinley Özer (*rdo grub chen 'jigs med phrin las 'od zer,* 1745–1821). Treasure-revealer, heart-son of Rigdzin Jigme Lingpa. Principle *Longchen Nyingtik* lineage holder.

Dölpopa Sherab Gyaltsen (*dol po pa shes rab rgyal mtshan,* 1292–1361). Sakya master, abbot of Jonang Monastery. Founder of the Jonang tradition, author of Shentong text, *Ocean of Definitive Meaning.*

Drakpa Gyaltsen (*grags pa rgyal mtshan,* 1147–1216). One of the Sakya tradition's five patriarchs, disciple of Sakya Pandita. Author of commentary on *Parting from the Four Clingings.*

Drime Ösel Lingpa (*dri med 'od gsal gling pa,* fl. 19th–20th century). Treasure-revealer, builder of Katok Bartrö and Rakchab Senge Ri Dorje Yutok Dzong retreats.

Drime Shingkyong (*dri med zhing skyong,* 1724–60). Gonpo Pel Chökyi Dorje. Reincarnation of Katok Dorje Den Monastery abbot Gyalse Sonam Deutsen. Revitalized Katok Monastery.

Dromtönpa Gyalwe Jungne (*'brom ston pa rgyal ba'i 'byung gnas,* 1005–64). Tibetan disciple and lineage holder of Atisha. Founded Radreng (Reting) Monastery in 1056.

Dza Patrul Rinpoche (*dza dpal sprul rin po che,* 1808–87). Orgyen Jigme Chökyi Wangpo. Fondly known as Abu Rinpoche. Meditation master, commentator on *Way of the Bodhisattva* and other texts, author of *Words of My Perfect Teacher.*

Dzogchen Tulku Rinpoche (*rdzogs chen sprul sku rin po che*, 1872–1935). Thubten Chökyi Dorje. Developed Shri Singha Buddhist College into a premier learning institution.

Fifth Dalai Lama, Lobzang Gyatso (*blo bzang rgya mtsho*, 1617–82). Seventeenth-century unifier, temporal ruler of Tibet.

Ganden Tri Rinpoche (*dga' ldan khri rin po che*, 1721–90). Ngawang Tsultrim. Sixth Regent of Tibet, tutor to the Thirteenth Dalai Lama, sixty-first abbot of **Ganden Monastery.**

Garab Dorje (*dga' rab rdo rje*). Also known as Prahevajra. First human lineage holder of the Great Perfection, author of *Three Statements That Strike the Vital Point,* teacher of Manjushrimitra.

Gemang Kyabgön Rinpoche (*dge mang skyabs mgon rin po che*, 1800–55). The first Dzogchen Gemang Rinpoche, Gyalse Shenpen Taye. Founder of **Gemang Monastery,** led rebuilding of **Dzogchen Monastery** in 1842, founded **Shri Singha Buddhist College.**

Gemang Ön Tenga (*dge mang dbon bstan dga'*, 1851–1900?). Orgyen Tendzin Norbu. Nephew of **Gyalse Shenpen Taye,** disciple of Dza Patrul Rinpoche, root teacher of **Khenpo Shenga,** Dilgo Khyentse Rinpoche's father.

Geshe Drapa (*dge bshes grwa pa*, 1012–90). Drapa Ngönshey. Founded Dratang Monastery in 1081. Treasure-revealer of *Four Tantras* of Tibetan medicine, established Phuntong Chenye, a tantric practice community.

Geshe Potawa (*dge bshes po ta ba*, 1027–1105). Rinchen Sal. One of three principle disciples of **Dromtönpa Gyalwe Jungne.** Disciples include Geshe Sharawa Yönten Drak and Geshe Langri Tangpa.

Golok Sonam Palden (*mgo log bsod nams dpal ldan*, fl. 19th–20th century). The Second Khyenrab of Dartang (Tarthang) Monastery.

Guru Chöwang (*gu ru chos dbang*, 1212–70). Chökyi Wangchuk. One of the Five Tertön Kings, treasure-revealer of *Lama Sangdu* treasure cycle, commentator on the treasure tradition. Built Samdrup Dewachenpo Temple at Lhalung Monastery.

Gyalse Shenpen Thaye (*rgyal sras gzhan phan mtha' yas*, 1800–55/69?). Kushok Gemang Rinpoche. Supervised the 1842 reconstruction of **Dzogchen Monastery,** established **Shri Singha College.** Disciple of Fourth Dzogchen Rinpoche and

Dodrubchen Jigme Trinley Özer. Disciples included Dza Patrul Rinpoche, Do Khyentse Yeshe Dorje, and Khenchen Pema Dorje.

Jamgön Mipam Rinpoche (*'jam mgon mi pham rin po che,* 1846–1912). Polymath, scholar, and meditation master, Rimé advocate. Student of Dza Patrul Rinpoche and Jamyang Khyentse Wangpo.

Jamyang Khyentse Wangpo (*'jam dbyangs mkhyen brtse'i dbang po,* 1820–92). Meditation master, treasure-revealer, and leader of the Rimé movement.

Jatsön Nyingpo (*'ja' tshon snying po,* 1585–1656). Also known as Letro Lingpa. Treasure-revealer of *Könchok Chidü,* a Padmasambhava treasure cycle.

Jigme Gyalwey Nyugu (*'jigs med rgyal ba'i myu gu,* 1765–1843). Master of the Longchen Nyingtik, Dza Patrul Rinpoche's teacher, inspiration for Patrul's *Words of My Perfect Teacher.*

Katok Situ Rinpoche (*ka thog si tu rin po che,* 1820–79?). Chökyi Lodrö Orgyen Tenpa Namgyal. The Second Katok Situ incarnation, disciple of Dza Patrul Rinpoche. *See* Nyoshul Khenpo, *Marvelous Garland of Rare Gems,* 465–66.

Khamtrul Ngawang Kunga Tendzin (*khams sprul ngag dbang kun dga' bstan 'dzin,* 1680–1728). The third Khamtrul incarnation. Master and commentator of Mahamudra, founded Drukpa Kagyü seat, Khampagar, also known as Pal Püntsok Chökor Ling Monastery.

Khedrub Je (*mkhas grub rje,* 1385–1438). Khedrub Gelek Palzang. One of Tsongkhapa's two main heirs, abbot of Ganden Monastery, First Panchen Lama incarnation.

Khenpo Gyaltsen Özer (*mkhan po rgyal mtshan 'od zer,* b. 1862). Khen Rinpoche Dorje Dzinpa Gyaltsen Özer. Katok meditation master, lineage holder of the *Longsel Dorje Nyingpo* cycle.

Khenpo Könchok Özer (*mkhan po dkon mchog 'od zer,* 1837?–1897?). Purtsa Khenpo Akön. Eleventh abbot of Shri Singha College, student of Dza Patrul Rinpoche.

Khenpo Kunpel (*mkhan po kun dpal,* 1872–1943). Author of *Nectar of Manjushri's Speech,* a commentary on *Way of the Bodhisattva,* and biographies of Dza Patrul Rinpoche and Jamgön Mipam Rinpoche.

Khenpo Shenga (*mkhan po gzhan dga',* 1871–1927). Shenpen Chökyi Nangwa. Disciple of Ön Tendzin Norbu, revitalized Nyingmapa monastic education through authoring a shedra curriculum.

Khenpo Sonam Chödrub (*mkhan po bsod nams chos 'grub,* 1862–1944) Attended Shri Singha College, refused teaching appointment to continue studies. Biographer of Longchenpa, commentator on *Way of the Bodhisattva* and *Guhyagarbha Tantra.*

Khenpo Sonam Chöpel (*mkhan po bsod nams chos 'phel,* 1836–1910). Shedrub Chökyi Nangwa. Seventeenth abbot of Shri Singha College, disciple of Khenpo Akön.

King Ja of Sahor (*rgyal po ja,* fl. 6th century). Also known as Indrabhuti. Title refers to several kings. Key figure in early transmission of Mahayoga and Anuyoga lineages. *See* Dudjom Rinpoche, *Nyingma School,* 548–462.

King Suchandra (*chos rgyal zla ba bzang po*). First king of Shambhala, requested teachings from the Buddha, received the *Kalachakra Tantra.*

King Trisong Detsen (*khri srong de'u btsan,* fl. 9th century). Second Dharma King of Tibet. Invited Shantarakshita, Padmasambhava, and Vimalamitra to Tibet, establishing Buddhism in Tibet.

Kongnyön (*kong nyon*). Possibly Tangdrok Ön Pema Chokdrub, third reincarnation of Natsok Rangdrol. Prominent student of Rigdzin Jigme Lingpa.

Kshitigarbha (fl. 10th cent.). Also known as Bhumigarbha. Indian scholar, accompanied Atisha to Tibet.

Kumaraja (*ku ma ra dza,* 1266–1343). Root teacher of Longchenpa and Rangjung Dorje, disciple of Melong Dorje.

Lama Özer (*bla ma 'od zer*). Possibly Khenpo Könchok Özer.

Lama Rigdzin (*bla ma rig dzin,* fl 19th-20th century). Disciple of Lungtok Tenpey Nyima Gyaltsen Pelzangpo.

Langri Tangpa (*glang ri thang pa,* 1054–1123). Kadampa master, author of *Eight Verses of Training the Mind,* founded Langtang Monastery.

Lerab Lingpa (*las rab gling pa,* 1856–1926). Nyakla Sögyal. Treasure-revealer, student of Lungtok Tenpey Nyima Gyaltsen Pelzangpo, teacher of the Thirteenth Dalai Lama.

Lhatsün Namkha Jigme (*lha btsun nam mkha' ' jigs med,* 1597–1653?). Dzogchen master, treasure-revealer, introduced the Great Perfection to Sikkim. *See* Dudjom Rinpoche, *Nyingma School,* 818–20.

Lilavajra (*sgeg pa'i rdo rje,* fl. 8th century). Mahayoga master, teacher of **Buddh-aguhya.** Commentator on *Chanting the Names of Manjushri* and *Guhyagarbha Tantra.*

Lingda Norko (*gling mda' nor kho,* fl. 20th century). Student of **Lungtok Tenpey Nyima Gyaltsen Pelzangpo.**

Lingtsang Khenpo (*gling tshang mkhen po*). Possibly Khenchen Gyurme Tubten Jamyang Drakpa (c. 1883–1945).

Lobzang Gyatso. *See* **Fifth Dalai Lama, Lobzang Gyatso.**

Longchenpa (1308–1364). Also known as Longchen Rabjampa, Drime Öser (*klong chen rab 'byams pa, dri med 'od zer*). Major teacher of the Nyingma school, disciple of the great mystic Kumaraja. Prolific writer who systematized all the teachings of the Great Perfection and authored the Seven Treasuries (*mdzod bdun*). Source of the Longchen Nyingtik tradition.

Longsel Dorje Nyingpo (*klong gsal rdo rje snying po,* 1625–92). Disciple of Düdül Dorje, treasure-revealer, helped to restore **Katok Dorje Den Monastery.**

Lungtok Tenpey Nyima Gyaltsen Pelzangpo (*lung rtogs bstan pa'i nyi ma rgyal mtshan dpal bzang po,* 1829–1901). Dzogchen master, Khenpo Ngakchung's root teacher, heart-son of **Dza Patrul Rinpoche.**

Maitripa (c. 1007–85). Indian mahasiddha of the Mahamudra lineage, disciple of Naropa and Saraha and teacher of **Marpa Chökyi Wangchuk.**

Majawa Jangchup Tsöndru (*rma bya ba byang chub brtson 'grus,* d. 1185). Author of *Ornament of Reason,* a commentary on **Nagarjuna's** *Root Verses of the Middle Way.*

Marpa Chökyi Wangchuk (*mar pa chos kyi dbang phyug,* 1012–96). Also known as Marpa the Translator. Translator, disciple of Naropa, teacher of Milarepa, and Tibetan source of the Kagyü lineage.

Mingyur Namkhai Dorje (*mi 'gyur nam mkha'i rdo rje,* 1793–1870). Fourth Dzog-chen Rinpoche, teacher of Jamyang Khyentse Wangpo, Do Khyentse Yeshe Dorje, Dza Patrul Rinpoche, and Jamgön Mipam Rinpoche.

Minling Lochen Dharmashri (*smin gling lo chen d+ha rma shri,* 1654–1718). Nyingma scholar and commentator on *Guhyagarbha Tantra.* Brother, spiritual heir of **Minling Terdak Lingpa.**

Minling Terdak Lingpa (*smin gling gter bdag gling pa*, 1646–1714). Gyurme Dorje. Disciple and teacher of the Fifth Dalai Lama, treasure-revealer, founder of **Mindroling Monastery**.

Minyak Kunzang Sonam (*mi nyag kun bzang bsod nams*, 1823–1901). Thubten Chökyi Drakpa. Geluk scholar, disciple of **Dza Patrul Rinpoche**, commentator on *Way of the Bodhisattva* and *Thirty-Seven Practices of a Bodhisattva*.

Nagarjuna (*slob dpon klu sgrub*, fl. 3rd century). Indian master, Madhyamaka philosopher. Author of *Root Verses of the Middle Way*. Nagarjuna and **Asanga** are called the Twin Chariots of Mahayana.

Naktar Tulku Sonam Chödrub (*nag thar sprul sku bsod nams chos grub*, fl. 19th–20th century). Student of **Lungtok Tenpey Nyima Gyaltsen Pelzangpo**.

Nesar Jamyang Khyentse Wangchuk (*gnas gsar 'jam dbyangs mkhyen rtse dbang phyug*, 1524–68). Abbot of Zhalu Monastery. Treasure-revealer, author of treasure-cycle liturgical and instructional texts.

Ngamdzong Tönpa (*ngam rdzong ston pa*, fl 12th century). Disciple of Milarepa, lineage holder of the Ngamdzong Whispered Lineage.

Ngari Panchen Pema Wangyal (*mnga' ris pan chen padma dbang rgyal*, 1487–1542/3). Treasure-revealer, author of the *Ascertainment of the Three Vows*.

Ngawang Palden Chökyong (*ngag dbang dpal ldan chos skyong*, 1702–69). Sakya master, thirty-fourth abbot of Ngor Monastery. Student of **Rigdzin Jigme Lingpa**, teacher of Second Dzogchen Rinpoche, Gyurme Tekchok Tendzin.

Ngawang Tenzin (*ngag dbang bstan 'dzin*, 1858–1914). Tutop Lingpa. Treasure-revealer, lineage holder of *Longchen Nyingtik* and **Nyakla Pema Düdül**.

Nyakla Pema Düdül (*nyag bla pad ma bdud 'dul*, 1816–72). Dzogchen master, treasure-revealer, teacher of **Adzom Drukpa**.

Nyangben Tingdzin Zangpo (*nyang ban ting 'dzin bzang po*, fl. 8th century). Disciple of **Padmasambhava** and **Vimalamitra**.

Nyang-rel Nyima Özer (*nyang ral nyi ma 'od zer*, 1124?-1192?). Treasure-revealer, first of the Five Tertön Kings. Revealed a biography of **Padmasambhava**.

Ön Tendzin Norbu (*dbon bstan 'dzin nor bu*, 1841–1900). Orgyen Tendzin Norbu.

Gemang scholar, disciple of **Dza Patrul Rinpoche,** nephew of **Gyalse Shenpen Taye,** teacher of Khenpo Yönten Gyatso.

Padmasambhava (8th century). Literally "Lotus-Born." Also known as Guru Rinpoche ("Precious Guru") or the Second Buddha. Indian Buddhist mahasiddha from Oddiyana who brought Vajrayana Buddhism to Tibet and neighboring countries at the invitation of the Abbot Shantarakshita and King Trisong Detsen. Regarded as the founder of the Nyingma tradition.

Patrul Rinpoche. See **Dza Patrul Rinpoche.**

Pema Norbu (*pad ma nor bu,* 1887–1932). Pema Kunzang Tendzin Norbu, the ninth throne-holder of Palyul lineage. *See* Jamgön Kongtrül, *Treasury of Knowledge: Buddhism's Journey,* 107–15.

Pema Wangchen (*padma dbang chen*). Son and lineage holder of **Guru Chöwang.**

Princess Pemasel (*lha lcam pad ma gsal*). Daughter of **King Trisong Detsen.** First recipient of the *Khandro Nyingtik* treasure cycle, revealed by her later incarnation Pema Ledreltsel (1231?–1307?).

Rigdzin Jigme Lingpa (*rig 'dzin 'jigs med gling pa,* 1729–98). Also known as Khyentse Özer. Meditation master, treasure-revealer of the *Longchen Nyingtik* cycle, author of *Yeshe Lama* and *Treasury of Precious Qualities.*

Rinchen Lingpa (*rin chen gling pa,* fl. 19th–20th century). Here, refers to treasure-revealer of Yel-le Gar Monastery, not Tertön Rinchen Lingpa (1313–92).

Rongtön Sheja Kunrig (*rong ston shes bya kun rig,* 1367–1449). Sakya scholar, especially of sutra and the *Prajnaparamita.* Founded Penpo Nalanda Monastery in 1436, teacher of **Sakya Chokden** and Gorampa Sonam Senge.

Sakya Chokden (*sa skya mchog ldan,* 1428–1507). Serdok Panchen. Abbot of Serdokchen Monastery, Sakya scholar.

Sakya Dakchen (*sa skya bdag chen*). Here, refers to Twenty-Second Sakya Trizin, Duchö Labrangpa Salo Jampel Dorje Kunga Sonam (1485–1533).

Sakya Panchen (*sa skya pan chen,* 1182–1251). Sakya Pandita Kunga Gyeltsen. The fourth of the five patriarchs of Sakya.

Shantarakshita (*zhi ba 'tsho,* b. 705). Abbot of Vikramashila Monastery in India. Invited to Tibet by **King Trisong Detsen,** founded **Samye Monastery,** ordained the first Tibetan monks.

Shechen Rabjam Rinpoche (*zhe chen rab 'byams rin po che*). Here, the fifth incarnation, Gyurme Pema Tekchok Tenpey Gyaltsen (1864–1909).

Shübu Palseng (*shud bu dpal seng*). Palgyi Senge of Shübu. Minister of King Trisong Detsen, one of the twenty-five disciples of Padmasambhava.

Sudhana (*phags pa nor bzang*). Indian youth whose quest for enlightenment is featured in the *Gandavyuha* chapter of *Avatamsakasutra*.

Tartse Pönlop (*thar rtse dpon slob*, 1847–1914). Pönlop Jamyang Loter Wangpo. Sakya compiler of *Compendium of Tantras,* publisher of first edition of *Explanation for Private Disciples.*

Trom Drubtop (*khrom grub thob*). Possibly Tromge Jigme Dongak Tendzin (fl. 19th century).

Tsangnakpa Tsöndrü Senge (*gtsan nag pa brtson 'grus seng ge*, d. 1185). Kadampa logician and scholar of Sangpu Neutok Monastery.

Tsangtönpa Dorje Gyaltsen (*gtsan ston pa rdo rje rgyal mstan*, 1126–1216). Second abbot of Katok Dorje Den Monastery. Disciple of Dampa Deshek, helped build Katok Monastery.

Tsongkhapa (1357–1419). Also known as Lobsang Drakpa (*blo bzang grags pa*) or Je Rinpoche. Famous master and prolific writer inspired by the Kadam tradition of Atisha. Founder of the Geluk school of Tibetan Buddhism.

Tsarchen Losal Gyatso (*tshar chen blo gsal rgya mtsho*, 1502–66). Thirteenth Shalu Khenchen. Founder of Dra Drangmoche Monastery, Tsar branch of the Sakya tradition. Teacher of Jamyang Khyentse Wangchuk and the Third Dalai Lama.

Vajraghantapada (*rdo rje dril bu pa*). One of the Eighty-Four Mahasiddhas, previous incarnation of Jamyang Khyentse Wangpo.

Venerable Öntrul (*rje dbon sprul*). Katok Öntrul Tsultrim Yönten Gyatso or his predecessor, Khenpo Pema Gyaltsen.

Vimalamitra (8th century). Indian adept who received the Great Perfection transmission from Shri Singha and Jnanasutra. Spread these teachings in Tibet at the invitation of King Trisong Detsen. Source of Vima Nyingtik tradition. Upon leaving Tibet, he promised to send an emanation once every hundred years to revitalize the Buddhist doctrine.

Wu Öd Yeshe Bum (*dbu 'od ye shes 'bum*, 1242?–1328?). Fifth abbot of **Katok Dorje Den Monastery.** Scholar and teacher of Highest Yoga Tantra.

Yeshe Gyaltsen (*ye shes rgyal mtshan*, b. 1395). Also known as Katokpa Yeshe Gyaltsen. Fifteenth abbot of **Katok Dorje Den Monastery,** scholar and master of Nyingma Kama tradition.

Yeshe Tsogyal (*ye shes mtsho rgyal*, ca. 757–817). Female buddha who attained the Rainbow Body. Main disciple and Tibetan consort of **Padmasambhava.** Recorded and concealed many of Padmasambhava's teachings.

Yudrönma (*rdo rje gyu sgron ma*). Also known as Dorje Yudrönma. One of the Twelve Tenma Sisters, protectors of the Nyingma lineage, guardians of Tibet. Often appears holding a five-colored long-life arrow and divinatory mirror.

GLOSSARY OF ENUMERATIONS

Two

two aims (*don gnyis*). Also called the two kinds of benefit: (1) personal or self (*rang*); and (2) altruistic or other (*gzhan*).

two notions of self (*bdag gnyis*). (1) Self of individual persons (*gang zag gi bdag*); and (2) self of phenomena (*chos kyi bdag*).

two *Nyingtik Child Cycles* (*snying thig bu yig gnyis*). Two sections of the famous four-part compilation of Dzogchen scriptures known as the *Nyingtik Yabshi* (*snying thig ya bzhi*): (1) *Lama Yangtik* (*bla ma yang thig*), which is **Longchenpa**'s two-volume collection of commentaries on Vimalamitra's *Vima Nyingtik* (*bi ma snying thig*); and (2) *Khandro Yangtik* (*mkha' 'gro yang thig*), which is **Longchenpa**'s two-volume collection of commentaries on **Padmasambhava**'s *Khandro Nyingtik*. **Longchenpa** also wrote two volumes of commentary that relate to both lineages, entitled *Zabmo Yangtik* (*zab mo yang thig*).

two *Nyingtik Mother Cycles* (*snying thig ma yig gnyis*). (1) Vimalamitra's *Sangwa Nyingtik* (*gsang ba snying thig*); and (2) **Padmasambhava**'s *Khandro Nyingtik* (*mkha' 'gro snying thig*).

two stages of meditation (*sgom rim gnyis*). (1) The generation or development stage (*bskyes rim*); and (2) the completion or perfection stage (*rdzogs rim*).

two stains (*glo bur dri ma*). Temporary obscurations caused by (1) disturbing emotions (*nyon mongs*); and (2) mistaken views about phenomena (*phyin ci log*).

two superior truths (*lhag pa'i bden gnyis*). (1) Superior relative truth (*lhag pa'i kun rdzob*), the establishment through valid cognition that sights, sounds, and awareness are the magical display of wisdom; and (2) superior ultimate truth (*lhag pa'i don dam*), the ascertainment of the inseparability of the space of reality and wisdom, which is realized through the insight that discerns ultimate truth.

two truths (*bden gnyis*). (1) Conventional truth (*kun rdzob bden pa*); and (2) absolute truth (*don dam bden pa*).

twofold path of the luminous Great Perfection (*rdzogs chen lam gnyis*). The two aspects of instruction in the Great Perfection pith-instructional class (*man ngag sde*): (1) The practice of Kadak Trekchö, "Cutting Through to Primordial Purity" (*ka dag khregs chod*). Through this practice, the wisdom aspect, one cuts through the stream of delusion, the thoughts of past, present, and future, by revealing a naked awareness devoid of dualistic fixation. To recognize this view through applying the precious instructions of one's lama and sustain it uninterruptedly throughout all aspects of life is the very essence of the Great Perfection; and (2) the practice of Trekchö forms the basis for the second aspect of Great Perfection instruction, the skillful means aspect, that of Ösel Tögal, "Direct Crossing to Luminosity" (*'od gsal thod rgal*), also known as Lhündrup Tögal, "Direct Crossing to Spontaneous Presence" (*lhun grub thod rgal*). Through the discipline of Tögal, which is more a fruition than a practice, the practitioner actualizes all the different aspects of enlightenment within a single lifetime. He or she uses specific and exceptionally powerful physical and visual exercises to incite four specific visionary experiences. Both Trekchö and Tögal require the direct guidance of a qualified master.

twofold superior evenness (*lhag pa'i mnyam pa gnyis*). (1) Qualified and unqualified emptiness are both spontaneously present as the identity of the seven riches of the superior ultimate truth; and (2) incorrect and correct relative truth are both equal as the superior relative truth in being the mandala of kayas and wisdoms. See Padmasambhava and Jamgön Kongtrul, *Light of Wisdom: Vol. II,* 154.

THREE

three appearances (*snang gsum*). (1) Object (*bzung ba'i yul*); (2) subjective consciousness (*'dzin pa'i sems*); and (3) body (*'gro ba'i lus*). Respectively associated with the desire realm as the variable coarse appearance of body (*lus rags pa snang ba 'dod khams*); blissful semi-appearance of speech of the pure form realm (*ngag phyed snang ba gzugs khams*); and formless realm, which is the intangible appearance of mind (*sems kyi snang ba ma myong ba gzugs med khams*).

three aspects of logic (*rtags kyi tshul gsum*). (1) Property of the subject (*phyogs chos*); (2) forward pervasion (*rjes 'gro*); and (3) counterpervasion (*ldog khyab*).

three aspects of objective perception (*yul gsum gyad du gyur pa*). Level of increasing proficiency in meditative perception of the deity as successively (1) mental, (2) visual, and (3) tactile object.

three capacities of practitioner (*dbang po gsum*). (1) Superior (*rab*); (2) middling (*'bring*); and (3) inferior (*tha ma*).

three classes of sublime being (*'phags pa gsum*). (1) Shravakas (*nyan thos*); (2) pratyekabuddhas (*rang rgyal*); and (3) bodhisattvas (*byang chub sems dpa'*).

three classes of the Great Perfection (*rdzogs chen sde gsum*). (1) Mind class (*sems sde*) on luminosity; (2) space class (*klong sde*) on emptiness; and (3) pith-instruction class (*man ngag sde*) emphasizing their indivisibility.

three distinctions (*phye ba gsum*). The distinctions between (1) universal ground (*kun gzhi*) and dharmakaya (*chos sku*); (2) mind (*sems*) and awareness (*rig pa*); and (3) relative truth (*kun rdzob bden pa*) and absolute truth (*don dam bden pa*).

three doors (*sgo gsum*). The three gross doors: (1) body (*lus*); (2) speech (*ngag*); (3) and mind (*yid*); the three subtle doors: (1) channels (*rtsa*); (2) energies (*rlung*); and (3) vital nuclei (*thig le*).

three dualistic concepts (*'khor gsum*). (1) Subject (*byed po*); (2) object (*byed pa*); and (3) action (*bya ba*).

three foundations of monastic discipline (*'dul ba gzhi gsum*). (1) Lay (*dge bsnyen*); (2) novice (*dge tshul*); and (3) full monastic ordination (*dge slong*).

three higher empowerments (*dbang gong ma gsum*). (1) Secret empowerment (*gsang dbang*); (2) insight and wisdom empowerment (*shes rab ye shes kyi bang*); and (3) word empowerment (*tshigs dbang*).

three inner tantra classes (*nang rgyud sde gsum*). Three approaches: (1) generation (*bskyed rim*); (2) completion (*rdzogs rim*); and (3) Great Perfection (*rdzogs pa chen po*); or the three yogas: (1) Maha (*rnal 'byor chen po*); (2) Anu (*rjes su rnal 'byor*); and (3) Ati (*shin tu rnal 'byor*).

Three Jewels (*dkon mchog gsum*). (1) Buddha (*sangs rgyas*); (2) Dharma (*chos*); and (3) Sangha (*dge 'dun*).

three kayas (*sku gsum*). (1) Dharmakaya (*chos sku*); (2) Sambhogakaya (*longs sku*); and (3) Nirmanakaya (*sprul sku*). Within the context of the Great Perfection, in terms of the ground of spiritual experience, these three are respectively known as: (1) the essential nature (*ngo bo*); (2) its natural expression (*rang bzhin*); and (3) its compassion (*thugs rje*), which is the raison d'être for the appearance of buddhas within the world. In terms of the path, they respectively denote bliss, radiance, and nonthought; in terms of the result of spiritual experience, they are properly known as the three kayas. Among them, the dharmakaya is free from elaborate constructs and endowed with the twenty-one sets of qualities. The sambhogakaya is of the nature of light and endowed with perfect major and minor marks, perceptible only to advanced bodhisattvas. The nirmanakaya manifests in the mundane world, in forms perceptible to both pure and impure beings.

three levels of existence (*sa gsum*). Three regions above, on, and below the earth: (1) the celestial abode of gods, (2) the terrestrial abode of humans, and (3) the subterranean abode of nagas.

three levels of vows (*sdom gsum*). Also called the three precepts: the precepts, trainings, and samayas of (1) Pratimoksha, (2) Bodhisattva, and (3) Mantra.

three lineages (*brgyud gsum*). (1) Mind Lineage of the Conquerors (*rgyal ba'i dgongs brgyud*); (2) Symbol Lineage of the Vidyadharas (*rig 'dzin brda brgyud*); and (3) Whispered Lineage of Individuals (*gang zag snyan brgyud*).

three methods of pleasing (a teacher) (*mnyes pa gsum*). (1) Material offerings, (2) service, and (3) spiritual practice; or (1) imbibing the teachings, (2) meditating on the teachings, and (3) integrating the teachings in all activities.

three monastic robes (*chos gos gsum*, Skt. *tricivara*). The three monastic robes comprise the lower robe, or undergarment (Skt. *antaravasaka*); the upper robe (Skt. *uttarasanga*); and the outer robe (Skt. *sangati*). From the first century c.e., these three monastic garments have been regularly used in representations of the Buddha, with the outer robe usually the most visible garment and the undergarment protruding at the bottom. The upper robe is barely visible within the folds of the outer robe.

three pitakas (*sde snod gsum*). The (1) Vinaya, (2) Sutra, and (3) Abhidharma collections of the Buddhist Canon.

Three Protectors of Mantra (*sngags srung gsum*). (1) Ekajati, (2) Rahula, and (3) Dorje Lekpa.

three purities (*dag pa gsum*). In Mahayoga, the (1) purity of the outer world (*snod dag pa*); (2) purity of its inner contents (*bcud dag pa*); and (3) purity of the mindstream (*rgyud rnams dag pa*).

three realms (*khams gsum*). (1) The desire realm (*'dod khams*); (2) the form realm (*gzugs khams*); and (3) the formless realm (*gzugs med khams*).

three ritual activities of vajra reality (*rdo rje'i cho ga gsum*). (1) The vajra, symbolizing body; (2) syllables such as HUM, symbolizing speech; and (3) ornaments and costumes, symbolizing mind.

Three Roots (*rtsa ba gsum*). (1) The lama (*bla ma*); (2) tutelary deity (*yi dam*); and (3) dakini (*mkha' 'gro*). Respectively, these confer blessings, accomplishments, and enlightened activities.

three secrets (*gsang ba gsum*). (1) Vajra body (*sku rdo rje*); (2) speech (*gsung rdo rje*); and (3) mind (*thugs rdo rje*).

Three Sources of the Teachings (*bstan pa'i btsas gsum*). Teachings of buddha body, speech, and mind as described in Longchenpa's Dzogchen tradition: (1) the vajra represents Dharmakaya, (2) a four-digit-size book represents Sambhogakaya, and (3) a buddha image represents Nirmanakaya.

three vehicles (*theg pa gsum*). The first three of the nine vehicles (*theg pa rim pa dgu*): those of the (1) shravakas (*nyan thos theg pa*); (2) pratyekabuddhas (*rang rgyal theg pa*); and (3) bodhisattvas (*byang chub sems dpa' theg pa*).

three stabilities (*ting nge 'dzin rnam gsum*). In Mahayoga: (1) the yoga of great emptiness, which is wisdom; (2) the apparitional display of compassion, which is skillful means; (3) and the seals of the meditational deities, which are subtle and coarse in their appearances.

three stages of conferral of novitiate vows (*tshig gsum rim nod*). (1) Preparation, (2) actual conferral of the ordination, and (3) subsequent advice. Also, three levels of ordination: (1) laity, (2) novitiate, and (3) full-fledged ordination.

three supreme methods (*sbyor dngos rjes gsum*). Requisites for spiritual practice: (1) altruistic motivation, (2) practicing without objective reference or conceptual fabrication, and (3) dedicating the merit for the sake of all beings.

three syllables (*'bru gsum*). OM AH HUM, the seed-syllables for the (1) buddha body (*sku*); (2) speech (*gsung*); and (3) mind (*thugs*) of all buddhas.

three times (*dus gsum*). (1) Past, (2) present, and (3) future.

three trainings (*bslab pa gsum*). (1) Training in moral discipline (*tshul khrims*); (2) stability (*ting nge 'dzin*); and (3) insight (*shes rab*).

three virtues (*dge ba gsum*). (1) Generosity (*sbyin pa*); (2) moral discipline (*tshul khrims*); and (3) meditation (*sgom*).

three ways of the wise (*mkhas tshul gsum*). (1) Teaching, (2) debate, and (3) composition (*'chad rtsod rtsom*).

three *Yangtik* teachings (1) *Khandro Yangtik* (*mkha' 'gro yang thig*); (2) *Lama Yangtik* (*bla ma yang thig*); and (3) *Zabmo Yangtik* (*zab mo yang thig*); **Longchenpa's** commentaries on *Khandro Nyingtik* (*mkha' 'gro snying thig*) and *Vima Nyingtik* (*bi ma snying thig*).

threefold kindness (*bka' drin gsum*). The three kindnesses of a spiritual master. In sutra: (1) giving precepts (*sdom pa*); (2) reading-transmissions (*lung*); and (3) guidance (*khrid*). In tantra: (1) conferring empowerments (*dbang bskur*); (2) explaining the tantras (*rgyud bshad*); and (3) imparting pith instructions (*man ngag gnang ba*).

threefold motionlessness (*mi gyo ba gsum*). (1) Motionlessness of body, (2) speech, and (3) mind.

threefold pure scrutiny (*dpyad gsum*). Analysis that is like the purification of gold through (1) smelting, (2) cutting, and (3) polishing.

threefold sky practice (*nam mkha' sum phrug*). Dzogchen meditation practice that integrates (1) the outer purity of the sky with (2) the inner purity of the ultimate nature and (3) the secret purity of the luminous essence (*'od gsal snying po*).

FOUR

four awakenings (*mngon byang bzhi*). (1) Moon seat (*zla gdan*); (2) the seed-syllables of speech (*gsung yig 'bru*); (3) the symbolic implements of mind (*thugs phyag mtshan*); and (4) the perfect body of the deity (*sku yongs rdzogs*).

four basic precepts (*rtsa ba bzhi*). The basic precepts of ordained individuals: (1) killing, (2) stealing, (3) sexual activity, and (4) falsely proclaiming oneself as a spiritual teacher.

Four Branches of the Nyingtik (*snying thig ya bzhi*). See *Four Nyingtik Motherand-Child Cycles.*

four circular empowerments (*zlum po bzhi dbang*). General empowerments, called "circular" because of the implements used: (1) vase, (2) skull, (3) mirror, and (4) torma.

four clingings (*zhen pa bzhi*). Also known as the four attachments. (1) Clinging to this life, (2) clinging to the three realms, (3) clinging to self-interest, and (4) grasping.

four concentrations (*bsam gtan bzhi*). The four dhyanas: (1) the first, which possesses both ideas and scrutiny (*rtog pa dang bcas shing dpyod pa dang bcas pa'i bsam gtan dang po*); (2) the second, which possesses no ideas but scrutiny alone (*rtog pa med la dpyod pa tsam dang bcas pa bsam gtan gnyis pa*); (3) the third of mental action, which is devoid of ideas and scrutiny (*rtog pa dang dpyod pa yang med pa yid la byed pa bsam gtan gsum pa*); and (4) the fourth of mental action, which is united with delight (*dga' ba sdud pa yid la byed pa'i bsam gtan bzhi pa*).

four defeats (*pham pa bzhi*). (1) Sex (*mi tshangs spyod pa*); (2) stealing (*ma byin len pa*); (3) killing (*srog gcog pa*); and (4) lying (*rdzun smra ba*).

four demons (*bdud bzhi*). (1) Negative emotions, (2) the psychophysical aggregates, (3) the Lord of Death, and (4) the subtle attachments of a god's son.

four empowerments (*dbang bzhi*). (1) Vase (*bum dbang*); (2) secret (*gsang dbang*); (3) insight-wisdom (*shes rab ye shes kyi dbang*); and (4) word (*tshig dbang*) empowerments.

four female gatekeepers (*sgo ma bzhi*). Goddesses who guard the four gates of the Secret Mantra mandala: (1) the Hook Lady (*lcags kyu ma*); (2) the Noose Lady (*zhags pa ma*); (3) the Chain Lady (*lcags sgrog ma*); and (4) the Bell Lady (*dril bu ma*).

Four Great Feasts (*'gyed chen bzhi*). Also called the four ways of cutting. These are profound methods for severing attachment to the ego by offering one's body to the **four types of guests** through visualization. They are practiced respectively at dawn, noon, evening, and night: (1) the white feast (*dkar 'gyed*); (2) the red feast (*dmar 'gyed*); (3) the variegated feast (*khra 'gyed*); and (4) the black feast (*nag 'gyed*).

four immeasurables (*tshad med bzhi*). (1) Loving-kindness (*byams pa*); (2) compassion (*snying rje*); (3) sympathetic joy (*dga 'ba*); and (4) equanimity (*btang snyoms*).

four kinds of realization (*rtogs bzhi*). According to Mahayoga: (1) the single basis (*rgyu gcig pa*); (2) the manner of seed-syllables (*yig 'bru'i tshul*); (3) consecration (*byin gyis rlabs*); and (4) direct perception (*mngon sum pa*).

four kinds of Vidyadhara (*rig 'dzin rnam bzhi*). (1) Vidyadhara of Maturation (*rnam smin rig 'dzin*); (2) Vidyadhara with Power over the Life Span (*tshe dbang rig 'dzin*); (3) Vidyadhara of the Great Seal (*phyag chen rig 'dzin*); and (4) Vidyadhara of Spontaneous Presence (*lhun grub rig 'dzin*).

four lamps of Tögal (*sgron ma bzhi*). (1) The far-reaching water lamp (*rgyang zhags chu yi sgron ma*) as a gateway that causes the arising of the three other lamps through the eyes, with the help of the light channels (*'od rtsa*); (2) the lamp of the basic space of awareness (*rig pa dbyings kyi sgron ma*) as a ground for the arising of the external, a space of projection for the two following other lamps; (3) the lamp of empty vital nuclei (*thig le stong pa'i sgron ma*) as a support (the shape of colored vital nuclei that join together or form groups, and that comes forth inside the second lamp) that activates the arising; and (4) the lamp of naturally occurring insight (*shes rab rang* *byung gi sgron ma*), which is not actually "lighting up" but is the naturally occurring insight itself.

Four Medical Tantras (*rgyud bzhi*). The basis of Tibet's medical tradition, written by Yutok Yönten Gönpo: (1) the Root Tantra (*rtsa rgyud*); (2) the Explanatory Tantra (*bshad rgyud*); (3) the Pith Instruction Tantra (*man ngag rgyud*); and (4) the Subsequent Tantra (*phyi ma'i rgyud*).

four modes (*tshul bzhi*). The four methods or aspects of meaning: (1) the literal mode, in words (*tshig gi tshul*); (2) the general or outer mode (*phyi'i tshul*); (3) the hidden mode (*sbas pa'i tshul*); and (4) the ultimate mode (*mthar thug gi tshul*).

four modes of birth (*skyes gnas bzhi*). (1) Womb-birth, (2) egg-birth, (3) warmth-and-moisture birth, and (4) miraculous birth.

four modes of evenness (*mnyam pa bzhi*). (1) Emptiness, (2) the unity of appearances and emptiness, (3) freedom from constructs, and (4) evenness itself.

four modes of gathering beings (*bsdu ba rnam bzhi*). (1) Generosity, (2) pleasing speech, (3) meaningful conduct, and (4) accordant meaning.

Four Noble Truths (*bden bzhi*). (1) The truth of suffering (*sdug bsngal bden pa*); (2) the truth of the origin of suffering (*kun 'byung bden pa*); (3) the truth of the cessation of suffering (*'gog pa'i bden pa*); and (4) the truth of the **eightfold path** (*lam gyi bden pa*).

Four Nyingtik Mother-and-Child Cycles (*snying thig ma bu bzhi*). Also known as *Nyingtik Yabshi*, the four sections of the Nyingtik. They comprise: the *Vima Nyingtik*, the *Khandro Nyingtik*, the *Lama Yangtik*, and the *Khandro Yangtik*. The *Vima Nyingtik* and *Khandro Nyingtik* are known as the "mother" *Nyingtik* texts, and the *Lama Yangtik* and *Khandro Yangtik* are known as "child" texts. *See* **two *Nyingtik* Child Cycles** and **two *Nyingtik* Mother Cycles.**

four patron deities of the Kadampas (*bka' gdams lha bzhi*). (1) Shakyamuni, (2) Akshobhya, (3) Avalokitesvara, and (4) Tara.

four powers (*stobs bzhi*). (1) Power of support (deity visualization); (2) power of regret (remorse for past negative actions); (3) power of resolution (resolving never to commit such acts again); and (4) power of action (offsetting negativity through accomplishing positive actions).

four root downfalls. *See* **four defeats.**

four stakes that bind the life force (*srog sdom gzer bzhi*). From Yoga Tantra and Mahayoga: (1) the stake of unchanging wisdom-mind; (2) the stake of stability in the deity; (3) the stake of the essential mantra recitation; and (4) the stake of enlightened activity.

four supports (*dpung bzhi*). (1) Firm aspiration (being firmly convinced of the benefits of the goal and the drawbacks of not achieving it); (2) steadfastness (convinced that one is capable of the goal, applying oneself steadily, even though the rate of progress may fluctuate); (3) joy (satisfaction in advancing); and (4) rest (taking a break in order to refresh oneself).

four thoughts that turn the mind (*blo ldog rnam bzhi*). (1) Reflecting on the difficulty of obtaining the unique freedoms and advantages of this precious human birth; (2) reflecting on death and impermanence, and recognizing the urgency to practice the Dharma; (3) reflecting on the defects of samsara; and (4) reflecting on past actions, their causes and results.

four transfixions (*thal 'byin bzhi*). (1) Wisdom-awareness kila (*rig pa ye shes kyi phur pa*); (2) enlightened-mind kila (*byang chub sems kyi phur pa*); (3) immeasurable-compassion kila (*tshad med snying rje'i phur pa*); and (4) substantial kila (*'dus byas rdzas kyi phur pa*).

four types of guests (*mgron po bzhi*). (1) The Three Jewels, (2) protective deities, (3) sentient beings of the six realms, and (4) those to whom we owe karmic debts.

four visions (*snang ba bzhi*). Four visionary appearances that arise in Dzogchen Tögal practice: (1) the vision of the direct perception of reality (*chos nyid mngon sum gi snang ba*); (2) the vision of ever-increasing meditative experience (*nyams gong 'phel ba'i snang ba*); (3) the vision of the culmination of awareness (*rig pa tshad phebs kyi snang ba*); and (4) the vision of the cessation of clinging in reality (*chos nyid du 'dzin pa zad pa'i snang ba*).

four ways of freely resting (*cog bzhag gzhi*). Also translated as the "four ways of leaving things as they are" in Dzogchen practice: (1) the view of a freely resting mountain (*ri bo cog bzhag gi lta ba*); (2) the wisdom intention of a freely resting ocean (*rgya mtsho cog bzhag gi dgongs pa*); (3) the pith instructions for freely resting awareness (*rig pa cog bzhag gi man ngag*); and (4) the techniques, which entail the total presence of visionary appearances (*snang ba cog bzhag gi thabs*).

four wheels (*'khor lo bzhi*). (1) The secret wheel, connected with the abiding nature of mind, (2) the wheel of existence, connected with the navel, (3) the cutting wheel, connected with the arms of the deity, and (4) the emanational wheel, connected with the legs and feet of the deity.

fourfold refuge (*skyabs 'gro bzhi skor ma*). (1) The Lama, (2) the Buddha, (3) the Dharma, and (4) the Sangha. Alternatively: (1) the Three Jewels, (2) the Three Roots, (3) the subtle channels, energies, and vital nuclei, and (4) the essence, nature, and capacity, the latter being the three aspects of the sugatagarbha according to the Great Perfection system.

FIVE

five aggregates (*phung po lnga*). The five aspects that comprise the physical and mental constituents of a sentient being: (1) form (*gzugs*); (2) feeling (*tshor ba*); (3) conception (*'du shes*); (4) formation (*'du byed*); and (5) consciousness (*rnam shes*).

five awakenings (*mngon byang lnga*). The successive steps of visualization employed in the generation stage of meditation: (1) the moon cushion emerging from the Sanskrit vowels, (2) the sun cushion emerging from the Sanskrit consonants, (3) the seed-syllable of buddha speech, (4) the hand implements emblematic of buddha mind, and (5) the complete body of the yidam deity. The moon cushion represents the mirrorlike wisdom, the sun cushion represents the wisdom of evenness, the seed-syllable and symbolic qualities represent the wisdom of discernment, the combination of all of these represents the wisdom of accomplishment, and the complete form of the deity represents the wisdom of the space of reality.

five bovine products (*ba byung lnga*). (1) Urine, (2) dung, (3) milk, (4) butter, and (5) curd. In traditional Indian culture, the cow is a sacred symbol of fecundity and is often regarded as a manifestation of Lakshmi, the goddess of wealth and plenty. A mixture of these five substances is added to saffron water and sprinkled over the mandala plate.

five buddha families (*rgyal ba rigs lnga*). The buddha families are traditionally displayed as the mandala of the five tathagatas, or buddhas. Each of the buddhas in the mandala embodies one of the five different aspects of enlightenment: (1) at the center of the mandala is Vairochana, lord of the buddha family, who is white and represents the wisdom of all-encompassing space; (2) in the east of the mandala is Akshobya, lord of the vajra family, who is blue and represents mirrorlike wisdom; (3) in the south of the mandala is Ratnasambhava, buddha of the ratna family, who is yellow and represents the wisdom of equanimity; (4) in the west of the mandala is Amitabha, buddha of the padma family, who is red and represents the wisdom of discernment; and (5) in the north of the mandala is Amogasiddhi, buddha of the karma family, who is green and represents all-accomplishing wisdom.

five classes of downfalls (*ltung ba sde lnga*). The 253 vows of a fully ordained monk in the Mulasarvastivadan school of the Vinaya are broadly divided into five categories or classes: (1) the four defeats, (2) the thirteen remainders, (3) the one hundred twenty downfalls, (4) the four matters to be confessed individually, and (5) the **one hundred twelve misdeeds.**

five colors (*ka dog lnga*). (1) Red, (2) yellow, (3) green, (4) blue, and (5) white.

five elements (*'byung ba lnga*). (1) Earth, (2) water, (3) fire, (4) wind, and (5) ether.

five faults (*nyes pa lnga*). The five shortcomings that impede concentration are (1) laziness (*le lo*); (2) forgetting the instructions (*gdams ngag brjed pa*); (3) dullness and agitation (*bying rgod*); (4) nonapplication of remedies (*'du mi byed pa*); and (5) overapplication of remedies (*ha cang 'du byed pa*).

Five Great Kings (*rgyal po sku lnga*). Aspects of the protector deity Pehar.

five great radiances (*gdangs chen lnga*). These are the five distinctly colored radiances of the five wisdoms of buddha mind: white, red, yellow, green, and blue.

five heinous crimes (*mtshams med lnga*). Also translated as the "five crimes of immediate retribution": (1) killing one's father, (2) killing one's mother, (3) killing an arhat, (4) drawing blood from a buddha with bad intentions, and (5) causing a schism in the monastic community (by repudiating the Buddha's teachings, drawing monastics away from them, and enlisting them in one's own newly founded religion).

five kinds of offerings (*mchod pa rnam lnga*). In general, these are equivalent to offerings of the five sense pleasures (Tib. *dod pa'i yon tan lnga,* Skt. *pancakamaguna*), namely: (1) a mirror representing visual forms (Tib. *gzugs,* Skt. *rupa*); (2) a lute representing sounds (Tib. *sgra,* Skt. *sapda*), (3) a conch filled with perfume representing smells (Tib. *dri,* Skt. *gandha*); (4) fruits representing tastes (Tib. *ro,* Skt. *rasa*); and (5) silken cloths representing tangibles (Tib. *reg bya,* Skt. *sparsa*). By extension, this enumeration can also refer to the eight external offerings symbolized by the eight offering goddesses: (1) drinking water, (2) washing water, (3) flowers, (4) incense, (5) lamps, (6) perfume, (7) food, and (8) a conch.

five knowings (*shes pa lnga*). (1) Knowing the lama as the Buddha, (2) knowing all the lama's actions as buddha activities, (3) knowing that for oneself the lama is even kinder than the Buddha, (4) knowing that the lama is the embodiment of all objects of refuge, and (5) knowing that if we pray to the lama, we will attain realization without needing to rely upon anyone else.

five paths (*lam lnga*). The Paths of (1) Accumulation, (2) Joining, (3) Seeing, (4) Cultivation, and (5) No-More-Learning. These five paths cover the entire process from sincerely beginning Dharma practice to attaining complete enlightenment.

five perfections (*phun sum tshogs pa lnga*). The setting or context in which the tantras are expounded, comprised of (1) the perfect place (buddha realms); (2) the perfect teacher (buddhas); (3) the perfect assembly (male and female bodhisattvas, meditational deities, and so forth); (4) the perfect teaching (tantras); and (5) the perfect time (indefinite time).

five phases of the generation stage (*bskyed pa rim pa lnga*). (1) Great emptiness (*stong pa chen po*); (2) great compassion (*snying rje chen po*); (3) the single seal (*phyag rgya gcig pa*); (4) the elaborate seal (*phyag rgya spros bcas*); and (5) the attainment of the mandala clusters (*tshom bu tshogs sgrub*).

five planetary aspects (*gza' lnga*). (1) Mars, (2) Mercury, (3) Jupiter, (4) Venus, and (5) Saturn.

five poisons (*dug lnga*). The five toxic emotions: (1) desire, (2) anger, (3) delusion, (4) pride, and (5) envy.

five sciences (*rig pa'i gnas lnga*). Five major Buddhist sciences: (1) craftsmanship, (2) logic, (3) grammar, (4) medicine, and (5) spirituality. Five minor Buddhist sciences: (1) synonyms, (2) mathematics and astrology, (3) performance and drama, (4) poetry, and (5) composition.

five sections of the (inner) preliminary practices (*sngon 'gro 'bum lnga*). The preliminary, preparatory, or foundational "practices" or "disciplines" (Skt. *sadhana*) common to all four schools of Tibetan Buddhism, and also to Bön. Often referred to as ngöndro, they establish the foundation for the more advanced and rarefied Vajrayana sadhana, which are held to engender realization and the embodiment of enlightenment. The outer preliminaries consist of the **four thoughts that turn the mind:** (1) precious human birth (2) impermanence, (3) karma, and (4) suffering. The inner preliminaries comprise one hundred thousand accumulations of (1) taking refuge, (2) generating bodhichitta, (3) meditating on Vajrasattva and reciting his **hundred-syllable mantra,** (4) offering the mandala, as well as (5) guru yoga with one or ten million recitations of the vajra guru mantra.

five spiritual degenerations (*snyigs ma lnga*). (1) The degeneration of views due to the decline in the virtue of renunciates implies wrong or mistaken views; (2) the degeneration of negative emotions due to the decline in the virtue of householders implies coarse-natured minds influenced by strong and obdurate negative emotions; (3) the degeneration of time due to the diminution of resources implies a declining Aeon of Strife; (4) the degeneration of life span due to the decline of the sustaining life force implies a reduction of the life span to only ten years; and (5) the degeneration of beings implies the decline of body due to its inferior shape and lesser size, the decline of merit due to a diminution of power and splendor, the decline of mind due to a diminution of intellectual sharpness, power of recollection, and diligence.

five thought-free states (*rtog med kyi gnas skabs lnga*). (1) Sleep (*gnyid*); (2) unconsciousness (*dran med*); (3) absorption of cessation (*'gog pa'i snyoms 'jug*); (4) absorption devoid of perception (*'du shes med pa'i snyoms 'jug*); and (5) being in the realm of the conceptionless gods (*'du shes med pa'i lha yul*).

Five Vidyadharas of the Symbol Lineage (*brda brgyud rig 'dzin lnga*). (1) Garab Dorje, (2) Manjushrimitra, (3) Shri Singha, (4) Vimalamitra, and (5) Jnanasutra.

five wisdoms (*ye shes lnga*). (1) Wisdom of the space of reality that is the natural purity of the aggregate of consciousness, free from delusion (*chos dbyings kyi ye shes*); (2) mirrorlike wisdom to which all the objects of the five senses appear spontaneously as in a mirror (*me long gi ye shes*); (3) wisdom of evenness that experiences the three types of feelings (good, bad, and indifferent) as of one taste (*mnyam nyid kyi ye shes*); (4) wisdom of discernment that accurately identifies names and forms (*sor rtog pa'i ye shes*); and (5) all-accomplishing wisdom that accomplishes enlightened activities and their purposes (*bya ba grub pa'i ye shes*).

Six

six branch precepts (*yan lag drug*). To refrain from (1) drinking alcohol, (2) eating after noon, (3) dancing, (4) jewelry, (5) high beds, and (6) accepting gold and silver.

six classes of beings (*'gro ba rigs drug*). (1) Hell beings, (2) pretas, (3) animals, (4) human beings, (5) asuras, and (6) gods.

six intermediate states (*bar do drug*). The six bardos: (1) the natural bardo of this life (*skyes gnas bar do*); (2) the bardo of dreams (*rmi lam bar do*); (3) the bardo of meditation (*bsam gtan bar do*); (4) the painful bardo of dying (*'chi kha bar do*); (5) the luminous bardo of dharmata (*chos nyid bar do*); and (6) the karmic bardo of becoming (*srid pa'i bar do*).

six limits (*mtha' drug*). Also called the six parameters, these are the views of the (1) expedient meaning (*drang don*) and (2) definitive meaning (*nges don*); (3) the implied (*dgongs pa can*) and (4) the not implied (*dgongs pa can ma yin pa*); (5) the literal (*sgra ji bzhin pa*) and (6) the nonliteral (*sgra ji bzhin pa ma yin pa*). Together with the **four modes** (*tshul bzhi*), they form the indispensable keys for unlocking the meaning of the tantras.

six phases of the completion stage in the Guhyasamaja system of Highest Yoga Tantra. (1) Isolation of body (*lus dben*); (2) isolation of speech (*ngag dben*);

(3) isolation of mind (*sems dben*); (4) luminosity (*'od gsal*); (5) illusory body (*sgyu lus*); and (6) unity (*zung 'jug*).

six-syllable mantra. OM MA NI PAD ME HUM. The mantra of Avalokitesvara.

six transcendent perfections (*phar phyin drug*). (1) Generosity (*byin pa*); (2) discipline (*tshul khrims*); (3) patience (*bzod pa*); (4) diligence (*brtson 'grus*); (5) concentration (*bsam gtan*); and (6) insight (*shes rab*).

SEVEN

seven aspects of royal wealth (*nor bu cha bdun*). (1) King's earrings, (2) queen's earrings, (3) rhino horn, (4) a stick of coral, (5) ivory, (6) minister's earrings, and (3) three-eyed banded chalcedony.

seven aspects of spiritual wealth (*dkor bdun / don dam dkor bdun*). (1) The ultimate truth of the space of reality, (2) the ultimate truth of wisdom, and the fivefold ultimate truth of the result, namely: (3) buddha body, (4) speech, (5) mind, (6) qualities, and (7) activities.

seven branches (*yan lag bdun*). (1) Homage, (2) offering, (3) confession, (4) rejoicing, (5) requesting teachers to turn the Wheel of Dharma, (6) requesting them not to pass into nirvana, and (7) dedication of merit.

seven branches of enlightenment (*byang chub yan lag bdun*). Also called the seven bodhi-factors: (1) perfect mindfulness (*dran pa yang dag*); (2) full discernment of phenomena (*chos rab tu rnam 'byed*); (3) perfect diligence (*brtson 'grus yang dag*); (4) perfect delight (*dga' ba yang dag*); (5) perfect pliancy (*shin tu sbyangs pa yang dag*); (6) concentration (*ting nge 'dzin*); and (7) impartiality (*btang snyoms*).

seven impure bodhisattva levels (*ma dag sa bdun*). Among the **ten bodhisattva levels** (*sa bcu*), the attainments of the first seven are considered reversible owing to the persistence of subtle pride, whereas those of the highest three levels are deemed to be irreversible.

Seven-Line Prayer (*tshig bdun gsol 'debs*). See *Seven Vajra Verses.*

seven vajra qualities (*rdo rje'i chos bdun*). (1) Invulnerable (*mi chod pa*); (2) indestructible (*mi shigs pa*); (3) real (*bden pa*); (4) solid (*sra ba*); (5) stable (*brtan pa*); (6) unobstructed (*thogs pa med pa*); and (7) invincible (*mi pham pa*).

Seven Vajra Verses (*rdo rje'i tshig bdun*). Also called the *Seven-Line Prayer,* this is the famous supplication to **Padmasambhava** in seven lines that begins: "On the northwest border of Oddiyana . . ."

sevenfold pith instructions of cause and effect (*rgyu 'bras man ngag bdun ldan*). (1) Recognizing all beings as our mothers, (2) remembering their kindness, (3) repaying their kindness, (4) cultivating great love, (5) cultivating great compassion, (6) exceptional resolve, and (7) the altruistic aim of bodhichitta.

EIGHT

eight applications (*'du shes brgyad*). (1) Faith (*dad pa*); (2) resolve (*'dun pa*); (3) endeavor (*rtsol ba*); (4) pliancy (*shin sbyangs*); (5) mindfulness (*dran pa*); (6) introspection (*shes bzhin*); (7) application (*'du byed pa*); and (8) nonapplication (*'du mi byed pa*).

eight auspicious substances (*bkra shis rdzas brgyad*). (1) A mirror, (2) bezoars, (3) curd / yogurt, (4) kusha (*Panicum dactylon*) grass, (5) wood apple fruit, (6) right-coiling white conch, (7) vermilion powder, and (8) white mustard seed.

eight auspicious symbols (*bkra shis rtags brgyad*). (1) An umbrella, (2) golden fish, (3) a wish-fulfilling vase, (4) a lotus flower, (5) a right-coiling white conch, (6) a knot of prosperity, (7) a victory banner, and (8) a Dharma Wheel.

Eight Close Sons (*nye ba'i sras brgyad*). The bodhisattvas (1) Ksitigarbha, (2) Maitreya, (3) Samantabhadra, (4) Akasagarbha, (5) Avalokitesvara, (6) Manjusrikumarabhuta, (7) Nivaranaviskambhin, and (8) Vajrapani.

eight great charnel grounds (*dur khrod chen po brgyad*). (1) In the east, Most Fierce (*gtum drag*); (2) in the north, Dense Thicket (*tsang tsing 'khrigs pa*); (3) in the west, Blazing Vajra (*rdo rje 'bar ba*); (4) in the south, Endowed with Skeletons (*keng rus can*); (5) in the northeast, Wild Cries of Ha Ha (*ha ha rgod pa*); (6) in the southeast, Auspicious Grove (*mer bkra shis tshal*); (7) in the southwest, Black Darkness (*mun pa drag po*); and (8) in the northwest, Resounding with Kili Kili (*ki li ki li'i sgra sgrog pa*).

Eight Heruka Sadhanas (*sgrub pa bka' brgyad*). Also called the *Eight Commands* or the *Eight Sadhana Sections / Teachings:* (1) Yamantaka, the wrathful Manjushri, the deity of body (*'jam dpal sku*); (2) Hayagriva, the deity of speech (*pad ma gsung*); (3) Vishuddha, the deity of mind (*yang dag thugs*); (4) Vajramrita, the deity of enlightened qualities (*bdud rtsi yon tan*); (5) Vajrakila, the deity of enlightened activity (*phur ba 'phrin las*); (6) Matarah, the deity of calling and dispatching (*ma mo rbod gtong*); (7) the worldly deities of offering and praise (*'jig rten mchod bstod*); and (8) the worldly deities of wrathful mantras (*mod pa drag sngags*). These comprise the eight chief yidam deities of Mahayoga and their corresponding tantras and sadhanas, transmitted to **Padmasambhava** by the **eight vidyadharas.**

eight manifestations of Padmasambhava (*gu ru mtshan brgyad*). Eight forms of Guru Rinpoche: (1) Shakya Senge, (2) **Padmasambhava**, (3) Nyima Özer, (4) Senge

Dradrok, (5) Dorje Drollö, (6) Tsokye Dorje, (7) Padma Gyalpo, and (8) Loden Choksey.

eight modes of consciousness (*rnam shes tshogs brgyad*). The eight avenues of ordinary consciousness: the five sense consciousnesses (sight, sound, smell, taste, touch), (6) mind consciousness, (7) ego consciousness, and (8) all-ground consciousness.

eight ordinary concerns (*'jig rten chos brgyad*). The preoccupations of ordinary beings: (1) gain and (2) loss; (3) pleasure and (4) pain; (5) praise and (6) blame; (7) fame and (8) infamy.

eight serious branch downfalls (*yan lag sbom po'i ltung ba brgyad*). Also called the eight major transgressions: (1) relying on a consort who has not matured through empowerment and samaya, (2) physically or verbally fighting during a feast-offering ceremony, (3) receiving the nectar of an unauthorized consort, (4) failing to reveal the Secret Mantra to a qualified recipient, (5) teaching something other than what has been requested by a faithful aspirant, (6) staying seven complete days with a shravaka, (7) proclaiming oneself to be a tantric adept when the yoga of primordial wisdom has not been realized, and (8) teaching unsuitable recipients.

eight vidyadharas (*rig 'dzin brgyad*). (1) Manjushrimitra, (2) Nagarjuna, (3) Humkara, (4) Vimalamitra, (5) Prabhahasti, (6) Dhanasanskrita, (7) Shintamgarbha, and (8) Guhyachandra.

eight wrathful kings (*khro bo brgyad*). Wrathful deities of the four cardinal and four intermediate directions.

eightfold path (*'phags lam yan lag brgyad*). (1) Perfect view, (2) perfect thought, (3) perfect speech, (4) perfect goals, (5) perfect livelihood, (6) perfect effort, (7) perfect mindfulness, and (8) perfect stability.

NINE

nine vehicles (*theg pa rim pa dgu*). A Tibetan classification of Buddhist teachings into nine sequential spiritual approaches: (1) Shravaka, (2) Pratyekabuddha, (3) Bodhisattva, (4) Kriya, (5) Upa, (6) Yoga, (7) Mahayoga, (8) Anuyoga, and (9) Atiyoga. The first two are Hinayana; the third is Mahayana; the next three are called the Three Outer Tantras; and the last three are called the Three Inner Tantras.

nine techniques for sustaining mental calm (*sems zhi bar gnas pa'i thabs dgu*). (1) Mental placement (*sems 'jog pa*); (2) perpetual placement (*rgyun 'jog*); (3) integrated placement (*bslan 'jog*); (4) intensified placement (*nye bar 'jog pa*); (5) control (*'dul* *ba*); (6) calmness (*zhi ba*); (7) quiescence (*rnam zhi*); (8) one-pointedness (*rtse gcig*); and (9) equanimity (*mnyam bzhag*).

TEN

ten bodhisattva levels (*sa bcu*). The ten bhumis according to Anuyoga: the levels of (1) Indefinite Transformation (*'gyur ba ma nges pa*); (2) Basis of Reliance (*brten pa gzhi'i sa*); (3) Important Purification (*gal chen sbyong ba'i sa*); (4) Continuity of Training (*bslab pa rgyun gyi sa*); (5) Supporting Merit (*bsod nams rten gyi sa*); (6) Superior Progress through Reliance (*brten pas khyad par du 'gro ba'i sa*); (7) The Level That Gives Birth to the Result with Respect to the Aftermath of Inner Radiance on the Path of Insight (*mthong lam 'od gsal las langs pa'i rjes la dmigs pa 'bras bu skye ba'i sa*); (8) Unchanging Abidance (*gnas pa mi 'gyur ba'i sa*); (9) Expanding Reality (*bdal ba chos nyid*); and (10) Riding on Perfection (*rdzogs pa ci chibs kyi sa*).

ten cardinal treasures (*phug nor bcu*). The ten guiding principles of past saints: (1) leave your mind to the Dharma, (2) leave your Dharma to a beggar's life, (3) live your beggar's life until death, (4) leave your death to a cave, (5) cast yourself out from your place among others, (6) take your place among the dogs, (7) find a place among celestial beings, (8) embrace unswerving determination, (9) embrace indifference to what others may think of you, and (10) retain wisdom.

ten coarse precepts (*rags pa bcu*). This is the code of monastic discipline for monks. It consists of the five precepts: (1) no killing, (2) no stealing, (3) no sexual activity, (4) no lying, and (5) no intoxicants, as well as five further restrictions designed specifically for members of the ordained Sangha: (6) no eating after noon, (7) no adorning the body with anything other than monastic robes, (8) no participating or attending public entertainments, (9) no sleeping in high or luxurious beds, and (10) no touching or using money, gold, or silver.

ten directions (*phyogs bcu*). The four cardinal directions, the four intermediate directions, the zenith and the nadir.

ten nonvirtues (*mi dge ba bcu*). (1) Taking life, (2) taking what is not given, (3) sexual misconduct, (4) lying, (5) speaking divisively, (6) speaking harshly, (7) gossiping, (8) coveting, (9) harboring ill will, and (10) harboring wrong views.

ten transcendent perfections (*phar phyin bdu*). Also known as the ten paramitas, these comprise the **six transcendent perfections:** (1) generosity; (2) discipline; (3) patience; (4) diligence; (5) concentration; and (6) insight—plus (7) skillful means (*thabs*); (8) strength / power (*stobs*); (9) aspiration (*smon lam*); and (10) wisdom (*ye shes*).

TWELVE

twelve oath-bound Matarah mother goddesses (*dam can ma mo bcu gnyis*). Mamos or matrikas constitute a large class of fierce female deities. Although they predate Buddhism, they have been assimilated to the Matrika, a type of sorcerer of the charnel grounds. These black goddesses personify natural forces that become destructive when disturbed. They carry bags full of disease germs and comprise the retinue of the Great Dharma Protectresses.

Twelve Teachers of the Great Perfection (*rdzogs chen ston pa bcu gnyis*). (1) Youth of Sublime Light (*ston pa khye'u snang ba dam pa*); (2) Youth of Immutable Light (*ston pa khye'u 'od mi 'khrugs pa*); (3) Protector against Fear (*ston pa 'jigs pa skyob*); (4) Youthful Tender Grace (*ston pa gzhon nu rol pa rnam par brtse ba*); (5) Vajradhara (*ston pa rdo rje 'chang*); (6) Powerful Warrior Youth (*ston pa gzhon nu dpa' bo*); (7) Wrathful Sage King (*ston pa drang srong khros pa'i rgyal po*); (8) Sublime Golden Light (*ston pa gser 'od dam pa*); (9) Lovingly Playful Intelligence (*ston pa brtse bas rol pa'i blo gros*); (10) Kashapa the Elder (*ston pa 'od srung bgres po*); (11) Truly Perfected King (*ston pa mngon rdzogs rgyal po*); and (12) Shakyamuni (*ston pa sha kya thub pa*).

Twelve Tenma Sisters (*bstan ma bcu gnyis*). Female protector deities of Tibet, bound under oath by Padmasambhava at Asura Cave. They consist of four female demons, four menmos, and four yakshinis. They are said to take care of us like sisters.

THIRTEEN

thirteen mandalas of the Kama (*bka' ma'i dkyil 'khor bcu gsum*). These comprise the principal cycles contained in the distant lineage of the orally transmitted Kama (*ring brgud bka' ma*) of the Nyingma school. The entire collection currently includes 120 volumes in its most extensive compilation. *See* bibliography of texts referenced by the author under NK; for a history of their transmission, *see* Dudjom Rinpoche, *Nyingma School*, 597–739.

SIXTEEN

sixteenfold delight (*dga' ba bcu drug*). (1) Delight, (2) supreme delight, (3) special delight, and (4) innate delight, each of which has four subsidiary aspects; for example, the delight of delight and the delight of supreme delight.

TWENTY

twenty-four sacred lands (*gnas nyer bzhi*). The twenty-four sacred power-places of ancient India and the Himalayan world are divided into three sets of eight, corresponding to buddha body, speech, and mind. In no particular order, they include: (1)

Jalandhara, (2) Oddiyana, (3) Paurnagiri, (4) Kamarupa, (5) Purimalaya, (6) Sindhu, (7) Nagara, (8) Munmuni, (9) Karunyapataka, (10) Devikota, (11) Karmarapataka, (12) Kulata, (13) Arbuda, (14) Godavari, (15) Himadri, (16) Harikela, (17) Lampaka, (18) Kanci, (19) Saurashtra, (20) Kalinga, (21) Kokana, (22) Caritra, (23) Koshala, and (24) Vindhyakaumarapaurika.

twenty-five disciples (*rje 'bangs nyer lnga*). The twenty-five main disciples of Guru **Padmasambhava** are generally enumerated as: (1) Khandro Yeshe Tsogyal, (2) Gyalwa Chokyang, (3) Namkhai Nyingpo, (4) Palgyi Senge, (5) Yeshe Yang, (6) Yeshe De, (7) Palgyi Dorje, (8) King Trisong Deutsen, (9) Karchen Palgyi Wangchuk, (10) Yudra Nyingpo, (11) Ma Rinchen Chok, (12) Sangye Yeshe, (13) Dorje Dudjom, (14) Gyalwa Lodrö, (15) Denma Tsemang, (16) Kawa Paltsek, (17) Ödren Wangchuk, (18) Jnanakumaravajra, (19) Sokpo Lhapel Shönnu, (20) Langdro Könchok Jungney, (21) Gyalwa Jangchup, (22) Drenpa Namkha Wangchuk, (23) Kyeuchung Khading, (24) Chokru Lu'i Gyaltsen, and (25) Tingdzin Zangpo.

THIRTY

thirty-six precepts (*bslab bya so drug*). The vows of novice ordination for monks and nuns. One should avoid: (1) taking a human life; (2) killing an animal or insect; (3) for selfish reasons, doing an action that may kill an animal or insect and not caring about it (for example, using water that contains insects without straining it; digging a hole in the earth without considering the creatures that might die as a result; cutting grass; overburdening an animal, which causes its death); (4) while doing something for others, doing an action that might kill an animal or insect and not caring about it; (5) sexual intercourse; (6) stealing, taking what has not been given (this includes borrowing things and not returning them, not paying fees and taxes); (7) lying in which one claims to have spiritual realizations or powers that one does not have; (8) accusing a pure bhikshu or bhikshuni of transgressing one of the **four basic precepts** when he or she has not; (9) insinuating that a pure bhikshu or bhikshuni has transgressed one of the four basic precepts when he or she has not; (10) causing disunity among the sangha community through untrue slander or taking sides in a disagreement; (11) supporting someone who is creating disunity in the sangha community, taking sides in the dispute; (12) doing actions that obliterate laypeople's faith in the sangha (for example, complaining untruthfully to laypeople that action brought by the sangha against oneself was unfair); (13) telling others lies; (14) criticizing the storekeeper in the monastery for giving more to those who are near to him or her instead of sharing them with all, when this is not the case; (15) criticizing the storekeeper in the monastery, directly or by insinuation, of not giving oneself a share of the food or other things equal to that given to other monastics, when this is not the case; (16) claiming that a monastic gave a teaching in return for a little food, which is not the case; (17) criticizing a bhikshu or bhikshuni by saying that he or she transgressed a precept in the second group (Skt. *sanghavasesa*) when this is not the case; (18) abandoning the training (for example, rejecting the good advice of a nun or monk, or criticizing the *Pratimoksha Sutra*); (19) covering the vegetables with rice, or covering the rice with vegetables; (20) taking intoxicants; (21) singing with self-attachment or for nonsensical reasons; (22) dancing with self-attachment or for nonsensical reasons; (23) playing music with self-attachment or for nonsensical reasons; (24) wearing ornaments; (25) wearing cosmetics; (26) wearing perfumes; (27) wearing rosary-like jewelry, wearing flower garlands; (28) sitting on an expensive throne; (29) sitting on an expensive bed; (30) sitting on a high throne; (31) sitting on a high bed; (32) eating after midday (exceptions: if one is ill, if one is traveling, or if one cannot meditate properly without food); (33) touching gold, silver, or precious jewels (includes money); (34) wearing laypeople's clothing and ornaments; letting one's hair grow long; (35) not wearing the robes of a Buddhist monastic; and (36) disrespecting or not following the guidance of one's ordination master.

thirty-seven factors of supreme enlightenment (*byang chub mchog gi chos sum cu rtsa bdun*). These are the four essential recollections, the four correct trainings, the **four supports** for miraculous ability, the five faculties, the five powers, the **seven branches** of enlightenment, and the **eightfold path.**

EIGHTY

eighty inherent thought processes (*rang bzhin brgyad cu'i rtog tshogs*). Thirty-three thought processes resulting from anger, forty from desire, and seven from delusion.

Eighty-Four Mahasiddhas (*grub thob brgyad cu rtsa bzhi*). These are the eighty-four great Buddhist siddhas of ancient India.

ONE HUNDRED

one hundred twelve misdeeds. The fifth class of downfalls in the Mulasarvastivadan school of the Vinaya. See **five classes of downfalls.**

Bibliography of Texts
Referenced by the Author

ABBREVIATIONS

BST   Buddhist Sanskrit Texts. Darbhanga, Bihar; Mithila Institute of Post-Graduate Studies and Research in Sanskrit Learning.

Chi.   Chinese

DgK   The Derge *Kangyur (sde dge bka' 'gyur)*. Xylograph edition. Edited by Situ Chökyi Jungney. 103 vols. Freely accessible online at www. tbrc.org.

DgNGB   The Derge xylograph edition of the *Collected Tantras of the Nying-mapa (rnying ma'i rgyud 'bum)*. Edited by Katok Getse Gyurme Tsewang Chokdrub. 26 vols. Catalogue by Thubten Chödar. Beijing: Mi rigs dpe skrun khang, 2000.

DgT   The Derge *Tengyur (sde dge bstan 'gyur)*. Xylograph edition. Edited by Zhuchen Tsultrim Rinchen. 213 vols. Freely accessible online at www.tbrc.org.

DZ   *gdams ngag mdzod*. 12 vols. Delhi: N. Lungtok and N. Gyaltsan, 1971.

NK   The *Collected Nyingma Transmitted Teachings (rnying ma'i bka' ma)*. Currently 120 vols. in the most extended edition *(shin tu rgyas pa)*. Compiled by Khenpo Münsel and Khenpo Jamyang of Katok. Chengdu, 1999.

NL   Not located, though possibly extant.

P   *The Tibetan Tripitaka*. Peking edition. 168 vols. Tokyo-Kyoto: Suzuki Research Foundation, 1955–61.

RTD   *Treasury of Revealed Teachings (rin chen gter mdzod)*. Compiled by Jamgön Kongtrul. Palpung xylographic edition, republished in

72 vols. Also, His Holiness Dilgo Khyentse edition in 36 vols. and the Shechen edition in 70 vols.

Skt.　　　　Sanskrit

T　　　　H. Ui et al. *A Complete Catalogue of the Tibetan Buddhist Canon.* Tohoku University catalogue of the *Derge* edition of the canon. Sendai: 1934.

Tib.　　　Tibetan

Tingkye NGB　The *gting skyes* edition of the *rning ma'i rgyud 'bum* published in 36 vols. by Dilgo Khyentse Rinpoche (Thimphu, 1973).

TBRC　　Tibetan Buddhist Resource Center (www.tbrc.org). An organization established by E. Gene Smith, dedicated to the preservation, digitization, online cataloguing, and dissemination of Tibetan literature of all traditions. Based in Cambridge, Massachusetts.

SCRIPTURAL ANTHOLOGIES: VINAYA, SUTRA, AND TANTRA

Kangyur
bka' 'gyur
The Collected Translations of the Transmitted Teachings. The TBRC digital library (www.tbrc.org) includes six versions, freely accessible online, such as the Derge Parphud xylograph edition of 1733 (103 vols.), which is catalogued in *A Complete Catalogue of the Tibetan Buddhist Canons.* Originally compiled by Butön Rinchendrub of Shalu (1290–1364) and integrating the extant canonical works of Sanskrit origin to which he then had access, the *Kangyur* survives in both manuscript and xylographic editions. The former include the Tshalpa manuscript and the renowned fifteenth-century Serdri (gilded) *Kangyur Thempangma* from Gyantse (*rgyal rtse gser bris bka' 'gyur them spangs ma*), from which many of the later xylographic editions stem. Among them are the versions of Narthang, Lhasa, Peking, Derge, Lithang, Chone, Ugra, Phudrak, and Stog Palace, along with the new collated edition, Kangyur Pedurma, published by Chengdu in 2009 in 108 vols.

Mind Class of the Great Perfection
rdzog chen sems kyi sde
A class of tantra texts, belonging to the Great Perfection, which emphasize the fundamental nature of mind (*sems nyid*). In the Derge edition of the *Nyingma Collected Tantras,* these comprise 54 distinct texts (vols. 5–6), headed by the *Tantra of the All-Accomplishing King (kun byed rgyal po'i rgyud).*

Nyingma Collected Tantras
rnying ma'i rgyud 'bum
Among extant versions, reference is principally made in the present work to the

Derge xylographic edition, which was prepared between 1794 and 1798, under the editorial guidance of Getse Pandita Gyurme Tsewang Chodrub of Katok and Pema Namdak, in 26 long-folio volumes (414 texts), and catalogued in Thubten Chödar, *rnying ma rgyud 'bum gyi dkar chag gsal ba'i me long* (Beijing: Mi rigs dpe skrun khang, 2000). Other well-known manuscript versions include the Tingkye edition, published in Delhi in 1973 by Dilgo Khyentse Rinpoche, in 36 short volumes, and catalogued in Kaneko (1982). The history of the various strands of compilation is discussed in Gyurme Dorje, "Introduction to the Guhyagarbha Tantra" (revised 2005), which is available online at the Wisdom Books reading room.

Seventeen Tantras of the Great Perfection
rdzogs pa chen po rgyud bcu bdun
A class of tantra texts, comprising the *Unsurpassedly Secret Cycle (yang gsang bla med kyi skor)* of the Pith Instructional Class, which is one of the three subdivisions of the Great Perfection *(man ngag gi sde)*, also known as the *Sangwa Nyingtik, "Secret Heart Essence."* In the Derge edition of the *Nyingma Collected Tantras,* these comprise seven tantra texts in vol. 3 and ten tantra texts in vol. 4. The following translations follow those of Erik Pema Kunzang and the sequence is according to the *Vima Nyingtik:* (1) Dra Talgyur Root Tantra *(sgra thal 'gyur gyi rgyud)*; (2) Tantra of Graceful Auspiciousness *(bkra shis mdzes ldan gyi rgyud)*; (3) Tantra of the Mind Mirror of Samantabhadra *(kun tu bzang po thugs kyi me long gi rgyud)*; (4) Blazing Lamp Tantra *(sgron ma 'bar ba'i rgyud)*; (5) Tantra of the Heart Mirror of Vajrasattva *(rdo rje sems dpa'i snying gi me long gi rgyud)*; (6) Tantra of Self-Manifest Awareness *(rig pa rang shar gyi rgyud)*; (7) Tantra of Studded Jewels *(nor bu 'phra bkod kyi rgyud)*; (8) Tantra of Pointing-Out Instructions *(ngo sprod spras pa'i rgyud)*; (9) Tantra of the Six Spheres of Samantabhadra *(kun tu bzang po klong drug pa'i rgyud)*; (10) Tantra of No Letters *(yi ge med pa'i rgyud)*; (11) Tantra of the Perfected Lion *(seng ge rtsal rdzogs chen po'i rgyud)*; (12) Pearl Garland Tantra *(mu tig phreng ba'i rgyud)*; (13) Tantra of Self-Liberated Awareness *(rig pa rang grol gyi rgyud)*; (14) Tantra of Piled Gems *(rin chen spungs pa'i rgyud)*; (15) Tantra of Shining Relics *(sku gdung 'bar ba'i rgyud)*; (16) Union of the Sun and Moon Tantra *(nyi zla kha sbyor gyi rgyud)*; (17) Tantra of Self-Existing Perfection *(rdzogs pa rang byung chen po'i rgyud)*; with the addition of (18) Tantra of the Black Wrathful Goddess *(nag mo khros ma'i rgyud)*.

INDIVIDUAL SCRIPTURES: VINAYA, SUTRA, AND TANTRA

Gathering of the Great Assembly
tshogs chen 'dus pa
NK, vols. 19–28, 90–99. These derive from the principal Anuyoga text entitled *General Sutra That Gathers All Wisdom Intentions (mdo dgongs pa 'dus pa).* DgK (rnying rgyud), vol. KA, 86b–290*aff.,* T 829; DgNGB, vol. JA (7), 110b–314*aff.*

General Sutra That Gathers All Wisdom Intentions
spyi mdo dgongs pa 'dus pa
See *Sutra That Gathers All Wisdom Intentions*

General Tantra Entitled Sutra That Gathers All Wisdom Intentions
rgyud spyi mdo dgongs 'dus
See below *Sutra That Gathers All Wisdom Intentions*

Heart Sutra
bhagavatiprajnaparamitahrdaya
bcom ldan 'das ma shes rab kyi pha rol tu phyin pa'i snying po
DgK (shes phyin), vol. KA, 144b–146a*ff.*, T 21

Kalachakra Tantra
paramadibuddhoddhotasri kalacakratantraraja
mchog gi dang po'i sangs rgyas las phyung ba rgyud kyi rgyal po dpal dus kyi
'khor lo
DgK (rgyud 'bum), vol. KA, 22b–128b*ff.*, T 362. Also known as the *Concise Kalachakra Tantra* (*bsdus rgyud*), when contrasted with the longer *Root Kalachakra Tantra* (*rTsa rgyud*), which is no longer extant, apart from references to it that are found in Pundarika's commentary (T 1347). Translations include: chap. 1 in Newman, *The Outer Wheel of Time;* chap. 2 in Wallace, *The Inner Kalacakratantra.*

Guhyagarbha, King of Tantras, Definitive with Respect to the Real
guhyagarbhatattvaviniscayamahatantra
gsang ba'i snying po de kho na nyid nges pa'i rgyud kyi rgyal po
DgK (rnying rgyud), vol. KHA, 110b–132a*ff.*, T 832; DgNGB, vol. TA (9),
1–31b*ff.;* Tingkye NGB, vol. 14. Tibetan text edited and translated in Dorje,
Guhyagarbhatantra. See also the revised introduction to that work at the Wisdom Books online reading room.

Peaceful and Wrathful Deities of the Magical Net
sgyu 'phrul zhi khro
See *Tantra of the Magical Net of Vajrasattva*

Praise to Manjushri Entitled You Whose Intelligence
aryamanjusribhattarakaprajnabuddhivardhana-nama-dharani
rje btsun 'phags pa 'jam dpal gyi shes rab dang blo 'phel ba zhes bya ba'i gzungs
[short title: gang gi blo ma]
DgK (gzungs 'dus), vol. E, 167b–168a*ff.*, T 895

Praise to the Twenty-One Taras
sgrol ma nyer gcig la bstod pa
Contained in chapter 3 of the *Tantra of Tara's Manifold Activities*

Prajnaparamita in Eight Thousand Lines
astasahasrikaprajnaparamita
shes rab kyi pha rol tu phyin pa brgyad stong pa
DgK (shes phyin), vol. KA 1b–286*aff.*, T 12. Translated in Conze, *Three Phases of Buddhist Philosophy.*

Prajnaparamita in One Hundred Thousand Lines
satasahasrikaprajnaparamita
shes rab kyi pha rol tu phyin pa stong phrag brgya pa
DgK (shes phyin), vol. KA, 1b-A*ff.*, 395*aff.* (12 vols.), T 8

Prayer of Good Conduct
bhadracaryapranidanaraja
bzang po spyod pa'i smon lam (gyi rgyal po)
DgK (gzungs 'dus), vol. VAM, 262b–66*aff.*, T 1095 (also T 44, part 4)

Prayer of Maitreya
'phags pa byams pa'i smon lam
DgK (gzungs 'dus), vol. VAM, 266a–267*aff.*, T 1096

Profound Heart Sutra
zab mdo
See *Heart Sutra of Insight*

Retentive Mantra of the Offering Clouds
pujamegha-nama-dharani
mchod pa'i sprin zhes bya ba'i gzungs
DgK (gzungs 'dus), vol. VA, 239a–239b*ff.*, T 1068

Root Tantra of Vajrakila
vajrakilamulatantra
phur ba rtsa rgyud rdo rje khros pa
DgNGB, vol. VA (1), 169a–183b*ff.*

Sutra of the Array of Buddha Akshobhya's Pure Realm
aksobhyatathagatasya vyuha-nama-mahayanasutra
sangs rgyas mi 'khrugs pa'i zhing gi bkod pa'i mdo
DgK (dkon brtsegs), vol. KHA, 1b–70*aff.*, T 50

Sutra of the Vows of Individual Liberation
pratimoksasutra
so sor thar pa'i mdo
DgK ('dul ba), vol. CA, 1b–29b*ff.*, T 2

Sutra That Gathers All Wisdom Intentions
mdo dgongs pa 'dus pa (short title)

DgNGB, vol. 7, no. 1, 1–110*aff.*; also DgK (rnying rgyud), vol. KHA, 86b–290a*ff.*, T 829. The principal tantra-text of Anuyoga.

Tantra of Glorious Heruka Galpo
'jigs rten las 'das pa'i mdo/ dpal he ru ka gal po'i rgyud
DgNGB, vol. TSHA (15), 278a–300ff. and vol. DZA (1), 1–258*bff.*

Tantra of Hevajra
hevajratantra
dgyes rdor rgyud kyi brtag pa
DgK (rgyud 'bum), vol. NGA, 1b–30*aff.*, T 417–18. Translated in Snellgrove, *The Hevajra Tantra.*

Tantra of Immaculate Confession
dri med bshags rgyud
NK, vol. 18

Tantra of No Letters
yi ge med pa'i rgyud
DgNGB, vol. GA (6), 145a–152*bff.* See also *Seventeen Tantras.*

Tantra of Peaceful Deities
zhi ba lha rgyud
NK, vol. 82, p. 191–210

Tantra of Tara's Manifold Activities
sarvatathagatamatotaravisvakarmabhavatantra
sgrol ma las sna tshogs pa'i rgyud
DgK ('gyud 'bum), vol. TSHA, 202a–217a*ff.*, T 726

Tantra of the Brilliant Sun of the Clear Expanse
klong gsal 'bar ma nyi ma'i rgyud
('jigs gling) NGB, vol. CHA (13)

Tantra of the Great Magical Net of Manjushri
'jam dpal sgyu 'phrul drva ba chen po
See *Tantra of the Litany of Manjushri's Names*

Tantra of the Litany of Manjushri's Names
manjusrinamasangiti
'jam dpal mtshan brjod kyi rgyud
DgK (rgyud 'bum), vol. KA, 1b–13*bff.*, T 360; DgNGB, vol. THA (3), 123a–135a*ff.*
Also known as the *Tantra of the Great Magical Net of Manjushri.* Translated in Davidson, *The Litany of Names of Manjushri;* and Wayman, *Chanting the Names of Manjushri.*

Tantra of the Magical Net of Vajrasattva
vajrasattvamayajalatantra
rdo rje sems dpa sgyu 'phrul dra ba'i rgyud
DgNGB, vols. 9–11. One of the four primary divisions of the cycle of the tantras of the Magical Net (*Mayajala*). According to Longchen Rabjampa, this division includes the following main texts:
1. The *Guhyagarbha Tantra* [DgNGB, vol. TA (9), 1–31b*ff.;* Tingkye NGB, vol. 14; DgK (rnying rgyud), vol. KHA, 110b–132a*ff.*, T 832], which presents mind and wisdom as naturally manifesting.
2. The *Forty-Chapter Tantra from the Magical Net* [DgNGB, vol. THA (10), 135a–182b*ff.;* Tingkye NGB, vol. 14], which perfectly presents buddha activities.
3. The *Eight-Chapter Tantra from the Magical Net* [DgNGB, vol. THA (10), 114a–123a*ff.;* Tingkye NGB, vol. 14], which perfectly presents the mandalas.
4. The *Tantra of the Spiritual Teacher from the Magical Net* [DgNGB, vol. DA (11), 34b–60a*ff.;* Tingkye NGB, vol. 14; DgK (rnying rgyud), vol. GA, 34b–60a*ff.*, T 837], which clearly presents the empowerments.
5. The *Tantra of Supplementary Points from the Magical Net* [DgNGB, vol. THA (10), 182b–238b*ff.;* Tingkye NGB, vol. 14], which emphatically presents the commitments.
6. The *Eighty-Chapter Tantra from the Magical Net* [DgNGB, vol. DA (11), 148b–248b*ff.;* Tingkye NGB, vol. 14; DgK (rnying rgyud), vol. KHA, 198b–298b*ff.*, T 834], which extensively presents buddha qualities.
7. The *Mirror of Indestructible Reality* [Derge, vol. DA (11), 82b–148a*ff.;* Tingkye NGB, vol. 15, DgK (rnying rgyud), vol. KHA 132b–198a*ff.*, T 833], which clearly presents the symbolic body colors and handheld implements of the hundred deities.
8. The *Infinite Tantra from the Magical Net* [DgNGB, vol. THA (10), 279b–313*ff.;* Tingkye NGB, vol. 15], which clearly presents the generation stage of meditation.
9. The *Penetrating Tantra from the Magical Net* [DgNGB, vol. DA (11), 249a–294a*ff.;* Tingkye NGB, vol. 15], which clearly presents the path of skillful means.
Nowadays, the root and explanatory tantras of the *Magical Net* (*sgyu 'phrul drva ba rtsa bshad kyi rgyud*) altogether comprise nineteen distinct texts, which are all contained in DgNGB, vols. 9–11; and Tingkye NGB, vols. 14–16 and 19. For further detail, see Dorje, *Guhyagarbhatantra.*

Tantra of the Ocean of Dakinis
dakarnavamahayoginitantraraja
mkha 'gro rgya mtsho rnal 'byor ma'i rgyud
DgK (rgyud 'bum), vol. KHA, 137a–264b*ff.*, T 372. An explanatory tantra pertaining to Chakrasamvara. Apabhramsa version edited in Chaudhuri, *Studies in the Apabhramsa Texts.*

Tantra of the Secret Assembly
guhyasamajatantra
gsang ba 'dus pa'i rgyud
DgK (rgyud 'bum), vol. CA, 90a–157b*ff.*, T 442–43; DgNGB, vol. NA (12), 89a–157a*ff.*, BST 9 (1965). Translated in Freemantle, *A Critical Study of the Guhyasamaja Tantra.*

Tantra of the Wrathful Protectress of Mantra
sngags srung khros ma'i rgyud
Possibly to be identified with *sngags kyi srung ma dpal e ka dza ti' rgyud,* Dg NGB, vol. ZA (11), 307a–380*ff.*

Verse Summation of the Prajnaparamita
prajnaparamitasancayagatha
shes rab kyi pha rol tu phyin pa sdud pa tshigs su bcad pa [short title: mdo sdud pa]
DgK (shes phyin), vol. KA 1b–10b*ff.*, T 13. Translated in Conze, *The Perfection of Wisdom in Eight Thousand Lines.*

COMMENTARIAL ANTHOLOGIES OF INDIC ORIGIN

Tengyur
bstan 'gyur
The Collected Translations of Classical Treatises. The TBRC digital library includes four versions, which are freely accessible online, including the Derge xylograph edition of 1737–44 (213 vols.), compiled and edited by Shuchen Tsultrim Rinchen, which is catalogued in *A Complete Catalogue of the Tibetan Buddhist Canons.* Other important versions include the Peking edition in 185 vols., republished with a catalogue by Suzuki Research Foundation, Tokyo-Kyoto, 1955–61; and the new collated edition, Tengyur Pedurma in 120 vols., Chengdu, 1995–2005.

INDIVIDUAL TREATISES OF INDIC ORIGIN

ANUBHUTISVABHAVA (A.K.A. ANUBHUTISVARUPA, FL. 13TH CENTURY)

Grammar of Sarasvata
sarasvatavyakaranasutra
brda sprod pa dbyangs can gyi mdo
DgT (sgra mod), vol. SE, 1b–9a*ff.*, T 4297

ASANGA (FL. LATE 4TH TO EARLY 5TH CENTURY)

Compendium of Abhidharma
abhidharmasamuccaya

chos mngon pa kun las btus pa
DgT (sems tsam), vol. RI, 44b–120aff., T 4049
Translated in Boin-Webb, *Abhidharmasamuccaya*.

Five Sections of the Yogacharya Levels
yogacaryabhumipancavarga
rnal 'byor spyod pa'i sa sde lnga
DgT (sems tsam), vols. ZHI–HI (9 vols., T 4035–42), comprising the three treatises of the *Actual Foundation of the Yogacharya Level (yogacarabhumivastu)*,
namely: *Yogacharya Level (yogacarabhumi*, T 4035); *Shravaka Level (sravakab-
humi*, T 4036); and *Bodhisattva Level (bodhisattvabhumi*, T 4037); along with
Summation of Ascertainment (yogacarabhumiviniscayasamgrahani, T 4038);
Summation of the Ground (yogacarabhumivastusamgrahani, T 4039); *Summation of Training Based on the Yogacharya Levels (yogacarabhumivinayasamgrah-
ani*, T 4040); *Summation of Enumerated Categories Derived from the Yogacharya
Levels (yogacarabhumiparyayasamgrahani*, T 4041); and *Summation of Exegeses
Based on the Yogacharya Levels (yogacarabhumivivaranasamgrahani*, T 4042).

Summary of the Mahayana
mahayanasamgraha
theg pa chen po bsdus pa
DgT (sems tsam), vol. RI, 1b–43aff., T 4048. Translated in Keenan, *The Summary of the Great Vehicle*.

AVALOKITAVRATA (FL. 7TH CENTURY)

Commentary on the Lamp of Insight
prajnapradipatika
shes rab sgron ma rgya cher 'grel pa
DgT (dbu ma), vols. VA–ZA (3 vols.), T 3859

BUDDHAGUHYA (FL. 7TH TO 8TH CENTURY)

Extensive and Short Stages of the Path of the Magical Net
mayajalapathakrama
lam rim che chung
The longer and shorter versions of this text are found in NK, vols. 80–82. The
former is also found in P4720 and the latter in DZ, vol. 1, p. 1–15

CHANDRAKIRTI (FL. 7TH CENTURY)

Auto-Commentary on the Introduction to the Middle Way
madhyamakavatarabhasya
dbu ma la 'jug pa'i bshad pa
DgT (dbu ma), vol. 'A, 220b–348aff., T 3862

Clearly Worded Commentary on the Fundamental Stanzas of the Madyamaka
mulamadhyamakavrttiprasannapada
dbu ma rtsa ba'i 'grel pa tshig gsal ba
DgT (dbu ma), vol. 'A, 1b–200*aff.*, T 3860. Translated in Sprung, *Lucid Exposition of the Middle Way.*

Commentary on the Four Hundred Stanzas on the Middle Way
bodhisattvayogacaracatuhsatakatika
byang chub sems dpa' rnal 'byor spyod pa bzhi brgya pa'i rgya cher 'grel pa
DgT (dbu ma), vol. YA, 30b–239*aff.*, T 3865

Introduction to the Middle Way
madhyamakavatara
dbu ma la 'jug pa
DgT (dbu ma), vol. 'A, 201b–219*aff.*, T 3861. Translated in Huntington and Wangchen, *Emptiness of Emptiness;* also in Changchub and Nyingpo, *Lady of the Lotus-Born.*

DANDIN (FL. 6TH CENTURY)

Mirror of Poetics
kavyadarsa
snyan ngag me long
DgT (sgra mdo), vol. SE, 318a–341*aff.*, T 4301. Sanskrit edited with English commentary in Ray, *Mahakavi Dandi's Sri Premcandra Tarkavagisaviracita Tikasametah.*

DHARMAKIRTI (FL. EARLY 7TH CENTURY)

Exposition of Valid Cognition
pramanavarttikakarika
tshad ma rnam 'grel gyi tshig le'u byas pa
DgT (tshad ma), vol. CE, 94b–151*aff.*, T 4210. English translation in chap. 2 of Nagatomi, *A Study of Dharmakīrti's Pramāṇavārttika.*

DHARMAPALA (CA. 530–61)

Commentary on the Four Hundred Stanzas on the Middle Way
dbu ma bzhi brgya pa'i 'grel ba
Possibly to be identified with his *Door Illuminating the Hundred Teachings of the Greater Vehicle* (Chi. *da cheng bai fa ming men lun,* Tib. *theg pa chen po'i chos brgya gsal pa'i sgo'i bstan bcos*), DgT (sems tsam), vol. SHI, 145a–146b*ff.*, T 4063

GUNAPRABHA (FL. 7TH CENTURY)

Root Sutra of Monastic Discipline
vinayamulasutra
'dul ba mdo rtsa
DgT, vol. VU, 1b–100*aff.*, T 4117

INDRABHUTI (A.K.A. KING JA, FL. 6TH CENTURY)

Array of the Path of the Magical Net
mayapathavyavasthapana
lam rnam bkod
NK, vol. 83

Prophetic Declaration
lung bstan ma
See Dudjom Rinpoche, *Nyingma School,* 457–59

JINAPUTRA (A.K.A. RAJAPUTRA OR YOGAMITRA, DATES UNCERTAIN)

Commentary on the Recollection of the Three Jewels
triratnastotravrtti
dkon mchog rjes dran 'grel
DgT, vol. KA, 105a–109b*ff.*, T 1145

Explanation of the Compendium of Abhidharma
abhidharmasamuccayabhasya
mngon pa chos kun las btus pa'i bshad pa
DgT (sems tsam), vol. LI, 1b–117a*ff.*, T 4053

Exposition of the Compendium of Abhidharma
abhidharmasamuccayavyakhya
mngon pa chos kun las btus pa'i rnam par bshad pa
DgT (sems tsam), vol. LI, 117a–293a*ff.*, T 4054

KAMALASILA (740–95)

Three Stages of Meditation
tribhavanakrama
sgom rim gsum ka de kho na nyid bsdus pa'i dka' 'grel
DgT (dbu ma), vol. KI, 22a–68b*ff.*, T 3915–17

LILAVAJRA (A.K.A VILASAVAJRA, FL. 7TH CENTURY)

Clarification of Samaya
samayavivyakti
dam tshig gsal bkra
NK, vol. 89, P 4744

Subtle Unfolding of Samaya
samayanusayanirdesa
dam tshig phra rgyas
NK, vol. 89, P 4745

MAITREYA

Distinction between Middle and Extremes
madhyantavibhaga
dbus mtha' rnam par 'byed pa'i tshig le'u byas pa
DgT (sems tsam), vol. PHI, 40b–45a*ff.*, T 4021
Translated in Dharmachakra Translation Committee, *Middle Beyond Extremes.*

Distinction between Phenomena and Reality
dharmadharmatavibhaga
chos dang chos nyid rnam par 'byed pa
DgT (sems tsam), vol. PHI, 46b–49a*ff.*, T 4021
Translated in Dharmachakra Translation Committee, *Middle Beyond Extremes.*

Five Treatises of Maitreya
byams chos sde lnga
Comprising the five individual works listed here

Ornament of Emergent Realization
abhisamayalamkara-nama-prajnaparamitopadesasastrakarika
shes rab kyi pha rol tu phyin pa'i man ngag gi bstan bcos mngon par rtogs pa'i rgyan
DgT (shes phyin), vol. KA, 1b–13a*ff.*, T 3786
Translated in Conze, *Abhisamayalamkara;* and Khenchen Thrangu, *The Ornament of Clear Realization.*

Ornament of the Sutras of the Greater Vehicle
mahayanasutralamkarakarika
theg pa chen po mdo sde'i rgyan zhes bya ba'i tshig le'ur byas pa
DgT (sems tsam), vol. PHI, 1b–39a*ff.*, T 4020
Translated in Jamspal et al., The Universal Vehicle Discourse Literature.

Two Distinctions
'byed rnam gnyis
Comprising the *Distinction between Middle and Extremes* and the *Distinction between Phenomena and Reality*

Unsurpassed Continuum of the Mahayana
mahayanottaratantrasastra
theg pa chen po rgyud bla ma'i bstan bcos
DgT (sems tsam), vol. PHI, 54b–73a*ff.*, T 4024

Translated in Takasaki, *A Study on the Ratnagotravibhaga;* and Holmes, *The Changeless Nature.*

MUDGARAGOMIN (FL. 2ND CENTURY)

Praise to the Exalted One
visesastava
khyad par 'phags bstod (khyad par du 'phags pa'i bstod pa)
DgT (bstod tshogs), vol. KA, 1b–4b*ff.,* T 1109

NAGARJUNA (FL. 2ND CENTURY)

Auto-Commentary on the Fundamental Stanzas of the Middle Way Entitled Fear-lessness in All Respects
mulamadhyamakavrttyakutobhaya
dbu ma rtsa ba'i 'grel pa ga las 'jigs med
DgT (dbu ma), vol. TSA, 29b–99a*ff.,* T 3829

Five Collections of the Reasoning of the Middle Way
madhyamakayuktikaya
dbu ma rigs tshogs
Comprising the *Fundamental Stanzas of the Middle Way Entitled Insight* (*pra-jna-nama-mulamadhyamakakarika,* T 3824); the *Sixty Verses on Reason* (*yukti-sasthaka,* T 3827); the *Seventy Verses on Emptiness* (*sunyatasaptati,* T 3827); the *Refutation of Disputed Topics* (*vigrahavyavartani,* T 3828); and the *Technique of Pulverization* (*vaidalyasutra,* T 3826)

Fundamental Stanzas of the Middle Way Entitled Insight
prajna-nama-mulamadhyamakakarika
dbu ma rtsa ba'i tshig le'u byas pa
DgT (dbu ma), vol. TSA, 1b–19a*ff.,* T 3824
Translated in Padmakara, *The Root Stanzas on the Middle Way;* also Streng, *Emptiness;* Inada, *Nagarjuna;* Kalupahana, *A Path of Righteousness;* Garfield, *The Fundamental Wisdom of the Middle Way;* and Batchelor, *Verses from the Center.*

Prayer in Twenty Verses from the Precious Garland of Kingly Advice
rajaparikatharatnavalyudbhavapranidhanagathavimsaka
rgyal po la gtam bya bar in po che'i phreng ba las byung ba'i smon lam nyi shu pa
DgT (sna tshogs), vol. NO, 318a–319a*ff.,* T 4388

Treatise on Human Behavior Entitled Point of Human Sustenance
nitisastrajantuposanabindu
lugs kyi bstan bcos skye bo gso thig
DgT (thun mong), vol. NGO, 113a–116b*ff.,* T 4330
Translated from the Mongolian in Frye, *A Drop of Nourishment.*

Treatise on Human Behavior Entitled Stem of Insight
nitisastraprajnadanda
lugs kyi bstan bcos shes rab sdong bu
DgT (thun mong), vol. NGO, 103a–113a*ff.*, T 4329
Translated in Dharma Publishing, *Nagarjuna and Sakya Pandit*

PURNAVARDHANA

Commentary on the Treasury of Abhidharma
abhidharmakosatikalaksananusarini
chos mngon pa'i mdzod kyi 'grel bshad mtshan nyid kyi rjes su 'brang ba
DgT (mngon pa), vol. CU, 1b–347a*ff.*, T 4093

SANKARAPATI

Praise to He Who Surpasses the Gods
devatisayastotra
lha las phul byung
DgT (bstod tshogs), vol. KA, 43b–45a*ff.*, T 1112

SHAKYAPRABHA

*Commentary on Monastic Discipline: The Novitiate of the Mulasarvastivada
Entitled Sunlight*
aryamulasarvastivadisramanerakarikavrttiprabhavati
'phags pa gzhi thams cad yod par smra ba'i dge tshul gyi tshig le'u byas pa'i 'grel
pa 'od ldan [short title: 'dul tik]
DgT ('dul ba), vol. AU, 74a–162b*ff.*, T 4125

SHANTARAKSHITA (725–83)

Auto-Commentary on the Ornament of the Middle Way
madhyamakalamkaravrtti
dbu ma rgyan gyi 'grel pa
DgT (dbu ma), vol. SA, 56b–84a*ff.*, T 3885. Translated in Ichigo,
Madhyamakalamkara.

Ornament of the Middle Way
madhyamakalamkara
dbu ma rgyan gyi tshig le'u byas pa
DgT (dbu ma), vol. SA, 53a–56b*ff.*, T 3884
Translated in Chandrakirti and Mipam, *Introduction to the Middle Way;* also
Blumenthal, *Ornament of the Middle Way;* and Doctor, *Speech of Delight.*

SHANTIDEVA (FL. LATE 7TH–EARLY 8TH-CENTURY)

Way of the Bodhisattva
bodhisattvacaryavatara
byang chub sems dpa'i spyod pa la 'jug pa
DgT (dbu ma), vol. LA, 1b–40aff., T 3871
Translated in Padmakara, *The Way of the Bodhisattva;* also Matics, *Entering the Path of Enlightenment;* Batchelor, *A Guide to the Bodhisattva's Way of Life;* Crosby and Skilton, *The Bodhicaryāvatāra;* Wallace and Wallace, *A Guide to the Bodhisattva Way of Life.*

SHRI SINGHA

Great Garuda Soaring in Space
khyung chen mkha' lding
See under Longchen Rabjampa

VASUBANDHU (CA. LATE 4TH TO EARLY 5TH CENTURY)

Auto-Commentary on the Treasury of Abhidharma
abhidharmakosabhasya
chos mngon pa'i mdzod kyi bshad pa
DgT (mngon pa), vol. KU, 26b–258aff., T 4090
Translated from the French in Lamotte, *Karmasiddhi Prakarana*

Dissertation on the Thirty Verses
trimsikakarikaprakarana
sum cu pa'i tshig le'u byas pa
DgT (sems tsam), vol. SHI, 1b–3aff., T 4055
Translated from the Chinese in Cook, *Three Texts on Consciousness Only;* also Anacker, *Seven Works of Vasubandhu;* and Kochumuttom, *A Treatise in Twenty Stanzas.*

Treasury of Abhidharma
abhidharmakosakarika
chos mngon pa'i mdzod kyi tshig le'ur byas pa
DgT (mngon pa), vol. KU, 1b–25aff., T 4089
Translated from the French in Lamotte, *Karmasiddhi Prakarana*

VIMALAMITRA (FL. LATE 8TH TO EARLY 9TH CENTURY)

Commentary on Monastic Discipline on the Sutra of the Vows of Individual Liberation
pratimoksasutratika-vinayasamuccaya
so sor thar ba'i mdo rgya cher 'grel pa 'dul ba kun las btus pa [short title: 'dul tik]
DgT (pu), vol. KU, 1b–150aff., T 4106

Commentary on the Litany of the Names of Manjushri
'jam dpal mtshan brjod kyi 'grel pa
NK, vol. 60

COMMENTARIAL ANTHOLOGIES OF TIBETAN ORIGIN

Collected Nyingma Transmitted Teachings
rnying ma'i bka' ma
Currently comprising 120 vols. in the most extended edition (*bka' ma shin tu rgyas pa*), compiled by Khenpo Münsel and Khenpo Jamyang of Katok. Chengdu, 1999

INDIVIDUAL TREATISES OF TIBETAN ORIGIN

ALAK NAMKHA GYATSO (FL. 19TH CENTURY)

Cycle of Minor Manuscripts
yig cha phran bu'i skor
NL

Cycle of Sealed Guidance
bka' rgya can gyi khrid skor
NL

ALAKSHA TENDAR (1759–1831)

Commentary on the Precious Treasury of Qualities
yon tan mdzod kyi 'grel pa bka' gnad rdo rje'i rgya mdud 'grol byed legs bzhad gser gyi thur ma
NK, vol. 56

ANONYMOUS

Commentary on the Threefold Razor Tantras
spu gri'i rnam gsum gyi rgyud 'grel
NL

Khechari according to the Sakya Tradition
sa lugs mkha' spyod (1 vol.)
NL

New Treasures: Three Aspects of Wrath
gter gsar drag po rnam gsum
NL

One Thousand Vajrakila Reversals
phur pa stong bzlog
NL

Thirteen Offering Liturgies of the Nyingma Transmitted Teachings
bka' ma'i mchod khag bcu gsum
NL

Anthology

Texts on the Protector Sage Loktri
loktri'i gzhung in 1 vol. [full title: sde brgyad 'joms byed lokripala'i chos skor]
2 vols., Bir: Tsöndü Seng-ge, 1979–85; also RTD, vol. 54

Anthology of Four Indian and Tibetan Scholars

Narrow Path to the Fortress
rdzong 'phrang [srog gsum gyi chings kyi man ngag sogs]
NK, vol. 29

Bartröpa Tashi Rinchen of Katok

Guidance on Dong Chadralwa's Four Stages of Yoga
rnal 'byor bzhi rim gyi khrid
NL

Bö Khepa Mipam Gelek Namgyal (1618–85)

Ornament of the Middle Chapters of the Mirror of Poetics
snyan ngag le'u bar pa'i rgyan
In *Literary Arts in Ladakh,* 1972–76.
Cf. *Commentary and Proverbs Based on the Mirror of Poetics*
snyan ngag me long gi 'grel pa dang dper brjod
In *snyan ngag rtsa 'grel,* Qinghai: Mi rigs dpe skrun khang, 1981

Chimchen Jampelyang (fl. 13th century, d. 1267)

Commentary on the Treasury Entitled Ornament of Abhidharma [also entitled the
Greater Chim Commentary on the Treasury of Abhidharma]
mdzod 'grel mngon pa'i rgyan
Beijing: Krung go'i bod rig pa dpe skrun khang, 1989

Chimchung Lobzang Drak (1299–1375)

Ocean of Eloquence Elucidating Abhidharma [also entitled the *Lesser Chim Commentary on the Treasury of Abhidharma*]
chos mngon pa gsal byed legs pas bshad pa'i rgya mtsho
In *dpal ldan sa skya pa'i gsung rab,* vol. 17, Beijing: Mi rigs dpe skrun khang, in
collaboration with Qinghai: Mi rigs dpe skrun khang, 2004

CHOKGYUR DECHEN LINGPA (1829–70)

Dispelling of Obstacles from the Path
bar chad lam sel
In *gsang chen snga 'gyur ba'i bka' gter zhal 'don phyogs bsgrigs*, p. 71–78

Spontaneous Fulfillment of Wishes
bsam pa lhun grub ma
In *gsang chen snga 'gyur ba'i bka' gter zhal 'don phyogs bsgrigs*, p. 78–80

Yamantaka Lord of Life: The Meteorite Scorpion (revelation)
gshin rje tshe bdag lcags sdig
RTD, vol. 27, p. 165–318

CHÖYING TOBDEN DORJE (1785–1848)

Commentary on the Litany of the Names of Manjushri
'jam dpal mtshan brjod kyi 'grel pa
NL

DALAI LAMA (THE FIFTH), LOBZANG GYATSO (1617–82)

Compendium of Eloquence on Mind Training
blo sbyong legs bshad kun 'dus
N. Topgyal, *blo sbyong legs bshad kun 'dus;* also in Jamyang Khyentse Wangpo, *blo sbyong legs bshad kun 'dus kyi 'chad thabs utpala gsar pa'i do shal*, vol. 11, p. 1–66

Hundred Deities of Tushita
dga' ldan lha brgya ma
Original not located, but extant version is found in the *Collected Works* of the Seventh Dalai Lama

Reversal of Imminent Events, according to the Ritual Arrangement of the Fifth Dalai Lama
rgyal mchog lnga pa chen po'i chog sgrigs la brten nas 'char ka yang bzlog
NL

Ritual Arrangement of the Red and Black Vajra Yamari
rgyal mchog lnga pa chen po'i chog sgrigs la brten nas gshin rje king kang dmar nag
NL

DARMO MENRAMPA LOBZANG CHÖDRAK (1636–1710)

Sealed Instructions on Medical Science
man ngag bka' rgya ma

In *bod kyi gso ba rig pa'i gna' dpe phyogs sgrigs dpe tshogs,* vol. 32, Beijing: Mi rigs dpe skriun khang, 2006

DODRUB JIGME TRINLEY ÖZER (1745–1821)

Drop of Water in the Ocean
yon tan mdzod kyi sgo lcags 'byed byed bsdud 'grel rgya mtsho'i chu thigs [rin chen lde mig]
Authorship jointly attributed to Rigdzin Jigme Lingpa
In *yon tan mdzod rtsa 'grel,* Chengdu: Sichuan mi rigs dpe skrun khang, 1998, p. 133–639; also NK, vols. 53–54

DOLPOPA SHERAB GYALTSEN (1292–1361)

Commentary on the Unsurpassed Continuum of the Mahayana
rgyud bla ma dol tik [full title: theg pa chen po rgyud bla ma'i bstan bcos legs bshad nyi ma'i 'od zer]
Thimphu: Kusang topgyay, 1976

DONG CHADRALWA SONAM DÖNDRUB OF KATOK

Detailed Instructions on the Mind Class of the Great Perfection
Full title: sgyu 'phrul gsang ba snying po'i grol lam rdzogs pa chen po bram ze lugs ces grags pa sems sde'i pra khrid kyi man ngag zab don snying po mun sel dpal gyi sgron me
A commentary on Prahevajra's *rdzogs pa chen po sems sde'i pra khrid kyi man ngag,* contained in *ka thog snyan brgyud khrid yig,* vol. 2, p. 1–866

Four Stages of Yoga
rnal 'byor bzhi rim
NL

DORJE LINGPA (1346–1405)

Blazing Clear Expanse
klong gsal 'bar ma
Possibly to be identified with *klong gsal 'bar ma nyi ma'i gsang rgyud*
NK, vol. 110

DRAKPA GYALTSEN (1147–1216)

Parting from the Four Clingings
zhen pa bzhi bral
In *sa skya bka' 'bum,* vol. 9, Dehra Dun: Sakya Center, 1992–93, p. 605–10

DRAPA GESHE NGAWANG TSERING (FL. 19TH CENTURY)

Advice on the Ten Cardinal Treasures of the Kadampas
bka' gdams phug nor bcu'i zhal gdams (also known as: bslab bya srid pa'i 'ching
ba gcod pa'i phug nor bcu)
In Potala Archive: *Collected Works* of Ngawang Tsering, vol. 12, 3ff.

DRAPA NGÖNSHEY (1012–90)

Four Medical Tantras (revelation)
grva thang rgyud bzhi
In *bod kyi gso ba rig pa'i gna' dpe phyogs bsgrigs dpe tshogs,* vol. 20, Beijing: Mi rigs
dpe skrun khang, 2005

DROMTÖNPA GYALWA JUNGNEY (1004–64) ET AL.

Father and Son Teachings of the Kadam School
bka' gdams pha chos bu chos
2 vols., Ziling: Qinghai mi rigs dpe skrun khang, 1994

Jewel Rosary of the Bodhisattva's Former Lives
byang chub sems dpa'i skyes rabs nor bu'i phreng ba
In *Father and Son Teachings of the Kadam School,* vol. 1, p. 607–10

DÜDÜL DORJE (1615–72)

Blazing Lotus Light (revelation)
pad ma 'od 'bar [full title: dam chos sprul sku snying thig las padma 'od 'bar]
In *rin chen gter mdzod chen mo,* Delhi: Shechen Publications, 2007–8

Dorje Drollö (revelation)
bdud 'dul gter byon gro lod [full title: dam chos sprul sku snying thig las gu ru
rdo rje gro lod kyi las byang nor bu'i phreng ba]
In *rin chen gter mdzod chen mo,* Delhi: Shechen Publications, 2007–8

Treasure Revelations in Nine Volumes (revelations)
bdud 'dul pod dgu
Republished in 8 vols. by Bairo Tulku: Darjeeling, 1976; also in 12 vols. by
Kagyud Sungrab Nyamso Khang: Darjeeling, 1997

Vajrakila (revelation)
bdud phur [full title: yang gsang mkha' 'gro'i snying thig las snying thig tshe
yang phur gsum]
In *phur pa phyogs sgrigs,* vol. 20

DUMPA GYA SHANGTROM (B. 1016)

Yamantaka Lord of Life: Imitation Meteorite (revelation)
gshin rje tshe bdag lcags 'dra
RTD, vol. 26, p. 1–417

GARWANG SHIGPO LINGPA (1524–83)

Great Compassionate One: Cycle of Teachings That Liberate from Samsara (revelation)
thugs rje chen po 'khor ba la sgrol gyi chos skor
2 vols., Gangtok: Sherab Gyaltsen Lama, 1976

GENDÜN DRUBPA (FIRST DALAI LAMA, 1391–1474)

Commentary on the Root Sutra of Monastic Discipline Entitled Jewel Garland
'dul tïk rin chen phreng ba
Beijing: Mi rigs dpe skrun khang, 1999

Hundred Thousand Anecdotes of Monastic Discipline
'dul ba'i gleng 'bum chen mo
Ziling: Qinghai mi rigs dpe skrun khang, 1990

GORAMPA SONAM SENGE (1429–89)

Commentary on Difficult Points in the Analysis of the Three Vows
sdom gsum gyi dka' 'grel [full title: sdom gsum rab dbye'i rnam bshad rgyal ba'i
gsung rab kyi dgongs pa gsal ba].
In the *Collected Works of Go* (*rams bsod nams seng ge*), vol. 9, Dzongsar: Khamye
Lobling, 2004

*Commentary on Difficult Points in the Ornament of Emergent Realization Entitled
Explanatory Clarification*
mngon rtogs rgyan gi dka' 'grel rnam bshad rab gsal
In *Collected Works of Go* (*rams bsod nams seng ge*), vols. 7–8.

*Commentary on the Introduction to the Middle Way, Entitled Dispelling the Dark-
ness of Inferior Views*
'jug tik lta ngan mun sel
In *Collected Works of Go* (*rams bsod nams seng ge*), vol. 5, Dzongsar: Khamye
Lobling, 2004, p. 475–754

Overview of the Middle Way according to the Mahayana
theg mchog dbu ma'i spyi don
Probably *lta ba'i shan 'byed theg mchog gnad kyi zla zer,* in *Collected Works of Go
rams bsod names seng ge*, vol. 5, p. 755–858

GURU CHÖWANG (1212–70)

Buddhasamayoga (revelation)
sangs rgyas mnyam sbyor lcags smyug ma
2 vols., Paro: Urgyen Tempai Gyaltsen, 1980; also Potala Archive ms. edition,
vol. 5, nos. 19–20 (dkar chags, p. 149)

Eight Heruka Sadhanas: Consummation of All Secrets (revelation)
bka' brgyad gsang ba yongs rdzogs
In *bka' brgyad phyogs bsgrigs,* 4 vols., Chengdu: Thubten Nyima, 2000; also
Potala Archive ms. edition, vols. 1–2 and 4, comprising 140 texts (*dkar chags,*
p. 143–45)

Hundred Thousand Names of the Buddha (revelation)
sangs rgyas kyi mtshan 'bum
Ziling: Kumbum Jampaling, 2000. Cf. Ratna Lingpa's *dus gsum sangs rgyas
stong rtsa'i mtshan 'bum,* in his *Collected Revelations,* vol. 7; also Khenpo Ngakchung's *mtshan 'bum gyi lag len thar lam gsal byed* in his *Collected Works,* vol. 3.

Perfection of the Seats of the Five Stages (revelation)
rim lnga gdan rdzogs [a.k.a.: rim lnga gdan thog gcig ma / chos dbang bka'
brgyad gsang rdzogs rim lnga]
RTD, vol. 23, no. 1, p. 1–5

Quintessential Embodiment of the Great Compassionate One (revelation)
thugs rje chen po yang snying 'dus pa
RTD, vol. 34, nos. 1–9, p. 1–234

Secret Embodiment of the Guru (revelation)
bla ma gsang 'dus
RTD, vol. 7, p. 461–614; also Potala Archive ms. edition, vol. 3, comprising 16
distinct texts (*dkar chags,* p. 145–46)

Tantra of the Great Elucidation of Freedom from Constructs (revelation)
spros bral don gsal chen po'i rgyud
DgNGB, vol. KA (1). A tantra-text of the Yangtik cycle.

Vajrakila: The Supremely Secret Razor (revelation)
yang gsang spu gri / phur pa chos dbang spu gri
One of the *Three Razor Scriptures* (*spu gri rnam gsum*), alongside the revelations
of Rigdzin Godemchen and Pema Lingpa
In *phur pa phyogs bsgrigs,* vol. 10, Chengdu: Bod kyi shes rig zhib 'jug khang,
2002, p. 1–234

GYALSE SHENPEN TAYE (1800–55)

Analysis of the Five Psychophysical Aggregates
phung lnga'i rab dbye
NL

GYALTSAB DHARMA RINCHEN (1364–1432)

Commentary on the Way of the Bodhisattva
spyod 'jug dar tik [long title: spyod 'jug rnam bshad rgyal sras 'jug ngogs]
Sarnath: Geden Chilekhang, 1973

Ornament of the Essence of Explanation of the Prajnaparamita
phar phyin rnam bshad snying rgyan
2 vols., Lanzhou: Gansu mi rigs dpe skrun khang, 2000

GYURME TSEWANG CHOKDRUB (1761–1829)

Explanatory Guide to the General Meaning of the Guhyagarbha Tantra, Entitled Ocean of Eloquence
gsang bas nying po'i spyi don gyi bshad pa'i zin bris bla ma'i man ngag don gsal snying po legs bshad rol mtsho
NK, vol. 77, p. 153–349

Spike of Unity of the Stages of Meditation
bskyed rim cho ga dang sbyar ba'i gsal byed zung 'jug snye ma
In *ka thog snyan brgyud khrid chen bcu gsum*, vol. 10 (THA), p. 319–420

JAMGÖN KONGTRÜL (1813–99)

Collection of Clear Vajrakila Commentaries
phur tik bum nag gi 'grel pa
NL. Possibly his commentary on the *Root Tantra of Vajrakila*, which is contained in NK, vol. 12, and immediately precedes the *phur tik bum nag*.
Commentary on the Profound Inner Meaning
zab mo nang don gyi 'grel pa
In *bka' brgyud pa'i gsung rab*, vol. 20, p. 45–322
Ziling: Qinghai mi rigs dpe skrun khang, 2001

Commentary on the Two-Chaptered Hevajra Tantra
btags gnyis kyi 'grel pa
In *bka' brgyud pa'i gsung rab*, vol. 18, p. 659–1095
Ziling: Qinghai mi rigs dpe skrun khang, 2001
Commentary on the Unsurpassed Continuum of the Mahayana
rgyud bla ma'i 'grel pa
In *bka' brgyud pa'i gsung rab*, vol. 16, p. 1–217
Ziling: Qinghai mi rigs dpe skrun khang, 2001

Explanation of the Rays of the Sun
nyi ma'i 'od zer gyi rnam bshad
NL

Infinite Ocean of Knowledge
shes bya mtha' yas pa'i rgya mtsho

Prose auto-commentary on the *Treasury of Knowledge*
3 vols. Beijing: Mi rigs dpe skrun khang, 1982
Translated in the ten-volume *Treasury of Knowledge* series

Sixteenfold Vital Nuclei Empowerments of the Kadam Tradition
bka' gdams thig le bcu drug
In *gdams ngag mdzod*, vol. 4, p. 283–316, entitled *bka'gdams thig le bcu drug gi sgrub thabs dbang bskur ba'i cho ga bklag pa chog tu bsdebs pa thugs rje rnam par rol pa'i rgyan*. According to *dung dkar tshig mdzod chen mo*, p. 166, Jamgön Kongtrül was the fountainhead of this empowerment transmission in eastern Tibet.

Treasury of Knowledge
shes bya kun khyab mdzod
3 vols., Beijing: Mi rigs dpe skrun khang, 1982
Translated in the ten-volume *Treasury of Knowledge* series

Treasury of Precious Instructions
gdams ngag mdzod
18 vols., Paro: Lama Ngodrup and Sherab Drimey, 1979–1981

Treasury of Precious Revelations (compilation)
rin chen gter mdzod chen mo
RTD (111 vols.); also Derge Parkhang xylographic edition (72 vols.), the Chengdu edition (63 vols.), and the new Shechen edition (70 vols., Delhi: 2007–9)

Treasury of Revelations, Restricted Section (compilation, in 3 vols)
gter mdzod lung bka' rgya ma

Yumka Khandrö Sangtik, "Secret Heart Essence of the Dakini": Transmitted Teachings of the Mother Consort (revelation)
yum bka' mkha' 'gro'i gsang thig
RTD, vol. 16, p. 1–300 passim

JAMGÖN MIPAM GYATSO (1846–1912)

Annotated Commentary on the Treasury of the Logical Reasoning of Valid Cognition
tshad ma rig gter gyi mchan 'grel
In *Collected Works*, vol. 5, p. 65–290

Clear Synopsis of the Great Secret Commentary on the Means for Attainment of Vishuddha Heruka
yang dag gsang 'grel chen mo'i don bsdus rab gsal / gsang 'grel don bsdus
In *Collected Works*, vol. 23, p. 347–512; also NK, vol. 61, p. 587–616; and Chengdu: Sichuan mi rigs dpe skrun khang, 2000

Collected Works of Jamgön Mipam
mi pham gsung 'bum
Lhasa: Potala Library imprint, 20 vols.; Paro: Lama Ngödrup and Sherab
Drimey, 1984–93 (27 vols.); Chengdu: Gangs can rig gzhung dpe rnying myur
skyobs lhan tshogs, 2007 (32 vols.); Gangtok: Sonam Topgyay Kazi, 1972 (15
vols.)

*Commentary on Difficult Points in the Eighteenth Chapter of the Treasury of Wish-
Fulfilling Gems*
le'u bco brgyad pa'i dka' 'grel
In *Collected Works*, vol. 17, p. 749–58

Commentary on Pulses and Urinalysis
rtsa chu'i 'grel pa
In *sman yig phyogs bsgrigs*, Chengdu: Sichuan mi rigs dpe skrun khang, 2006,
p. 21–91

Commentary on the Insight Chapter Entitled Water-Purifying Gem
spyod 'jug sher 'grel ke ta ka / sher le
In *Collected Works*, vol. 18, p. 1–160; also Byalakuppe: Ngagyur Nyingma Institute, 2002

Commentary on the Distinction between Middle and Extremes
dbu mtha' rnam 'byed kyi 'grel pa 'od zer phreng ba
In *Collected Works*, vol. 15, p. 297–414; also Byalakuppe: Ngagyur Nyingma
Institute, 2002

Commentary on the Distinction between Phenomena and Reality
chos dang chos nyid rnam 'byed kyi 'grel pa
In *Collected Works*, vol. 15, p. 241–90; also Byalakuppe: Ngagyur Nyingma
Institute, 2002

*Commentary on the Sutra of the Recollection of the Three Jewels Entitled Melody of
Inexhaustible Auspiciousness*
dkon mchog gsum rjes su dran pa'i mdo 'grel bkra shis mi zad pa'i sgra dbyangs
NK, vol. 45, p. 423–518; also in *Collected Works*, vol. 10, p. 1–66

*Commentary on the Verse Summation of the Prajnaparamita Integrating the Sutras
and Treatises*
sdud 'grel mdo sbyar
In *Collected Works*, vol. 14, p. 217–360

Explanation of the Deities of the Eight Heruka Sadhanas
bka' brgyad rnam bshad
In *Collected Works*, vol. 23, p. 513–700; also Chengdu: Sichuan mi rigs dpe skrun
khang, 2000

Gateway to Knowledge
mkhas pa'i tshul la 'jug pa'i sgo / mkhas 'jug
In *Collected Works of Jamgön Mipam,* vol. 17 (TSHA), p. 1–318. Also Ziling: Qinghai mi rigs dpe skrun khang, 1988, 1992. Translated in Erik Pema Kunsang, *Gateway to Knowledge.*

Instructions on the Mind: Holding Buddha in Your Hand
sems don sangs rgyas lag bcang [also known as: gdams ngag sangs rgyas lag bcang ma]
In *Collected Works,* vol. 19, p. 371–552

Light of the Sun: Response to Critiques
brgal lan nyin byed snang ba
Written in defense of his somewhat controversial commentary on chapter 9 of the *Way of the Bodhisattva*
In *Collected Works,* vol. 18, p. 161–274

Manifold Light Rays of the Praise Entitled You Whose Intelligence
gang blo ma'i 'od zer dgu phrug
See next entry

Manjushri according to the Mahayoga Tantra Tradition
'jam dpal rgyud lugs
In *Collected Works,* vol. 24 (item YA). Cf. also *rgyud lugs 'jam dpal zhi ba'i sgrub thabs ye shes snang ba mchog grub,* vol. 5, p. 1–18

Manjushri Offering Ritual
'jam dpal mchod chog [also known as: 'jam dpal gyi tshogs mchod]
NK, vol. 4, p. 525–48

Overview of the Guhyagarbha Entitled Luminous Essence
gsang snying spyi don 'od gsal snying po
NK, vol. 69; also in *Collected Works,* vol. 23, p. 97–320; and Chengdu: Sichuan mi rigs dpe skrun khang, 2000

Pebble Commentary on the Root Tantra
rtsa rgyud rde'u 'grel 'grems mya ngan med pa'i ljon shing
In *sman yig phyogs bsgrigs,* Chengdu: Sichuan mi rigs dpe skrun khang, 2006, p. 1–19

Practical Instructions on Herbal Medications
sngo sman lag khrid
Possibly identified with the chapters in *sman yig phyogs bsgrigs,* Chengdu: Sichuan mi rigs dpe skrun khang, 2006, p. 93ff.

Praise to Manjushri
'jam dpal dbyangs la bstod pa
NL

Prayer for the Spread of the Teachings
bstan rgyas smon lam
In *gsang chen snga 'gyur ba'i bka' gter zhal 'don phyogs bsgrigs*, Ziling: Qinghai mtsho lho dge 'os slob grva'i par khang, 1998

Reply to Lobzang Rabsel's Letter
rab lan [full title: mkhas mchog blo bzang rab gsal nas phul ba'i zhu shog dang le'i lan]
In *Collected Works*, vol. 18, p. 587–66

Sadanana
gdong drug las bro brdung ba
In *Collected Works*, vol. 29, p. 63–65

Short Commentary Entitled Definitive Excellence
nges legs 'grel chung [full title: so thar mdo yi mcgan 'grel nyung ngo nges legs them skas]
NK, vol. 45, p. 573–730

Summation of Philosophical Systems from the Treasury of Wish-Fulfilling Gems
yid bzhin mdzod kyi grub mtha' bsdus pa
In *Collected Works*, vol. 17, p. 599–672; also Byalakuppe: Ngagyur Nyingma Institute, 1999

Sword of Insight That Thoroughly Ascertains Reality
don rnam par nges pa shes rab ral gri
In *Collected Works*, vol. 17, p. 433–46

Sword That Cuts Through Doubts about Symbolism
brda shan byed the tshom gcod pa'i ral gri
In *Collected Works*, vol. 17, p. 407–32; also Byalakuppe: Namdroling Monastic Junior High School, 1997

JAMPA TRINLEY (FL. 18TH CENTURY)

Thread-Cross of Tara That Averts Battles
sgrol ma gyul mdos yig rnying gi dgongs pa
Kathmandu: Sachen International Community, 2005

JAMYANG KHYENTSE WANGPO (1820–92)

Commentary on You Whose Intelligence
gang gi blo ma'i 'grel pa
NL, but possibly equivalent to *'jam pa'i dbyangs kyi rnam bshad* in his *Collected Works*

Drubtop Nyingtik: Heart Essence of the Accomplished Master (revelation)
grub thob snying thig
Inspired by the vision of Tangtong Gyalpo
Thimphu: National Library of Bhutan, 1985

Gathering of All the Dakinis' Secrets (rediscovered revelation)
yang gter mkha' 'gro gsang ba kun 'dus
Gangtok: Gonpo Tseten Lama, 1976

Ösel Nyingtik, "Heart Essence of Luminosity" (revelation)
rtsa gsum 'od gsal snying thig
Paro: Kyichu Temple, 1982

Praise and Sadhana of Manjushri
'jam dpal bstod sgrub
NL

Two Stages of Visualization
dmigs rim gnyis
NL

Whispered Lineage Dakinis according to Tangtong Gyalpo
thang rgyal snyang brgyud mkha' 'gro
A rediscovered treasure (*yang gter*)
Full title: *Whispered Lineage of the Dakinis' Secret Conduct* (*gsang spyod mkha'
'gro'i snyan brgyud*)
See *Collected Works*, vol. 15, p. 399–402

JATSÖN NYINGPO (1585–1656)

Blazing Lotus Light (revelation)
padma 'od 'bar [gyi tshe sgrub]
RTD, vol. 6, p. 81–92; also *Collected Works*, vol. 1

Collected Revelations of Jatsön Nyingpo [*in Six Volumes*] (revelations)
'ja' tshon pod drug
Delhi, Pema Norbu Rinpoche, 1995; also published in 8 vols. by Taklung Tsetrul
Pema Wangyal, Darjeeling, 1978–82

Peaceful and Wrathful Deities (revelation)
'ja' tshon zhi khro [nges don snying po]

Collected Works, vol. 4

Union of All Precious Jewels (revelation)
[yang zab] dkon mchog spyi 'dus

Collected Works, vol. 1

KARMA CHAKME (C. 1650–78)

Concise Guidance on the Namchö Revelations
gnam chos khrid chung
NL, but possibly to be identified with Karma Chakme's *gnam chos dkar lugs zung 'jug pa,* contained in his *Collected Works,* p. 125–30

Oral Instructions for Mountain Retreat
ri chos mtshams kyi zhal gdams
Hong Kong: Tenma dpe sakrun khang, n.d.

Stallion for Selecting a Pure Realm
zhing khams 'dam pa'i rta pho [full title: bde ba can gyi zhing khams du 'gro ba'i gdams pa bya rgyal khyung gi rta pho
In *bde smon phyogs bsgrigs,* vol. 1 (new ed.), Chengdu: Sichuan mi rigs dpe skrun khang, 2007, p. 276–82

KARMA LINGPA (FL. 14TH CENTURY)

Concise Torma Empowerment Entitled Meaningful to Touch
gtor dbang reg pa don ldan
Written by Namkha Chökyi Gyatso and contained in the compilation below called *Peaceful and Wrathful Deities,* vol. 1, p. 161–64

Guidance Manual to the Six Intermediate States
bar do drug gi khrid yig
In the compilation below called *Peaceful and Wrathful Deities,* vol. 2, p. 303–432

Middle-Length Empowerment Entitled Natural Liberation of the Six Classes of Beings (revelation)
dbang 'bring pa 'gro drug rang grol
In the compilation below, vol. 2, p. 145–228

Peaceful and Wrathful Deities: Natural Liberation of Wisdom Mind (revelation)
zhi khro dgongs pa rang grol / kar gling zhi khro
Eighteen extant manuscript and printed versions have been identified, among which the most extensive is the three-volume compilation of Katok provenance, reproduced from the library of Düdjom Rinpoche and published in photo-off-set form (Delhi: Sherab Lama, 1975–76). The sixty-four texts contained within it are listed in Dorje, Coleman, and Jinpa, *Tibetan Book of the Dead,* 381–86.

Peaceful and Wrathful Deities: Natural Liberation through Encountering All Four Empowerments (revelation)
zhi khro dbang bzhi phrad tshad rang grol
In the above-mentioned compilation, vol. 1, p. 49–92

KATOK DRUNGPA (COMPILER)

Prayer Book of Katok Monastery
ka thog chos spyod [see: snga 'gyur rgyal ba kaë thog pa'i rgyun 'don phyogs sgrig]
Published in book form at Katok Monastery, with Chinese translation, n.p., n.d.

KATOKPA DAMPA DESHEK (1122–92)

Annotated Commentary on the Clarification of Samaya
dam tshig gsal dkra'i mchan 'grel
NK, vol. 89

Annotated Commentary on the General Sutra That Gathers All Wisdom Intentions
spyi mdo'i mchan 'grel
Possibly to be identified with his *mdo dgongs 'dus kyi bsdus don padma dkar po,*
NK, vol. 95, p. 123–268

Annotated Commentary on the Sutra of All-Inclusive Awareness
kun 'dus rig pa'i mdo'i mchan 'grel
NL

Commentary on the Difficult Points in the General Sutra That Gathers All Wisdom Intentions
spyi mdo dgongs pa 'dus pa'i dka' 'grel rdo rje'i tha ram 'byed pa'i lde'u mig
NK, vol. 95, p. 269–340

Commentary on the Guhyagarbha Entitled Words Spoken at Chimpu
gsang 'grel bka' mchims phu ma
NK, vols. 65–66

Commentary That Binds All the Vehicles
theg pa spyi chings
NK, vol. 58, p. 5–58

Exalted Meanings of the Same Wording
'dra mthun don 'phags [full title: 'dra mthun khyad 'phags ngang pa'i rgyan]
NK, vol. 114, p. 317–18

Miscellaneous Writings of Dampa Deshek and His Spiritual Heir Tsangtönpa
dam pa yab sras gsung 'thor bu
1 vol.

Sadhana of Lord Vinayaka
mgon po tshogs bdag kyi sgrub thabs [full title: legs ldan tshogs kyi bdag po mchod pa bdud las rnam rgyal]
NK, vol. 39

Topical Outline of the General Sutra That Gathers All Wisdom Intentions
[mdo dgongs pa 'dus pa'i] spyi don [full title: 'dus pa'i mdo'i khog dbub legs
bshad nyi ma'i snang ba]
NK, vol. 95, p. 75–122

Trio of the Peaceful and Wrathful Deities, and Vajrakila
zhi khro phur gsum
NK, vol. 15

Uncommon Exorcism of the Vitality of the Matarah
ma mo'i srog gtad thun min
Possibly contained in NK, vol. 39

*Uncommon Exorcism of the Vitality of the Seven Classes of Mamo in the Retinue of
Omniscient Ekajati*
kun mkhyen sde bdun gyi srog gtad thun min
Possibly contained in NK, vol. 39

KHAMTRÜL NGAWANG KUNGA TENDZIN (1680–1728)

Commentary on the Mirror of Poetics
snyan ngag me long gi 'grel pa
NL

KÖNCHOK TSULTRIM OF ZURTSO

Commentary on the Guhyagarbha Tantra
gsang snying 'grel
NL

KUNZANG SONAM OF MINYAK (A.K.A. TUBTEN CHÖKYI DRAKPA, 1823–1906)

General Explanation of the Insight Chapter
sher le'i spyi don [full title: spyod 'jug gi 'grel bshad rgyas sras yon tan bum
bzang]
Beijing: Gangs ljongs shes rig gi nying bcud, 1990

Prayer for Mind Training
blo sbyong smon lam
NL

LERAB LINGPA (1856–1926)

Prophetic Inventory
lung byang
Contained in his *Collected Works and Revelations* in 17 vols., Byalakuppe: Penor
Rinpoche, 1985

LOCHEN DHARMASHRI (1654–1718)

Great Commentary on the Ascertainment of the Three Vows Entitled the Wish-Fulfilling Spike
sdom gsun rnam nges kyi 'grel pa dpag bsam snye ma
NK, vol. 51; also in *gangs ti se shes rig spar khang*, n.p., n.d.

Oral Transmission of the Lord of Secrets
gsang bdag zhal lung
NK, vols. 74–75

Ornament of the Lord of Secrets' Wisdom Mind
gsang bdag dgongs rgyan
NK, vol. 76. Also in DgNGB, vol. TA (9), 31b–174b*ff.*, and in the *Collected Works of Lochen Dharmashri*, Dehra Dun edition, vol. 8, 1999, 90–337ff.

LONGCHEN RABJAMPA (1308–63)

Commentary on the Guhyagarbha Entitled Dispelling the Darkness of the Ten Directions
gsang 'grel phyogs bcu mun sel
New edition: Beijing: Krung go bod ri pa dpe skrun khang, *dpal brtsegs bod yig dpe rnying* series, 1 vol. (series no. 128), 2009; also NK, vol. 68
Translated in Dorje, *Guhyagarbhatantra*

Demonstration of the Vajra Path of Secret Conduct
gsang spyod rdo rje'i lam bstan
Contained in the *Khandro Yangtik*, vol. 4 (series no. 113), p. 1–15

Essence of Ultimate Meaning
nges don snying po
Contained in the *Khandro Yangtik*, vol. 4 (series no. 113), p. 16–21

Foundation Manual Recording Signs of Realization and Degrees of Progress (revelation of Prahevajra)
rtags yig tshad yig gzhi
In the *Khandro Nyingtik*, vol. 1 (series no. 110), p. 267–71; also vol. 2 (series no. 111), p. 173–75

Four Nyingtik Mother-and-Child Cycles (revelation)
snying thig ma bu bzhi / snying thig ya bzhi
Comprising the two *Nyingtik Mother Cycles* and the two *Nyingtik Child Cycles*
New edition: Beijing: Krung go bod ri pa dpe skrun khang, *dpal brtsegs bod yig dpe rnying* series, 12 vols. (series nos. 106–17), 2009

Golden Rosary of Nectar (revelation)
zhus lan bdud rtsi gser phreng
In the *Khandro Nyingtik*, vol. 1 (series no. 110), p. 349–68

Great Array of the Highest (revelation)
ati bkod pa chen po
An alternative title of the *Vima Nyingtik*

Great Garuda Soaring in Space
khyung chen mkha' lding
An instruction of Shri Simha
In the *Vima Nyingtik,* vol. 2 (series no. 107), p. 267–73

Guidance on the Khandro Yangtik Entitled Cloudbanks of the Ocean of Profound Meaning
mkha' 'gro yang tig gi khid zab don rgya mtsho'i sprin phung
Contained in the *Khandro Yangtik,* vol. 3 (series no. 112), p. 191–518

Guidance on the Secret Unwritten Whispered Lineage of the Zabmo Yangtik (revelation)
zab mo yang tig gsang ba yi ge med pa'i snyan brgyud kyi khrid [rnams]
Probably comprising the *snyan brgyud gnad kyi mdo chings,* vol. 1 (series no. 116), p. 318–24; as well as the *snyan brgyud thugs kyi me long* and the *snyan brgyud don gyi me long,* vol. 2 (series no. 117), p. 124–77

Illuminating Lamp (revelation)
[zangs yig can gyi] snang byed sgron ma
In the *Vima Nyingtik,* vol. 1 (series no. 106), p. 334–60

In All My Lives
bdag gis kyang gang du skye ba ma
NL

Khandro Nyingtik, "Heart Essence of the Dakini" (revelation of Padmasambhava)
mkha 'gro snying thig
Also entitled *Khandro Sangwa Nyingtik, "Secret Heart Essence of the Dakini"*
mkha' 'gro gsang ba snying thig
New edition (including texts from *mkha' 'gro yang tig*). Beijing: Krung go bod ri pa dpe skrun khang, *dpal brtsegs bod yig dpe rnying* series, 4 vols. (series nos. 110–13), 2009

Khandro Yangtik, "Dakini Quintessence" (revelation)
mkha' 'gro yang tig
New edition (labeled *mkha' 'gro snying thig*). Beijing: Krung go bod rig pa dpe skrun khang, *dpal brtsegs bod yig dpe rnying* series, 2 vols. (series nos. 112–13), 2009

Lama Yangtik, "Guru Quintessence" (revelation)
bla ma yang tig
New edition: Beijing: Krung go bod ri pa dpe skrun khang, *dpal brtsegs bod yig dpe rnying* series, 2 vols. (series nos. 114–15), 2009

Miscellaneous Writings
gsung thor bu
New edition: Beijing: Krung go bod ri pa dpe skrun khang, dpal brtsegs bod yig
dpe rnying series, 2 vols. (series nos. 129–30), 2009

Nyingtik Child Cycles (revelation)
snying thig bu
Comprising the *Lama Yangtik* and the *Khandro Yangtik,* along with the *Zabmo
Yangtik*

Nyingtik Mother Cycles (revelation)
snying thig ma
Comprising the *Vima Nyingtik* and the *Khandro Yangtik*

Precious Torch of Power (revelation)
rin po che dbang gi sgron ma
In the *Khandro Nyingtik*
Possibly to be identified with *dbang khrid nor bu sgron gsal,* vol. 1, p. 112–28, or
with *rin po che dbang gi phreng ba,* vol. 2, p. 389–462

Precious Treasury of Reality
chos dbyings rin po che'i mdzod
New edition: Beijing: Krung go bod ri pa dpe skrun khang, *dPal brtsegs bod yig
dpe rnying* series, 1 vol. (series no. 121), 2009

Translated in Barron, *The Precious Treasury.*

*Precious Treasury of Wish-Fulfilling Gems: A Treatise on the Pith Instructions of the
Mahayana*
theg pa chen po'i man ngag gi bstan bcos yid bzhin rin po che'i mdzod
In the *Seven Treasuries of Longchenpa (klong chen mdzod bdun)*
New edition: Beijing: Krung go bod ri pa dpe skrun khang, *dpal brtsegs bod yig
dpe rnying* series, 1 vol. (series no. 118), 2009
Ch. 1 translated in Lipman, "How Samsara Is Fabricated."

Resting in Illusion
sgyu ma ngal gso
NK, vol. 101
New edition: Beijing: Krung go bod ri pa dpe skrun khang, *dpal brtsegs bod yig
dpe rnying* series, 1 vol. (series no. 127), 2009, p. 1–174

Resting in the Nature of Mind
sems nyid ngal gso
New edition: Beijing: Krung go bod ri pa dpe skrun khang, *dpal brtsegs bod yig
dpe rnying* series, 2 vols. (series nos. 125–26), 2009

Sangwa Nyingtik, "Secret Heart Essence" (revelation)
gsang ba snying thig
Sometimes used as an alternative title of the *Vima Nyingtik*

Seven-Point Mind Training
[sngon 'gro] sems sbyong bdun [gyi don khrid]
In the *Lama Yangtik*, vol. 1 (series no. 114), p. 185–191

Seven Treasuries
mdzod bdun
Comprising the *Precious Treasury of Wish-Fulfilling Gems* (*yid bzhin rin po che'i mdzod*); the *Precious Treasury of the Abiding Nature* (*gnas lugs rin po che'i mdzod*); the *Precious Treasury of Philosophical Systems* (*grub mtha' rin po che'i mdzod*); the *Precious Treasury of Pith Instructions* (*man ngag rin po che'i mdzod*); the *Precious Treasury of Reality* (*chos dbyings rin po che'i mdzod*); the *Precious Treasury of the Supreme Vehicle* (*theg mchog rin po che'i mdzod*); and the *Precious Treasury of Word and Meaning* (*tshig don rin po che'i mdzod*).
New edition: Beijing: Krung go bod ri pa dpe skrun khang, *dpal brtsegs bod yig dpe rnying* series, 7 vols. (series nos. 118–24), 2009

Three Words That Strike the Key Points
tshig gsum gnad du brdeg pa
An instruction of Prahevajra in the *Vima Nyingtik*, vol. 1 (series no. 106), p. 200–3

Trilogy of Essential Guidance from the Lama Yangtik (revelation)
bla ma yang tig gi don khrid skor gsum
Comprising the *Preliminary Guidance on the Meaning of the Seven-Point Mind Training* (*sngon 'gro sems sbyong bdun gyi don khrid*); the *Main Practice That Is Guidance on the Meaning of the Luminous Essence* (*dngos gzhi 'od gsal snying po'i don khrid*); and the *Guidance on the Meaning of Atemporal Total Presence in Trekchö* (*khregs chod ye babs sor gzhag gi don khrid*)
Contained in the *Lama Yangtik*, vol. 1 (series no. 114), p. 185–228

Trilogy of Natural Liberation
rang grol skor gsum
Comprising *Natural Liberation of the Nature of Mind* (*sems nyid rang grol*); *Natural Liberation of Reality* (*chos nyid rang grol*); and *Natural Liberation of Evenness* (*mnyam nyid rang grol*)
New edition: Beijing: Krung go bod ri pa dpe skrun khang, *dpal brtsegs bod yig dpe rnying* series, 1 vol. (series no. 127), 2009, p. 365–479

Trilogy of Resting
ngal gso skor gsum
Comprising *Resting in the Nature of Mind* (*sems nyid ngal gso*); *Resting in Illusion* (*sgyu ma'i ngal gso*); and *Resting in Concentration* (*bsam gtan ngal gso*)

New edition: Beijing: Krung go bod ri pa dpe skrun khang, *dpal brtsegs bod yig dpe rnying* series, 3 vols. (series nos. 125–26, and 127), 2009, p. 1–364

Trilogy of Whispered-Lineage Instructions from the Lama Yangtik (revelation)
bla ma yang tig gi snyan brgyud skor gsum
Comprising the *Brief Instruction of the Whispered Lineage Entitled Natural Appearance of Wisdom* (*snyan brgyud chung ngu ye shes rang snang*); the *Middling Instruction of the Whispered Lineage Entitled Natural Appearance of Luminosity during the Intermediate State* (*snyan brgyud 'bring po bar do 'od gsal rang snang*); and the *Extensive Instruction of the Whispered Lineage Entitled Direct Natural Appearance of the Ultimate Meaning* (*snyan brgyud chen mo nges don mngon sum rang snang*)
Contained in the *Lama Yangtik*, vol. 2 (series no. 115), p. 194–241

Treasury of Pith Instructions
man ngag mdzod
New edition: Beijing: Krung go bod ri pa dpe skrun khang, *dpal brtsegs bod yig dpe rnying* series, 1 vol. (series no. 120), 2009, p. 337–464
Translated in Barron, *The Precious Treasury of Pith Instructions.*

Treasury of the Supreme Vehicle
theg mchog mdzod
New edition: Beijing: Krung go bod ri pa dpe skrun khang, *dpal brtsegs bod yig dpe rnying* series, 2 vols. (series no. 122–23), 2009

Vima Nyingtik, "Heart Essence of Vimalamitra" (revelation)
bi ma'i snying thig [a.k.a. *Sangwa Nyingtik*]
New edition: Beijing: Krung go bod ri pa dpe skrun khang, *dpal brtsegs bod yig dpe rnying* series, 4 vols. (nos. 106–9), 2009

White Lotus Auto-Commentary on the Precious Treasury of Wish-Fulfilling Gems: A Treatise on the Pith Instructions of the Mahayana
theg pa chen po'i man ngag gi bstan bcos yid bzhin rin po che'i mdzod kyi 'grel pa padma dkar po
In the *Seven Treasuries of Longchenpa* (*klong chen mdzod bdun*)
New edition: Beijing: Krung go bod ri pa dpe skrun khang, *dpal brtsegs bod yig dpe rnying* series, 2 vols. (series nos. 118–19), 2009

Zabmo Yangtik, "Profound Quintessence" (revelation)
zab mo yang tig
New edition: Beijing: Krung go bod ri pa dpe skrun khang, *dpal brtsegs bod yig dpe rnying* series, 2 vols. (nos. 116–17), 2009

Longsel Nyingpo (1625–82)

Collected Revelations and Works in Twelve Volumes
zab gter gsung 'bum
Darjeeling: Kagyud sungrab nyamso khang, 1997

Eight Heruka Sadhanas (revelation)
bka' brgyad drag po bde gshegs yongs 'dus
In *Collected Revelations and Works*, vols. 7–8

Great Compassionate One (revelation)
thugs rje chen po yang gsang bla med
In *Collected Revelations and Works*, vol. 9

Great Glorious Shri Devi's Prosperity Sadhana with Prosperity Pledges and Vows
(revelation)
dpal chen mo'i gyang sgrub gyang gta' sdom pa bcas

Longevity Sadhana: Unexcelled Supreme Secret (revelation)
tshe sgrub yang gsang bla med
In *Collected Revelations and Works*, vol. 2, p. 23–38

Middle-Length Commentary on the Preliminary Practices
sngon 'gro'i khrid 'bring pa [full title: thun mong sngon 'gro'i khrid kyi ngag
'don]
In *Collected Revelations and Works*, vol. 1, p. 185–212
Alternatively, it could refer to *sngon 'gro blo mdog rnam bzhi'i khrid 'khor ba
zhen log ma*, in *Collected Revelations and Works*, vol. 12, p. 243–354

Peaceful and Wrathful Deities (revelation)
[sku gsum] zhi khro
Part of the *Vajra Essence* cycle, in *Collected Revelations and Works*, vol. 1

Red and Black Indestructible Yamari (revelation)
gshin rje king kang dmar nag
In *Collected Revelations and Works*, vol. 2

Red Lion-Faced Dakini (revelation)
seng ha dmar mo
Preserved in the *Collected Works* of Khakhyab Dorje, vol. 6, Paro: Lama Ngodup,
1979–81, p. 403–20

Supplicatory Prayer to the Hundred Thousand Names of the Buddha
sangs rgyas mtshan 'bum gyi gsol 'debs
NL

Unlabelled Cycle
them med skor
In *Collected Revelations and Works,* vol. 5
Note that the contents of this cycle are actually districted throughout the preceding *Labeled Cycle* (*them byang gi skor*)

Vajra Essence (revelation)
rdo rje snying po
In *Collected Revelations and Works,* vol. 1; also *ka thog snyan brgyud khrid chen
bcu gsum skor,* vols. 11–13

Wrathful Guru Blazing Wisdom (revelation)
gur drag ye shes rab 'bar
In *Collected Revelations and Works,* vol. 10, p. 19–316, and vol. 13 (also vol. 5, etc.)

MAJAWA JANGCHUP TSÖNDRÜ (D. 1185)

Commentary on the Fundamental Stanzas of the Madyamaka
rma bya ba'i 'grel [full title: dbu ma rtsa ba shes rab kyi 'grel pa 'thad pa'i rgyan]
Rumtek: Dharma Chakra Center, 1975

MATI RATNA (FL. 16TH CENTURY)

Ten Thousand Reversals of Simhavaktra
ma ti'i seng gdong khri bzlog
Contained in his *mkha' 'gro bdud 'dul drag mo'i sgrub skor,* Byalakuppe: Penor
Rinpoche, 1985

MENLUNGPA MIKYÖ DORJE (FL. 12TH CENTURY)

Commentary on the Guhyagarbha Tantra
gsang snying 'grel pa rgyud don rnam nges
NK, vol. 71, p. 5–499

MOKTSA DRUBTOB OF KATOK (FL. EIGHTEENTH TO NINETEENTH
CENTURIES)

Vajravarahi
rmog grub phag mo
NL

NAMCHÖ MINGYUR DORJE (1645–67)

Collected Revelations of Namchö [*in Thirteen Volumes*] (revelation)
nam chos pod bcu gsum
Paro: Dilgo Khyentsey Rinpoche, 1983

NAMKHA DORJE OF KATOK

Kham Tradition of Prahevajra's Detailed Guidance of the Mind Class
dga' rab rdo rje nas brgyud pa'i rdzogs pa chen po sems sde'i pra khrid khams lugs
NK, vol. 30

NAMKHA GYALTSEN OF PELBAR

Annotated Commentary on Buddhaguhya's Innermost Essence of the Mind
thugs thigs mchan 'grel [full title: man ngag thugs kyi thigs pa'i 'grel bshad nyi
ma'i 'od zer]
NK, vol. 87

NAMKHA PEL OF KATOK

Commentary on the Short Path of the Magical Net
lam chung 'grel [full title: sgyu 'phrul man ngag lam gyi rim pa'i 'grel bshad rin
po che'i chu dvangs]
NK, vol. 85

NAMKHA RINCHEN (FL. 13TH TO 14TH CENTURIES)

Commentary on the Guhyagarbha Tantra
gsang snying 'grel
NK, vols. 72–73

NGARI PANCHEN (1487–1543)

Guru as a Treasure Trove of Qualities
gu ru yon tan gter mdzod
RTD, vol. 11, nos. 1 and 7

Root Verses of the Ascertainment of the Three Vows
sdom gsum rnam nges rtsa ba
NK, vol. 51; also in *gangs ti se shes rig spar khang,* n.p., n.d.

NGAWANG CHÖDRAK (1572–1641)

Commentary on the Complete Analysis of the Three Vows
sdom gsum rab dbye'i 'grel pa [full title: sdom gsum kha skong gi rnam bshad
rgyan gyi me tog]
Beijing: Mi rigs dpe skrun khang, *dpal ldan sa skya pa'i gsung rab* series, vol. 12a,
2004, p. 181–311

NGAWANG PALZANG (A.K.A. KHENPO NGAKCHUNG / ÖSEL RINCHEN
NYINGPO PEMA LEDRELTSEL, 1879–1941)

Attainment of Medicinal Nectar: The Great Secret Swift Path
bdud rtsi sman sgrub gsang chen myur lam
NL

Collected Works [in Nine Volumes]
gsung 'bum
Chengdu 1990s

Commentary on the Buddha Mind of Samantabhadra: A Key to the Mother-and-Child Cycles of the Great Perfection
rdzogs pa chen po [ye shes bla ma'i spyi don snying thig] ma bu'i lde'u mig kun
bzang kyi thugs kyi ti ka
In *Collected Works,* vol. 9, p. 255–800

Definitive Structure of the Commitments: Taking Others as One's Own Child and Taking Oneself as Another's Child
bdag sras gzhan sras dam tshig rnam gzhag
In *Collected Works,* vol. 8, p. 440–76

Explanation of Yogic Inner Heat
snying thig gtum mo'i rnam bshad

Guide to the Valid Cognition of the Prasangika Tradition
thal 'gyur lugs kyi tshad ma'i zin bris
Possibly to be equated with the texts in *Collected Works,* vols. 6–7

A Guide to the Words of My Perfect Teacher
kun bzang bla ma'i zhal lung gi zin bris
Chengdu: Sichuan mi rigs spe skrun khang, 1996
Translated in Ngawang Palzang, *Guide to the Words of My Perfect Teacher*

Heart-Drop of the Dakinis: Guide to the Whispered Lineage of All-Surpassing Realization: Unwritten Pith Instructions That Are the Ornament of the Wisdom Mind of Samantabhadra
thod rgal gyi snyan brgyud kyi zin bris kun tu bzang po'i dgongs rgyan yig med
u pa de sha mkha' 'gro'i thugs kyi ti la ka
In *Collected Works,* vol. 9, p. 161–254

Heart Treasury of the Guru Vidyadharas of the Three Lineages (revelation)
brgyud gsum rig 'dzin bla ma'i thugs mdzod
Possibly a reference to his revelation entitled *brgyud gsum rig 'dzin skong ba
tshangs pa'i dbyangs,* contained in *Collected Works,* vol. 3, p. 365–72

*Light of the Sun: A Commentary on the Inner Writings of Both Trekchö and Tögal
according to the Lama Yangtik*

bla ma yang tig gi gnyis ka'i yang yig gi 'grel pa nyi ma'i snang ba
Possibly including the *gzhi khregs chod skabs kyi zin bris bstan pa'i nyi ma'i zhal lung snyan brgyud chu bo'i bcud 'dus,* contained in *Collected Works,* vol. 9, p. 1–160

Manifold Display of Great Bliss: A Ritual Purification from the Eight Heruka Sadhanas (revelation)
bka' brgyad rgyun khyer las byang bde chen rnam rol
In *Collected Works,* vol. 3, p. 129–46

Manual on Yogic Exercises, according to the Nyingtik
snying thig gi 'khrul 'khor

Notes on the Essential Chapters on the Provisional and Ultimate Meanings
drang nges snying po'i skabs kyi brjed byang
Possibly to be equated with the texts in *Collected Works,* vol. 7

Notes on the Guidance of the Five Stages
rim lnga'i khrid kyi brjed byang [full title: dpal gsang ba 'dus pa'i rdzogs rim rim pa lnag pa'i snyan brgyud klu grub zhal lung]
In *Collected Works,* vol. 8, p. 127–272

Notes on the Kalachakra Tantra
dus 'khor gyi brjed byang
NL

Nubchen: Guru Sadhana
gnubs chen gyi bla sgrub
In *Collected Works,* vol. 3, p. 101–28; also vol. 8, p. 350–84

Offering Liturgy of the Five Great Kings
rgyal chen sku lnga'i gsol mchod
Based on the oral teachings of Dodrub Jigme Trinley Özer
In *Collected Works,* vol. 5, p. 823–24

Praise to Manjughosha
'jam pa'i dbyangs la bstod pa

Sadhana of Achala from the Sixteenfold Nuclei Empowerments of the Kadam Whispered Lineage
snyan brgyud thig le bcu drug las mi gyo ba'i sgrub thabs
In *Collected Works,* vol. 3, p. 153–72

Sadhana of Guru Vidyadhara alongside the Eight Heruka Sadhanas
bka' brgyad bla ma rig 'dzin sgrub pa
In *Collected Works,* vol. 3, p. 1–39

Structural Presentation of the Refutations of Valid Cognition
tshad ma'i ldog pa'i rnam bzhag
In *Collected Works,* vol. 8, p. 55–68

Tantra of the Wheel of Lightning (revelation of Prahevajra)
nam mkha' glog gi 'khor lo'i rgyud
NL

NGEDÖN TENDZIN ZANGPO OF DZOGCHEN (1759–92)

White Path to Liberation: Guidance according to the Khandro Yangtik
mkha' 'gro yang tig gi khrid thar lam dkar po
NL

NUBCHEN SANGYE YESHE (FL. 8TH–9TH CENTURIES)

Lamp for the Eye of Concentration
bsam gtan mig sgron
NK, vol. 104, p. 573–1078

Pearl Garland Empowerment Liturgy for the General Sutra That Gathers All Wisdom Intentions
mu tig phreng ba
NL

NYAKLA PEMA DÜDÜL (1816–72)

Profound Teaching: All-Pervasive Natural Liberation (revelation)
zab chos mkha' khyab rang grol
In *Collected Revelations of nyag bla padma bdud 'dul,* vol. 1 (of 5)

NYANG-REL NYIMA ÖZER (1136–1204)

Black Wrathful Mother Krodhakali (revelation)
khros ma nag mo
RTD, vol. 54

Embodiment of the Sugatas of the Eight Heruka Sadhanas (revelation)
bka' brgyad bde gshegs 'dus pa
Short title: *Eight Heruka Sadhanas*
sgrub pa bka' brgyad
One of the three main revelatory cycles of the *Eight Heruka Sadhanas* (*bka' brgyad rnam gsum*), alongside those of Guru Chöwang and Rigdzin Godemchen
In *bka' brgyad phyogs bsgrigs,* 12 vols., Chengdu: Thubten Nyima, 2000; also Tsamdrak ms. edition in 13 vols., Paro: Lama Ngodup, 1979–80

Fusing the Vitality of the Vidyadharas (revelations)
rig 'dzin srog mthud
RTD, vol. 54, no. 29

Key to the Commands of the Transmitted Teachings
bka' bsgo lde mig
In the *Embodiment of the Sugatas of the Eight Heruka Sadhanas*, vol. 3, p. 471–526

Purging of the Mark of Impending Death (revelation)
bka' brgyad khram phyis
In the *Embodiment of the Sugatas of the Eight Heruka Sadhanas*
NL

Storehouse of Secret Mantra Scriptures
gsang sngags lung gi bang mdzod
In the *Embodiment of the Sugatas of the Eight Heruka Sadhanas*, vol. 3, Chengdu:
Zenkar Rinpoche, 2000, p. 55–152

Wild Cocongrass
[gsang sngags bka'i] tha ram
In the *Embodiment of the Sugatas of the Eight Heruka Sadhanas*, vol. 3, p. 153–332

NYELPA DELEKPEL

Empowerment Liturgy of the Transmitted Teachings Entitled Jewel Rosary
dbang bka' rin po che'i phreng ba
NK, vol. 92

ÖNTRUL RINPOCHE TSULTRIM YÖNTEN GYATSO OF KATOK (FL. 20TH CEN-
TURY)

Annotated Commentary on the Root Sutra of Monastic Discipline
'dul ba mdo rtsa'i mchan 'grel
NL

ORGYEN CHÖDRAK (B. 1676)

Guide to the Ornament of the Lord of Secrets' Wisdom Mind
gsang bdag dgongs rgyan spyi don zin bris
NK, vol. 76

ORGYEN LINGA OF YARJE (CA. 1323–60)

Chronicles of Padma
padma bka' thang
Chengdu: Sichuan mi rigs dpe skrun khang, 1987

ORGYEN TENDZIN NORBU (B. 1851)

Annotated Commentary on Chandrakirti's Auto-Commentary on the Introduction to the Middle Way
zla grags 'jug pa'i rang 'grel gyi mchan 'grel
NL

PADAMPA SANGYE (FL. 11TH CENTURY)

Thirty-Verse Prayer
smon lam sum cu pa
NL

PADMASAMBHAVA

Narrative History Entitled Heap of Precious Gems
gtam rgyud rin chen spungs pa [full title: spyi chos mdo sngags thun mong gi lam rim rin chen spungs pa]
NK, vol. 82, p. 137–72

Secret Commentary on the Sadhana of Vishuddha Heruka
yang dag grub pa'i gsang 'grel
NK, vol. 61

PANCHEN LOBZANG CHÖGYAN (1567–1662)

Aiming at Loving-Kindness
dmigs rtse ma
Preserved in the *Collected Works of Panchen Palden Yeshe,* vol. 5, p. 453–60

Remembrance of Circumstances
[dge slong gi] dus dran [full title: dge slong gi bslab bya sogs nye bar mtho ba 'ga' zhig
In his *Collected Works,* vol. 4, Delhi: Mongolian Lama Gurudeva, 1973, p. 433–58

PATRÜL ORGYEN JIGME CHÖKYI WANGCHUK (1808–87)

Benefits of Reading the Mahayana Sutras
theg chen mdo mthong phan yon
Collected Works, vol. 3, p. 338–72

Calling the Lama from Afar
bla ma rgyang 'bod
Collected Works, vol. 3, p. 94–137

Collected Works [in Eight Volumes]
gsung 'bum
Chengdu: Sichuan mi rigs dpe skrun khang, 2003

Commentarial Explanation of the Ornament of Emergent Realization: Prajnaparamita
shes rab kyi pha rol tu phyin pa mngon rtogs rgyan gyi 'grel bshad / rtsa 'grel
Chengdu: Sichuan mi rigs dpe skrun khang, 1997

Commentary on Difficult Points in Drop of Water in the Ocean
rgya mtsho'i chu thigs kyi dka' 'grel
Collected Works, vol. 4, p. 25–172

Commentary on Difficult Points Entitled Guidance on the Deities of the Generation Stage
bskyed rim lha'i khrid kyi dka' gnad cung zad bshad pa
Collected Works, vol. 4, p. 390–418
Commentary on the Way of the Bodhisattva
byang chub sems dpa'i spyod pa la 'jug pa'i sgom rim rab gsal nyi ma
NK, vol. 48, p. 5–24

Discourse on Virtuous Action in the Beginning, Middle, and End
thog mtha' bar dge'i gtam
Collected Works, vol. 8, p. 127–73

Display of the Three Realms: The Melodious Voice of Brahma
khams gsum rol pa tshangs pa'i sgra dbyangs
Collected Works, vol. 4, p. 419–35

Drumbeat of the Gods: Advice for Retreat
dben gtam lha yi rnga sgra
Collected Works, vol. 1, p. 351–65

Essential Guide to Resting in the Nature of Mind
sems nyid ngal gso'i don khrid
Also entitled: sems nyid ngal gso'i bsdus don padma dkar po'i zil mngar
Collected Works, vol. 3, p. 1–53

Explanation Entitled Profound Pith Instructions of the Object of Severance: Wild Laughter of the Dakinis
gcod yul mkha' 'gro'i gad rgyangs kyi man ngag zab mo
Collected Works, vol. 5, p. 226–43

Guidance on the View of the Middle Way according to the Mahayana
theg chen dbu ma'i lta khrid
Collected Works, vol. 3, p. 293–304

Guide to the Seventeen Foundations of Monastic Discipline
gzhi bcu bdun zin bris
Collected Works, vol. 3, p. 84–104

Overview of the Ornament of Emergent Realization of the Transcendent Perfections
sher phyin mngon rtogs rgyan gyi spyi don
Collected Works, vol. 6

Selected Works of Kadam
bka' gdams gsung gi gces bsdus
NL

Special Qualities of the Learned and Glorious King
mkhas pa sri rgyal po'i khyad chos
A commentary on the *Three Words That Strike the Key Points* (*tshig gsum gnad bsdeg*)
Collected Works, vol. 5, p. 206–25

Stages of Meditation on the Transcendent Perfections
sher phyin sgom rim
Collected Works, vol. 5, p. 450–92

Word-for-Word Commentary on the Ornament of Emergent Realization of the Transcendent Perfections
sher phyin mngon rtogs rgyan a bu'i tshig 'grel
Collected Works, vol. 5, p. 244–418

The Words of My Perfect Teacher
kun bzang bla ma'i zhal lung
Collected Works, vol. 7

PEMA LINGPA (1450–1521)

Vajrakila Razor (revelation)
pad gling spu gri [full title: phur pa yang gsang bla med srog gi spu gri]
Collected Revelations of Pema Lingpa in Twenty-One Volumes, vol. 16, Thimphu: Kunsang Topgay, 1975–76; also in *phur pa phyogs sgrigs*, vol. 10, nos. 29–31

RASHAK SONAM DORJE

Peak Arising of the Matarah (revelation)
ma mo sgang shar
NL. Possibly in RTD (Shechen ed.), vol. KHI (32)

RATNA LINGPA (1403–79)

Answers to Tsogyal's Questions (revelation)
mtsho rgyal zhus lan
Collected Revelations, vol. 3
Translated in Padmasambhava and Jamgön Kongtrül, *Light of Wisdom: Vol. II*

Collected Revelations of Ratna Lingpa [*in Thirteen Volumes*]
ratna gling pa gter chos pod bcu gsum
Republished in 19 vols., Darjeeling: Taklung Tsetrul Pema Wangyal, 1977–79

Great Compassionate One (revelation)
thugs rje chen po [gsang ba 'dus pa]
Collected Revelations, vols. 6–7

Guru Sadhana (revelation)
bla sgrub [see: thugs sgrub yang snying 'dus pa'i skor]
Collected Revelations, vol. 3

Longevity Sadhana (revelation)
tshe sgrub [gsang ba 'dus pa]
Collected Revelations, vol. 13

Longsel Nyingtik, "Heart Essence of the Clear Expanse" (revelation)
klong gsal snying thig
Collected Revelations, vols. 11–12

Vajrakila: The Unsurpassedly Supreme Secret (revelation)
phur pa yang gsang bla med
Collected Revelations, vol. 10; also in *phur pa phyogs sgrigs,* vol. 16

RIGDZIN GODEMCHEN NGÖDRUB GYALTSEN (1337–1409)

Collected Revelations of the Northern Treasures [*in Six Volumes*]
byang gter pod drug
Extant in the Potala ms. edition (10 vols.)

Essential Guidance of the Sky-Faced One
gnam zhal don khrid [full title: sgrub chen bka' brgyad rang byung rang shar gyi
snying po gnam zhal 'don khrid]
In *Naturally Arising Wrathful Deities of the Eight Heruka Sadhanas;* also in
RTD (Shechen ed.), vol. 15, p. 303–34

Five Nails (revelation)
[byang gter sngon 'gro] zer lnga
RTD (Shechen ed.), vol. 12, p. 39–56; also in *thugs sgrub drag po rtsal gyi chos skor,*
vol. 3, Gangtok: Bari Longsal Lama, 1980, p. 429–46

Naturally Arising Wrathful Deities of the Eight Heruka Sadhanas (revelation)
bka' brgyad drag po rang byung rang shar
One of the three main revelatory cycles of the *Eight Heruka Sadhanas* (*bka' brgyad rnam gsum*), alongside those of Guru Chöwang and Nyang-rel Nyima Özer
In *bka' brgyad phyogs bsgrigs,* 4 vols. Chengdu: Thubten Nyima, 2000

Showering Blessings on Great Sacred Places
gnas chen byin 'bebs rab gnas
In *thugs sgrub drag po rtsal gyi chos skor,* vol. 2, Gangtok: Bari Longsal Lama, 1980, p. 17–24

Unimpeded Realization of the Great Perfection (revelation)
rdzogs pa chen po dgongs pa zang thal
5 vols., Simla: Thub bstan rdo rje brag e wam chos sgar, 2000

Vajrakila Razor according to the Northern Treasures (revelation)
byang gter spu gri [full title: dpal rdo rje phur pa spu gri nag po rab tu gsang ba'i rgyud]
One of the three main Vajrakila Razor revelations (spu gri rnam gsum), alongside those of Guru Chöwang and Pema Lingpa
In *phur pa phyogs sgrigs,* vols. 12–14, especially vol. 13 (no. 15), p. 135–58

RIGDZIN JIGME LINGPA (1730–98)

Billionfold Mandala Offering (revelation)
[klong snying gi] stong chen gyi mandala
In *Preliminary Practices of the Longchen Nyingtik*

Collected Works and Revelations [*in Nine Volumes*]
'jigs gling pod dgu
Derge xylograph edition; also 12 vols. in *a 'dzom par ma* edition

Coming of Age of the Six Transcendental Perfections: An Explanation on the Object of Severance: Wild Laughter of the Dakinis (revelation)
gcod yul mkha' 'gro'i gad rgyangs kyi bshad pa phyin drug lang tsho
Collected Works (*a 'dzoms par ma*), vol. 12, p. 57–62

Consorts Mahakala and Shri Devi (revelation)
[bka' srung] ma mgon lcam dral
In *Collected Works and Revelations,* vol. 8 (BE), p. 155–72ff.

Continuation Tantra Entitled Experiencing the Wisdom Mind of Samantabhadra (revelation)
rgyud phyi ma lung kun tu bzang po'i dgongs nyams
In *Collected Works and Revelations,* vol. 8 (ZU), p. 377–84ff.

Great Compassionate One: Natural Liberation of Suffering (revelation)
[gsang sgrub] thugs rje chen pos dug bsngal rang grol
In *Collected Works and Revelations,* vol. 7 (THI–THE), p. 811–36ff.

Great Display Torma Exorcism (revelation)
rol pa chen po'i gtor bzlog
In *Collected Works and Revelations,* vol. 11 (TSO), p. 5–86

Guidance on the Uncommon Preliminaries according to the Longchen Nyingtik Entitled Foundations of Mindfulness (revelation)
[rdzogs pa chen po] klong chen snying thig gi thun mong ma yin pa'i sngon 'gro'i khrid yig dran pa nyer bzhag
In *Collected Works and Revelations*, vol. 12, p. 241–72

[Guru] Embodiment of Vidyadharas (revelation)
[bla ma / nang grub] rig 'dzin 'dus pa
In *Collected Works and Revelations*, vol. 7 (DA), 175–84ff.

Guru Sadhana Sealed with a Vital Nucleus (revelation)
[yang gsang] bla sgrub thig le rgya can
In *Collected Works and Revelations*, vol. 8 (DE), 1–4ff.

Guru Yoga of the Longchen Nyingtik (revelation)
klong chen snying thig gi bla ma'i rnal 'byor [full title: phyi sgrub bla ma'i rnal 'byor yid bzhin nor bu]
In *Collected Works and Revelations*, vol. 7 (JA), 111–18ff.

Instruction on the Channels and Energies (revelation)
klong snying rtsa lung [rig 'dzin 'khrul 'khor sbas don gsal ba]
In *Collected Works and Revelations*, vol. 8 (VO), 323–34ff.

Lion's Roar That Cuts through Errors and Deviations (revelation)
[snying thig sgom pa'i bya bral gyi] gol shor tshar gcod senge'i nga ro
In *Collected Works and Revelations*, vol. 8 (YE), 681–92ff.

Longchen Nyingtik: Heart Essence of Longchenpa (revelation) (alternatively translated as *Heart Essence of the Vast Expanse*)
klong chen snying thig
In *Collected Works and Revelations*, vols. 7–8

Longevity Sadhana: A Drink from the Vase of Immortality (revelation)
tshe sgrub bdud rtsi'i bum bcud [full title: rig 'dzin tshe sgrub bdud rtsi bum bcud]
In *Collected Works and Revelations*, vol. 10 (THA), p. 227–34

Naked Perception of the Abiding Nature (revelation)
[rdzogs chen] gnas lugs cer mthong
In *Collected Works and Revelations*, vol. 8 (YO), 693–98ff.

Object of Severance: Wild Laughter of the Dakinis (revelation)
gcod yul mkha' 'gro'i gad rgyangs
In *Collected Works and Revelations*, vol. 8 (ZHU), 337–48ff.

Oral Transmission of Great Glorious Heruka (revelation)
[yo ga gsum gyi spyi chings] dpal chen zhal lung
In *Collected Works and Revelations*, vol. 7 (NGO), 471–78ff.

Ornament of Nagendra's Wisdom Mind
[sgrol ma mandal bzhi pa'cho ga] klu dbang dgongs rgyan
In *Collected Works and Revelations;* also NK, vol. 4, p. 5–40

Path of the Wish-Fulfilling Jewel: A Scroll of the Whispered Lineage
snyan brgyud shog dril yid bzhin nor bu'i lam
In *Collected Works and Revelations,* vol. 8 (VE), 315–22ff.

Practical Application of Guidance [*on the Common Preliminaries according to the Longchen Nyingtik*] (revelation)
[rdzogs chen snying thig gi thun mong sngon 'gro'i] khrid kyi lag len 'debs lugs
In *Collected Works and Revelations,* vol. 12 ('O), p. 209–40

Precious Treasury of Qualities
yon tan rin po che'i mdzod [dga' ba'i char]
In *Collected Works and Revelations,* vol. 1, 1–102ff.
Auto-commentary in vols. 1–2

Preliminary Practices of the Longchen Nyingtik (revelation)
snying thig gi sngon 'gro
In *Collected Works and Revelations,* vol. 8 (ZO), 389–466ff.

Reversing the Reception Party of the Dakinis (revelation)
mkha' 'gro'i sun bzlog [full title: yum ka mkha' 'gro bde chen rgyal mo las mkha' 'gro'i bsun zlog ngo mtshar snang ba]
Collected Works and Revelations, vol. 7 (SHA), 7ff.

[*Sadhana of Buddha Mind*]: *Embodiment of the Great Glorious Wrathful Heruka* (revelation)
[rig 'dzin thugs sgrub drag po] dpal chen 'dus pa
In *Collected Works and Revelations,* vol. 7 (CI–CE), 481–512ff.

Staircase to Akanishta (revelation)
don 'grel [bskyed rim rnam gzhag] 'og min bsgrod pa'i them skas
In *Collected Works and Revelations,* vol. 7 (TU), p. 713–48

Staircase to Liberation: Seven Mind Trainings in the Longchen Nyingtik (revelation)
klong snying sems sbyong bdun pa [full title: sems sbyong rnam bdun gyi don khrid thar pa'i them skas]
In *Collected Works and Revelations,* vol. 12 ('O), p. 103–208

Tantra of the Wisdom Expanse (revelation)
[klong chen snying thig gi] ye shes klong gi rgyud
In *Collected Works and Revelations,* vol. 8 (ZHO), p. 355–68

Thread-Cross of Mahakali and Mahakala That Averts Worldly Battles (revelation)
ma mgon gyul mdos [kyi bca' gzhi]
vol. 11 (a dzom par ma), p. 611–16
In *Collected Works and Revelations,* vol. 11 (TSO), p. 611–16

Transmitted Teachings of the Father (revelation)
yab bka'
See *Guru Embodiment of Vidyadharas*

Transmitted Teachings of the Mother: Queen of Great Bliss (revelation)
yum ka / bka' bde chen rgyal mo
In *Collected Works and Revelations*, vol. 7 (TSA–GU), p. 217ff., and especially
vol. RA, p. 271–86

Vajrakila according to the Tantra Tradition
phur pa rgyud lugs
In *Collected Works and Revelations*, vol. 6; also in *phur pa phyogs sgrigs*, vol. 8

Vajrakila: Subjugator of the Hordes of Demons (revelation)
phur ba bdud dpung zil gnon
In *Collected Works and Revelations*, vol. 7 (CHE), p. 535–48ff.

Wrathful Guru with the Fiery Hayagriva and Garuda (revelation)
[bla ma] drag po rta khyung 'bar ba
In *Collected Works and Revelations*, vol. 8 (DO–NU), p. 5–26ff.

Wondrous Ocean of Advice on Mountain Retreat (revelation)
ri chos zhal gdams ngo mtshar rgya mtsho
In *Collected Works and Revelations*, vol. 8 (RI), p. 699–708ff.

Words of the Omniscient One (revelation)
kun mkhyen zhal lung [bdud rtsi'i thigs pa]
In *Collected Works and Revelations*, vol. 8 (YU), p. 663–80ff.

Yeshe Lama (revelation)
[gdod ma'i mgon po'i lam gyi rim pa'i khrid yig] ye shes bla ma
In *Collected Works and Revelations*, vol. 8 ('E), p. 519–618ff.

RINCHEN LINGPA (FL. 19TH–20TH CENTURIES)

Black Manjushri: Lord of Life (revelation)
'jam dpal tshe bdag
NL

Peaceful and Wrathful Manjushri
'jam dpal zhi drag
NL

Variegated Vajra Garuda (revelation)
rdo rje khyung khra
NL

Yama Dharmaraja (revelation)
gshin rje chos rgyal
NL

ROK SHERAB Ö (1166–1244)

Vajrakila according to the Rok Tradition
rog lugs phur pa ['i gzhung pod phrin las rol pa'i bang mdzod]
NK, vol. 11

RONGTÖN SHEJA KUNRIG (1367–1449)

Collected Works
10 vols., Jyekundo: Gangs ljongs rig rgyan gsung rab par khang, 2004

Commentaries on the Two Distinctions
'byed rnam gnyis rong ston ti ka
Comprising *dbus mtha' rnam 'byed rnam bshad and chos dang chos nyid rnam 'byed rnam bshad, Collected Works*, vol. 7, p. 537–654

Commentary on the Prajnaparamita
sher phyin [stong phrag brgya pa'i] rnam 'grel
Collected Works, vols. 4–5

Meditation Stages in the Exposition of Valid Cognition
tshad ma [rnam 'grel gyi] sgom rim
Collected Works, vol. 1, p. 144–49

Meditation Stages in the Five Treatises of Maitreya
byams chos sde lnga'i sgom rim
Three texts, *Collected Works*, vol. 1, p. 98–107

RONGZOMPA CHÖKYI ZANGPO (FL. 11TH CENTURY)

Collected Works
rong zom chos bzang gig sung 'bum
2 vols., Chengdu: Sichuan mi rigs dpe skrun khang, 1999

Establishing Appearances as Divine
snang ba lhar sgrub
Collected Works, vol. 1, p. 557–68; also NK, vol. 78

Introduction to the Mahayana Way
theg chen tshul la 'jug pa
Collected Works, vol. 1, p. 415–555; also NK, vol. 78

Rare and Precious Commentary on the Guhyagarbha Tantra
dkon mchog 'grel
Collected Works, vol. 1, p. 31–250; also NK, vol. 67

Sakya Pandita Kunga Gyaltsen (1182–1251)

Analysis of the Three Vows
sdom gsum rab dbye
In *dpal ldan sa skya'i gsung rabs,* vol. 12a, p. 1–127

Treasure of Valid Logical Reasoning
[tshad ma] rigs gter
In *Collected Works of Sapen Kunga Gyaltsen* (*gangs can rig mdzod*), vol. 24, p. 1–53; with auto-commentary, Lhasa: Bod ljongs bod yig dpe rnying dpe skrun khang, 1992, p. 55–538. Other versions include SK, vol. 5, no. 1, 1968; Lhasa: Bod ljongs mi dmangs dpe skrun khang, 1989; Beijing: Mi rigs dpe skrun khang, 1989; and Sichuan: Mi rigs dpe skrun khang, 1995.

Sangye Gyatso (1653–1705)

Blue Beryl Treatise on Medicine [*Clarifying the Four Tantras That Are the Wisdom Mind of Bhaishajyaguru*]
[gso ba rig pa'i bstan bcos sman bla'i dgongs rgyan rgyud bzhi'i gsal byed] baidurya sngon po'i mallika
2 vols., Lhasa: Bod ljongs mi dmangs dpe skrun khang, 1982. Illustrated extracts translated in Parfianovitch, Dorje, and Meyer, *Tibetan Medical Paintings,*.

Sealed Supplement of the Pith Instructional Tantra
man ngag bka' rgya lhan thabs
In *man ngag lhan thabs dang lde mig,* Beijing: Mi rigs dpe skrun khang (Bod kyi gso ba rig pa'i gna' dpe phyogs bsgrigs dpe tshogs, series no. 14), 2005

Sangye Lingpa (1340–96)

Beautiful Flower Garland Ritual Sadhana (revelation)
las byang me tog phreng mdzes [full title: phrin las lam khyer bsdus pa me tog phreng mdzes]
In *bla ma dgongs 'dus,* vol. 1, p. 479–516; also in *bla ma dgonsg 'dus las byang me tog phreng mdzes kyi mngon rtogs cug zad spros pa dang nyer mkho'i zur 'debs nyung ngu rin chen snying po'i ze'u 'bru,* Paro: Lama Ngödrup, 1979–81; and RTD, vol. 9, p. 387–416.

Embodiment of the Master's Realization [*in Thirteen Volumes*] (revelation)
bla ma dgongs 'dus
Gangtok: Sonam Topgay Kazi, 1972; later republished at Thimphu in 18 vols.

Longevity Sadhana: Sealed with the Sun and Moon (revelation)
tshe sgrub nyi zla [kha sbyor] rgya can
RTD, vol. 29, p. 337–81

Mind Quintessence of the Kila Sadhana (revelation)
phur sgrub thugs kyi nying khu
RTD, vol. 49, p. 363–501; also in *phur pa phyogs bsgrigs,* vol. 10, p. 235–40

Sunset Heat
las byang tsha ba dmar thag
In *bla ma dgongs 'dus,* vol. 10, p. 1–76

Tantra of the Sole Heir to the Buddhas (revelation)
sangs rgyas [thams cad kyi] sras gcig gi rgyud
DgNGB, vol. PHA (13), 159b–168a*ff.*

SAZANG MATI PANCHEN (1294–1376)

Commentary on the Compendium of Abhidharma
mngon pa kun btus kyi 'grel pa
2 vols., Beijing: Mi rigs dpe skrun khang, 2007

SHAKYA CHOKDEN OF ZILUNG (1428–1507)

Golden Lancet of Questions and Answers
dris lan gser thur
Collected Works of Gser-mdog Pan-chen, vol. 6, Thimphu: Kunzang Topgey, 1975

SHAKYA DORJE (GREAT ABBOT OF KATOK)

Commentary on Difficult Points in the Explanation That Binds All the Vehicles
theg pa spyi chings kyi dka' 'grel [full title: theg pa mtha' thams cad kyi on gsal
bar ston pa'i chos gyi gter mdzod chen po kun 'dus rig pa'i sgron me]
NK, vol. 57

SHERAB ÖZER (1518–84)

Vital Nucleus of Liberation
grol thig [dgongs pa rang grol]
2 vols.
RTD, vol. 3, p. 647–96 passim

SHENPEN CHÖKYI NANGWA (A.K.A. KHENPO SHENGA, 1871–1927)

Annotated Sutra on the Vows of Individual Liberation
sor mdo mchan 'grel / can
Collected Works, vol. 2, Chengdu: Sichuan mi rigs dpe skrun khang, 2006, p.
1–128; also Byalakuppe: Ngagyur Nyingma Institute, 2002

Commentary on the Introduction to the Middle Way
dbu ma 'jug pa'i 'grel [mchan legs bshad zla ba'i 'od zer]
Collected Works, vol. 8, Chengdu: Sichuan mi rigs dpe skrun khang, 2006

SITU CHÖKYI GYATSO (1880–1926)

*Concise Summary of Jamgön Mipam's Ashoka Tree, Entitled Pebble Commentary on
the Root Tantra*
ljong shing stong thun
NL

Concise Summary of Jamgön Mipam's Sword of Insight
ral gri'i stong thun
NL

Concise Summary of Jamgön Mipam's Venomous Snake
dug sbrul gyi stong thun
NL

SITU CHÖKYI JUNGNEY (1700–74)

Collected Works of Situ Chökyi Jungney
si tu chos kyi 'byung gnas kyi gsung 'bum
14 vols., Sansal, Kangra: Sungrab Nyamso Khang, 1990

*Great Commentary on Grammar and Spelling Entitled Beautiful Pearl Garland, a
Necklace of the Learned*
sum rtags 'grel chen mkhas pa'i mgul rgyan mu tig phreng mdzes
In *Collected Works of Situ Chökyi Jungney*, vol. 6 (CHA), no. 3, p. 86

TAKSHAMPA NÜDEN DORJE (B. 1655)

Chronicles of Tsogyal (revelation)
mtsho rgyal bka' thang [full title: mkhar chen bza' mkha' 'gro ye shes mtsho
rgyal gyi rnam thar]
In *bka' thang dri ma med pa'i rgyan*, Lhasa: Bod ljongs mi rigs dpe skrun khang,
2006
Translated in Changchub and Nyingpo, *Lady of the Lotus-Born*; Dowman, *Sky
Dancer*; and Nyingpo, *Mother of Knowledge*

TEKCHEN DRODÖN THARCHIN (A.K.A. GARWANG LERABTSEL, FL. 18TH
CENTURY)

Banishing King Spirits through the Wrathful Guru (revelation)
gur drag rgyal rdzongs
Contained in his *bla ma thugs sgrub yon tan kun 'byung las rgyal rdzong bskrad
pa'i 'khor lo*, Potala Archive ms. collection, no. 01373

TERDAK LINGPA (1646–1714)

Collected Revelations of Minling Terchen in Six Volumes (revelations)
smin gter pod drug
Potala Archive has extant ms. version in 5 vols.; also *Collected Works* in 16 vols.,
Dehra Dun: Khocchen Tulku, 1998

Excellent Wish-Fulfilling Vase
'dod 'jo bum bzang
Delhi: B. Jamyang Norbu, 1972–73; also Gangtok: Sherab Gyaltsen, 1977

Inspection of the Wishing Cow of Excellent Virtue
[rten gsum rab gnas] dge legs 'dod 'jo dngos lta
In his *Collected Works,* vol. 16, p. 337–402; also in Dudjom Rinpoche's *bka' ma,*
vol. 21, p. 61–124

Vajrasattva according to the Mindroling Tradition (revelation)
smin gling rdor sems
Collected Works, vol. 7; also RTD, vol. 3, p. 231–566

TOKDEN LHAKSAM TENPEI GYALTSEN OF PALPUNG (B. 19TH CENTURY)

Commentary on the Sword of Insight That Thoroughly Ascertains Reality
don rnam par nges pa shes rab ral gri'i 'grel pa
Byalakuppe: Penor Rinpoche, 1984

Guide to the Sword That Cuts Through Doubts about Symbolism
brda shan 'byed the tshom gcod pa'i ral gri'i zin bris
NL, but there is an annotated commentary (*mchan 'grel*): Byalakuppe: Namdroling Monastic Jr. High School, 1997

TOKMEY ZANGPO (1295–1369)

Commentary on the Way of the Bodhisattva
spyod 'jug thogs 'grel [legs par bshad pa'i rgya mtsho]
Lhasa: Bod ljongs mi dmangs dpe skrun khang, 2008

TRULSHIK WANGDRAK GYATSO (FL. 17TH CENTURY, D. 1640?)

Miscellaneous Writings
gsung 'thor bu
See his *Collected Works,* Byalakuppe: Penor Rinpoche, 1984

TSANGTÖNPA DORJE GYALTSEN (1126–1216)

Annotated Commentary on the Propensity for the Commitments
dam tshig phra rgyas kyi mchan 'grel
NK, vol. 89

Commentary on the Lamp for the Eye of Concentration
bsam gtan mig sgron khrid
Perhaps this refers to his *rdzogs pa chen po sa gcig pa'i 'grel pa don gsal nyi ma* or
his *rdzogs pa chen po'i gal gnad* (both in NK, vol. 103)

TSONAWA SHERAB ZANGPO (FL. 13TH CENTURY)

Ocean Commentary on Monastic Discipline
'dul ba mtsho tik [full title: 'dul ba mdo rtsa'i 'grel pa legs bshad nyi ma'i 'od zer]
Beijing: Krung g'i bod kyi shes rig rig dpe skrun khang, 1993

TSONGKHAPA LOBZANG DRAKPA (1357–1419)

Collected Works
18 vols., Tashilhunpo edition (*dpe rnying*), Dharamsala: Sherig Parkhang, 1997

Commentary on the Insight Chapter
shes tik [full title: spyod 'jug shes rab le'u tika blo gsal ba]
Collected Works, vol. 16, p. 807–80

Commentary on the Introduction to the Middle Way
'jug tik [full title: dbu ma 'jug pa'i rnam bshad dgongs pa rab gsal]
Collected Works, vol. 16, p. 3–578

Extensive and Concise Stages of the Path to Enlightenment
byang chub lam rim che chung
Comprising the *Great Treatise on the Stages of the Path* (*Collected Works,* vol.
13) and the *Lesser Treatise on the Stages of the Path* (*Collected Works,* vol. 14, p.
3–440)

Golden Rosary of Eloquence
[mngon rtogs rgyan 'grel] legs bzhad gser phreng
Collected Works, vol. 17, and vol. 18, p. 3–578; also Ziling: Qinghai mi rigs dpe
skrun khang, 1986

Great Treatise on the Stages of the Path
lam rim chen mo
Collected Works, vol. 13; also Ziling: Qinghai mi rigs dpe skrun khang, 1985

Guidance on the Five Stages
rim lnga'i khrid [full title: gsang 'dus rdzogs rim rim lnga gdan rdzogs kyi dmar
khrid]
Collected Works, vol. 8, p. 201–342

Ocean of Reasoning [*: A Commentary on the Fundamental Stanzas of the Middle Way*]
[dbu ma rtsa ba'i tshig le'ur byas pa shes rab ces bya ba'i rnam bshad] rigs pa'i
rgya mtsho
Collected Works, vol. 15, p. 3–568

Precepts for Fully Ordained Monks and Novices Entitled Soaring the Vaults of the Heavens
dge tshul slong gi bslab bya gnam rtsed lding ma
Collected Works, vol. 1, p. 753–936

Stages of the Path of the Secret Mantra
gsang sngags lam rim
Collected Works, vol. 3; also Ziling: Qinghai mi rigs dpe skrun khang, 1995

YAGTÖN SANGYEPEL (1350–1414)

Commentary on the Prajnaparamita
sher phyin [mngon rtogs rgyan gyi] gyag 'grel
Delhi: Ngawang Topgyay, 1973

YESHE GYALTSEN PUBORWA OF KATOK (B. 1395)

Commentary on the Explanation That Binds All the Vehicles Entitled Rays of the Sun
theg pa spyi chings kyi 'grel pa [nyi ma 'od zer]
NK, vol. 58

Ocean of Mahamudra Pith Instructions
phyag chen man ngag rgya mtsho
In *ka thog snyan brgyud khrid chen bcu gsum,* vol. 1, p. 651–62

YESHE TSOGYAL (FL. 8TH–9TH CENTURIES)

Collection of Clear Vajrakilaya Commentaries
phur tik 'bum nag
NK, vol. 12; also *phur pa phyogs bsgrigs,* vol. 5, p. 1–344

YUNGTÖN DORJEPEL (1284–1365)

Ornate Flower Commentary on the Guhyagarbha Tantra
gyung tik rgyan gyi me tog
NK, vol. 70

ZURMO GENDÜN BUM (FL. 14TH CENTURY)

Commentary on the Guhyagarbha Tantra
gsang snying 'grel
NL

REFERENCE BIBLIOGRAPHY

Allione, Tsultrim. *Women of Wisdom.* London: Routledge, 1984.

Anacker, Stefan. *Seven Works of Vasubandhu.* Delhi: Motilal Banarsidass, 1984.

Anon. *Gsang chen snga 'gyur ba'i bka' gter zhal 'don phyogs bsgrigs.* Qinghai: mTsho lho dge 'os slob grva'i par khang, 1998.

Batchelor, Stephen. *A Guide to the Bodhisattva's Way of Life.* Dharamsala: Library of Tibetan Works and Archives, 1979.

———. *Verses from the Center: A Buddhist Vision of the Sublime.* New York: Riverhead Books, 2000.

Baumer, Christoph. *Bon: Tibet's Ancient Religion.* Trumbell, Conn: Weatherhill, 2002.

Beer, Robert. *The Encyclopedia of Tibetan Symbols and Motifs.* Boston: Shambhala, 1999.

———. *The Handbook of Tibetan Buddhist Symbols.* Boston: Shambhala, 2003.

Blumenthal, James. *The Ornament of the Middle Way: A Study of the Madhyamaka Thought of Śāntarakṣita.* Ithaca, N.Y.: Snow Lion, 2004.

Boin-Webb, Sara. *Abhidharmasamuccaya: The Compendium of the Higher Teaching (Philosophy).* (English translation of the French). Fremont, Calif.: Asian Humanities Press, 2001.

Boord, Martin J. *A Bolt of Lightning from the Blue: The Vast Commentary on Vajrakila That Clearly Defines the Essential Points.* Ithaca, N.Y.: Snow Lion, 2002.

Brown, Daniel P. and Robert A. F. Thurman. *Pointing Out the Great Way: The Stages of Meditation in the Mahamudra Tradition.* Boston: Wisdom, 2006.

Bryant, Barry. *The Wheel of Time Sand Mandala: Visual Scripture of Tibetan Buddhism.* Ithaca, N.Y.: Snow Lion, 2002.

Chandrakirti and Jamgön Mipam. *Introduction to the Middle Way: Chandrakirti's Madhyamakavatara with Commentary by Ju Mipam.* Translated by the Padmakara Translation Group. Boston: Shambhala, 2005.

Chaudhuri, Nagendra N. *Studies in the Apabhramsa Texts of the Dakarnava.* Calcutta: Metropolitan Printing and Publishing House, 1935.

Cook, Francis H. *Three Texts on Consciousness Only.* Berkeley: Numata Center for Buddhist Translation and Research, 1999.

Conze, Edward, trans. *Abhisamayalamkara*. Rome: Is. M.E.O., 1954.
———. *Buddhist Thought in India: Three Phases of Buddhist Philosophy*. London: Allen &Unwin, 1983.
———, trans. *The Perfection of Wisdom in Eight Thousand Lines and Its Verse Summary*. Columbia, Mo.: South Asia Books, 1973
Crosby, Kate and Andrew Skilton. *The Bodhicaryāvatāra*. Oxford: Oxford University Press, 1996.
Davidson, Ronald M. "The Litany of Names of Manjushri." *Tantric and Taoist Studies in Honour of R. A.Stein* vol. 1. Edited by Michel Strickmann. Institut Belge Des Hautes Etudes Chinoises, 1981.
de Nebesky-Wojkowitz, René. *Oracles and Demons of Tibet: The Cult and Iconography of the Tibetan Protective Deities*. Graz: Akademische Druck-u. Verlagsanstalt, 1975. Reprint of 1956 edition.
Dharmachakra Translation Committee, trans. *Middle Beyond Extremes: Maitreya's Madhyantavibhaga with Commentaries by Khenpo Shenga and Ju Mipham*. Ithaca, N.Y.: Snow Lion, 2006.
Dilgo Khyentse. *Brilliant Moon: The Autobiography of Dilgo Khyentse*. Translated by Ani Jinpa Palmo. Boston: Shambhala, 2008.
———. *The Wish-Fulfilling Jewel: The Practice of Guru Yoga according to the Longchen Nyingthig Tradition*. Translated by the Padmakara Translation Group. Boston: Shambhala, 1988.
Doctor, Thomas H., trans. *Speech of Delight: Mipham's Commentary of Shantarakshita's Ornament of the Middle Way*. By Jamgon Mipham. Ithaca: Snow Lion Publications, 2004.
Dorje, Gyurme. "The Guhyagarbhatantra and Its XIVth Century Commentary Phyogs-bcu mun-sel." 3 vols. PhD Diss., University of London, 1987.
———. *Tibetan Elemental Divination Paintings: Illuminated Manuscript from the White Beryl of Sangs-Rgyas Rgya-Mtsho*. London: Eskenazi & Fogg, 2001.
Dorje, Gyurme, Graham Coleman, and Thupten Jinpa, trans. *The Tibetan Book of the Dead: First Complete English Translation*. London: Penguin Classics, 2005.
Dorje, Gyurme, Tashi Tsering, Heather Stoddard, and André Alexander. *Jokhang: Tibet's Most Sacred Buddhist Temple*. London: Hansjorg Mayer, 2010.
Dowman, Keith. *Masters of Mahamudra: Songs and Histories of the Eighty-Four Buddhist Siddhas*. Albany: State University of New York Press, 1986.
———. *Sky Dancer: The Secret Life and Songs of the Lady Yeshe Tsogyal*. New York: Viking, 1984.
Dreyfus, Georges B. J. *Recognizing Reality: Dharmakirti's Philosophy and Its Tibetan Interpretations*. Albany: State University of New York Press, 1997.
Drigung Kyapgön Chetsang. *The Practice of Mahamudra*. Ithaca, N.Y.: Snow Lion, 2009.
Duckworth, Douglas. *Mipam on Buddha-Nature: The Ground of the Nyingma Tradition*. Albany: State University of New York Press, 2008.

———. *Jamgon Mipam: His Life and Teachings.* Boston: Shambhala, 2011.

Dudjom Rinpoche. *The Nyingma School of Tibetan Buddhism: Its Fundamentals and History.* Translated by Gyurme Dorje and Matthew Kapstein. Boston: Wisdom Publications. 1st ed. (2 vols.), 1991; 2nd ed. (1 vol.), 2002. Citations refer to the first edition.

Duff, Lotsawa Tony. *Gampopa's Mahamudra: The Five Part Mahamudra of the Kagyus.* Portland, Ore.: Padma Karpo Translation Committee, 2008.

Dungkar Lonzang Trinle. *Dung dkar tshig mdzod chen mo.* Beijing: Krung go bod rig pa dpe skrun khang, 2002.

Dunne, John D. *Foundations of Dharmakirti's Philosophy.* Boston: Wisdom, 2004.

Fremantle, F. *A Critical Study of the Guhyasamaja Tantra* (PhD thesis). University of London, 1971.

Frye, Stanley, trans. *A Drop of Nourishment for People, and Its Commentary, The Jewel Ornament.* By Nagarjuna. Dharamsala: Library of Tibetan Works and Archives, 1981.

Fuchs, Rosmarie. *Buddha Nature.* Ithaca, New York: Snow Lion, 2000.

Garfield, Jay L. *The Fundamental Wisdom of the Middle Way: Nagarjuna's Mulamadhyamakakarika.* Oxford: Oxford University Press, 1995.

Gö Lotsawa. *The Blue Annals by Gö Lotsawa.* Translated by George de Roerich and Gedün Choepel. Calcutta: Royal Asiatic Society of Bengal, 1949. Reprinted by Delhi: Motilal Banarsidass, 1976 and 1979.

Gruschke, Andreas. *The Cultural Monuments of Tibet's Outer Provinces: Kham.* 2 vols. Bangkok: White Lotus Press, 2004.

Gyalwa Changchub and Namkhai Nyingpo. *Lady of the Lotus-Born: The Life and Enlightenment of Yeshe Tsogyal.* Translated by the Padmakara Translation Group. Boston: Shambhala, 2002.

Gyatso, Janet. *Apparitions of the Self: The Secret Autobiographies of a Tibetan Visionary.* Princeton, N.J.: Princeton University Press, 1998.

His Holiness the Dalai Lama. *Kalachakra Tantra: Rite of Initiation.* Translated by Jeffrey Hopkins. Boston: Wisdom, 1985.

Holmes, Ken and Katia, trans. *The Changeless Nature (Uttaratantra).* Newcastle, UK: Karma KagyuTrust, 1985.

Huntington, C. W., Jr. with Geshe Namgyal Wangchen. *The Emptiness of Emptiness: An Introduction to Early Indian Madhyamika.* Honolulu: University of Hawai'i Press, 1989.

Ichigo, Masamichi, ed. *Madhyamakālaṁkāra of Śāntarakṣita with his own commentary of Vritti and with the subcommentary of Panjika of Kamalasila.* Kyoto: Bruneido, 1985.

Inada, Kenneth K., trans. and ed. *Nagarjuna: A Translation of His Mulamadhyamakakarika.* Tokyo: The Hokuseido Press, 1970.

Jamgön Kongtrül, *The Treasury of Knowledge.* 10 vols. Ithaca, N.Y.: Snow Lion, 1995–2012.

Jamgön Kongtrül. *The Treasury of Knowledge: Buddhism's Journey to Tibet.* (Books 2, 3, and 4.) Translated by Ngawang Zangpo. Ithaca, N.Y.: Snow Lion, 2010.

———. *The Treasury of Knowledge: Indo-Tibetan Classical Learning & Buddhist Phenomenology.* (Book 6, parts 1 and 2.) Translated by Gyurme Dorje. Ithaca, N.Y.: Snow Lion, 2013.

———. *The Treasury of Knowledge: Frameworks of Buddhist Philosophy.* (Book 6, part 3.) Translated by Elizabeth M. Callahan. Ithaca, N.Y.: Snow Lion, 2007.

Jamgön Mipham. *Luminous Essence: A Guide to the Guhyagarbha Tantra.* Translated by the Dharmachakra Translation Committee. Ithaca, N.Y.: Snow Lion, 2009.

———. *White Lotus: An Explanation of the Seven-Line Prayer to Guru Padmasambhava.* Translated by the Padmakara Translation Group. Boston: Shambhala, 2007.

Jamspal, L. et al., trans. *The Universal Vehicle Discourse Literature.* New York: Columbia University Press, 2004.

Jarigpa Lobzang Namgyal. *dga' ldan khri pa rim byon gyi rnam thar mdor bsdus.* Lhasa: Bod ljongs mi rigs dpe skrun khang, 2008.

Jigme Chöki Dorje. *Bod brgyud nang bstan lha thsogs chen mo* [*Encyclopedia of Tibetan Buddhist iconography*]. Zi-lin: Mtsho snon mi rigs dpe skrun khan [Blue Lake People's Printing Press], 2001.

Jigme Samdrub. *Khams phyogs dkar mdzes khul gyi dgon sde so so'i lo rgyus gsal bar bshad pa nang bstan gsal ba'i me long.* 3 vols. Beijing / Chengdu: Krung go'i bod kyi shes rig zhib 'jug lte gnas, 1995.

Kalupahana, David J. *A Path of Righteousness: Dhammapada: An Introductory Essay, together with the Pali Text, English Translation, and Commentary.* Lanham, Md.: University Press of America, 1986.

Keenan, John P., trans. *The Summary of the Great Vehicle.* BDK English Tripitaka, 46-III. Berkeley, Calif.: Numata Center for Buddhist Translation and Research, 2003.

Khenchen Kunzang Palden and Minyak Kunzang Sonam. *Wisdom: Two Buddhist Commentaries.* Translated by the Padmakara Translation Group. Saint Léon-sur-Vézère: Editions Padmakara, 1993.

Khenchen Thrangu Rinpoche. *The Ornament of Clear Realization: A Commentary on the Prajnaparamita of the Maitreya Buddha.* Auckland, New Zealand: Zhyi-sil Chokyi Ghatsal, 2004.

Kochumuttom, Thomas A., trans. and ed. *A Treatise in Twenty Stanzas and its Explanation, in A Buddhist Doctrine of Experience.* Delhi: Motilal Banarsidass Publishers, 1982.

Konchok Gyaltsen, Khenpo. *Garland of Mahamudra Practices.* Ithaca, N.Y.: Snow Lion, 2002.

Kongtrül Lodrö Taye, Jamgön. *Myriad Worlds.* The Treasury of Knowledge, Book 1. Ithaca: Snow Lion, 2003.

Kvaerne, Per. *The Bon Religion of Tibet: The Iconography of a Living Tradition.* Chicago: Serindia, 1995.

Lamotte, Etienne. *History of Indian Buddhism.* Translated by Sara Webb-Boin. Louvain: Peeters Press, 1988.

———. *Karmasiddhi Prakarana: The Treatise on Action by Vasubandhu.* Translated by Leo Pruden. Berkeley, Calif.: Asian Humanities Press, 1988.

Lingpa, Jigme, Patrul Rinpoche, and Getse Mahapandita. *Deity, Mantra, and Wisdom: Development Stage Meditation in Tibetan Buddhist Tantra.* Translated by the Dharmachakra Translation Committee. Ithaca, N.Y.: Snow Lion, 2007.

Longchen Rabjam. *The Precious Treasury of the Basic Space of Phenomena.* Trans. Richard Barron. Junction City, Calif.: Padma Publishing, 2001.

Lonchenpa. "How Samsara is Fabricated from the Ground of Being." Trans. Kennard Lipman. In *Crystal Mirror* 5. Emeryville, Calif.: Dharma Publishing, 1977.

———. *The Precious Treasury of Pith Instructions.* Trans. Richard Barron. Junction City, Calif.: Padma Publishing, 2006.

Mipham Gyatso, Jamgon Ju. *Gateway to Knowledge: The Treatise Entitled The Gate for Entering the Way of the Pandita.* Trans. Chökyi Nyima Rinpoche and Erik Pema Kunsang. Hong Kong: Rangjung Yeshe Publications, 1997–2002.

Nagatomi, Masatoshi. *A Study of Dharmakīrti's Pramāṇavārttika: An English Translation and Annotation of the Pramāṇavārttika Book I.* PhD dissertation, Harvard University, 1957.

Namkhai Nyingpo. *Mother of Knowledge: The Enlightenment of Yeshe Tsogyal.* Translated by Tarthang Tulku. Berkeley, Calif.: Dharma Publishing, 1983.

Newman, J. R. *The Outer Wheel of Time: Vajrayana Buddhist Cosmology in the Kalacakra Tantra.* PhD dissertation, University of Wisconsin–Madison, 1987. (UMI number 8723348).

Ngawang Palzang, Khenpo. *A Guide to the Words of My Perfect Teacher.* Translated by the Padmakara Translation Group. Boston: Shambhala, 2004.

Norbu, Chögyal Namkhai. *Dream Yoga and the Practice of Natural Light.* Edited by Michael Katz. Ithaca, N.Y.: Snow Lion, 1992.

———. *Dzogchen: The Self-Perfected State.* Ithaca, N.Y.: Snow Lion Publications, 1996.

Nordrang Orgyan. *Chos rnam kun btus* [Compendium of Buddhist numeric terms]. 3 vols. Beijing: Krung go'i bod rig pa dpe skrun khang, 2008.

Nyima, Tudeng, ed. *An Encyclopaedic Tibetan-English Dictionary: Volume 1 (Ka–Nya).* Translated by Gyurme Dorje and Tudeng Nyima. Beijing/London: The Nationalities Publishing House and The School of Oriental and African Studies. 2001.

Nyoshul Khenpo. *A Marvelous Garland of Rare Gems: Biographies of Masters of Awareness in the Dzogchen Lineage.* Translated by Richard Barron. Junction City, Calif.: Padma, 2005.

Padmakara Translation Group, trans. *The Root Stanzas on the Middle Way.* Saint-Léon-sur-Vézère, France: Editions Padmakara, 2008.

Padmasambhava. *Natural Liberation: Padmasambhava's Teachings on the Six Bardos* by Padmasambhava. Commentary by Gyatrul Rinpoche. Translated by B. Alan Wallace. Boston: Wisdom, 1998.

Padmasambhava and Jamgön Kongtrul. *Light of Wisdom: Vol. II.* Translated by Erik Pema Kunsang. Berkeley, Calif.: North Atlantic Books, 2004. First published 1986 by Rangjung Yeshe.

Parfionovitch, Yuri, Gyurme Dorje, and Fernand Meyer. *Tibetan Medical Paintings: Illustrations to the Blue Beryl Treatise of Sangye Gyamtso (1653–1705).* New York: Abrams, 1992.

Patrul Rinpoche. *A Brief Guide to the Stages and Paths of the Bodhisattvas.* In vol. 4 of the *Collected Works.* Translated by Adam Pearcy. Rigpa Translations, 2007. http://www.lotsawahouse.org/tibetan-masters/patrul-rinpoche/stages-and -path.

——. *The Words of My Perfect Teacher: A Complete Translation of a Classic Introduction to Tibetan Buddhism.* Translated by the Padmakara Translation Group. New Haven, Conn.: Yale University Press, 1994. Rev. ed. 1998, 2010. Citations refer to 1994 edition.

Perdue, Daniel E. *Debate in Tibetan Buddhism.* Ithaca, N.Y.: Snow Lion, 1992.

Phuntsho, Karma. *Mipham's Dialectics and the Debates on Emptiness: To Be, Not to Be, or Neither.* London: Routledge, 2005.

Ray, Kumudranjan, S. Jain, eds. *Mahakavi Dandi's Sri Premcandra Tarkavagisavi-racitaTikasametah.* Delhi: Oriental Book Centre, 2004.

Ruegg, David Seyfort. *The Literature of the Madhyamaka School of Philosophy in India.* Wiesbaden: Otto Harrassowitz, 1981.

Shabkar Tsogdruk Rangdrol. *The Life of Shabkar: The Autobiography of a Tibetan Yogin.* Translated by Matthieu Ricard. Asian ed. Delhi: Shechen Publications, 1997.

Shantideva. *Entering the Path of Enlightenment: The Bodhicayavatara of the Buddhist Poet Shantideva.* Translated and with an introduction by Marion L. Matics. London: Macmillan, 1970.

——. *A Guide to the Bodhisattva Way of Life.* Trans. Wallace, Vesna A. and Wallace, B. Alan. Ithaca: Snow Lion Publications, 1997.

——. *The Way of the Bodhisattva.* Trans. Padmakara Translation Group. Boston: Shambhala Publications, 1997.

Shantarakshita and Jamgön Mipam. *The Adornment of the Middle Way: Shantarakshita's Madhyamakalankara with Commentary by Jamgön Mipam.* Translated by the Padmakara Translation Group. Boston: Shambhala, 2005.

Smith, E. Gene. *Among Tibetan Texts: History and Literature of the Himalayan Plateau.* Boston: Wisdom, 2001.

Snellgrove, David L., trans. *The Hevajra Tantra.* London Oriental Series, vol. 6. London: Oxford University Press, 1959.

Sprung, Mervyn, T. R. V. Murti, U. S. Vyas, trans. *Lucid Exposition of the Middle Way: The Essential Chapters from the Prasannapada of Candrakirti.* Vol. 18 of Routledge Library Editions: Buddhism Series. New York: Routledge, 1979.

Stanley, John, David R. Loy, and Gyurme Dorje, eds. *A Buddhist Response to the Climate Emergency*. Boston: Wisdom, 2009.

Stearns, Cyrus. *The Buddha from Dölpo: A Study of the Life and Thought of the Tibetan Master Dolpopa Sherab Gyaltsen*. Rev. ed. Tsadra Series. Ithaca, N.Y.: Snow Lion, 2010.

———. *Tangtong Gyalpo: King of the Empty Plain*. Ithaca, N.Y.: Snow Lion, 2007.

Stein, Rolf A. *Recherches sur l'épopée et le Barde au Tibet*. Paris: Presses Universitaires de France, 1959.

Streng, Frederick J. *Emptiness: A Study in Religious Meaning*. Nashville: Abingdon Press, 1967.

Takasaki, Jikido, trans. *A Study on the Ratnagotravibhaga (Uttaratantra)*. Rome: Is. M.E.O., 1966.

Tāranātha, Jo Nang. *The Seven Instruction Lineages*. Edited and translated by David Templeman. Dharamsala: Library of Tibetan Works and Archives, 1983.

Tarthang Tulku. *Kum Nye Tibetan Yoga: A Complete Guide to Health and Well-Being*. Berkeley, Calif.: Dharma Publishing, 1978.

Tendzin Lungtok Nyima. *sNga 'gyur rdzogs chen chos 'byung chen mo*. Beijing: Krung g'i bod rig pa dpe skrun khang, 2004.

Tertön Sögyal [Lerab Lingpa]. *The Collected Visionary Revelations and Textual Rediscoveries (gter chos) of Las-rab-gling-pa, alias Nag-bla Bsod-rgal (1856–1926)*. 17 vols. Bylakuppe: Pema Norbu Rinpoche, 1985.

Trungpa, Chögyam. *Journey Without Goal: The Tantric Wisdom of the Buddha*. Boston: Shambhala, 2000. First published 1981.

———. *The Rain of Wisdom*. Translated by the Nalanda Translation Committee. Boston: Shambhala, 1999.

Tsele, Natsok Rangdrol. *Mirror of Mindfulness*. Translated by Erik Pema Kunzang. Boston: Shambhala, 1989.

Tsering Lama Jampal Zangpo. *A Garland of Immortal Wish-Fulfilling Trees: The Palyul Tradition of Nyingmapa*. Ithaca, N.Y.: Snow Lion, 1988.

Tsewang Rigzin, Khenpo. *The Story of the Vajra Dharmapalas*. Dehra Dun: Ngagyur Nyingma College, 2003.

Tulku Thondup. *Masters of Meditation and Miracles: Lives of the Great Buddhist Masters of India and Tibet*. Buddhayana Series. Boston: Shambhala, 1999.

———. *The Practice of Dzogchen*. Ithaca, N.Y.: Snow Lion, 1996.

Ui, H., et al. *A Complete Catalogue of the Tibetan Buddhist Canons*. Sendai: Tohoku University, 1934.

Vose, Kevin A. *Resurrecting Chandrakirti: Disputes in the Tibetan Creation of Prasangika*. Boston: Wisdom, 2009.

Wallace, V. A. *The Inner Kalacakratantra. A Buddhist Tantric View of the Individual*. London: Oxford University Press, 2001.

Wayman, Alex, trans. *Chanting the Names of Manjusri: The Manjusri-Nama-Samgiti*. Buddhist Tradition Series. Delhi: Motilal Barnarsidass, 1985.

Yeshe Dorje. *Nyag bla padma bdud 'dul gyi rnam thar dang mgur 'bum*. Chengdu: Sichuan mi rigs dpe skrun khang, 1998.

Yudra Nyingpo, comp. *The Great Image: The Life Story of Vairochana the Translator.* Translated by Ani Jinpa Palmo. Boston: Shambhala, 2004.

Yuthok, Lama Choedak. *The Life of Mahasiddha Virupa.* Canberra: Gorum Publications, 1997.

INDEX

སྔགས་སྲུང་ཨེ་ཀ་ཛ་ཊི་མ།

EKAJATI, THE PROTECTRESS OF MANTRA